Solutions Manual (Chapters 1-17)

Accounting
TWENTY-FIRST EDITION

OR

Financial Accounting
NINTH EDITION

CARL S. WARREN • JAMES M. REEVE • PHILIP E. FESS

Verified by

Alice Sineath
Forsyth Technical Community College

Patricia Holmes
Des Moines Area Community College

THOMSON

SOUTH-WESTERN

Australia · Canada · Mexico · Singapore · Spain · United Kingdom · United States

THOMSON

SOUTH-WESTERN

Solutions Manual Chapters 1 – 17 to accompany Accounting 21e or Financial Accounting 9e

Carl S. Warren, James M. Reeve, Philip E. Fess

VP/Editorial Director:
Jack W. Calhoun

VP/Editor-in-Chief:
George Werthman

Publisher:
Rob Dewey

Executive Editor:
Sharon Oblinger

Sr. Developmental Editor:
Ken Martin

Marketing Manager:
Keith Chassé

Sr. Production Editor:
Deanna Quinn

Media Technology Editor:
Jim Rice

Media Developmental Editor:
Sally Nieman

Media Production Editors:
Robin Browning, Kelly Reid

Manufacturing Coordinator:
Doug Wilke

Cover Design:
Michelle Kunkler, Michael H. Stratton

Cover Illustration
Matsu

Production House:
Litten Editing and Production

Printer:
West Group

For permission to use material from this text or product, submit a request online at http://www.thomsonrights.com

For more information
contact South-Western,
5191 Natorp Boulevard,
Mason, Ohio 45040.
Or you can visit our Internet site at:
http://www.swlearning.com

CONTENTS

CHAPTER 1
INTRODUCTION TO ACCOUNTING AND BUSINESS

CLASS DISCUSSION QUESTIONS

1. The objective of most businesses is to maximize profits. Profit is the difference between the amounts received from customers for goods or services provided and the amounts paid for the inputs used to provide those goods or services.

2. A manufacturing business changes basic inputs into products that are then sold to customers. A service business provides services rather than products to customers. A restaurant such as Applebee's has characteristics of both a manufacturing and a service business in that Applebee's takes raw inputs such as cheese, fish, and beef and processes them into products for consumption by their customers. At the same time, Applebee's provides services of waiting on their customers as they dine.

3. The corporate form allows the company to obtain large amounts of resources by issuing stock. For this reason, most companies that require large investments in property, plant, and equipment are organized as corporations.

4. The business strategy of KIA is a low-cost strategy. In contrast, the business strategy of Porche is a differentiation strategy. The difference in strategies is directly reflected in the prices of the autos. For example, you can purchase a KIA for under $10,000 while the entry level Porche begins at over $40,000.

5. Super Wal-Mart will compete for customers using a low-cost strategy. The size and buying power of Wal-Mart Corporation provides Wal-Mart a competitive advantage over your friend in the ability to offer low prices. Thus, your friend should attempt to compete using a differentiation strategy. For example, your friend could offer personalized service to customers such as knowing customers' names, friendly atmosphere, home delivery of medicines, help in filing insurance forms, 24-hour call service, etc.

6. eBay offers value to its customers by developing a Web-based community in which buyers and sellers are brought together in an efficient format to browse, buy, and sell items such as collectibles, automobiles, high-end or premium art items, jewelry, consumer electronics, and a host of practical and miscellaneous items.

7. The stakeholders of a business normally include owners, managers, employees, customers, creditors, and the government.

8. Simply put, the role of accounting is to provide information for managers to use in operating the business. In addition, accounting provides information to other stakeholders to use in assessing the economic performance and condition of the business.

9. No. The business entity concept limits the recording of economic data to transactions directly affecting the activities of the business. The payment of the interest of $3,600 is a personal transaction of Deana Moran and should not be recorded by First Delivery Service.

10. The land should be recorded at its cost of $112,000 to Elrod Repair Service. This is consistent with the cost concept.

11. a. No. The offer of $600,000 and the increase in the assessed value should not be recognized in the accounting records.

    b. Cash would increase by $600,000, land would decrease by $500,000, and owner's equity would increase by $100,000.

12. An account receivable is a claim against a customer for goods or services sold. An account payable is an amount owed to a creditor for goods or services purchased. Therefore, an account receivable in the records of the seller is an account payable in the records of the purchaser.

13. The business incurred a net loss of $35,000.

14. The business realized net income of $80,000.

15. Net income or net loss
Owner's equity at the end of the period
Cash at the end of the period

1

EXERCISES

Ex. 1–1

1. manufacturing	6. manufacturing	11. service
2. service	7. service	12. manufacturing
3. merchandise	8. manufacturing	13. merchandise
4. service	9. merchandise	14. service
5. service	10. manufacturing	15. manufacturing

Ex. 1–2

1. a—low cost	6. b—differentiation	11. a—low cost
2. a—low cost	7. b—differentiation	12. b—differentiation
3. b—differentiation	8. c—combination	13. a—low cost
4. b—differentiation	9. a—low cost	14. a—low cost
5. c—combination	10. b—differentiation	15. c—combination

Ex. 1–3

As in many ethics issues, there is no one right answer. The local newspaper reported on this issue in these terms: "The company covered up the first report, and the local newspaper uncovered the company's secret. The company was forced to not locate here (Collier County). It became patently clear that doing the least that is legally allowed is not enough."

Ex. 1–4

1. B	5. B	9. X
2. B	6. F	10. B
3. E	7. X	
4. F	8. E	

Ex. 1–5

Coca-Cola owners' equity: $24,501 − $12,701 = $11,800
PepsiCo owners' equity: $23,474 − $14,183 = $9,291

Ex. 1–6

Toys "R" Us $9,397 – $5,367 = $4,030
Estée Lauder $3,417 – $1,955 = $1,462

Ex. 1–7

a. $96,500 ($25,000 + $71,500)
b. $67,750 ($82,750 – $15,000)
c. $19,500 ($37,000 – $17,500)

Ex. 1–8

a. $275,000 ($475,000 – $200,000)
b. $310,000 ($275,000 + $75,000 – $40,000)
c. $233,000 ($275,000 – $15,000 – $27,000)
d. $465,000 ($275,000 + $125,000 + $65,000)
e. Net income: $45,000 ($425,000 – $105,000 – $275,000)

Ex. 1–9

a. owner's equity
b. liability
c. asset
d. asset
e. owner's equity
f. asset

Ex. 1–10

a. Increases assets and increases owner's equity.
b. Increases assets and increases owner's equity.
c. Decreases assets and decreases owner's equity.
d. Increases assets and increases liabilities.
e. Increases assets and decreases assets.

Ex. 1–11

a. (1)   Total assets increased $80,000.

   (2)   No change in liabilities.

   (3)   Owner's equity increased $80,000.

b. (1)   Total assets decreased $30,000.

   (2)   Total liabilities decreased $30,000.

   (3)   No change in owner's equity.

Ex. 1–12

1. increase
2. decrease
3. increase
4. decrease

Ex. 1–13

1. c
2. c
3. d
4. c
5. e
6. a
7. e
8. a
9. e
10. e

Ex. 1–14

a. (1)   Sale of catering services for cash, $25,000.

    (2)   Purchase of land for cash, $10,000.

    (3)   Payment of expenses, $16,000.

    (4)   Purchase of supplies on account, $800.

    (5)   Withdrawal of cash by owner, $2,000.

    (6)   Payment of cash to creditors, $10,600.

    (7)   Recognition of cost of supplies used, $1,400.

b. $13,600 ($18,000 – $4,400)

c. $5,600 ($64,100 – $58,500)

d. $7,600 ($25,000 – $16,000 – $1,400)

e. $5,600 ($7,600 – $2,000)

Ex. 1–15

It would be incorrect to say that the business had incurred a net loss of $21,750. The excess of the withdrawals over the net income for the period is a decrease in the amount of owner's equity in the business.

Ex. 1–16

Company M

Owner's equity at end of year	
($1,200,000 – $650,000)	$550,000
Owner's equity at beginning of year	
($750,000 – $300,000)	450,000
Net income (increase in owner's equity)	$100,000

Company N

Increase in owner's equity (as determined for M)	$100,000
Add withdrawals..	60,000
Net income	$160,000

Company O

Increase in owner's equity (as determined for M)	$100,000
Deduct additional investment..	150,000
Net loss..	$ (50,000)

Company P

Increase in owner's equity (as determined for M)	$100,000
Deduct additional investment..	150,000
	$ (50,000)
Add withdrawals	60,000
Net income	$ 10,000

Ex. 1–17

Balance sheet items: 1, 3, 4, 8, 9, 10

Ex. 1–18

Income statement items: 2, 5, 6, 7

Ex. 1–19

MADRAS COMPANY
Statement of Owner's Equity
For the Month Ended April 30, 2006

Leo Perkins, capital, April 1, 2006............................		$297,200
Net income for the month	$73,000	
Less withdrawals...	12,000	
Increase in owner's equity...		61,000
Leo Perkins, capital, April 30, 2006............................		$358,200

Ex. 1–20

HERCULES SERVICES
Income Statement
For the Month Ended November 30, 2006

Fees earned		$232,120
Operating expenses:		
Wages expense...	$100,100	
Rent expense	35,000	
Supplies expense	4,550	
Miscellaneous expense	3,150	
Total operating expenses....................................		142,800
Net income		$ 89,320

Ex. 1–23

Balance sheet: b, c, e, f, h, i, j, l, m, n, o
Income statement: a, d, g, k

Ex. 1–24

1. b–investing activity
2. a–operating activity
3. c–financing activity
4. a–operating activity

Ex. 1–25

1. All financial statements should contain the name of the business in their heading. The statement of owner's equity is incorrectly headed as "Jerry Maris" rather than Caddis Realty. The heading of the balance sheet needs the name of the business.

2. The income statement and statement of owner's equity cover a period of time and should be labeled "For the Month Ended July 31, 2006."

3. The year in the heading for the statement of owner's equity should be 2006 rather than 2005.

4. The balance sheet should be labeled as of "July 31, 2006," rather than "For the Month Ended July 31, 2006."

5. In the income statement, the miscellaneous expense amount should be listed as the last operating expense.

6. In the income statement, the total operating expenses are incorrectly subtracted from the sales commissions, resulting in an incorrect net income amount. The correct net income should be $4,900. This also affects the statement of owner's equity and the amount of Jerry Maris, capital, that appears on the balance sheet.

7. In the statement of owner's equity, the additional investment should be added first to Jerry Maris, capital, as of July 1, 2006. The net income should be presented next, followed by the amount of withdrawals, which is subtracted from the net income to yield a net increase in owner's equity.

8. Accounts payable should be listed as a liability on the balance sheet.

9. Accounts receivable and supplies should be listed as assets on the balance sheet.

10. The balance sheet assets should equal the sum of the liabilities and owner's equity.

Ex. 1–25   Concluded

Corrected financial statements appear as follows:

CADDIS REALTY
Income Statement
For the Month Ended July 31, 2006

Sales commissions		$51,900
Operating expenses:		
Office salaries expense	$32,400	
Rent expense	11,000	
Automobile expense	2,500	
Supplies expense	300	
Miscellaneous expense	800	
Total operating expenses		47,000
Net income		$ 4,900

CADDIS REALTY
Statement of Owner's Equity
For the Month Ended July 31, 2006

Jerry Maris, capital, July 1, 2006		$10,400
Additional investment during July	$ 2,500	
Net income for July	4,900	
	$ 7,400	
Less withdrawals during July	2,000	
Increase in owner's equity		5,400
Jerry Maris, capital, July 31, 2006		$15,800

CADDIS REALTY
Balance Sheet
July 31, 2006

Assets		Liabilities	
Cash	$ 3,300	Accounts payable	$ 3,800
Accounts receivable	14,300		
Supplies	2,000	**Owner's Equity**	
		Jerry Maris, capital	15,800
		Total liabilities and	
Total assets	$19,600	owner's equity	$19,600

Ex. 1–26

   a. 2003: $10,209 ($30,011 – $19,802)

       2002: $8,312 ($26,394 – $18,082)

   b. 2003: 0.52 ($10,209 ÷ $19,802)

       2002: 0.46 ($8,312 ÷ $18,082)

   c. The ratio of liabilities to stockholders' equity increased from 2002 to 2003, indicating an increase in risk for creditors. However, the assets of The Home Depot are more than sufficient to satisfy creditor claims.

Ex. 1–27

   a. 2003: $7,807 ($16,109 – $8,302

       2002: $6,674 ($13,736 – $7,062)

   b. 2003: 1.06 ($8,302 ÷ $7,807)

       2002: 1.06 ($7,062 ÷ $6,674)

   c. The margin of safety for creditors has remained approximately the same from 2002 to 2003. In both years, creditors have more at stake in Lowe's than do stockholders, since the ratio exceeds one.

   d. Lowe's ratio of liabilities to stockholders' equity (1.06) is much higher than that of The Home Depot (0.52 and 0.46), indicating that creditors of Lowe's are more at risk than creditors of The Home Depot.

PROBLEMS

Prob. 1–1A

1.

		Assets			= Liabilities +		Owner's Equity	
	Cash +	Accounts Receivable +	Supplies	=	Accounts Payable	+	Duane Mays, Capital	
a.	+18,000						+18,000	Investment
b.			+ 950		+ 950			
Bal.	18,000		950		950		18,000	
c.	– 575				– 575			
Bal.	17,425		950		375		18,000	
d.	+ 4,250						+ 4,250	Fees earned
Bal.	21,675		950		375		22,250	
e.	– 1,200						– 1,200	Rent expense
Bal.	20,475		950		375		21,050	
f.	– 975						– 600	Auto expense
							– 375	Misc. expense
Bal.	19,500		950		375		20,075	
g.	– 1,500						– 1,500	Salaries exp.
Bal.	18,000		950		375		18,575	
h.			– 725				– 725	Supplies exp.
Bal.	18,000		225		375		17,850	
i.		+ 6,350					+ 6,350	Fees earned
Bal.	18,000	6,350	225		375		24,200	
j.	– 2,000						– 2,000	Withdrawal
Bal.	16,000	6,350	225		375		22,200	

2. Owner's equity is the right of owners to the assets of the business. These rights are increased by owner's investments and revenues and decreased by owner's withdrawals and expenses.

Prob. 1–2A

1.

CHICKADEE TRAVEL SERVICE
Income Statement
For the Year Ended April 30, 2006

Fees earned..		$263,200
Operating expenses:		
Wages expense	$131,700	
Rent expense	37,800	
Utilities expense.....................................	22,500	
Supplies expense....................................	7,100	
Taxes expense..	5,600	
Miscellaneous expense...........................	2,950	
Total operating expenses.................		207,650
Net income		$ 55,550

2.

CHICKADEE TRAVEL SERVICE
Statement of Owner's Equity
For the Year Ended April 30, 2006

Adam Cellini, capital, May 1, 2005..................		$50,000
Net income for the year................................	$55,550	
Less withdrawals...	30,000	
Increase in owner's equity............................		25,550
Adam Cellini, capital, April 30, 2006		$75,550

3.

CHICKADEE TRAVEL SERVICE
Balance Sheet
April 30, 2006

Assets		Liabilities	
Cash.................................	$53,050	Accounts payable..........	$12,200
Accounts receivable.......	31,350		
Supplies..........................	3,350	Owner's Equity	
		Adam Cellini, capital	75,550
		Total liabilities and	
Total assets....................	$87,750	owner's equity	$87,750

Prob. 1–3A

1.

LINCHPIN COMPUTER SERVICES
Income Statement
For the Month Ended August 31, 2006

Fees earned..		$16,500
Operating expenses:		
Salaries expense	$4,000	
Rent expense	3,600	
Auto expense	1,550	
Supplies expense	650	
Miscellaneous expense.................................	750	
Total operating expenses...........................		10,550
Net income		$ 5,950

2.

LINCHPIN COMPUTER SERVICES
Statement of Owner's Equity
For the Month Ended August 31, 2006

Jeanine Sykes, capital, August 1, 2006		$ 0
Investment on August 1, 2006	$10,000	
Net income for August	5,950	
	$15,950	
Less withdrawals..	2,000	
Increase in owner's equity..		13,950
Jeanine Sykes, capital, August 31, 2006		$13,950

3.

LINCHPIN COMPUTER SERVICES
Balance Sheet
August 31, 2006

Assets		Liabilities	
Cash.................................	$ 6,600	Accounts payable..........	$ 940
Accounts receivable.......	7,500		
Supplies..........................	790	**Owner's Equity**	
		Jeanine Sykes, capital ..	13,950
		Total liabilities and	
Total assets.....................	$14,890	owner's equity	$14,890

Prob. 1–4A

1.

	Assets			= Liabilities +	Owner's Equity	
	Cash	+	Supplies =	Accounts Payable	+ Shad Menard, Capital	
a.	+15,000				+15,000	Investment
b.	– 2,400				– 2,400	Rent expense
Bal.	12,600				12,600	
c.	– 1,130				– 750	Auto expense
					– 380	Misc. expense
Bal.	11,470				11,470	
d.			+ 950	+ 950		
Bal.	11,470		950	950	11,470	
e.	+17,350				+17,350	Sales commissions
Bal.	28,820		950	950	28,820	
f.	– 580			– 580		
Bal.	28,240		950	370	28,820	
g.	– 3,600				– 3,600	Salaries expense
Bal.	24,640		950	370	25,220	
h.	– 1,500				– 1,500	Withdrawal
Bal.	23,140		950	370	23,720	
i.			– 675		– 675	Supplies expense
Bal.	23,140		275	370	23,045	

2.

CENTILLION REALTY
Income Statement
For the Month Ended August 31, 2006

Sales commissions		$17,350
Operating expenses:		
Office salaries expense	$3,600	
Rent expense	2,400	
Automobile expense	750	
Supplies expense	675	
Miscellaneous expense	380	
Total operating expenses		7,805
Net income		$ 9,545

Prob. 1–4A Concluded

CENTILLION REALTY
Statement of Owner's Equity
For the Month Ended August 31, 2006

Shad Menard, capital, August 1, 2006		$ 0
Investment on August 1, 2006	$15,000	
Net income for August	9,545	
	$24,545	
Less withdrawals..	1,500	
Increase in owner's equity...		23,045
Shad Menard, capital, August 31, 2006		$23,045

CENTILLION REALTY
Balance Sheet
August 31, 2006

Assets		Liabilities	
Cash...................................	$23,140	Accounts payable..........	$ 370
Supplies............................	275		
		Owner's Equity	
		Shad Menard, capital	23,045
		Total liabilities and	
Total assets......................	$23,415	owner's equity	$23,415

17

Prob. 1–5A

1.

		Assets			=	Liabilities	+	Owner's Equity
Cash	+	Accounts Receivable	+ Supplies	+ Land	=	Accounts Payable	+	Vince Fry, Capital
8,600	+	9,500	+ 1,875	+ 15,000	=	4,100	+	Vince Fry, Capital
			34,975		=	4,100	+	Vince Fry, Capital
			30,875		=			Vince Fry, Capital

2.

		Assets			=	Liabilities	+	Owner's Equity	
	Cash	+ Accounts Receivable	+ Supplies	+ Land	=	Accounts Payable	+	Vince Fry, Capital	
Bal.	8,600	9,500	1,875	15,000		4,100		30,875	
a.	− 4,000							− 4,000	Rent expense
Bal.	4,600	9,500	1,875	15,000		4,100		26,875	
b.		+ 8,150						+ 8,150	Dry cleaning sales
Bal.	4,600	17,650	1,875	15,000		4,100		35,025	
c.	− 2,680					− 2,680			
Bal.	1,920	17,650	1,875	15,000		1,420		35,025	
d.			+ 1,500			+ 1,500			
Bal.	1,920	17,650	3,375	15,000		2,920		35,025	
e.	+ 17,600							+ 17,600	Dry cleaning sales
Bal.	19,520	17,650	3,375	15,000		2,920		52,625	
f.	+ 8,450	− 8,450							
Bal.	27,970	9,200	3,375	15,000		2,920		52,625	
g.						+ 7,400		− 7,400	Dry cleaning expense
Bal.	27,970	9,200	3,375	15,000		10,320		45,225	
h.	− 4,725							− 2,800	Wages expense
								− 825	Truck expense
								− 710	Utilities expense
								− 390	Miscellaneous expense
Bal.	23,245	9,200	3,375	15,000		10,320		40,500	
i.			− 1,775					− 1,775	Supplies expense
Bal.	23,245	9,200	1,600	15,000		10,320		38,725	
j.	− 3,500							− 3,500	Withdrawal
Bal.	19,745	9,200	1,600	15,000		10,320		35,225	

19

Prob. 1–5A Concluded

3. a.

EUREKA DRY CLEANERS
Income Statement
For the Month Ended June 30, 2006

Dry cleaning sales		$25,750
Operating expenses:		
Dry cleaning expense	$7,400	
Rent expense	4,000	
Wages expense	2,800	
Supplies expense	1,775	
Truck expense	825	
Utilities expense	710	
Miscellaneous expense	390	
Total operating expenses		17,900
Net income		$ 7,850

b.

EUREKA DRY CLEANERS
Statement of Owner's Equity
For the Month Ended June 30, 2006

Vince Fry, capital, June 1, 2006		$30,875
Net income for June	$7,850	
Less withdrawals	3,500	
Increase in owner's equity		4,350
Vince Fry, capital, June 30, 2006		$35,225

c.

EUREKA DRY CLEANERS
Balance Sheet
June 30, 2006

Assets		Liabilities	
Cash	$19,745	Accounts payable	$10,320
Accounts receivable	9,200		
Supplies	1,600	**Owner's Equity**	
Land	15,000	Vince Fry, capital	35,225
		Total liabilities and	
Total assets	$45,545	owner's equity	$45,545

Prob. 1–6A

a. Wages expense, $4,300 ($9,560 – $1,920 – $1,600 – $1,080 – $660)

b. Net income, $9,240 ($18,800 – $9,560)

c. Terry Garcia, capital, June 1, 2006, $0

d. Investment on June 1, 2006, $36,000

e. Net income for June, $9,240

f. $45,240 ($36,000 + $9,240)

g. Withdrawals, $4,800

h. Increase in owner's equity, $40,440 ($45,240 – $4,800)

i. Terry Garcia, capital, June 30, 2006, $40,440

j. Land, $28,800 ($41,400 – $11,800 – $800)

k. Total assets, $41,400

l. Terry Garcia, capital, $40,440

m. Total liabilities and owner's equity, $41,400 ($960 + $40,440)

n. Cash received from customers, $18,800 ($9,400 + $9,400)

o. Net cash flow from operating activities, $9,400 ($11,800 – $31,200 + $28,800)

p. Net cash flow from financing activities, $31,200 ($36,000 – $4,800)

q. Net cash flow and June 30, 2006 cash balance, $11,800

Prob. 1–1B

1.

	Cash	+	Accounts Receivable	+ Supplies	=	Accounts Payable	+	Pamela Larsen, Capital	
			Assets		= Liabilities +			**Owner's Equity**	
a.	+15,000							+15,000	Investment
b.				+ 1,350		+ 1,350			
Bal.	15,000			1,350		1,350		15,000	
c.	+ 6,500							+ 6,500	Fees earned
Bal.	21,500			1,350		1,350		21,500	
d.	– 2,500							– 2,500	Rent expense
Bal.	19,000			1,350		1,350		19,000	
e.	– 700					– 700			
Bal.	18,300			1,350		650		19,000	
f.			+ 1,250					+ 1,250	Fees earned
Bal.	18,300		1,250	1,350		650		20,250	
g.	– 1,225							– 550	Auto expense
								– 675	Misc. expense
Bal.	17,075		1,250	1,350		650		19,025	
h.	– 1,800							– 1,800	Salaries exp.
Bal.	15,275		1,250	1,350		650		17,225	
i.				– 970				– 970	Supplies exp.
Bal.	15,275		1,250	380		650		16,255	
j.	– 1,500							– 1,500	Withdrawal
Bal.	13,775		1,250	380		650		14,755	

2. Owner's equity is the right of owners to the assets of the business. These rights are increased by owner's investments and revenues and decreased by owner's withdrawals and expenses.

Prob. 1–2B

1.

GRECO TRAVEL AGENCY
Income Statement
For the Year Ended December 31, 2006

Fees earned...		$ 188,000
Operating expenses:		
Wages expense	$56,800	
Rent expense	36,000	
Utilities expense	16,500	
Supplies expense	4,500	
Miscellaneous expense..	2,800	
Total operating expenses......................................		116,600
Net income		$ 71,400

2.

GRECO TRAVEL AGENCY
Statement of Owner's Equity
For the Year Ended December 31, 2006

Petrea Kraft, capital, January 1, 2006		$16,200
Net income for the year..	$71,400	
Less withdrawals...	47,000	
Increase in owner's equity...		24,400
Petrea Kraft, capital, December 31, 2006		$40,600

3.

GRECO TRAVEL AGENCY
Balance Sheet
December 31, 2006

Assets		Liabilities	
Cash...................................	$11,520	Accounts payable..........	$ 5,120
Accounts receivable........	31,200		
Supplies..........................	3,000	Owner's Equity	
		Petrea Kraft, capital	40,600
		Total liabilities and	
Total assets....................	$45,720	owner's equity	$45,720

Prob. 1–3B

1.

JACK-IN-THE-PULPIT FINANCIAL SERVICES
Income Statement
For the Month Ended January 31, 2006

Fees earned..		$31,400
Operating expenses:		
Rent expense	$6,000	
Salaries expense	5,000	
Auto expense	3,000	
Supplies expense	2,520	
Miscellaneous expense...	800	
Total operating expenses.......................................		17,320
Net income		$14,080

2.

JACK-IN-THE-PULPIT FINANCIAL SERVICES
Statement of Owner's Equity
For the Month Ended January 31, 2006

Lynn Rosberg, capital, January 1, 2006...........................		$ 0
Investment on January 1, 2006..	$30,000	
Net income for January..	14,080	
	$44,080	
Less withdrawals..	7,000	
Increase in owner's equity..		37,080
Lynn Rosberg, capital, January 31, 2006.........................		$37,080

3.

JACK-IN-THE-PULPIT FINANCIAL SERVICES
Balance Sheet
January 31, 2006

Assets		Liabilities	
Cash..................................	$27,200	Accounts payable..........	$ 1,180
Accounts receivable.......	10,400		
Supplies...........................	660	**Owner's Equity**	
		Lynn Rosberg, capital...	37,080
		Total liabilities and	
Total assets.....................	$38,260	owner's equity	$38,260

Prob. 1–4B

1.

	Assets			= Liabilities +	Owner's Equity	
	Cash	+	Supplies	= Accounts Payable	+ Beth Nesbit, Capital	
a.	+ 18,000				+ 18,000	Investment
b.			+ 1,650	+ 1,650		
Bal.	18,000		1,650	1,650	18,000	
c.	− 1,100			− 1,100		
Bal.	16,900		1,650	550	18,000	
d.	+ 25,200				+ 25,200	Sales commissions
Bal.	42,100		1,650	550	43,200	
e.	− 7,200				− 7,200	Rent expense
Bal.	34,900		1,650	550	36,000	
f.	− 10,000				− 10,000	Withdrawal
Bal.	24,900		1,650	550	26,000	
g.	− 2,250				− 1,500	Auto expense
					− 750	Misc. expense
Bal.	22,650		1,650	550	23,750	
h.	− 8,000				− 8,000	Salaries expense
Bal.	14,650		1,650	550	15,750	
i.			− 1,050		− 1,050	Supplies expense
Bal.	14,650		600	550	14,700	

2.

PATRIOTIC REALTY
Income Statement
For the Month Ended July 31, 2006

Sales commissions		$25,200
Operating expenses:		
Office salaries expense	$8,000	
Rent expense	7,200	
Automobile expense	1,500	
Supplies expense	1,050	
Miscellaneous expense	750	
Total operating expenses		18,500
Net income		$ 6,700

Prob. 1–4B Concluded

PATRIOTIC REALTY
Statement of Owner's Equity
For the Month Ended July 31, 2006

Beth Nesbit, capital, July 1, 2006		$ 0
Investment on July 1, 2006	$18,000	
Net income for July	6,700	
	$24,700	
Less withdrawals..	10,000	
Increase in owner's equity..		14,700
Beth Nesbit, capital, July 31, 2006		$14,700

PATRIOTIC REALTY
Balance Sheet
July 31, 2006

Assets		Liabilities	
Cash...............................	$14,650	Accounts payable..........	$ 550
Supplies...........................	600		
		Owner's Equity	
		Beth Nesbit, capital.......	14,700
		Total liabilities and	
Total assets.....................	$15,250	owner's equity	$15,250

Prob. 1–5B

1.

Assets				=	Liabilities	+	Owner's Equity
Cash +	Accounts Receivable +	Supplies +	Land =		Accounts Payable	+	Gloria Carson, Capital
7,150 +	12,880 +	3,400 +	20,000 =		6,360	+	Gloria Carson, Capital
	43,430			=	6,360	+	Gloria Carson, Capital
	37,070			=			Gloria Carson, Capital

Prob. 1–5B Continued

2.

	Assets				=	Liabilities +		Owner's Equity	
	Cash +	Accounts Receivable +	Supplies +	Land	=	Accounts Payable	+	Gloria Carson, Capital	
Bal.	7,150	12,880	3,400	20,000		6,360		37,070	
a.	+22,000							+22,000	Dry cleaning sales
Bal.	29,150	12,880	3,400	20,000		6,360		59,070	
b.	– 3,500							– 3,500	Rent expense
Bal.	25,650	12,880	3,400	20,000		6,360		55,570	
c.			+2,100			+2,100			
Bal.	25,650	12,880	5,500	20,000		8,460		55,570	
d.	– 4,800					–4,800			
Bal.	20,850	12,880	5,500	20,000		3,660		55,570	
e.		+11,700						+11,700	Dry cleaning sales
Bal.	20,850	24,580	5,500	20,000		3,660		67,270	
f.						+8,400		– 8,400	Dry cleaning expense
Bal.	20,850	24,580	5,500	20,000		12,060		58,870	
g.	– 6,570							– 3,400	Wages expense
								– 1,580	Truck expense
								– 960	Utilities expense
								– 630	Miscellaneous expense
Bal.	14,280	24,580	5,500	20,000		12,060		52,300	
h.	+10,100	–10,100							
Bal.	24,380	14,480	5,500	20,000		12,060		52,300	
i.			– 2,900					– 2,900	Supplies expense
Bal.	24,380	14,480	2,600	20,000		12,060		49,400	
j.	– 6,000							– 6,000	Withdrawals
Bal.	18,380	14,480	2,600	20,000		12,060		43,400	

Prob. 1–5B Concluded

3. a.

DAISY DRY CLEANERS
Income Statement
For the Month Ended March 31, 2006

Dry cleaning sales		$33,700
Operating expenses:		
Dry cleaning expense	$8,400	
Rent expense	3,500	
Wages expense	3,400	
Supplies expense	2,900	
Truck expense	1,580	
Utilities expense	960	
Miscellaneous expense	630	
Total operating expenses		21,370
Net income		$12,330

b.

DAISY DRY CLEANERS
Statement of Owner's Equity
For the Month Ended March 31, 2006

Gloria Carson, capital, March 1, 2006		$37,070
Net income for March	$12,330	
Less withdrawals	6,000	
Increase in owner's equity		6,330
Gloria Carson, capital, March 31, 2006		$43,400

c.

DAISY DRY CLEANERS
Balance Sheet
March 31, 2006

Assets		Liabilities	
Cash	$18,380	Accounts payable	$12,060
Accounts receivable	14,480		
Supplies	2,600	Owner's Equity	
Land	20,000	Gloria Carson, capital	43,400
		Total liabilities and	
Total assets	$55,460	owner's equity	$55,460

Continuing Problem   Concluded

2.

DANCIN MUSIC
Income Statement
For the Month Ended April 30, 2006

Fees earned...		$4,750
Operating expenses:		
Office rent expense	$ 1,000	
Music expense...	940	
Equipment rent expense..	650	
Advertising expense..	600	
Wages expense	400	
Utilities expense	300	
Supplies expense	180	
Miscellaneous expense...	150	
Total operating expenses.................................		4,220
Net income		$ 530

3.

DANCIN MUSIC
Statement of Owner's Equity
For the Month Ended April 30, 2006

Shannon Burns, capital, April 1, 2006		$ 0
Investment on April 1, 2006	$7,000	
Net income for April	530	
	$7,530	
Less withdrawals..	250	
Increase in owner's equity...		7,280
Shannon Burns, capital, April 30, 2006		$7,280

4.

DANCIN MUSIC
Balance Sheet
April 30, 2006

Assets		Liabilities	
Cash..............................	$6,160	Accounts payable..........	$ 250
Accounts receivable.......	1,200		
Supplies..........................	170	**Owner's Equity**	
		Shannon Burns, capital	7,280
		Total liabilities and	
Total assets....................	$7,530	owner's equity	$7,530

SPECIAL ACTIVITIES

Activity 1–1

1. Acceptable professional conduct requires that Sue Alejandro supply First National Bank with all the relevant financial statements necessary for the bank to make an informed decision. Therefore, Sue should provide the complete set of financial statements. These can be supplemented with a discussion of the net loss in the past year or other data explaining why granting the loan is a good investment by the bank.

2. a. Owners are generally willing to provide bankers with information about the operating and financial condition of the business, such as the following:

    -   Operating Information:
        -   description of business operations
        -   results of past operations
        -   preliminary results of current operations
        -   plans for future operations
    -   Financial Condition:
        -   list of assets and liabilities (balance sheet)
        -   estimated current values of assets
        -   owner's personal investment in the business
        -   owner's commitment to invest additional funds in the business

    Owners are normally reluctant to provide the following types of information to bankers:

    -   *Proprietary Operating Information.* Such information, which might hurt the business if it becomes known by competitors, might include special processes used by the business or future plans to expand operations into areas that are not currently served by a competitor.

    -   *Personal Financial Information.* Owners may have little choice here because banks often require owners of small businesses to pledge their personal assets as security for a business loan. Personal financial information requested by bankers often includes the owner's net worth, salary, and other income. In addition, bankers usually request information about factors that might affect the personal financial condition of the owner. For example, a pending divorce by the owner might significantly affect the owner's personal wealth.

Activity 1–1   Concluded

b. Bankers typically want as much information as possible about the ability of the business and the owner to repay the loan with interest. Examples of such information are described above.

c. Both bankers and business owners share the common interest of the business doing well and being successful. If the business is successful, the bankers will receive their loan payments on time with interest, and the owners will increase their personal wealth.

Activity 1–2

1. In a commodity business like poultry production, the dominant business strategy is a low-cost strategy. This is because customers cannot differentiate between chickens produced by different companies. The implication of a low-cost strategy is that you would put most of your emphasis on designing and running efficient operations. In addition, you would spend significant amounts of monies in research and development activities trying to discover and develop new ways to breed and raise bigger chickens with less feed.

2. A major business risk includes the selling of contaminated chickens and the possibility that competitors will develop lower-cost methods of breeding and raising chickens. Also, a major cost of raising chickens is the cost of feed. Thus, fluctuations in feed costs such as corn can dramatically influence the profitability of chicken production. To manage feed cost risk, chicken producers like Gold Kist enter into hedging transactions for feed that involve commodity futures and options. Finally, another major risk is that consumer tastes may change with the result that the demand for chicken products may decrease significantly.

3. Gold Kist could try to differentiate its products by emphasizing that it raises its chickens with only "natural" feeds without the use of artificial ingredients such as steroids, etc. Gold Kist could then sell its products as the "healthy choice" products.

Activity 1–3

The difference in the two bank balances, $180,000 ($240,000 – $60,000), may not be pure profit from an accounting perspective. To determine the accounting profit for the seven-month period, the revenues for the period would need to be matched with the related expenses. The revenues minus the expenses would indicate whether the business generated net income (profit) or a net loss for the period. Using only the difference between the two bank account balances ignores such factors as amounts due from customers (receivables), liabilities (accounts payable) that need to be paid for wages or other operating expenses, additional investments that Dr. Smith may have made in the business during the period, or withdrawals during the period that Dr. Smith might have taken for personal reasons unrelated to the business.

Some businesses that have few, if any, receivables or payables may use a "cash" basis of accounting. The cash basis of accounting ignores receivables and payables because they are assumed to be insignificant in amount. However, even with the cash basis of accounting, additional investments during the period and any withdrawals during the period have to be considered in determining the net income (profit) or net loss for the period.

Activity 1–4

1.

	Assets			=	Liabilities	+	Owner's Equity	
	Cash	+	Supplies	=	Accounts Payable	+	Dawn Ivy Capital	
a.	+ 1,000						+ 1,000	Investment
b.	– 320		+ 320					
Bal.	680		320				1,000	
c.	– 160						– 160	Rent expense
Bal.	520		320				840	
d.	– 140				+ 60		– 200	Rent expense
Bal.	380		320		60		640	
e.	+ 1,600						+ 1,600	Service revenue
Bal.	1,980		320		60		2,240	
f.	+ 300						+ 300	Service revenue
Bal.	2,280		320		60		2,540	
g.	– 600						– 600	Salary expense
Bal.	1,680		320		60		1,940	
h.	– 150						– 150	Misc. expense
Bal.	1,530		320		60		1,790	
i.	+ 600						+ 600	Service revenue
Bal.	2,130		320		60		2,390	
j.			– 170				– 170	Supplies expense
Bal.	2,130		150		60		2,220	
k.	– 800						– 800	Withdrawal
Bal.	1,330		150		60		1,420	

2.

DEUCE
Income Statement
For the Month Ended June 30, 2005

Service revenue		$2,500
Operating expenses:		
Salary expense	$600	
Rent expense	360	
Supplies expense	170	
Miscellaneous expense..	150	
Total operating expenses.....................................		1,280
Net income		$1,220

Activity 1–4   Continued

3.

DEUCE
Statement of Owner's Equity
For the Month Ended June 30, 2005

Dawn Ivy, capital, June 1, 2005		$ 0
Investment on June 1, 2005	$1,000	
Net income for June	1,220	
	$2,220	
Less withdrawals	800	
Increase in owner's equity		1,420
Dawn Ivy, capital, June 30, 2005		$1,420

4.

DEUCE
Balance Sheet
June 30, 2005

Assets		Liabilities	
Cash	$1,330	Accounts payable	$ 60
Supplies	150		
		Owner's Equity	
		Dawn Ivy, capital	1,420
		Total liabilities and	
Total assets	$1,480	owner's equity	$1,480

5.   a. Deuce would provide Dawn with $260 more income per month than work-
ing as a waitress. This amount is computed as follows:

Net income of Deuce, per month	$1,220
Earnings as waitress, per month:	
30 hours per week × $8 per hour × 4 weeks	960
Difference	$ 260

Activity 1–4 Concluded

b. Other factors that Dawn should consider before discussing a long-term arrangement with the Racquet Club include the following:

Dawn should consider whether the results of operations for June are indicative of what to expect each month. For example, Dawn should consider whether club members will continue to request lessons or use the ball machine during the winter months when interest in tennis may slacken. Dawn should evaluate whether the additional income of $260 per month from Deuce is worth the risk being taken and the effort being expended.

Dawn should also consider how much her investment in Deuce could have earned if invested elsewhere. For example, if the initial investment of $1,000 had been deposited in a money market or savings account at 3% interest, it would have earned $2.50 interest in June, or $30 for the year.

Note to Instructors: Numerous other considerations could be mentioned by students, such as the ability of Dawn to withdraw cash from Deuce for personal use. Unlike a money market account or savings account, some of her investment in Deuce will be in the form of supplies (tennis balls, etc.), which may not be readily convertible to cash. The objective of this case is not to mention all possible considerations, but rather to encourage students to begin thinking about the use of accounting information in making business decisions.

Activity 1–5

Note to Instructors: The purpose of this activity is to familiarize students with the certification requirements and their on-line availability.

Activity 1–6

	1998	1997	1996
Net cash flows from operating activities	positive	positive	negative
Net cash flows from investing activities	negative	negative	negative
Net cash flows from financing activities	positive	positive	positive

Start-up companies normally experience negative cash flows from operating and investing activities. Also, start-up companies normally have positive cash flows from financing activities—activities from raising capital.

Activity 1–7

As can be seen from the balance sheet data in the case, Enron was financed largely by debt as compared to equity. Specifically, Enron's stockholders' equity represented only 17.5% ($11,470 divided by $65,503) of Enron's total assets. The remainder of Enron's total assets, 82.5%, were financed by debt. When a company is financed largely by debt, it is said to be highly leveraged.

In late 2001 and early 2002, allegations arose as to possible misstatements of Enron's financial statements. These allegations revolved around the use of "special purpose entities" (partnerships) and related party transactions. The use of special purpose entities allowed Enron to hide a significant amount of additional debt off its balance sheet. The result was that Enron's total assets were even more financed by debt than the balance sheet indicated.

After the allegations of misstatements became public, Enron's stock rapidly declined and the company filed for bankruptcy. Subsequently, numerous lawsuits were filed against the company and its management. In addition, the Securities and Exchange Commission, the Justice Department, and Congress launched investigations into Enron.

Note to Instructors: The role of the auditors and board of directors of Enron might also be discussed. However, these topics are not covered in Chapter 1 but are covered in later chapters.

15. **a.** From the viewpoint of Kennon Storage, the balance of the checking account represents an asset.

b. From the viewpoint of Livingston Savings Bank, the balance of the checking account represents a liability.

EXERCISES

Ex. 2–1

Balance Sheet Accounts	Income Statement Accounts

<table>
<tr><td align="center"><u>Assets</u></td><td align="center"><u>Revenue</u></td></tr>
<tr><td>Flight Equipment</td><td>Cargo and Mail Revenue</td></tr>
<tr><td>Purchase Deposits
   for Flight Equipment*</td><td>Passenger Revenue</td></tr>
<tr><td>Spare Parts and Supplies</td><td align="center"><u>Expenses</u></td></tr>
<tr><td align="center"><u>Liabilities</u></td><td>Aircraft Fuel Expense</td></tr>
<tr><td>Accounts Payable</td><td>Commissions***</td></tr>
<tr><td>Air Traffic Liability**</td><td>Landing Fees****</td></tr>
<tr><td align="center"><u>Owner's Equity</u></td><td></td></tr>
<tr><td>None</td><td></td></tr>
</table>

    * Advance payments on aircraft purchases
   ** Passenger ticket sales not yet recognized as revenue
 *** Commissions paid to travel agents
**** Fees paid to airports for landing rights

Ex. 2–2

Account	Account Number
Accounts Payable	21
Accounts Receivable	12
Cash	11
Corey Krum, Capital	31
Corey Krum, Drawing	32
Fees Earned	41
Land	13
Miscellaneous Expense	53
Supplies Expense	52
Wages Expense	51

Ex. 2–3

Balance Sheet Accounts	Income Statement Accounts

Balance Sheet Accounts

1. Assets

11	Cash
12	Accounts Receivable
13	Supplies
14	Prepaid Insurance
15	Equipment

2. Liabilities

21	Accounts Payable
22	Unearned Rent

3. Owner's Equity

31	Millard Fillmore, Capital
32	Millard Fillmore, Drawing

Income Statement Accounts

4. Revenue

41	Fees Earned

5. Expenses

51	Wages Expense
52	Rent Expense
53	Supplies Expense
59	Miscellaneous Expense

Note: The order of some of the accounts within the major classifications is somewhat arbitrary, as in accounts 13–14 and accounts 51–53. In a new business, the order of magnitude of balances in such accounts is not determinable in advance. The magnitude may also vary from period to period.

Ex. 2–4

a. and b.

Transaction	Account Debited Type	Account Debited Effect	Account Credited Type	Account Credited Effect
(1)	asset	+	owner's equity	+
(2)	asset	+	asset	–
(3)	asset	+	asset	–
			liability	+
(4)	expense	+	asset	–
(5)	asset	+	revenue	+
(6)	liability	–	asset	–
(7)	asset	+	asset	–
(8)	drawing	+	asset	–
(9)	expense	+	asset	–

Ex. 2–5

(1)	Cash	40,000	
	Ira Janke, Capital		40,000
(2)	Supplies	1,800	
	Cash		1,800
(3)	Equipment	24,000	
	Accounts Payable		15,000
	Cash		9,000
(4)	Operating Expenses	3,050	
	Cash		3,050
(5)	Accounts Receivable	12,000	
	Service Revenue		12,000
(6)	Accounts Payable	7,500	
	Cash		7,500
(7)	Cash	9,500	
	Accounts Receivable		9,500
(8)	Ira Janke, Drawing	5,000	
	Cash		5,000
(9)	Operating Expenses	1,050	
	Supplies		1,050

Ex. 2–6

MALTA CO.
Trial Balance
February 28, 2006

Cash	23,150	
Accounts Receivable	2,500	
Supplies	750	
Equipment	24,000	
Accounts Payable		7,500
Ira Janke, Capital		40,000
Ira Janke, Drawing	5,000	
Service Revenue		12,000
Operating Expenses	4,100	
	59,500	59,500

45

Ex. 2–16

HALEAKALA PARK CO.
Trial Balance
March 31, 2006

Cash	17,450	
Accounts Receivable	37,500	
Supplies	2,100	
Prepaid Insurance	3,000	
Land	85,000	
Accounts Payable		18,710
Unearned Rent		9,000
Notes Payable		40,000
Neil Orzeck, Capital		86,640
Neil Orzeck, Drawing	20,000	
Fees Earned		310,000
Wages Expense	175,000	
Rent Expense	60,000	
Utilities Expense	41,500	
Supplies Expense	7,900	
Insurance Expense	6,000	
Miscellaneous Expense	8,900	
	464,350	464,350

Ex. 2–17

Inequality of trial balance totals would be caused by errors described in (b) and (d).

Ex. 2–18

ESCALADE CO.
Trial Balance
December 31, 2006

Cash...	13,375	
Accounts Receivable...	24,600	
Prepaid Insurance	8,000	
Equipment...	75,000	
Accounts Payable..		11,180
Unearned Rent...		4,250
Erin Capelli, Capital..		82,420
Erin Capelli, Drawing..	10,000	
Service Revenue..		83,750
Wages Expense	42,000	
Advertising Expense	7,200	
Miscellaneous Expense	1,425	
	181,600	181,600

Ex. 2–19

Error	(a) Out of Balance	(b) Difference	(c) Larger Total
1.	yes	$1,250	debit
2.	yes	18	credit
3.	yes	4,175	debit
4.	yes	800	credit
5.	no	—	—
6.	yes	180	credit
7.	no	—	—

Ex. 2–20

1. The debit column total is added incorrectly. The sum is $97,250, rather than $152,750.

2. The trial balance should be dated January 31, 2006, not for the month of January.

3. The Accounts Receivable balance should be in the debit column.

4. The Accounts Payable balance should be in the credit column.

5. The Susan Appleby, Drawing, balance should be in the debit column.

6. The Advertising Expense balance should be in the debit column.

A corrected trial balance would be as follows:

DINERO CO.
Trial Balance
January 31, 2006

Cash	7,500	
Accounts Receivable	16,400	
Prepaid Insurance	3,600	
Equipment	50,000	
Accounts Payable		1,850
Salaries Payable		1,250
Susan Appleby, Capital		43,200
Susan Appleby, Drawing	6,000	
Service Revenue		78,700
Salary Expense	32,810	
Advertising Expense	7,200	
Miscellaneous Expense	1,490	
	125,000	125,000

Ex. 2–21

a.	Gerald Owen, Drawing	15,000	
	Wages Expense		15,000
b.	Prepaid Rent	4,500	
	Cash		4,500

52

Ex. 2–22

a.	Supplies	550	
	Accounts Payable		550
	Prepaid Rent...	550	
	Miscellaneous Expense		550
b.	Cash	7,500	
	Accounts Payable		3,750
	Accounts Receivable...		3,750

Ex. 2–23

a.   1. Net sales: $4,694 million increase ($58,247 – $53,553)

                       8.8% increase ($4,694 ÷ $53,553)

    2. Total operating
       expenses: $1,063 million increase ($12,278 – $11,215)

                       9.5% increase ($1,063 ÷ $11,215)

b.   During the year ending February 2, 2003, the percent increase in total operating expenses (9.5%) is more than the percent increase in net sales (8.8%), an unfavorable trend.

Ex. 2–24

a.

KMART CORPORATION
Income Statement
For the Years Ending January 31, 2000 and 1999
(in millions)

			Increase (Decrease)	
	2000	**1999**	**Amount**	**Percent**
1. Sales	$37,028	$35,925	$ 1,103	3.1%
2. Cost of sales	(29,658)	(28,111)	1,547	5.5%
3. Selling, general, and admin.				
expenses	(7,415)	(6,514)	901	13.8%
4. Operating income (loss)				
before taxes...............................	$ (45)	$ 1,300	$(1,345)	(103.5%)

b. The horizontal analysis of Kmart Corporation reveals deteriorating operating results from 1999 to 2000. While sales increased by $1,103 million, a 3.1% increase, cost of sales increased by $1,547 million, a 5.5% increase. Selling, general, and administrative expenses also increased by $901 million, a 13.8% increase. The end result was that operating income decreased by $1,345 million, over a 100% decrease, and created a $45 million loss in 2000. Little over a year later, Kmart filed for bankruptcy protection. It has now emerged from bankruptcy, hoping to return to profitability.

PROBLEMS

Prob. 2–1A

1. and 2.

Cash			
(a)	17,500	(b)	4,000
(g)	3,725	(c)	2,200
9,410	*21,225*	(d)	660
		(f)	1,200
		(h)	1,800
		(i)	235
		(l)	1,300
		(m)	105
		(n)	200
		(o)	115
			11,815

Accounts Receivable			
(k)	3,500		

Supplies			
(d)	660		

Prepaid Insurance			
(f)	1,200		

Automobiles			
(b)	15,300		

Equipment			
(e)	5,200		

Notes Payable			
(n)	200	(b)	11,300
		11,100	

Accounts Payable			
(h)	1,800	(e)	5,200
		(j)	650
	4,050	*5,850*	

Shaun Wilcox, Capital			
		(a)	17,500

Professional Fees			
		(g)	3,725
		(k)	3,500
			7,225

Rent Expense			
(c)	2,200		

Salary Expense			
(l)	1,300		

Blueprint Expense			
(j)	650		

Automobile Expense			
(o)	115		

Miscellaneous Expense			
(i)	235		
(m)	105		
	340		

Prob. 2–2A Concluded

2.

Cash			
(a)	12,000	(d)	2,000
(c)	12,600	(e)	450
15,575	*24,600*	(f)	1,500
		(g)	2,075
		(h)	3,000
			9,025

Supplies			
(b)	850	(i)	605
245			

Accounts Payable			
(e)	450	(b)	850
		400	

Tim Cochran, Capital		
	(a)	12,000

Tim Cochran, Drawing	
(f)	1,500

Sales Commissions		
	(c)	12,600

Rent Expense	
(d)	2,000

Office Salaries Expense	
(h)	3,000

Automobile Expense	
(g)	1,700

Supplies Expense	
(i)	605

Miscellaneous Expense	
(g)	375

3.

STAR REALTY
Trial Balance
March 31, 2006

Cash	15,575	
Supplies	245	
Accounts Payable		400
Tim Cochran, Capital		12,000
Tim Cochran, Drawing	1,500	
Sales Commissions		12,600
Rent Expense	2,000	
Office Salaries Expense	3,000	
Automobile Expense	1,700	
Supplies Expense	605	
Miscellaneous Expense	375	
	25,000	25,000

4. a. $12,600

b. $7,680

c. $4,920

Prob. 2–3A

1.

	JOURNAL			Pages 1 and 2
Date	Description	Post. Ref.	Debit	Credit
2006				
July 1	Cash...	11	18,000	
	Leon Cruz, Capital.............................	31		18,000
5	Rent Expense..	53	1,500	
	Cash	11		1,500
10	Truck...	18	15,000	
	Cash	11		5,000
	Notes Payable.......................................	21		10,000
13	Equipment...	16	4,500	
	Accounts Payable	22		4,500
14	Supplies	13	975	
	Cash	11		975
15	Prepaid Insurance	14	3,000	
	Cash	11		3,000
15	Cash...	11	4,100	
	Fees Earned..	41		4,100
21	Accounts Payable..................................	22	2,400	
	Cash	11		2,400
24	Accounts Receivable	12	6,100	
	Fees Earned..	41		6,100
26	Truck Expense.......................................	55	580	
	Accounts Payable	22		580
27	Utilities Expense...................................	54	950	
	Cash	11		950
27	Miscellaneous Expense	59	315	
	Cash	11		315

Prob. 2–3A Continued

	JOURNAL			Pages 1 and 2

Date	Description	Post. Ref.	Debit	Credit
2006				
July 29	Cash..	11	3,420	
	Accounts Receivable	12		3,420
30	Wages Expense	51	2,500	
	Cash	11		2,500
31	Leon Cruz, Drawing............................	32	2,000	
	Cash	11		2,000

2.

Cash   **11**

		Post.			Balance	
Date	Item	Ref.	Dr.	Cr.	Dr.	Cr.
2006						
July 1	....	1	18,000	....	18,000	....
5	....	1	....	1,500	16,500	....
10	....	1	....	5,000	11,500	....
14	....	1	....	975	10,525	....
15	....	1	....	3,000	7,525	....
15	....	1	4,100	....	11,625	....
21	....	2	....	2,400	9,225	....
27	....	2	....	950	8,275	....
27	....	2	....	315	7,960	....
29	....	2	3,420	....	11,380	....
30	....	2	....	2,500	8,880	....
31	....	2	....	2,000	6,880	....

Accounts Receivable   **12**

Date	Item	Ref.	Dr.	Cr.	Dr.	Cr.
2006						
July 24	....	2	6,100	....	6,100	....
29	....	2	....	3,420	2,680	....

Prob. 2–3A Continued

Supplies   13

Date	Item	Post. Ref.	Dr.	Cr.	Balance Dr.	Balance Cr.
2006						
July 14	....	1	975	....	975	....

Prepaid Insurance   14

Date	Item	Post. Ref.	Dr.	Cr.	Balance Dr.	Balance Cr.
2006						
July 15	....	1	3,000	....	3,000	....

Equipment   16

Date	Item	Post. Ref.	Dr.	Cr.	Balance Dr.	Balance Cr.
2006						
July 13	....	1	4,500	....	4,500	....

Truck   18

Date	Item	Post. Ref.	Dr.	Cr.	Balance Dr.	Balance Cr.
2006						
July 10	....	1	15,000	....	15,000	....

Notes Payable   21

Date	Item	Post. Ref.	Dr.	Cr.	Balance Dr.	Balance Cr.
2006						
July 10	....	1	....	10,000	....	10,000

Accounts Payable   22

Date	Item	Post. Ref.	Dr.	Cr.	Balance Dr.	Balance Cr.
2006						
July 13	....	1	....	4,500	....	4,500
21	....	2	2,400	....	....	2,100
26	....	2	....	580	....	2,680

Leon Cruz, Capital   31

Date	Item	Post. Ref.	Dr.	Cr.	Balance Dr.	Balance Cr.
2006						
July 1	....	1	....	18,000	....	18,000

Leon Cruz, Drawing   32

Date	Item	Post. Ref.	Dr.	Cr.	Balance Dr.	Balance Cr.
2006						
July 31	....	2	2,000	....	2,000	....

Prob. 2–4A Continued

Accounts Payable 21

Date	Item	Post. Ref.	Dr.	Cr.	Balance Dr.	Balance Cr.
2006						
Aug. 1	Balance	✓	....	....	....	5,200
1		18	....	1,760	....	6,960
9		18	240	....	....	6,720
23		18	2,670	....	....	4,050

Unearned Rent 22

Date	Item	Post. Ref.	Dr.	Cr.	Balance Dr.	Balance Cr.
2006						
Aug. 31		19	....	1,500	....	1,500

Notes Payable 23

Date	Item	Post. Ref.	Dr.	Cr.	Balance Dr.	Balance Cr.
2006						
Aug. 31		19	....	65,000	....	65,000

Larissa Sanchez, Capital 31

Date	Item	Post. Ref.	Dr.	Cr.	Balance Dr.	Balance Cr.
2006						
Aug. 1	Balance	✓	....	....	....	39,700

Larissa Sanchez, Drawing 32

Date	Item	Post. Ref.	Dr.	Cr.	Balance Dr.	Balance Cr.
2006						
Aug. 1	Balance	✓	....	....	16,000	....
31		19	2,500	....	18,500	....

Fees Earned 41

Date	Item	Post. Ref.	Dr.	Cr.	Balance Dr.	Balance Cr.
2006						
Aug. 1	Balance	✓	....	....	....	224,000
31		19	....	41,900	....	265,900

Salary and Commission Expense 51

Date	Item	Post. Ref.	Dr.	Cr.	Balance Dr.	Balance Cr.
2006						
Aug. 1	Balance	✓	....	....	133,000	....
31		19	....	800	132,200	....
31		19	17,400	....	149,600	....

Prob. 2–4A Continued

Rent Expense 52

Date		Item	Post. Ref.	Dr.	Cr.	Balance Dr.	Balance Cr.
2006							
Aug.	1	Balance...............................	✓	....	....	17,500	....
	2	....	18	2,500	....	20,000	....

Advertising Expense 53

Date		Item	Post. Ref.	Dr.	Cr.	Balance Dr.	Balance Cr.
2006							
Aug.	1	Balance...............................	✓	....	....	14,300	....
	17	....	18	3,450	....	17,750	....

Automobile Expense 54

Date		Item	Post. Ref.	Dr.	Cr.	Balance Dr.	Balance Cr.
2006							
Aug.	1	Balance...............................	✓	....	....	6,400	....
	30	....	19	1,360	....	7,760	....

Miscellaneous Expense 59

Date		Item	Post. Ref.	Dr.	Cr.	Balance Dr.	Balance Cr.
2006							
Aug.	1	Balance...............................	✓	....	....	950	....
	29	....	19	350	....	1,300	....

Prob. 2–4A   Concluded

4.

FICKLE REALTY
Trial Balance
August 31, 2006

Cash	28,390	
Accounts Receivable	48,930	
Prepaid Insurance	6,400	
Office Supplies	2,520	
Land	75,000	
Accounts Payable		4,050
Unearned Rent		1,500
Notes Payable		65,000
Larissa Sanchez, Capital		39,700
Larissa Sanchez, Drawing	18,500	
Fees Earned		265,900
Salary and Commission Expense	149,600	
Rent Expense	20,000	
Advertising Expense	17,750	
Automobile Expense	7,760	
Miscellaneous Expense	1,300	
	376,150	376,150

Prob. 2–5A

1. Totals of preliminary trial balance:

	Debit	$59,291.40
	Credit	$45,229.20

2. Difference between preliminary trial balance totals: $14,062.20

3. Errors in trial balance:

    (a) Land debit balance was listed as $26,265.00 instead of $26,625.00.

    (b) Accounts Payable credit balance of $1,077.50 was listed as debit balance.

    (c) Wages Expense debit balance of $2,518.60 was listed as credit balance.

    (d) Advertising Expense of $275.00 was omitted.

4. Errors in account balances:

    (a) Shelly Felix, Drawing, balance of $1,350.00 was totaled as $1,500.00.

5. Errors in posting:

    (a) Rent Expense entry of July 1 for $1,540.00 was posted as $15,400.00 (slide).

    (b) Cash entry of July 15 for $1,785.50 was posted as $1,875.50 (transposition).

    (c) Service Revenue entry of July 31 for $1,276.10 was posted as $1,726.10 (transposition).

    (d) Utilities Expense entry of July 30 for $436.60 was posted as $4,366.00 (slide).

6.

July	31	Utilities Expense	52	210.00	
		Cash	11		210.00

7.

CYPRESS TV REPAIR
Trial Balance
July 31, 20—

Cash	8,706.00	
Supplies	997.90	
Prepaid Insurance	395.50	
Land	26,625.00	
Notes Payable		6,500.00
Accounts Payable		1,077.50
Shelly Felix, Capital		27,760.20
Shelly Felix, Drawing	1,350.00	
Service Revenue		8,000.40
Wages Expense	2,518.60	
Utilities Expense	646.60	
Advertising Expense	275.00	
Rent Expense	1,540.00	
Miscellaneous Expense	283.50	
	43,338.10	43,338.10

Prob. 2–6A

1.

ONYX VIDEOGRAPHY
Trial Balance
August 31, 2006

Cash..	4,500*	
Accounts Receivable..	10,200	
Supplies..	1,500	
Prepaid Insurance	1,140	
Equipment..	36,000	
Notes Payable		12,000
Accounts Payable..		3,720
Jerri Orr, Capital		21,600
Jerri Orr, Drawing..	9,000	
Fees Earned		118,680
Wages Expense	68,000	
Rent Expense...	13,900	
Advertising Expense	6,300	
Gas, Electricity, and Water Expense...............................	3,780	
Miscellaneous Expense	1,680	
	156,000	156,000

* $4,700 – $3,500 (a) + $3,300 (b)

2. No. The trial balance indicates only that the debits and credits are equal. Any errors that have the same effect on debits and credits will not affect the balancing of the trial balance.

Prob. 2–1B

1. and 2.

Cash			
(a)	18,000	(b)	1,500
(g)	2,750	(c)	1,500
10,780	*20,750*	(e)	1,050
		(f)	1,200
		(h)	140
		(i)	3,000
		(j)	450
		(m)	1,000
		(n)	130
			9,970

Accounts Receivable	
(l)	4,150

Supplies	
(e)	1,050

Prepaid Insurance	
(f)	1,200

Automobiles	
(c)	16,500

Equipment	
(d)	6,500

Notes Payable			
(j)	450	(c)	15,000
			14,550

Accounts Payable			
(i)	3,000	(d)	6,500
		(k)	525
	4,025		*7,025*

Christina Kiff, Capital			
		(a)	18,000

Professional Fees			
		(g)	2,750
		(l)	4,150
			6,900

Rent Expense	
(b)	1,500

Salary Expense	
(m)	1,000

Automobile Expense	
(n)	130

Blueprint Expense	
(k)	525

Miscellaneous Expense	
(h)	140

Prob. 2–2B   Concluded

2.

Cash			
(a)	9,000	(b)	2,000
(e)	10,750	(d)	290
12,080	19,750	(f)	1,880
		(g)	2,500
		(i)	1,000
			7,670

Sales Commissions			
		(e)	10,750

Office Salaries Expense			
(g)	2,500		

Supplies			
(c)	700	(h)	575
125			

Rent Expense			
(b)	2,000		

Accounts Payable			
(d)	290	(c)	700
		410	

Automobile Expense			
(f)	1,400		

Lela Peterson, Capital			
		(a)	9,000

Supplies Expense			
(h)	575		

Lela Peterson, Drawing			
(i)	1,000		

Miscellaneous Expense			
(f)	480		

3.

ACADIA REALTY
Trial Balance
January 31, 2006

Cash..	12,080	
Supplies..	125	
Accounts Payable...		410
Lela Peterson, Capital..		9,000
Lela Peterson, Drawing..	1,000	
Sales Commissions..		10,750
Office Salaries Expense...	2,500	
Rent Expense...	2,000	
Automobile Expense	1,400	
Supplies Expense...	575	
Miscellaneous Expense	480	
	20,160	20,160

4.   a. $10,750

   b. $6,955

   c. $3,795

Prob. 2–3B

1.

Date	Description	Post. Ref.	Debit	Credit
2006				
Nov. 2	Cash..	11	15,000	
	Nicole Oliver, Capital	31		15,000
5	Rent Expense....................................	53	1,750	
	Cash	11		1,750
6	Equipment..	16	8,500	
	Accounts Payable	22		8,500
8	Truck..	18	18,000	
	Cash	11		10,000
	Notes Payable...................................	21		8,000
10	Supplies	13	1,115	
	Cash	11		1,115
12	Cash..	11	7,500	
	Fees Earned.....................................	41		7,500
15	Prepaid Insurance	14	2,400	
	Cash	11		2,400
23	Accounts Receivable	12	3,950	
	Fees Earned.....................................	41		3,950
24	Truck Expense...................................	55	600	
	Accounts Payable	22		600
29	Utilities Expense................................	54	750	
	Cash	11		750
29	Miscellaneous Expense	59	310	
	Cash	11		310
30	Cash..	11	2,200	
	Accounts Receivable	12		2,200

Prob. 2–3B Continued

JOURNAL

Pages 1 and 2

Date	Description	Post. Ref.	Debit	Credit
2006				
Nov. 30	Wages Expense	51	2,700	
	Cash	11		2,700
30	Accounts Payable.................................	22	2,125	
	Cash	11		2,125
30	Nicole Oliver, Drawing	32	1,400	
	Cash	11		1,400

2.

GENERAL LEDGER

Cash   11

Date	Item	Post. Ref.	Dr.	Cr.	Balance Dr.	Balance Cr.
2006						
Nov. 2	....	1	15,000	....	15,000	....
5	....	1	....	1,750	13,250	....
8	....	1	....	10,000	3,250	....
10	....	1	....	1,115	2,135	....
12	....	1	7,500	....	9,635	....
15	....	1	....	2,400	7,235	....
29	....	2	....	750	6,485	....
29	....	2	....	310	6,175	....
30	....	2	2,200	....	8,375	....
30	....	2	....	2,700	5,675	....
30	....	2	....	2,125	3,550	....
30	....	2	....	1,400	2,150	....

Accounts Receivable   12

Date	Item	Post. Ref.	Dr.	Cr.	Balance Dr.	Balance Cr.
2006						
Nov. 23	....	1	3,950	....	3,950	....
30	....	2	....	2,200	1,750	....

Prob. 2–3B Continued

Supplies   13

Date	Item	Post. Ref.	Dr.	Cr.	Balance Dr.	Balance Cr.
2006						
Nov. 10	....	1	1,115	....	1,115	....

Prepaid Insurance   14

Date	Item	Post. Ref.	Dr.	Cr.	Balance Dr.	Balance Cr.
2006						
Nov. 15	....	1	2,400	....	2,400	....

Equipment   16

Date	Item	Post. Ref.	Dr.	Cr.	Balance Dr.	Balance Cr.
2006						
Nov. 6	....	1	8,500	....	8,500	....

Truck   18

Date	Item	Post. Ref.	Dr.	Cr.	Balance Dr.	Balance Cr.
2006						
Nov. 8	....	1	18,000	....	18,000	....

Notes Payable   21

Date	Item	Post. Ref.	Dr.	Cr.	Balance Dr.	Balance Cr.
2006						
Nov. 8	....	1	....	8,000	....	8,000

Accounts Payable   22

Date	Item	Post. Ref.	Dr.	Cr.	Balance Dr.	Balance Cr.
2006						
Nov. 6	....	1	....	8,500	....	8,500
24	....	1	....	600	....	9,100
30	....	2	2,125	....	....	6,975

Nicole Oliver, Capital   31

Date	Item	Post. Ref.	Dr.	Cr.	Balance Dr.	Balance Cr.
2006						
Nov. 2	....	1	....	15,000	....	15,000

Nicole Oliver, Drawing   32

Date	Item	Post. Ref.	Dr.	Cr.	Balance Dr.	Balance Cr.
2006						
Nov. 30	....	2	1,400	....	1,400	....

Prob. 2–4B Continued

Accounts Payable   21

Date	Item	Post. Ref.	Dr.	Cr.	Balance Dr.	Balance Cr.
2006						
Nov. 1	Balance................................	✓	....	....	....	23,020
2	....	18	....	1,675	....	24,695
17	....	18	9,100	....	....	15,595
20	....	18	400	....	....	15,195

Unearned Rent   22

Date	Item	Post. Ref.	Dr.	Cr.	Balance Dr.	Balance Cr.
2006						
Nov. 30	....	19	....	2,000	....	2,000

Notes Payable   23

Date	Item	Post. Ref.	Dr.	Cr.	Balance Dr.	Balance Cr.
2006						
Nov. 15	....	18	....	80,000	....	80,000

Drew Felkel, Capital   31

Date	Item	Post. Ref.	Dr.	Cr.	Balance Dr.	Balance Cr.
2006						
Nov. 1	Balance................................	✓	....	....	....	68,680

Drew Felkel, Drawing   32

Date	Item	Post. Ref.	Dr.	Cr.	Balance Dr.	Balance Cr.
2006						
Nov. 1	Balance................................	✓	....	....	2,000	....
30	....	19	7,500	....	9,500	....

Fees Earned   41

Date	Item	Post. Ref.	Dr.	Cr.	Balance Dr.	Balance Cr.
2006						
Nov. 1	Balance................................	✓	....	....	....	253,000
30	....	19	....	48,400	....	301,400

Salary and Commission Expense   51

Date	Item	Post. Ref.	Dr.	Cr.	Balance Dr.	Balance Cr.
2006						
Nov. 1	Balance................................	✓	....	....	148,200	....
27	....	19	....	700	147,500	....
30	....	19	24,000	....	171,500	....

Prob. 2–4B Continued

Rent Expense   52

Date	Item	Post. Ref.	Dr.	Cr.	Balance Dr.	Balance Cr.
2006						
Nov. 1	Balance..............................	✓	....	....	30,000	....
1	....	18	7,000	....	37,000	....

Advertising Expense   53

Date	Item	Post. Ref.	Dr.	Cr.	Balance Dr.	Balance Cr.
2006						
Nov. 1	Balance..............................	✓	....	....	17,800	....
23	....	18	2,050	....	19,850	....

Automobile Expense   54

Date	Item	Post. Ref.	Dr.	Cr.	Balance Dr.	Balance Cr.
2006						
Nov. 1	Balance..............................	✓	....	....	5,500	....
28	....	19	1,100	....	6,600	....

Miscellaneous Expense   59

Date	Item	Post. Ref.	Dr.	Cr.	Balance Dr.	Balance Cr.
2006						
Nov. 1	Balance..............................	✓	....	....	3,100	....
29	....	19	390	....	3,490	....

4.

BOOMERANG REALTY
Trial Balance
November 30, 2006

Cash	25,060	
Accounts Receivable	93,900	
Prepaid Insurance	7,000	
Office Supplies	3,375	
Land	90,000	
Accounts Payable		15,195
Unearned Rent		2,000
Notes Payable		80,000
Drew Felkel, Capital		68,680
Drew Felkel, Drawing	9,500	
Fees Earned		301,400
Salary and Commission Expense	171,500	
Rent Expense	37,000	
Advertising Expense	19,850	
Automobile Expense	6,600	
Miscellaneous Expense	3,490	
	467,275	467,275

Prob. 2–5B

1. Totals of preliminary trial balance:

	Debit	$59,291.40
	Credit	$45,229.20

2. Difference between preliminary trial balance totals: $14,062.20

3. Errors in trial balance:

    (a) Land debit balance was listed as $26,265.00 instead of $26,625.00.

    (b) Accounts Payable credit balance of $1,077.50 was listed as debit balance.

    (c) Advertising Expense of $275.00 was omitted.

4. Errors in account balances:

    (a) Shelly Felix, Drawing, balance of $1,350.00 was totaled as $1,500.00.

5. Errors in posting:

    (a) Rent Expense entry of July 1 for $1,540.00 was posted as $15,400.00 (slide).

    (b) Cash entry of July 15 for $1,785.50 was posted as $1,875.50 (transposition).

    (c) Service Revenue entry of July 31 for $1,276.10 was posted as $1,726.10 (transposition).

    (d) Utilities Expense entry of July 30 for $436.60 was posted as $4,366.00 (slide).

6.

July	31	Advertising Expense	53	175.00	
		Cash	11		175.00

7.

CYPRESS TV REPAIR
Trial Balance
July 31, 20—

Cash	8,741.00	
Supplies	997.90	
Prepaid Insurance	395.50	
Land	26,625.00	
Notes Payable		6,500.00
Accounts Payable		1,077.50
Shelly Felix, Capital		27,760.20
Shelly Felix, Drawing	1,350.00	
Service Revenue		8,000.40
Wages Expense	2,518.60	
Utilities Expense	436.60	
Advertising Expense	450.00	
Rent Expense	1,540.00	
Miscellaneous Expense	283.50	
	43,338.10	43,338.10

Prob. 2–6B

1.

MONTERO CARPET
Trial Balance
October 31, 2006

Cash...	4,000*	
Accounts Receivable..	8,575	
Supplies..	1,540	
Prepaid Insurance	770	
Equipment...	35,000	
Notes Payable		21,000
Accounts Payable...		5,475
Tyca Seagle, Capital...		21,825
Tyca Seagle, Drawing..	11,200	
Fees Earned		76,700
Wages Expense	43,540	
Rent Expense..	10,400	
Advertising Expense	4,480	
Gas, Electricity, and Water Expense....................	4,400	
Miscellaneous Expense	1,095	
	125,000	125,000

* $5,200 + $1,500 (a) – $2,700 (b)

2. No. The trial balance indicates only that the debits and credits are equal. Any errors that have the same effect on debits and credits will not affect the balancing of the trial balance.

CONTINUING PROBLEM

2. and 3.

		JOURNAL			Page 1

Date	Description	Post. Ref.	Debit	Credit
2006				
May 1	Cash..	11	3,000	
	Shannon Burns, Capital	31		3,000
1	Office Rent Expense	51	1,600	
	Cash	11		1,600
1	Prepaid Insurance	15	3,360	
	Cash	11		3,360
2	Cash..	11	1,200	
	Accounts Receivable	12		1,200
3	Cash..	11	4,800	
	Unearned Revenue............................	23		4,800
3	Accounts Payable..................................	21	250	
	Cash	11		250
4	Miscellaneous Expense	59	150	
	Cash	11		150
5	Office Equipment..................................	17	5,000	
	Accounts Payable	21		5,000
8	Advertising Expense	55	200	
	Cash	11		200
11	Cash..	11	600	
	Fees Earned....................................	41		600
13	Equipment Rent Expense	52	500	
	Cash	11		500
14	Wages Expense	50	1,200	
	Cash	11		1,200

Continuing Problem   Continued

2. and 3.

			Post.		
Date		Description	Ref.	Debit	Credit
2006					
May 16		Cash...	11	1,100	
		Fees Earned......................................	41		1,100
	18	Supplies	14	750	
		Accounts Payable	21		750
	21	Music Expense	54	240	
		Cash	11		240
	22	Advertising Expense	55	500	
		Cash	11		500
	23	Cash...	11	400	
		Accounts Receivable	12	1,160	
		Fees Earned......................................	41		1,560
	27	Utilities Expense...................................	53	560	
		Cash	11		560
	28	Wages Expense....................................	50	1,200	
		Cash	11		1,200
	29	Miscellaneous Expense	59	170	
		Cash	11		170
	30	Cash...	11	600	
		Accounts Receivable	12	600	
		Fees Earned......................................	41		1,200
	31	Cash...	11	2,000	
		Fees Earned......................................	41		2,000
	31	Music Expense	54	600	
		Cash	11		600
	31	Shannon Burns, Drawing......................	32	2,000	
		Cash	11		2,000

JOURNAL — Page 2

Continuing Problem   Continued

1. and 3.

Cash   11

Date	Item	Post. Ref.	Dr.	Cr.	Balance Dr.	Balance Cr.
2006						
May 1	Balance............................	✓	....	....	6,160	....
1	....	1	3,000	....	9,160	....
1	....	1	....	1,600	7,560	....
1	....	1	....	3,360	4,200	....
2	....	1	1,200	....	5,400	....
3	....	1	4,800	....	10,200	....
3	....	1	....	250	9,950	....
4	....	1	....	150	9,800	....
8	....	1	....	200	9,600	....
11	....	1	600	....	10,200	....
13	....	1	....	500	9,700	....
14	....	1	....	1,200	8,500	....
16	....	2	1,100	....	9,600	....
21	....	2	....	240	9,360	....
22	....	2	....	500	8,860	....
23	....	2	400	....	9,260	....
27	....	2	....	560	8,700	....
28	....	2	....	1,200	7,500	....
29	....	2	....	170	7,330	....
30	....	2	600	....	7,930	....
31	....	2	2,000	....	9,930	....
31	....	2	....	600	9,330	....
31	....	2	....	2,000	7,330	....

Accounts Receivable   12

Date	Item	Post. Ref.	Dr.	Cr.	Balance Dr.	Balance Cr.
2006						
May 1	Balance............................	✓	....	....	1,200	....
2	....	1	....	1,200	—	—
23	....	2	1,160	....	1,160	....
30	....	2	600	....	1,760	....

Supplies   14

Date	Item	Post. Ref.	Dr.	Cr.	Balance Dr.	Balance Cr.
2006						
May 1	Balance............................	✓	....	....	170	....
18	....	2	750	....	920	....

Prepaid Insurance   15

Date	Item	Post. Ref.	Dr.	Cr.	Balance Dr.	Balance Cr.
2006						
May 1	....	1	3,360	....	3,360	....

Continuing Problem   Continued

Office Equipment 17

Date	Item	Post. Ref.	Dr.	Cr.	Balance Dr.	Balance Cr.
2006						
May 5	....	1	5,000	....	5,000	....

Accumulated Depreciation—Office Equipment 18
This account is not used in Chapter 2.

Accounts Payable 21

Date	Item	Post. Ref.	Dr.	Cr.	Balance Dr.	Balance Cr.
2006						
May 1	Balance................................	✓	....	....	....	250
3	....	1	250	....	—	—
5	....	1	....	5,000	....	5,000
18	....	2	....	750	....	5,750

Wages Payable 22
This account is not used in Chapter 2.

Unearned Revenue 23

Date	Item	Post. Ref.	Dr.	Cr.	Balance Dr.	Balance Cr.
2006						
May 3	....	1	....	4,800	....	4,800

Shannon Burns, Capital 31

Date	Item	Post. Ref.	Dr.	Cr.	Balance Dr.	Balance Cr.
2006						
May 1	Balance................................	✓	....	....	....	7,000
1	....	1	....	3,000	....	10,000

Shannon Burns, Drawing 32

Date	Item	Post. Ref.	Dr.	Cr.	Balance Dr.	Balance Cr.
2006						
May 1	Balance................................	✓	....	....	250	....
31	....	2	2,000	....	2,250	....

Income Summary 33
This account is not used in Chapter 2.

Fees Earned 41

Date	Item	Post. Ref.	Dr.	Cr.	Balance Dr.	Balance Cr.
2006						
May 1	Balance................................	✓	....	....	....	4,750
11	....	1	....	600	....	5,350
16	....	2	....	1,100	....	6,450
23	....	2	....	1,560	....	8,010
30	....	2	....	1,200	....	9,210
31	....	2	....	2,000	....	11,210

Continuing Problem   Continued

Wages Expense   50

Date	Item	Post. Ref.	Dr.	Cr.	Balance Dr.	Balance Cr.
2006						
May 1	Balance................................	✓	....	....	400	....
14	....	1	1,200	....	1,600	....
28	....	2	1,200	....	2,800	....

Office Rent Expense   51

Date	Item	Post. Ref.	Dr.	Cr.	Balance Dr.	Balance Cr.
2006						
May 1	Balance................................	✓	....	....	1,000	....
1	....	1	1,600	....	2,600	....

Equipment Rent Expense   52

Date	Item	Post. Ref.	Dr.	Cr.	Balance Dr.	Balance Cr.
2006						
May 1	Balance................................	✓	....	....	650	....
13	....	1	500	....	1,150	....

Utilities Expense   53

Date	Item	Post. Ref.	Dr.	Cr.	Balance Dr.	Balance Cr.
2006						
May 1	Balance................................	✓	....	....	300	....
27	....	2	560	....	860	....

Music Expense   54

Date	Item	Post. Ref.	Dr.	Cr.	Balance Dr.	Balance Cr.
2006						
May 1	Balance................................	✓	....	....	940	....
21	....	2	240	....	1,180	....
31	....	2	600	....	1,780	....

Advertising Expense   55

Date	Item	Post. Ref.	Dr.	Cr.	Balance Dr.	Balance Cr.
2006						
May 1	Balance................................	✓	....	....	600	....
8	....	1	200	....	800	....
22	....	2	500	....	1,300	....

Supplies Expense   56

Date	Item	Post. Ref.	Dr.	Cr.	Balance Dr.	Balance Cr.
2006						
May 1	Balance................................	✓	....	....	180	....

Insurance Expense   57

This account is not used in Chapter 2.

Continuing Problem   Concluded

Depreciation Expense
58

Date	Item	Post. Ref.	Dr.	Cr.	Balance Dr.	Balance Cr.

This account is not used in Chapter 2.

Miscellaneous Expense
59

Date	Item	Post. Ref.	Dr.	Cr.	Balance Dr.	Balance Cr.
2006						
May 1	Balance	✓	....	....	150	....
4		1	150	....	300	....
29		2	170	....	470	....

4.

DANCIN MUSIC
Trial Balance
May 31, 2006

	Dr.	Cr.
Cash	7,330	
Accounts Receivable	1,760	
Supplies	920	
Prepaid Insurance	3,360	
Office Equipment	5,000	
Accounts Payable		5,750
Unearned Revenue		4,800
Shannon Burns, Capital		10,000
Shannon Burns, Drawing	2,250	
Fees Earned		11,210
Wages Expense	2,800	
Office Rent Expense	2,600	
Equipment Rent Expense	1,150	
Utilities Expense	860	
Music Expense	1,780	
Advertising Expense	1,300	
Supplies Expense	180	
Miscellaneous Expense	470	
	31,760	31,760

SPECIAL ACTIVITIES

Activity 2–1

Acceptable ethical conduct requires that Ross look for the difference. If Ross cannot find the difference within a reasonable amount of time, he should confer with his supervisor as to what action should be taken so that the financial statements can be prepared by the 5 o'clock deadline. Ross's responsibility to his employer is to act with integrity, objectivity, and due care, so that users of the financial statements will not be misled.

Activity 2–2

The following general journal entry should be used to record the receipt of tuition payments received in advance of classes:

Cash	XXXX	
Unearned Tuition Deposits		XXXX

Cash is an asset account, and Unearned Tuition Deposits is a liability account. As the classes are taught throughout the term, the unearned tuition deposits become earned revenue.

Activity 2–3

The journal is called the book of original entry. It provides a time-ordered history of the transactions that have occurred for the firm. This time-ordered history is very important because it allows one to trace ledger account balances back to the original transactions that created those balances. This is called an "audit trail." If the firm recorded transactions by posting ledgers directly, it would be nearly impossible to reconstruct actual transactions. The debits and credits would all be separated and accumulated into the ledger balances. Once the transactions become part of the ledger balances, the original transactions would be lost. That is, there would be no audit trail, and any errors that might occur in recording transactions would be almost impossible to trace. Thus, firms first record transaction debits and credits in a journal. These transactions are then posted to the ledger to update the account balances. The journal and ledger are linked using posting references. This allows an analyst to trace the transaction flow forward or backward, depending upon the need.

Activity 2–6

1. From our discussions in Chapter 1, the three possible business strategies that could be used are as follows:

   low-cost strategy
   differentiation strategy
   combination strategy

2. Real world examples of each strategy are as follows:

   low-cost strategy: Stein Mart, Wal-Mart, Kmart, Costco
   differentiation strategy: GAP, Limited, Old Navy, Talbots
   combination strategy: JCPenney, Sears, Dillards

3. The answers will vary among the students groups. Normally, venture capital firms demand a large percentage of ownership, which many times is the majority (over 50%) ownership.

Activity 2–7

Note to Instructors: The purpose of this activity is to familiarize students with the job opportunities available in accounting or in fields that require (or prefer) the employee to have some knowledge of accounting.

CHAPTER 3
THE MATCHING CONCEPT AND
THE ADJUSTING PROCESS

CLASS DISCUSSION QUESTIONS

1. a. Under cash-basis accounting, revenues are reported in the period in which cash is received and expenses are reported in the period in which cash is paid.
   b. Under accrual-basis accounting, revenues are reported in the period in which they are earned and expenses are reported in the same period as the revenues to which they relate.

2. a. 2006
   b. 2005

3. a. 2006
   b. 2005

4. The matching concept is related to the accrual basis.

5. Yes. The cash amount listed on the trial balance is normally the amount of cash on hand and needs no adjustment at the end of the period.

6. No. The amount listed on the trial balance, before adjustments, normally represents the cost of supplies on hand at the beginning of the period plus the cost of the supplies purchased during the period. Some of the supplies have been used; therefore, an adjustment is necessary for the supplies used before the amount for the balance sheet is determined.

7. Adjusting entries are necessary at the end of an accounting period to bring the ledger up to date.

8. Adjusting entries bring the ledger up to date as a normal part of the accounting cycle. Correcting entries correct errors in the ledger.

9. Five different categories of adjusting entries include deferred expenses (prepaid expenses), deferred revenues (unearned revenues), accrued expenses (accrued liabilities), accrued revenues (accrued assets), and fixed assets (depreciation).

10. Statement (b): Increases the balance of an expense account.

11. Statement (a): Increases the balance of a revenue account.

12. Yes, because every adjusting entry affects expenses or revenues.

13. a. The balance is the sum of the beginning balance and the amount of the insurance premiums paid during the period.
    b. The balance is the unexpired premiums at the end of the period.

14. a. The rights acquired represent an asset.
    b. The justification for debiting Rent Expense is that when the ledger is summarized in a trial balance at the end of the month and statements are prepared, the rent will have become an expense. Hence, no adjusting entry will be necessary.

15. a. The portion of the cost of a fixed asset deducted from revenue of the period is debited to Depreciation Expense. It is the expired cost for the period. The reduction in the fixed asset account is recorded by a credit to Accumulated Depreciation rather than to the fixed asset account. The use of the contra asset account facilitates the presentation of original cost and accumulated depreciation on the balance sheet.
    b. Depreciation Expense—debit balance; Accumulated Depreciation—credit balance.
    c. No, it is not customary for the balances of the two accounts to be equal in amount.
    d. Depreciation Expense appears in the income statement; Accumulated Depreciation appears on the balance sheet.

EXERCISES

Ex. 3–1

1. Accrued expense (accrued liability)
2. Deferred expense (prepaid expense)
3. Deferred revenue (unearned revenue)
4. Accrued revenue (accrued asset)
5. Accrued expense (accrued liability)
6. Accrued expense (accrued liability)
7. Deferred expense (prepaid expense)
8. Deferred revenue (unearned revenue)

Ex. 3–2

Account	Answer
Aaron Piper, Drawing	Does not normally require adjustment.
Accounts Receivable	Normally requires adjustment (AR).
Accumulated Depreciation	Normally requires adjustment (DE).
Cash	Does not normally require adjustment.
Interest Payable	Normally requires adjustment (AE).
Interest Receivable	Normally requires adjustment (AR).
Land	Does not normally require adjustment.
Office Equipment	Does not normally require adjustment.
Prepaid Rent	Normally requires adjustment (DE).
Supplies Expense	Normally requires adjustment (DE).
Unearned Fees	Normally requires adjustment (DR).
Wages Expense	Normally requires adjustment (AE).

Ex. 3–3

Supplies Expense	801	
Supplies		801

Ex. 3–4

$1,067 ($118 + $949)

Ex. 3–5

a. Insurance expense (or expenses) will be understated. Net income will be overstated.

b. Prepaid insurance (or assets) will be overstated. Owner's equity will be overstated.

Ex. 3–6

a.	Insurance Expense	1,215	
	Prepaid Insurance		1,215
b.	Insurance Expense	1,215	
	Prepaid Insurance		1,215

Ex. 3–7

a.	Insurance Expense	3,720	
	Prepaid Insurance		3,720
b.	Insurance Expense	3,720	
	Prepaid Insurance		3,720

Ex. 3–8

Unearned Fees	9,570	
Fees Earned		9,570

Ex. 3–9

a. Rent revenue (or revenues) will be understated. Net income will be understated.

b. Owner's equity at the end of the period will be understated. Unearned rent (or liabilities) will be overstated.

Ex. 3–10

a.	Salary Expense	9,360	
	Salaries Payable		9,360
b.	Salary Expense	12,480	
	Salaries Payable		12,480

Ex. 3–11

$59,850 ($63,000 − $3,150)

Ex. 3–12

a. Salary expense (or expenses) will be understated. Net income will be overstated.

b. Salaries payable (or liabilities) will be understated. Owner's equity will be overstated.

Ex. 3–13

a. Salary expense (or expenses) will be overstated. Net income will be understated.

b. The balance sheet will be correct. This is because salaries payable has been satisfied, and the net income errors have offset each other. Thus, owner's equity is correct.

Ex. 3–14

a.	Taxes Expense	945	
	Prepaid Taxes		945
	($1,260 ÷ 12) × 9 = $945		
	Taxes Expense	8,750	
	Taxes Payable		8,750
b.	$9,695 ($945 + $8,750)		

Ex. 3–15

$195,816,000 ($128,776,000 + $67,040,000)

Ex. 3–16

a. $503,000,000

b. 63% ($503,000,000 ÷ $798,000,000)

Ex. 3–17

	Error (a)		Error (b)	
	Over-stated	Under-stated	Over-stated	Under-stated
1. Revenue for the year would be	$ 0	$6,900	$ 0	$ 0
2. Expenses for the year would be	0	0	0	3,740
3. Net income for the year would be..........	0	6,900	3,740	0
4. Assets at December 31 would be	0	0	0	0
5. Liabilities at December 31 would be	6,900	0	0	3,740
6. Owner's equity at December 31 would be...	0	6,900	3,740	0

Ex. 3–18

$175,840 ($172,680 + $6,900 − $3,740)

Ex. 3–19

a. Accounts Receivable.. 11,500
    Fees Earned 11,500

b. No. If the cash basis of accounting is used, revenues are recognized only when the cash is received. Therefore, earned but unbilled revenues would not be recognized in the accounts, and no adjusting entry would be necessary.

Ex. 3–27

1. The accountant debited Accounts Receivable for $2,000, but did not credit Laundry Revenue. This adjusting entry represents accrued laundry revenue.

2. The accountant credited Laundry Equipment for the depreciation expense of $5,600, instead of crediting the accumulated depreciation account.

3. The accountant credited the prepaid insurance account for $1,700, but only debited the insurance expense account for $700.

4. The accountant did not debit Wages Expense for $850.

5. The accountant debited rather than credited Laundry Supplies for $1,100.

The corrected adjusted trial balance is shown below.

Minaret Laundry
Adjusted Trial Balance
May 31, 2006

Cash	2,500	
Accounts Receivable	9,500	
Laundry Supplies	650	
Prepaid Insurance	1,125	
Laundry Equipment	85,600	
Accumulated Depreciation		61,300
Accounts Payable		4,950
Wages Payable		850
Troy Jobe, Capital		32,450
Troy Jobe, Drawing	10,000	
Laundry Revenue		68,900
Wages Expense	25,350	
Rent Expense	15,575	
Utilities Expense	8,500	
Depreciation Expense	5,600	
Laundry Supplies Expense	1,100	
Insurance Expense	1,700	
Miscellaneous Expense	1,250	
	168,450	168,450

Ex. 3–28

a. (1) $620 million increase ($3,664 million – $3,044 million)

   20.4% increase ($620 million ÷ $3,044 million)

   (2) 2003: 6.3% ($3,644 million ÷ $58,247 million)

   2002: 5.7% ($3,044 million ÷ $53,553 million)

b. The net earnings increased during 2003 by 20.4%, a favorable trend. The percent of net earnings to net sales also increased—from 5.7% to 6.3%, a favorable trend.

Ex. 3–29

a. Dell Computer Corporation

	Amount	Percent
Net sales	$35,404,000	100.0
Cost of goods sold	(29,055,000)	82.1
Operating expenses	(3,505,000)	9.9
Operating income (loss)	$ 2,844,000	8.0

b. Gateway Inc.

	Amount	Percent
Net sales	$ 4,171,325	100.0
Cost of goods sold	(3,605,120)	86.4
Operating expenses	(1,077,447)	25.8
Operating income (loss)	$ (511,242)	(12.2)

c. Dell is more profitable than Gateway. Specifically, Dell's cost of goods sold of 82.1% is significantly less (4.3%) than Gateway's cost of goods sold of 86.4%. In addition, Gateway's operating expenses are over one-fourth of sales, while Dell's operating expenses are 9.9% of sales. The result is that Dell generates an operating income of 8.0% of sales, while Gateway generates a loss of 12.2% of sales. Obviously, Gateway must improve its operations if it is to remain in business and remain competitive with Dell.

PROBLEMS

Prob. 3–1A

1. a. Accounts Receivable 7,100
       Fees Earned   7,100

   b. Supplies Expense 1,860
       Supplies   1,860

   c. Wages Expense 1,380
       Wages Payable   1,380

   d. Unearned Rent 1,650
       Rent Revenue..   1,650

   e. Depreciation Expense 1,120
       Accumulated Depreciation   1,120

2. Adjusting entries are a planned part of the accounting process to update the accounts. Correcting entries are not planned, but arise only when necessary to correct errors.

Prob. 3–2A

a. Supplies Expense	1,420	
Supplies		1,420
b. Depreciation Expense	1,450	
Accumulated Depreciation		1,450
c. Rent Expense	9,500	
Prepaid Rent		9,500
d. Wages Expense	1,050	
Wages Payable		1,050
e. Unearned Fees	3,600	
Fees Earned		3,600
f. Accounts Receivable	7,100	
Fees Earned		7,100

Prob. 3–5A

1.

a.	Depreciation Expense—Building	3,600	
	Accumulated Depreciation—Building		3,600
b.	Depreciation Expense—Equipment	2,400	
	Accumulated Depreciation—Equipment		2,400
c.	Salaries and Wages Expense	2,170	
	Salaries and Wages Payable		2,170
d.	Insurance Expense	2,500	
	Prepaid Insurance		2,500
e.	Accounts Receivable	4,350	
	Fees Earned		4,350
f.	Supplies Expense	1,075	
	Supplies		1,075
g.	Unearned Rent	4,400	
	Rent Revenue		4,400

Prob. 3–5A   Concluded

2.

GRECO SERVICE CO.
Adjusted Trial Balance
December 31, 2006

Cash	4,200	
Accounts Receivable	24,950	
Prepaid Insurance	3,500	
Supplies	375	
Land	100,000	
Building	161,500	
Accumulated Depreciation—Building		79,300
Equipment	80,100	
Accumulated Depreciation—Equipment		37,700
Accounts Payable		7,500
Salaries & Wages Payable		2,170
Unearned Rent		2,800
Curtis Loomis, Capital		157,100
Curtis Loomis, Drawing	5,000	
Fees Earned		261,550
Rent Revenue		4,400
Salaries and Wages Expense	103,970	
Utilities Expense	28,200	
Advertising Expense	15,000	
Repairs Expense	12,100	
Depreciation Expense—Equipment	2,400	
Insurance Expense	2,500	
Depreciation Expense—Building	3,600	
Supplies Expense	1,075	
Miscellaneous Expense	4,050	
	552,520	552,520

Prob. 3–6A

1. a. Accounts Receivable.. 9,600
        Fees Earned..   9,600

    b. Depreciation Expense.. 3,500
        Accumulated Depreciation....................................   3,500

    c. Wages Expense... 1,450
        Wages Payable...   1,450

    d. Supplies Expense... 1,100
        Supplies...   1,100

2.

	Net Income	Total Assets	Total Liabilities	Total Owner's Equity
Reported amounts	$124,350	$500,000	$125,000	$375,000
Corrections:				
Adjustment (a)	+ 9,600	+ 9,600	0	+ 9,600
Adjustment (b)	− 3,500	− 3,500	0	− 3,500
Adjustment (c)	− 1,450	0	+ 1,450	− 1,450
Adjustment (d)	− 1,100	− 1,100	0	− 1,100
Corrected amounts	$127,900	$505,000	$126,450	$378,550

Prob. 3–1B

1. a. Supplies Expense.. 1,565
        Supplies 1,565

    b. Unearned Rent... 1,340
        Rent Revenue 1,340

    c. Wages Expense 2,150
        Wages Payable 2,150

    d. Accounts Receivable.. 11,278
        Fees Earned.. 11,278

    e. Depreciation Expense.. 1,000
        Accumulated Depreciation 1,000

2. Adjusting entries are a planned part of the accounting process to update the accounts. Correcting entries are not planned, but arise only when necessary to correct errors.

Prob. 3–2B

a.	Accounts Receivable	1,150	
	Fees Earned		1,150
b.	Supplies Expense	1,390	
	Supplies		1,390
c.	Rent Expense	6,000	
	Prepaid Rent		6,000
d.	Depreciation Expense	1,650	
	Accumulated Depreciation		1,650
e.	Unearned Fees	4,725	
	Fees Earned		4,725
f.	Wages Expense	2,180	
	Wages Payable		2,180

Prob. 3–3B

a.	Accounts Receivable	3,200	
	Fees Earned		3,200
b.	Supplies Expense	2,590	
	Supplies		2,590
c.	Depreciation Expense	3,850	
	Accumulated Depreciation		3,850
d.	Unearned Fees	1,000	
	Fees Earned		1,000
e.	Wages Expense	820	
	Wages Payable		820

Prob. 3–4B

2006

June 30	Supplies Expense	2,670	
	Supplies		2,670
30	Insurance Expense	2,550	
	Prepaid Insurance		2,550
30	Depreciation Expense—Equipment	7,020	
	Accumulated Depreciation—Equipment		7,020
30	Depreciation Expense—Automobiles	3,650	
	Accumulated Depreciation—Automobiles		3,650
30	Utilities Expense	420	
	Accounts Payable		420
30	Salary Expense	1,560	
	Salaries Payable		1,560
30	Unearned Service Fees	2,000	
	Service Fees Earned		2,000

Prob. 3–5B

1.

a.	Insurance Expense	3,200	
	Prepaid Insurance		3,200
b.	Supplies Expense	1,040	
	Supplies		1,040
c.	Depreciation Expense—Building	1,320	
	Accumulated Depreciation—Building		1,320
d.	Depreciation Expense—Equipment	4,100	
	Accumulated Depreciation—Equipment		4,100
e.	Unearned Rent	3,000	
	Rent Revenue		3,000
f.	Salaries and Wages Expense	1,760	
	Salaries and Wages Payable		1,760
g.	Accounts Receivable	3,200	
	Fees Earned		3,200

CONTINUING PROBLEM

1.

	JOURNAL			Page 3
Date	Description	Post. Ref.	Debit	Credit
2006				
May	31 Accounts Receivable	12	1,200[1]	
	Fees Earned...............................	41		1,200
	31 Supplies Expense...........................	56	750	
	Supplies	14		750
	31 Insurance Expense........................	57	140[2]	
	Prepaid Insurance......................	15		140
	31 Depreciation Expense...................	58	100	
	Accum. Depr.—Office Equip.	18		100
	31 Unearned Revenue.........................	23	2,400	
	Fees Earned...............................	41		2,400
	31 Wages Expense	50	130	
	Wages Payable...........................	22		130

[1] 30 hours × $40 = $1,200
[2] $3,360 ÷ 24 months = $140 per month

Continuing Problem   Continued

2.

Cash   **11**

Date	Item	Post. Ref.	Dr.	Cr.	Balance Dr.	Balance Cr.
2006						
May 1	Balance..................	✓	....	....	6,160	....
1	....	1	3,000	....	9,160	....
1	....	1	....	1,600	7,560	....
1	....	1	....	3,360	4,200	....
2	....	1	1,200	....	5,400	....
3	....	1	4,800	....	10,200	....
3	....	1	....	250	9,950	....
4	....	1	....	150	9,800	....
8	....	1	....	200	9,600	....
11	....	1	600	....	10,200	....
13	....	1	....	500	9,700	....
14	....	1	....	1,200	8,500	....
16	....	2	1,100	....	9,600	....
21	....	2	....	240	9,360	....
22	....	2	....	500	8,860	....
23	....	2	400	....	9,260	....
27	....	2	....	560	8,700	....
28	....	2	....	1,200	7,500	....
29	....	2	....	170	7,330	....
30	....	2	600	....	7,930	....
31	....	2	2,000	....	9,930	....
31	....	2	....	600	9,330	....
31	....	2	....	2,000	7,330	....

Accounts Receivable   **12**

Date	Item	Post. Ref.	Dr.	Cr.	Balance Dr.	Balance Cr.
2006						
May 1	Balance..................	✓	....	....	1,200	....
2	....	1	....	1,200	—	—
23	....	2	1,160	....	1,160	....
30	....	2	600	....	1,760	....
31	Adjusting................	3	1,200	....	2,960	....

Continuing Problem   Continued

Supplies   14

Date	Item	Post. Ref.	Dr.	Cr.	Balance Dr.	Balance Cr.
2006						
May 1	Balance..................	✓	....	....	170	....
18	....	2	750	....	920	....
31	Adjusting...............	3	....	750	170	....

Prepaid Insurance   15

2006						
May 1	....	1	3,360	....	3,360	....
31	Adjusting...............	3	....	140	3,220	....

Office Equipment   17

2006						
May 5	....	1	5,000	....	5,000	....

Accumulated Depreciation—Office Equipment   18

2006						
May 31	Adjusting...............	3	....	100	....	100

Accounts Payable   21

2006						
May 1	Balance..................	✓	....	....	....	250
3	....	1	250	....	—	—
5	....	1	....	5,000	....	5,000
18	....	2	....	750	....	5,750

Wages Payable   22

2006						
May 31	Adjusting...............	3	....	130	....	130

Unearned Revenue   23

2006						
May 3	....	1	....	4,800	....	4,800
31	Adjusting...............	3	2,400	....	....	2,400

Continuing Problem   Continued

Shannon Burns, Capital   31

Date		Item	Post. Ref.	Dr.	Cr.	Balance Dr.	Balance Cr.
2006							
May	1	Balance..................	✓	....	....	....	7,000
	1	....	1	....	3,000	....	10,000

Shannon Burns, Drawing   32

Date		Item	Post. Ref.	Dr.	Cr.	Balance Dr.	Balance Cr.
2006							
May	1	Balance..................	✓	....	....	250	....
	31	....	2	2,000	....	2,250	....

Income Summary   33

This account is not used in Chapter 3.

Fees Earned   41

Date		Item	Post. Ref.	Dr.	Cr.	Balance Dr.	Balance Cr.
2006							
May	1	Balance..................	✓	....	....	....	4,750
	11	....	1	....	600	....	5,350
	16	....	2	....	1,100	....	6,450
	23	....	2	....	1,560	....	8,010
	30	....	2	....	1,200	....	9,210
	31	....	2	....	2,000	....	11,210
	31	Adjusting................	3	....	1,200	....	12,410
	31	Adjusting................	3	....	2,400	....	14,810

Wages Expense   50

Date		Item	Post. Ref.	Dr.	Cr.	Balance Dr.	Balance Cr.
2006							
May	1	Balance..................	✓	....	....	400	....
	14	....	1	1,200	....	1,600	....
	28	....	2	1,200	....	2,800	....
	31	Adjusting................	3	130	....	2,930	....

Office Rent Expense   51

Date		Item	Post. Ref.	Dr.	Cr.	Balance Dr.	Balance Cr.
2006							
May	1	Balance..................	✓	....	....	1,000	....
	1	....	1	1,600	....	2,600	....

Activity 3–4

a. There are several indications that adjusting entries were not recorded before the financial statements were prepared, including:

1. All expenses on the income statement are identified as "paid" items and not as "expenses."

2. No expense is reported on the income statement for depreciation, and no accumulated depreciation is reported on the balance sheet.

3. No supplies, accounts payable, or wages payable are reported on the balance sheet.

b. Likely accounts requiring adjustment include:

1. Truck (for depreciation).

2. Supplies (paid) expense for supplies on hand.

3. Insurance (paid) expense for unexpired insurance.

4. Wages accrued.

5. Utilities accrued.

Activity 3–5

Note to Instructors: The purpose of this activity is to familiarize students with behaviors that are common in codes of conduct. In addition, this activity addresses an actual ethical dilemma for students.

Activity 3–6

1. The answers will vary among the student groups. The objective of this case is to generate student interest and discussion of business strategies.

    The advantages of the "do-it-yourself" strategy are as follows:

    a. This strategy requires less capital equipment and training of employees. For example, expensive automotive diagnostic equipment will not have to be purchased and Auto-Mart will not have to train its employees in auto repair and service. That is, it will be easier to staff the stores with sales personnel than with mechanics.

    b. This strategy emphasizes low costs and has worked well for other companies in the industry, such as AutoZone, Pep Boys, and the automobile departments of Wal-Mart and Kmart.

    The advantages of the "do-it-for-me" strategy are as follows:

    a. Demographically, the population of the United States is aging and is becoming more affluent. In the future, such demographics mean that more customers will be less willing to fix their own cars. That is, they would rather pay someone to fix their cars for them.

    b. Increased complexity of cars makes it more difficult for customers to repair their own cars.

    c. The margins are typically higher for service and maintenance than for retail parts (i.e., service and maintenance are more profitable).

    d. Kmart recently shut down hundreds of repair and service centers, thus providing an opportunity to offer Kmart customers "do-it-for-me" service.

2. Examples of "do-it-yourself" include AutoZone, Pep Boys, and Napa Auto Parts in the automotive industry. In the home improvement industry, examples include Home Depot and Lowe's.

    Examples of "do-it-for-me" include automotive dealerships and repair and service centers located at Sears, Wal-Mart, and Kmart. Other automotive examples include Mr. Transmission, Midas Muffler, and Brake-0.

CHAPTER 4
COMPLETING THE ACCOUNTING CYCLE

CLASS DISCUSSION QUESTIONS

1. a. The financial statements are the most important output of the accounting cycle.
    b. Yes, all companies have an accounting cycle that begins with analyzing and journalizing transactions and ends with a post-closing trial balance. However, companies may differ in how they implement the steps in the accounting cycle. For example, while most companies use computerized accounting systems, some companies may use manual systems.

2. No. The work sheet is a device used by the accountant to facilitate the preparation of statements and the recording of adjusting and closing entries.

3. Net loss. The expenses exceed the revenues.

4. Net income. The revenues exceed the expenses by $68,500.

5. a. Current assets are composed of cash and other assets that may reasonably be expected to be realized in cash or sold or consumed in the near future through the normal operations of the business.
    b. Property, plant, and equipment is composed of assets used in the business that are of a permanent or relatively fixed nature.

6. Current liabilities are liabilities that will be due within a short time (usually one year or less) and that are to be paid out of current assets. Liabilities that will not be due for a comparatively long time (usually more than one year) are called long-term liabilities.

7. Revenue, expense, and drawing accounts are generally referred to as temporary accounts.

8. Closing entries are necessary at the end of an accounting period (1) to transfer the balances in temporary accounts to permanent accounts and (2) to prepare the temporary accounts for use in accumulating data for the following accounting period.

9. Adjusting entries bring the accounts up to date, while closing entries reduce the revenue, expense, and drawing accounts to zero balances for use in accumulating data for the following accounting period.

10. (1) The first entry closes all income statement accounts with credit balances by transferring the total to the credit side of Income Summary.
    (2) The second entry closes all income statement accounts with debit balances by transferring the total to the debit side of Income Summary.
    (3) The third entry closes Income Summary by transferring its balance, the net income or net loss for the year, to the owner's capital account.
    (4) The fourth entry closes the drawing account by transferring its balance to the owner's capital account.

11. The purpose of the post-closing trial balance is to make sure that the ledger is in balance at the beginning of the next period.

12. The natural business year is the fiscal year that ends when business activities have reached the lowest point in the annual operating cycle.

13. January is more likely to have a lower level of business activity than is December for a department store. Therefore, the additional work to adjust and close the accounts and prepare the financial statements can more easily be performed at the end of January than at the end of December.

14. All the companies listed are general merchandisers whose busiest time of the year is during the holiday season, which extends through most of December. Traditionally, the lowest point of business activity for general merchandisers will be near the end of January and the beginning of February. Thus, these companies have chosen their natural business year for their fiscal years.

15. Yes. If a company has positive working capital, then its current assets must exceed its current liabilities. Thus, the current ratio will always be greater than one.

EXERCISES

Ex. 4–1

e, c, g, b, f, a, d

Ex. 4–2

   a.   Income statement: 3, 8, 9
   b.   Balance sheet: 1, 2, 4, 5, 6, 7, 10

Ex. 4–3

   a.   Asset: 1, 4, 5, 6, 10
   b.   Liability: 9, 12
   c.   Revenue: 2, 7
   d.   Expense: 3, 8, 11

Ex. 4–4

  1. f
  2. c
  3. b
  4. h
  5. g
  6. j
  7. a
  8. i
  9. d
10. e

Ex. 4–5

ITHACA SERVICES CO.
Work Sheet
For the Year Ended January 31, 2006

	Account Title	Trial Balance Dr.	Trial Balance Cr.	Adjustments Dr.	Adjustments Cr.	Adjusted Trial Balance Dr.	Adjusted Trial Balance Cr.	
1	Cash	8				8		1
2	Accounts Receivable	50		(a) 7		57		2
3	Supplies	8			(b) 5	3		3
4	Prepaid Insurance	12			(c) 6	6		4
5	Land	50				50		5
6	Equipment	32				32		6
7	Accum. Depr.—Equip.		2		(d) 5		7	7
8	Accounts Payable		26				26	8
9	Wages Payable		0		(e) 1		1	9
10	Terry Dagley, Capital		112				112	10
11	Terry Dagley, Drawing	8				8		11
12	Fees Earned		60		(a) 7		67	12
13	Wages Expense	16		(e) 1		17		13
14	Rent Expense	8				8		14
15	Insurance Expense	0		(c) 6		6		15
16	Utilities Expense	6				6		16
17	Depreciation Expense	0		(d) 5		5		17
18	Supplies Expense	0		(b) 5		5		18
19	Miscellaneous Expense	2				2		19
20	Totals	200	200	24	24	213	213	20

Ex. 4–6

ITHACA SERVICES CO.
Work Sheet
For the Year Ended January 31, 2006

	Account Title	Adjusted Trial Balance Dr.	Adjusted Trial Balance Cr.	Income Statement Dr.	Income Statement Cr.	Balance Sheet Dr.	Balance Sheet Cr.	
1	Cash	8				8		1
2	Accounts Receivable	57				57		2
3	Supplies	3				3		3
4	Prepaid Insurance	6				6		4
5	Land	50				50		5
6	Equipment	32				32		6
7	Accum. Depr.—Equip.		7				7	7
8	Accounts Payable		26				26	8
9	Wages Payable		1				1	9
10	Terry Dagley, Capital		112				112	10
11	Terry Dagley, Drawing	8				8		11
12	Fees Earned		67		67			12
13	Wages Expense	17		17				13
14	Rent Expense	8		8				14
15	Insurance Expense	6		6				15
16	Utilities Expense	6		6				16
17	Depreciation Expense	5		5				17
18	Supplies Expense	5		5				18
19	Miscellaneous Expense	2		2				19
20	Totals	213	213	49	67	164	146	20
21	Net income (loss)			18			18	21
22				67	67	164	164	22

Ex. 4–7

ITHACA SERVICES CO.
Income Statement
For the Year Ended January 31, 2006

Fees earned...		$67
Expenses:		
Wages expense	$17	
Rent expense	8	
Insurance expense	6	
Utilities expense	6	
Depreciation expense	5	
Supplies expense	5	
Miscellaneous expense....................................	2	
Total expenses.......................................		49
Net income		$18

ITHACA SERVICES CO.
Statement of Owner's Equity
For the Year Ended January 31, 2006

Terry Dagley, capital, February 1, 2005		$112
Net income for the year..	$18	
Less withdrawals...	8	
Increase in owner's equity...		10
Terry Dagley, capital, January 31, 2006		$122

ITHACA SERVICES CO.
Balance Sheet
January 31, 2006

Assets			Liabilities		
Current assets:			Current liabilities:		
Cash............................	$ 8		Accounts payable	$26	
Accounts receivable...	57		Wages payable............	1	
Supplies	3		Total liabilities.........		$ 27
Prepaid insurance	6				
Total current assets.		$ 74			
Property, plant, and			Owner's Equity		
equipment:			Terry Dagley, capital.......		122
Land.............................		$50			
Equipment...................	$32				
Less accum. depr.	7	25			
Total property, plant,					
and equipment		75	Total liabilities and		
Total assets....................		$149	owner's equity..........		$149

Ex. 4–8

2006

Jan.	31	Accounts Receivable	7	
		Fees Earned		7
	31	Supplies Expense	5	
		Supplies..		5
	31	Insurance Expense	6	
		Prepaid Insurance...		6
	31	Depreciation Expense..	5	
		Accumulated Depreciation—Equipment......		5
	31	Wages Expense..	1	
		Wages Payable...		1

Ex. 4–9

2006

Jan.	31	Fees Earned..	67	
		Income Summary...		67
	31	Income Summary	49	
		Wages Expense		17
		Rent Expense		8
		Insurance Expense		6
		Utilities Expense		6
		Depreciation Expense		5
		Supplies Expense		5
		Miscellaneous Expense		2
	31	Income Summary	18	
		Terry Dagley, Capital		18
	31	Terry Dagley, Capital..	8	
		Terry Dagley, Drawing		8

Ex. 4–10

LARYNX MESSENGER SERVICE
Income Statement
For the Year Ended June 30, 2006

Fees earned..		$273,700
Operating expenses:		
Salaries expense	$77,100	
Rent expense	22,500	
Utilities expense	6,500	
Depreciation expense	5,200	
Supplies expense	2,750	
Insurance expense	1,500	
Miscellaneous expense..	1,350	
Total operating expenses....................................		116,900
Net income		$156,800

Ex. 4–11

SIROCCO SERVICES CO.
Income Statement
For the Year Ended March 31, 2006

Service revenue		$103,850
Operating expenses:		
Wages expense	$56,800	
Rent expense	21,270	
Utilities expense	11,500	
Depreciation expense	8,000	
Insurance expense	4,100	
Supplies expense	3,100	
Miscellaneous expense..	2,250	
Total operating expenses....................................		107,020
Net loss..		$ (3,170)

Ex. 4–12

a.

FEDEX CORPORATION
Income Statement
For the Year Ended May 31, 2002
(in millions)

Revenues..		$15,327
Operating expenses:		
Salaries and employee benefits...............................	$6,467	
Rentals and landing fees	1,524	
Fuel...	1,009	
Maintenance and repairs	980	
Depreciation and amortization	806	
Purchased transportation..	562	
Other operating expenses	3,168	
Total operating expenses...		14,516
Income from operations..		$ 811
Interest expense	$ 56	
Other expenses..	52	108
Net income before income tax..		$ 703
Less provision for income taxes.....................................		260
Net income		$ 443

b. The income statements are very similar. The actual statement includes some
additional information (i.e., earnings per share).

Ex. 4–13

SYNTHESIS SYSTEMS CO.
Statement of Owner's Equity
For the Year Ended October 31, 2006

Suzanne Jacob, capital, November 1, 2005.....................		$173,750
Net income for year..	$44,250	
Less withdrawals..	12,000	
Increase in owner's equity..		32,250
Suzanne Jacob, capital, October 31, 2006		$206,000

Ex. 4–14

BOBCAT SPORTS
Statement of Owner's Equity
For the Year Ended August 31, 2006

John Kramer, capital, September 1, 2005		$210,300
Net loss for year	$49,650	
Plus withdrawals	16,000	
Decrease in owner's equity		65,650
John Kramer, capital, August 31, 2006		$144,650

Ex. 4–15

a. Current asset: 1, 3, 5, 6

b. Property, plant, and equipment: 2, 4

Ex. 4–16

Since current liabilities are usually due within one year, $165,000 ($13,750 × 12 months) would be reported as a current liability on the balance sheet. The remainder of $335,000 ($500,000 – $165,000) would be reported as a long-term liability on the balance sheet.

Ex. 4–23

Mar. 31	Fees Earned	180,700	
	Income Summary		180,700
31	Income Summary	285,200	
	Wages Expense		180,000
	Rent Expense		75,000
	Supplies Expense		24,000
	Miscellaneous Expense		6,200
31	Emil Carr, Capital	104,500	
	Income Summary		104,500
31	Emil Carr, Capital	50,000	
	Emil Carr, Drawing		50,000

Ex. 4–24

a. Accounts Receivable

b. Accumulated Depreciation

c. Cash

e. Equipment

f. Estella Hall, Capital

i. Supplies

k. Wages Payable

Ex. 4–25

RHOMBIC REPAIRS CO.
Post-Closing Trial Balance
March 31, 2006

Cash	9,225	
Accounts Receivable	33,300	
Supplies	1,980	
Equipment	63,000	
Accumulated Depreciation—Equipment		19,980
Accounts Payable		11,250
Salaries Payable		2,700
Unearned Rent		5,400
Angie Hammill, Capital		68,175
	107,505	107,505

Ex. 4–26

a. 2003 working capital: $3,882 ($11,917 – $8,035)

2002 working capital: $3,860 ($10,361 – $6,501)

2003 current ratio: 1.48 ($11,917 ÷ $8,035)

2002 current ratio: 1.59 ($10,361 ÷ $6,501)

b. The working capital increased slightly during 2003, a favorable trend. The current ratio decreased slightly during 2003, an unfavorable trend. Before reaching a more definitive conclusion concerning Home Depot's ability to meet its current obligations, the working capital and current ratio should be compared with past years, industry averages, and similar firms in the industry. It appears, however, that Home Depot's 2003 working capital and current ratio are adequate.

Ex. 4–27

a.

	2002	2001
Working capital	($143,034)	($159,453)
Current ratio	0.81	0.80

b. 7 Eleven has negative working capital as of December 31, 2002 and 2001. In addition, the current ratio is below one at the end of both years. While the working capital and current ratios have improved from 2001 to 2002, creditors would likely be concerned about the ability of 7 Eleven to meet its short-term credit obligations. This concern would warrant further investigation to determine whether this is a temporary issue (for example, an end-of-the-period phenomenon) and the company's plans to address its working capital shortcomings.

Appendix Ex. 4–28

a. (1) Sales Salaries Expense... 6,480
      Salaries Payable 6,480

   (2) Accounts Receivable... 10,250
      Fees Earned 10,250

b. (1) Salaries Payable 6,480
      Sales Salaries Expense 6,480

   (2) Fees Earned 10,250
      Accounts Receivable............................. 10,250

Appendix Ex. 4–29

a. (1) Payment (last payday in year)

   (2) Adjusting (accrual of wages at end of year)

   (3) Closing

   (4) Reversing

   (5) Payment (first payday in following year)

b. (1) Wages Expense 45,000
      Cash... 45,000

   (2) Wages Expense 18,000
      Wages Payable 18,000

   (3) Income Summary....................................... 1,120,800
      Wages Expense 1,120,800

   (4) Wages Payable... 18,000
      Wages Expense 18,000

   (5) Wages Expense 43,000
      Cash... 43,000

Prob. 4–1A

1.

DYNAMITE LAUNDRY
Work Sheet
For the Year Ended July 31, 2006

Account Title	Trial Balance Dr.	Cr.	Adjustments Dr.	Cr.	Adjusted Trial Balance Dr.	Cr.	Income Statement Dr.	Cr.	Balance Sheet Dr.	Cr.
1 Cash	2,900				2,900				2,900	
2 Laundry Supplies	7,500			(c) 5,750	1,750				1,750	
3 Prepaid Insurance	4,800			(d) 2,400	2,400				2,400	
4 Laundry Equipment	109,050				109,050				109,050	
5 Accum. Depreciation		41,100		(b) 6,800		47,900				47,900
6 Accounts Payable		6,100				6,100				6,100
7 David Duffy, Capital		37,800				37,800				37,800
8 David Duffy, Drawing	2,000				2,000				2,000	
9 Laundry Revenue		165,000				165,000		165,000		
10 Wages Expense	71,400		(a) 1,200		72,600		72,600			
11 Rent Expense	36,000				36,000		36,000			
12 Utilities Expense	13,650				13,650		13,650			
13 Misc. Expense	2,700				2,700		2,700			
14	250,000	250,000								
15 Wages Payable				(a) 1,200		1,200				1,200
16 Depreciation Expense			(b) 6,800		6,800		6,800			
17 Laundry Supp. Expense			(c) 5,750		5,750		5,750			
18 Insurance Expense			(d) 2,400		2,400		2,400			
19			16,150	16,150	258,000	258,000	139,900	165,000	118,100	93,000
20 Net income							25,100			25,100
21							165,000	165,000	118,100	118,100

149

Prob. 4–1A Continued

2.

DYNAMITE LAUNDRY
Income Statement
For the Year Ended July 31, 2006

Laundry revenue		$165,000
Operating expenses:		
Wages expense	$72,600	
Rent expense	36,000	
Utilities expense	13,650	
Depreciation expense	6,800	
Laundry supplies expense	5,750	
Insurance expense	2,400	
Miscellaneous expense	2,700	
Total operating expenses		139,900
Net income		$ 25,100

DYNAMITE LAUNDRY
Statement of Owner's Equity
For the Year Ended July 31, 2006

David Duffy, capital, August 1, 2005		$37,800
Net income for the year	$25,100	
Less withdrawals	2,000	
Increase in owner's equity		23,100
David Duffy, capital, July 31, 2006		$60,900

DYNAMITE LAUNDRY
Balance Sheet
July 31, 2006

Assets			Liabilities		
Current assets:			Current liabilities:		
Cash	$ 2,900		Accounts payable	$6,100	
Laundry supplies	1,750		Wages payable	1,200	
Prepaid insurance	2,400		Total liabilities		$ 7,300
Total current assets		$ 7,050			
Property, plant, and equipment:					
			Owner's Equity		
Laundry equipment	$109,050		David Duffy, capital		60,900
Less accum. depr.	47,900	61,150	Total liabilities and		
Total assets		$68,200	owner's equity		$68,200

Prob. 4–1A   Concluded

3.

Adjusting Entries

2006

July	31	Wages Expense	1,200	
		Wages Payable		1,200
	31	Depreciation Expense	6,800	
		Accumulated Depreciation		6,800
	31	Laundry Supplies Expense	5,750	
		Laundry Supplies		5,750
	31	Insurance Expense	2,400	
		Prepaid Insurance		2,400

4.

Closing Entries

2006

July	31	Laundry Revenue	165,000	
		Income Summary		165,000
	31	Income Summary	139,900	
		Wages Expense		72,600
		Rent Expense		36,000
		Utilities Expense		13,650
		Miscellaneous Expense		2,700
		Depreciation Expense		6,800
		Laundry Supplies Expense		5,750
		Insurance Expense		2,400
	31	Income Summary	25,100	
		David Duffy, Capital		25,100
	31	David Duffy, Capital	2,000	
		David Duffy, Drawing		2,000

Prob. 4–3A   Continued

2.

LITHIUM SERVICES CO.
Income Statement
For the Month Ended March 31, 2006

Revenues:		
Service revenue	$43,484	
Rent revenue	100	
Total revenues		$43,584
Operating expenses:		
Wages expense	$15,300	
Rent expense	3,910	
Utilities expense	1,728	
Supplies expense	1,347	
Depreciation expense—building	625	
Depreciation expense—equipment	200	
Insurance expense	150	
Miscellaneous expense	2,307	
Total operating expenses		25,567
Net income		$18,017

LITHIUM SERVICES CO.
Statement of Owner's Equity
For the Month Ended March 31, 2006

Natasha Morrow, capital, March 1, 2006		$52,825
Additional investment during the month		5,000
Total		$57,825
Net income for the month	$18,017	
Less withdrawals	2,000	
Increase in owner's equity		16,017
Natasha Morrow, capital, March 31, 2006		$73,842

Prob. 4–3A   Continued

LITHIUM SERVICES CO.
Balance Sheet
March 31, 2006

Assets				Liabilities		
Current assets:				**Current liabilities:**		
Cash		$ 4,509		Accounts payable	$5,141	
Accounts receivable		4,050		Wages payable	501	
Supplies		300		Unearned rent	2,100	
Prepaid insurance		1,650		Total liabilities		$ 7,742
Total current assets			$10,509			
Property, plant, and equipment:				**Owner's Equity**		
Land		$20,000		Natasha Morrow, capital		73,842
Building	$55,500					
Less accumulated depreciation	24,025	31,475				
Equipment	$30,000					
Less accumulated depreciation	10,400	19,600				
Total property, plant, and equipment			71,075	Total liabilities and		
Total assets			$81,584	owner's equity		$81,584

155

Prob. 4-3A   Continued

3.   JOURNAL   Page 26

Date		Post. Ref.	Debit	Credit
2006	**Adjusting Entries**			
Mar. 31	Accounts Receivable	12	1,500	
	Service Revenue	41		1,500
31	Supplies Expense..................................	52	1,347	
	Supplies......................................	13		1,347
31	Insurance Expense.................................	57	150	
	Prepaid Insurance.............................	14		150
31	Depreciation Expense—Building	54	625	
	Accumulated Depr.—Building	17		625
31	Depreciation Expense—Equipment..........	56	200	
	Accumulated Depr.—Equipment	19		200
31	Unearned Rent..................................	23	100	
	Rent Revenue.................................	42		100
31	Wages Expense.................................	51	501	
	Wages Payable................................	22		501

4.   JOURNAL   Page 27

Date		Post. Ref.	Debit	Credit
2006	**Closing Entries**			
Mar. 31	Service Revenue...	41	43,484	
	Rent Revenue..	42	100	
	Income Summary	33		43,584
31	Income Summary...	33	25,567	
	Wages Expense	51		15,300
	Rent Expense	53		3,910
	Utilities Expense	55		1,728
	Miscellaneous Expense	59		2,307
	Supplies Expense	52		1,347
	Insurance Expense	57		150
	Depreciation Expense—Building	54		625
	Depreciation Expense—Equipment	56		200
31	Income Summary...	33	18,017	
	Natasha Morrow, Capital........................	31		18,017
31	Natasha Marrow, Capital............................	31	2,000	
	Natasha Morrow, Drawing....................	32		2,000

Prob. 4–3A Continued

3. and 4.

Cash   11

Date	Item	Post. Ref.	Dr.	Cr.	Balance Dr.	Balance Cr.
2006						
Mar. 1	Balance..................	✓	....	....	2,259	....
3	....	23	....	910	1,349	....
4	....	23	5,000	....	6,349	....
5	....	23	....	86	6,263	....
7	....	23	800	....	7,063	....
8	....	23	400	....	7,463	....
8	....	23	....	2,584	4,879	....
8	....	23	1,695	....	6,574	....
10	....	24	....	510	6,064	....
12	....	24	....	2,319	3,745	....
15	....	24	2,718	....	6,463	....
16	....	24	....	1,000	5,463	....
19	....	24	....	2,135	3,328	....
22	....	24	....	370	2,958	....
22	....	24	3,992	....	6,950	....
24	....	25	....	527	6,423	....
26	....	25	....	2,480	3,943	....
30	....	25	....	156	3,787	....
30	....	25	....	26	3,761	....
31	....	25	....	1,000	2,761	....
31	....	25	2,029	....	4,790	....
31	....	25	....	281	4,509	....

Accounts Receivable   12

Date	Item	Post. Ref.	Dr.	Cr.	Balance Dr.	Balance Cr.
2006						
Mar. 1	Balance..................	✓	....	....	2,200	....
7	....	23	....	800	1,400	....
8	....	23	....	400	1,000	....
22	....	24	1,550	....	2,550	....
31	Adjusting................	26	1,500	....	4,050	....

Prob. 4–3A Continued

Supplies

13

Date	Item	Post. Ref.	Dr.	Cr.	Balance Dr.	Balance Cr.
2006						
Mar. 1	Balance..................	✓	....	....	610	....
10	....	24	510	....	1,120	....
27	....	25	527	....	1,647	....
31	Adjusting..............	26	....	1,347	300	....

Prepaid Insurance

14

Date	Item	Post. Ref.	Dr.	Cr.	Balance Dr.	Balance Cr.
2006						
Mar. 1	Balance..................	✓	....	....	420	....
22	....	24	1,380	....	1,800	....
31	Adjusting..............	26	....	150	1,650	....

Land

15

Date	Item	Post. Ref.	Dr.	Cr.	Balance Dr.	Balance Cr.
2006						
Mar. 1	Balance..................	✓	....	....	20,000	....

Building

16

Date	Item	Post. Ref.	Dr.	Cr.	Balance Dr.	Balance Cr.
2006						
Mar. 1	Balance..................	✓	....	....	55,500	....

Accumulated Depreciation—Building

17

Date	Item	Post. Ref.	Dr.	Cr.	Balance Dr.	Balance Cr.
2006						
Mar. 1	Balance..................	✓	....	....	....	23,400
31	Adjusting..............	26	....	625	....	24,025

Equipment

18

Date	Item	Post. Ref.	Dr.	Cr.	Balance Dr.	Balance Cr.
2006						
Mar. 1	Balance..................	✓	....	....	29,250	....
3	....	23	750	....	30,000	....

Accumulated Depreciation—Equipment

19

Date	Item	Post. Ref.	Dr.	Cr.	Balance Dr.	Balance Cr.
2006						
Mar. 1	Balance..................	✓	....	....	....	10,200
31	Adjusting..............	26	....	200	....	10,400

Prob. 4–3A   Continued

Accounts Payable   21

Date	Item	Post. Ref.	Dr.	Cr.	Balance Dr.	Balance Cr.
2006						
Mar. 1	Balance...............	✓	....	....	....	8,625
3	....	23	....	750	....	9,375
8	....	23	2,584	....	....	6,791
19	....	24	2,135	....	....	4,656
31	....	25	....	485	....	5,141

Wages Payable   22

Date	Item	Post. Ref.	Dr.	Cr.	Balance Dr.	Balance Cr.
2006						
Mar. 31	Adjusting..............	26	....	501	....	501

Unearned Rent   23

Date	Item	Post. Ref.	Dr.	Cr.	Balance Dr.	Balance Cr.
2006						
Mar. 1	Balance...............	✓	....	....	....	2,200
31	Adjusting..............	26	100	....	....	2,100

Natasha Morrow, Capital   31

Date	Item	Post. Ref.	Dr.	Cr.	Balance Dr.	Balance Cr.
2006						
Mar. 1	Balance...............	✓	....	....	....	52,825
4	....	23	....	5,000	....	57,825
31	Closing..............	27	....	18,017	....	75,842
31	Closing..............	27	2,000	....	....	73,842

Natasha Morrow, Drawing   32

Date	Item	Post. Ref.	Dr.	Cr.	Balance Dr.	Balance Cr.
2006						
Mar. 16	....	24	1,000	....	1,000	....
31	....	25	1,000	....	2,000	....
31	Closing..............	27	....	2,000	—	—

Income Summary   33

Date	Item	Post. Ref.	Dr.	Cr.	Balance Dr.	Balance Cr.
2006						
Mar. 31	Closing..............	27	....	43,584	....	43,584
31	Closing..............	27	25,567	....	....	18,017
31	Closing..............	27	18,017	....	—	—

Prob. 4–3A Continued

Service Revenue   41

Date	Item	Post. Ref.	Dr.	Cr.	Balance Dr.	Balance Cr.
2006						
Mar. 8	....	23	....	9,695	....	9,695
15	....	24	....	7,718	....	17,413
22	....	24	....	8,992	....	26,405
22	....	24	....	7,550	....	33,955
31	....	25	....	8,029	....	41,984
31	Adjusting..............	26	....	1,500	....	43,484
31	Closing	27	43,484	....	—	—

Rent Revenue   42

Date	Item	Post. Ref.	Dr.	Cr.	Balance Dr.	Balance Cr.
2006						
Mar. 31	Adjusting..............	26	....	100	....	100
31	Closing	27	100	....	—	—

Wages Expense   51

Date	Item	Post. Ref.	Dr.	Cr.	Balance Dr.	Balance Cr.
2006						
Mar. 12	....	24	7,319	....	7,319	....
26	....	25	7,480	....	14,799	....
31	Adjusting..............	26	501	....	15,300	....
31	Closing	27	....	15,300	—	—

Supplies Expense   52

Date	Item	Post. Ref.	Dr.	Cr.	Balance Dr.	Balance Cr.
2006						
Mar. 31	Adjusting..............	26	1,347	....	1,347	....
31	Closing	27	....	1,347	—	—

Rent Expense   53

Date	Item	Post. Ref.	Dr.	Cr.	Balance Dr.	Balance Cr.
2006						
Mar. 3	....	23	3,910	....	3,910	....
31	Closing	27	....	3,910	—	—

Depreciation Expense—Building   54

Date	Item	Post. Ref.	Dr.	Cr.	Balance Dr.	Balance Cr.
2006						
Mar. 31	Adjusting..............	26	625	....	625	....
31	Closing	27	....	625	—	—

Prob. 4–3A   Continued

Utilities Expense 55

Date	Item	Post. Ref.	Dr.	Cr.	Balance Dr.	Balance Cr.
2006						
Mar. 5	....	24	586	....	586	....
30	....	25	456	....	1,042	....
31	....	25	686	....	1,728	....
31	Closing	27	....	1,728	—	—

Depreciation Expense—Equipment 56

Date	Item	Post. Ref.	Dr.	Cr.	Balance Dr.	Balance Cr.
2006						
Mar. 31	Adjusting	26	200	....	200	....
31	Closing	27	....	200	—	—

Insurance Expense 57

Date	Item	Post. Ref.	Dr.	Cr.	Balance Dr.	Balance Cr.
2006						
Mar. 31	Adjusting	26	150	....	150	....
31	Closing	27	....	150	—	—

Miscellaneous Expense 59

Date	Item	Post. Ref.	Dr.	Cr.	Balance Dr.	Balance Cr.
2006						
Mar. 30	....	25	1,026	....	1,026	....
31	....	25	1,281	....	2,307	....
31	Closing	27	....	2,307	—	—

Prob. 4–3A   Concluded

5.

LITHIUM SERVICES CO.
Post-Closing Trial Balance
March 31, 2006

Cash	4,509	
Accounts Receivable	4,050	
Supplies	300	
Prepaid Insurance	1,650	
Land	20,000	
Building	55,500	
Accumulated Depreciation—Building		24,025
Equipment	30,000	
Accumulated Depreciation—Equipment		10,400
Accounts Payable		5,141
Wages Payable		501
Unearned Rent		2,100
Natasha Morrow, Capital		73,842
	116,009	116,009

Prob. 4–4A

1.

HERITAGE COMPANY
Work Sheet
For the Year Ended April 30, 2006

Account Title	Trial Balance Dr.	Trial Balance Cr.	Adjustments Dr.	Adjustments Cr.	Adjusted Trial Balance Dr.	Adjusted Trial Balance Cr.	Income Statement Dr.	Income Statement Cr.	Balance Sheet Dr.	Balance Sheet Cr.
1 Cash	3,200				3,200				3,200	
2 Accounts Receivable	10,500		(a) 2,800		13,300				13,300	
3 Prepaid Insurance	1,800			(b) 450	1,350				1,350	
4 Supplies	1,350			(c) 700	650				650	
5 Land	50,000				50,000				50,000	
6 Building	136,500				136,500				136,500	
7 Acc. Depr.—Building		50,700		(d) 1,620		52,320				52,320
8 Equipment	92,700				92,700				92,700	
9 Acc. Depr.—Equipment		36,300		(e) 3,500		39,800				39,800
10 Accounts Payable		6,500				6,500				6,500
11 Unearned Rent		3,000	(g) 1,500			1,500				1,500
12 Shelby Powers, Capital		212,500				212,500				212,500
13 Shelby Powers, Drawing	10,000				10,000				10,000	
14 Fees Revenue		191,000		(a) 2,800		193,800		193,800		
15 Salaries & Wages Exp.	96,200		(f) 1,800		98,000		98,000			
16 Advertising Expense	63,200				63,200		63,200			
17 Utilities Expense	18,000				18,000		18,000			
18 Repairs Expense	12,500				12,500		12,500			
19 Misc. Expense	4,050				4,050		4,050			
20	500,000	500,000								
21 Insurance Expense			(b) 450		450		450			
22 Supplies Expense			(c) 700		700		700			
23 Depr. Exp.—Building			(d) 1,620		1,620		1,620			
24 Depr. Exp.—Equip.			(e) 3,500		3,500		3,500			
25 Sal. & Wages Payable				(f) 1,800		1,800				1,800
26 Rent Revenue				(g) 1,500		1,500		1,500		
27			12,370	12,370	509,720	509,720	202,020	195,300	307,700	314,420
28 Net loss								6,720	6,720	
29							202,020	202,020	314,420	314,420

163

2.

Accounts Receivable	2,800	
Fees Revenue		2,800
Insurance Expense	450	
Prepaid Insurance		450
Supplies Expense	700	
Supplies		700
Depreciation Expense—Building	1,620	
Accumulated Depreciation—Building		1,620
Depreciation Expense—Equipment	3,500	
Accumulated Depreciation—Equipment		3,500
Salaries and Wages Expense	1,800	
Salaries and Wages Payable		1,800
Unearned Rent	1,500	
Rent Revenue		1,500

3.

HERITAGE COMPANY
Adjusted Trial Balance
April 30, 2006

Cash	3,200	
Accounts Receivable	13,300	
Prepaid Insurance	1,350	
Supplies	650	
Land	50,000	
Building	136,500	
Accumulated Depreciation—Building		52,320
Equipment	92,700	
Accumulated Depreciation—Equipment		39,800
Accounts Payable		6,500
Unearned Rent		1,500
Salaries and Wages Payable		1,800
Shelby Powers, Capital		212,500
Shelby Powers, Drawing	10,000	
Fees Revenue		193,800
Rent Revenue		1,500
Salaries and Wages Expense	98,000	
Advertising Expense	63,200	
Utilities Expense	18,000	
Repairs Expense	12,500	
Depreciation Expense—Equipment	3,500	
Insurance Expense	450	
Supplies Expense	700	
Depreciation Expense—Building	1,620	
Miscellaneous Expense	4,050	
	509,720	509,720

Prob. 4–4A   Continued

4.

HERITAGE COMPANY
Income Statement
For the Year Ended April 30, 2006

Revenues:		
Fees revenue...	$193,800	
Rent revenue...	1,500	
Total revenues...		$195,300
Operating expenses:		
Salaries and wages expense.....................................	$ 98,000	
Advertising expense..	63,200	
Utilities expense...	18,000	
Repairs expense...	12,500	
Depreciation expense—equipment............................	3,500	
Depreciation expense—building................................	1,620	
Supplies expense...	700	
Insurance expense...	450	
Miscellaneous expense...	4,050	
Total operating expenses.....................................		202,020
Net loss...		$ 6,720

5.

HERITAGE COMPANY
Statement of Owner's Equity
For the Year Ended April 30, 2006

Shelby Powers, capital, May 1, 2005...............................		$212,500
Net loss for the year	$ 6,720	
Add withdrawals	10,000	
Decrease in owner's equity		16,720
Shelby Powers, capital, April 30, 2006............................		$195,780

Prob. 4-4A   Concluded

6.

HERITAGE COMPANY
Balance Sheet
April 30, 2006

Assets

Current assets:
Cash	$ 3,200	
Accounts receivable	13,300	
Prepaid insurance	1,350	
Supplies	650	
Total current assets		$ 18,500

Property, plant, and equipment:
Land		$50,000	
Building	$136,500		
Less accum. depreciation	52,320	84,180	
Equipment	$ 92,700		
Less accum. depreciation	39,800	52,900	
Total property, plant, and equipment			187,080
Total assets			$205,580

Liabilities

Current liabilities:
Accounts payable	$6,500	
Salaries and wages payable	1,800	
Unearned rent	1,500	
Total liabilities		$ 9,800

Owner's Equity

Shelby Powers, capital	195,780
Total liabilities and owner's equity	$205,580

7. $195,300 ÷ $205,580 = 95%

167

Prob. 4–5A Continued

Supplies Expense   52

Date	Item	Post. Ref.	Dr.	Cr.	Balance Dr.	Balance Cr.
2006						
Dec. 31	Adjusting...........	26	4,570	....	4,570	....
31	Closing..............	27	....	4,570	—	—

Rent Expense   53

Date	Item	Post. Ref.	Dr.	Cr.	Balance Dr.	Balance Cr.
2006						
Dec. 31	Balance.............	✓	....	....	8,100	....
31	Closing.............	27	....	8,100	—	—

Depreciation Expense—Equipment   54

Date	Item	Post. Ref.	Dr.	Cr.	Balance Dr.	Balance Cr.
2006						
Dec. 31	Adjusting............	26	5,080	....	5,080	....
31	Closing.............	27	....	5,080	—	—

Truck Expense   55

Date	Item	Post. Ref.	Dr.	Cr.	Balance Dr.	Balance Cr.
2006						
Dec. 31	Balance.............	✓	....	....	6,350	....
31	Closing.............	27	....	6,350	—	—

Depreciation Expense—Trucks   56

Date	Item	Post. Ref.	Dr.	Cr.	Balance Dr.	Balance Cr.
2006						
Dec. 31	Adjusting............	26	3,500	....	3,500	....
31	Closing.............	27	....	3,500	—	—

Insurance Expense   57

Date	Item	Post. Ref.	Dr.	Cr.	Balance Dr.	Balance Cr.
2006						
Dec. 31	Adjusting............	26	1,000	....	1,000	....
31	Closing.............	27	....	1,000	—	—

Miscellaneous Expense   59

Date	Item	Post. Ref.	Dr.	Cr.	Balance Dr.	Balance Cr.
2006						
Dec. 31	Balance.............	✓	....	....	2,195	....
31	Closing.............	27	....	2,195	—	—

Prob. 4–5A Continued

2.

PABLO REPAIRS
Work Sheet
For the Year Ended December 31, 2006

	Trial Balance Dr.	Trial Balance Cr.	Adjustments Dr.	Adjustments Cr.	Adjusted Trial Balance Dr.	Adjusted Trial Balance Cr.	Income Statement Dr.	Income Statement Cr.	Balance Sheet Dr.	Balance Sheet Cr.	
1 Cash	2,825				2,825				2,825		1
2 Supplies	5,820			(a) 4,570	1,250				1,250		2
3 Prepaid Insurance	2,500			(b) 1,000	1,500				1,500		3
4 Equipment	44,200				44,200				44,200		4
5 Acc. Depr.—Equipment		12,050		(c) 5,080		17,130				17,130	5
6 Trucks	45,000				45,000				45,000		6
7 Acc. Depr.—Trucks		27,100		(d) 3,500		30,600				30,600	7
8 Accounts Payable		2,015				2,015				2,015	8
9 Jason Hoyt, Capital		32,885				32,885				32,885	9
10 Jason Hoyt, Drawing	5,000				5,000				5,000		10
11 Service Revenue		75,950				75,950		75,950			11
12 Wages Expense	28,010		(e) 900		28,910		28,910				12
13 Rent Expense	8,100				8,100		8,100				13
14 Truck Expense	6,350				6,350		6,350				14
15 Misc. Expense	2,195				2,195		2,195				15
16	150,000	150,000									16
17 Supplies Expense			(a) 4,570		4,570		4,570				17
18 Insurance Expense			(b) 1,000		1,000		1,000				18
19 Depr. Exp.—Equip.			(c) 5,080		5,080		5,080				19
20 Depr. Exp.—Trucks			(d) 3,500		3,500		3,500				20
21 Wages Payable				(e) 900		900				900	21
22			15,050	15,050	159,480	159,480	59,705	75,950	99,775	83,530	22
23 Net income							16,245			16,245	23
24							75,950	75,950	99,775	99,775	24

Prob. 4–5A   Continued

3.

Date			Post. Ref.	Debit	Credit
		Adjusting Entries			
2006					
Dec.	31	Supplies Expense......................................	52	4,570	
		Supplies...	13		4,570
	31	Insurance Expense.....................................	57	1,000	
		Prepaid Insurance.................................	14		1,000
	31	Depreciation Expense—Equipment...........	54	5,080	
		Accumulated Depreciation—Equip.	17		5,080
	31	Depreciation Expense—Trucks..................	56	3,500	
		Accumulated Depreciation—Trucks	19		3,500
	31	Wages Expense	51	900	
		Wages Payable.......................................	22		900

Prob. 4–5A   Continued

4.

PABLO REPAIRS
Adjusted Trial Balance
December 31, 2006

Cash	2,825	
Supplies	1,250	
Prepaid Insurance	1,500	
Equipment	44,200	
Accumulated Depreciation—Equipment		17,130
Trucks	45,000	
Accumulated Depreciation—Trucks		30,600
Accounts Payable		2,015
Wages Payable		900
Jason Hoyt, Capital		32,885
Jason Hoyt, Drawing	5,000	
Service Revenue		75,950
Wages Expense	28,910	
Supplies Expense	4,570	
Rent Expense	8,100	
Depreciation Expense—Equipment	5,080	
Truck Expense	6,350	
Depreciation Expense—Trucks	3,500	
Insurance Expense	1,000	
Miscellaneous Expense	2,195	
	159,480	159,480

Prob. 4–5A Continued

5.

PABLO REPAIRS
Income Statement
For the Year Ended December 31, 2006

Service revenue		$75,950
Operating expenses:		
Wages expense	$28,910	
Rent expense	8,100	
Truck expense	6,350	
Depreciation expense—equipment	5,080	
Supplies expense	4,570	
Depreciation expense—trucks	3,500	
Insurance expense	1,000	
Miscellaneous expense	2,195	
Total operating expenses		59,705
Net income		$16,245

PABLO REPAIRS
Statement of Owner's Equity
For the Year Ended December 31, 2006

Jason Hoyt, capital, January 1, 2006		$32,885
Net income for the year	$16,245	
Less withdrawals	5,000	
Increase in owner's equity		11,245
Jason Hoyt, capital, December 31, 2006		$44,130

Prob. 4–5A   Continued

PABLO REPAIRS
Balance Sheet
December 31, 2006

Assets				Liabilities			
Current assets:				**Current liabilities:**			
Cash		$ 2,825		Accounts payable		$2,015	
Supplies		1,250		Wages payable		900	
Prepaid insurance		1,500		Total liabilities			$ 2,915
Total current assets			$ 5,575				
Property, plant, and equipment:				**Owner's Equity**			
Equipment	$44,200			Jason Hoyt, capital			44,130
Less accumulated depr.	17,130	$27,070					
Trucks	$45,000						
Less accumulated depr.	30,600	14,400					
Total property, plant, and equipment			41,470	Total liabilities and owner's equity			$47,045
Total assets			$47,045				

175

Prob. 4–5A   Concluded

6.

Date		Post. Ref.	Debit	Credit
	JOURNAL			**Page 27**
	Closing Entries			
2006				
Dec. 31	Service Revenue..	41	75,950	
	Income Summary	33		75,950
31	Income Summary...	33	59,705	
	Wages Expense	51		28,910
	Supplies Expense................................	52		4,570
	Rent Expense	53		8,100
	Depreciation Expense—Equipment	54		5,080
	Truck Expense	55		6,350
	Depreciation Expense—Trucks............	56		3,500
	Insurance Expense	57		1,000
	Miscellaneous Expense	59		2,195
31	Income Summary...	33	16,245	
	Jason Hoyt, Capital.............................	31		16,245
31	Jason Hoyt, Capital	31	5,000	
	Jason Hoyt, Drawing	32		5,000

7.

PABLO REPAIRS
Post-Closing Trial Balance
December 31, 2006

	Debit	Credit
Cash...	2,825	
Supplies..	1,250	
Prepaid Insurance	1,500	
Equipment..	44,200	
Accumulated Depreciation—Equipment		17,130
Trucks...	45,000	
Accumulated Depreciation—Trucks		30,600
Accounts Payable..		2,015
Wages Payable		900
Jason Hoyt, Capital		44,130
	94,775	94,775

Prob. 4–1B

1.

THE UTOPIA LAUNDROMAT
Work Sheet
For the Year Ended October 31, 2006

	Trial Balance Dr.	Trial Balance Cr.	Adjustments Dr.	Adjustments Cr.	Adjusted Trial Balance Dr.	Adjusted Trial Balance Cr.	Income Statement Dr.	Income Statement Cr.	Balance Sheet Dr.	Balance Sheet Cr.	
1 Cash	4,600				4,600				4,600		1
2 Laundry Supplies	7,850			(a) 6,600	1,250				1,250		2
3 Prepaid Insurance	3,600			(b) 1,800	1,800				1,800		3
4 Laundry Equipment	120,000				120,000				120,000		4
5 Accumulated Depr.		62,700		(c) 5,500		68,200				68,200	5
6 Accounts Payable		4,100				4,100				4,100	6
7 Cecily Farner, Capital		46,450				46,450				46,450	7
8 Cecily Farner, Drawing	3,500				3,500				3,500		8
9 Laundry Revenue		96,750				96,750		96,750			9
10 Wages Expense	43,400		(d) 2,160		45,560		45,560				10
11 Rent Expense	16,400				16,400		16,400				11
12 Utilities Expense	8,500				8,500		8,500				12
13 Miscellaneous Exp.	2,150				2,150		2,150				13
14	210,000	210,000									14
15 Laundry Supplies Exp.			(a) 6,600		6,600		6,600				15
16 Insurance Expense			(b) 1,800		1,800		1,800				16
17 Depreciation Expense			(c) 5,500		5,500		5,500				17
18 Wages Payable				(d) 2,160		2,160				2,160	18
19			16,060	16,060	217,660	217,660	86,510	96,750	131,150	120,910	19
20 Net income							10,240			10,240	20
21							96,750	96,750	131,150	131,150	21

177

Prob. 4–1B Continued

2.

THE UTOPIA LAUNDROMAT
Income Statement
For the Year Ended October 31, 2006

Laundry revenue		$96,750
Operating expenses:		
Wages expense	$45,560	
Rent expense	16,400	
Utilities expense	8,500	
Laundry supplies expense	6,600	
Depreciation expense	5,500	
Insurance expense	1,800	
Miscellaneous expense	2,150	
Total operating expenses		86,510
Net income		$10,240

THE UTOPIA LAUNDROMAT
Statement of Owner's Equity
For the Year Ended October 31, 2006

Cecily Farner, capital, November 1, 2005		$46,450
Net income for the year	$10,240	
Less withdrawals	3,500	
Increase in owner's equity		6,740
Cecily Farner, capital, October 31, 2006		$53,190

THE UTOPIA LAUNDROMAT
Balance Sheet
October 31, 2006

Assets			Liabilities		
Current assets:			Current liabilities:		
Cash	$ 4,600		Accounts payable	$4,100	
Laundry supplies	1,250		Wages payable	2,160	
Prepaid insurance	1,800		Total liabilities		$ 6,260
Total current assets		$ 7,650			
Property, plant, and					
equipment:			Owner's Equity		
Laundry equipment	$120,000		Cecily Farner, capital		53,190
Less accum. depr.	68,200	51,800	Total liabilities and		
Total assets		$59,450	owner's equity		$59,450

Prob. 4–1B   Concluded

3.

Adjusting Entries

2006

Oct.	31	Laundry Supplies Expense	6,600	
		Laundry Supplies		6,600
	31	Insurance Expense	1,800	
		Prepaid Insurance...		1,800
	31	Depreciation Expense.......................................	5,500	
		Accumulated Depreciation...........................		5,500
	31	Wages Expense...	2,160	
		Wages Payable..		2,160

4.

Closing Entries

2006

Oct.	31	Laundry Revenue	96,750	
		Income Summary		96,750
	31	Income Summary	86,510	
		Wages Expense		45,560
		Rent Expense		16,400
		Utilities Expense		8,500
		Miscellaneous Expense		2,150
		Laundry Supplies Expense		6,600
		Insurance Expense		1,800
		Depreciation Expense		5,500
	31	Income Summary	10,240	
		Cecily Farner, Capital		10,240
	31	Cecily Farner, Capital	3,500	
		Cecily Farner, Drawing...................................		3,500

Prob. 4–2B

1.

Closing Entries

2006

June 30	Service Fees Earned		180,000	
	Rent Revenue		3,000	
	Income Summary			183,000
30	Income Summary		169,500	
	Salary Expense			133,500
	Rent Expense			18,000
	Supplies Expense			4,000
	Depreciation Expense—Equipment			3,500
	Utilities Expense			3,200
	Taxes Expense			3,100
	Insurance Expense			2,400
	Miscellaneous Expense			1,800
30	Income Summary		13,500	
	Bruce Driskell, Capital			13,500
30	Bruce Driskell, Capital		8,000	
	Bruce Driskell, Drawing			8,000

2.

THE ALLIGATOR COMPANY
Statement of Owner's Equity
For the Year Ended June 30, 2006

Bruce Driskell, capital, July 1, 2005		$71,410
Net income for the year	$13,500	
Less withdrawals	8,000	
Increase in owner's equity		5,500
Bruce Driskell, capital, June 30, 2006		$76,910

3. $22,000 net loss. The $30,000 decrease is caused by the $8,000 withdrawals and a $22,000 net loss.

Prob. 4–3B

1.

LITHIUM SERVICES CO.
Work Sheet
For the Month Ended March 31, 2006

#	Account Title	Trial Balance Dr.	Trial Balance Cr.	Adjustments Dr.	Adjustments Cr.	Adjusted Trial Balance Dr.	Adjusted Trial Balance Cr.	Income Statement Dr.	Income Statement Cr.	Balance Sheet Dr.	Balance Sheet Cr.
1	Cash	4,509				4,509				4,509	
2	Accounts Receivable	2,550		(a) 1,250		3,800				3,800	
3	Supplies	1,647			(b) 1,247	400				400	
4	Prepaid Insurance	1,800			(c) 150	1,650				1,650	
5	Land	20,000				20,000				20,000	
6	Building	55,500				55,500				55,500	
7	Acc. Depr.—Building		23,400		(d) 500		23,900				23,900
8	Equipment	30,000				30,000				30,000	
9	Acc. Depr.—Equipment		10,200		(e) 150		10,350				10,350
10	Accounts Payable		5,141				5,141				5,141
11	Unearned Rent		2,200	(f) 200			2,000				2,000
12	N. Morrow, Capital		57,825				57,825				57,825
13	N. Morrow, Drawing	2,000				2,000				2,000	
14	Service Revenue		41,984		(a) 1,250		43,234		43,234		
15	Wages Expense	14,799		(g) 601		15,400		15,400			
16	Rent Expense	3,910				3,910		3,910			
17	Utilities Expense	1,728				1,728		1,728			
18	Misc. Expense	2,307				2,307		2,307			
19		140,750	140,750								
20	Supplies Expense			(b) 1,247		1,247		1,247			
21	Insurance Expense			(c) 150		150		150			
22	Depr. Exp.—Building			(d) 500		500		500			
23	Depr. Exp.—Equipment			(e) 150		150		150			
24	Rent Revenue				(f) 200		200		200		
25	Wages Payable				(g) 601		601				601
26				4,098	4,098	143,251	143,251	25,392	43,434	117,859	99,817
27	Net income							18,042			18,042
28								43,434	43,434	117,859	117,859

Prob. 4–3B   Continued

2.

LITHIUM SERVICES CO.
Income Statement
For the Month Ended March 31, 2006

Revenues:		
Service revenue	$43,234	
Rent revenue	200	
Total revenues		$43,434
Operating expenses:		
Wages expense	$15,400	
Rent expense	3,910	
Utilities expense	1,728	
Supplies expense	1,247	
Depreciation expense—building	500	
Depreciation expense—equipment	150	
Insurance expense	150	
Miscellaneous expense	2,307	
Total operating expenses		25,392
Net income		$18,042

LITHIUM SERVICES CO.
Statement of Owner's Equity
For the Month Ended March 31, 2006

Natasha Morrow, capital, March 1, 2006		$52,825
Additional investment during the month		5,000
Total		$57,825
Net income for the month	$18,042	
Less withdrawals	2,000	
Increase in owner's equity		16,042
Natasha Morrow, capital, March 31, 2006		$73,867

Prob. 4-3B   Continued

LITHIUM SERVICES CO.
Balance Sheet
March 31, 2006

Assets

Current assets:

Cash		$ 4,509
Accounts receivable		3,800
Supplies		400
Prepaid insurance		1,650
Total current assets		$10,359

Property, plant, and equipment:

Land		$20,000
Building	$55,500	
Less accum. depreciation	23,900	31,600
Equipment	$30,000	
Less accum. depreciation	10,350	19,650
Total property, plant, and equipment		71,250
Total assets		$81,609

Liabilities

Current liabilities:

Accounts payable	$5,141	
Wages payable	601	
Unearned rent	2,000	
Total current liabilities		$ 7,742

Owner's Equity

Natasha Morrow, capital		73,867
Total liabilities and owner's equity		$81,609

Prob. 4–3B   Continued

3.   JOURNAL   Page 26

Date		Post. Ref.	Debit	Credit
2006	**Adjusting Entries**			
Mar. 31	Accounts Receivable	12	1,250	
	Service Revenue	41		1,250
31	Supplies Expense.................................	52	1,247	
	Supplies..	13		1,247
31	Insurance Expense.................................	57	150	
	Prepaid Insurance..............................	14		150
31	Depreciation Expense—Building	54	500	
	Accum. Depreciation—Building	17		500
31	Depreciation Expense—Equipment...........	56	150	
	Accum. Depreciation—Equipment	19		150
31	Unearned Rent.................................	23	200	
	Rent Revenue	42		200
31	Wages Expense	51	601	
	Wages Payable.................................	22		601

4.   JOURNAL   Page 27

Date		Post. Ref.	Debit	Credit
2006	**Closing Entries**			
Mar. 31	Service Revenue..	41	43,234	
	Rent Revenue...	42	200	
	Income Summary	33		43,434
31	Income Summary..	33	25,392	
	Wages Expense	51		15,400
	Rent Expense	53		3,910
	Utilities Expense	55		1,728
	Miscellaneous Expense	59		2,307
	Supplies Expense	52		1,247
	Insurance Expense	57		150
	Depreciation Expense—Building	54		500
	Depreciation Expense—Equip..............	56		150
31	Income Summary..	33	18,042	
	Natasha Morrow, Capital......................	31		18,042
31	Natasha Morrow, Capital	31	2,000	
	Natasha Morrow, Drawing.....................	32		2,000

Prob. 4–3B   Continued

3. and 4.

Cash 11

Date		Item	Post. Ref.	Dr.	Cr.	Balance Dr.	Balance Cr.
2006							
Mar.	1	Balance..................	✓	....	....	2,259	....
	3	....	23	....	910	1,349	....
	4	....	23	5,000	....	6,349	....
	5	....	23	....	86	6,263	....
	7	....	23	800	....	7,063	....
	8	....	23	400	....	7,463	....
	8	....	23	....	2,584	4,879	....
	8	....	23	1,695	....	6,574	....
	10	....	24	....	510	6,064	....
	12	....	24	....	2,319	3,745	....
	15	....	24	2,718	....	6,463	....
	16	....	24	....	1,000	5,463	....
	19	....	24	....	2,135	3,328	....
	22	....	24	....	370	2,958	....
	22	....	24	3,992	....	6,950	....
	24	....	25	....	527	6,423	....
	26	....	25	....	2,480	3,943	....
	30	....	25	....	156	3,787	....
	30	....	25	....	26	3,761	....
	31	....	25	....	1,000	2,761	....
	31	....	25	2,029	....	4,790	....
	31	....	25	....	281	4,509	....

Accounts Receivable 12

Date		Item	Post. Ref.	Dr.	Cr.	Balance Dr.	Balance Cr.
2006							
Mar.	1	Balance..................	✓	....	....	2,200	....
	7	....	23	....	800	1,400	....
	8	....	23	....	400	1,000	....
	22	....	24	1,550	....	2,550	....
	31	Adjusting................	26	1,250	....	3,800	....

Prob. 4–3B Continued

Supplies   13

Date	Item	Post. Ref.	Dr.	Cr.	Balance Dr.	Balance Cr.
2006						
Mar. 1	Balance..................	✓	....	....	610	....
10	....	24	510	....	1,120	....
27	....	25	527	....	1,647	....
31	Adjusting................	26	....	1,247	400	....

Prepaid Insurance   14

Date	Item	Post. Ref.	Dr.	Cr.	Balance Dr.	Balance Cr.
2006						
Mar. 1	Balance..................	✓	....	....	420	....
22	....	24	1,380	....	1,800	....
31	Adjusting................	26	....	150	1,650	....

Land   15

Date	Item	Post. Ref.	Dr.	Cr.	Balance Dr.	Balance Cr.
2006						
Mar. 1	Balance..................	✓	....	....	20,000	....

Building   16

Date	Item	Post. Ref.	Dr.	Cr.	Balance Dr.	Balance Cr.
2006						
Mar. 1	Balance..................	✓	....	....	55,500	....

Accumulated Depreciation—Building   17

Date	Item	Post. Ref.	Dr.	Cr.	Balance Dr.	Balance Cr.
2006						
Mar. 1	Balance..................	✓	....	....	....	23,400
31	Adjusting................	26	....	500	....	23,900

Equipment   18

Date	Item	Post. Ref.	Dr.	Cr.	Balance Dr.	Balance Cr.
2006						
Mar. 1	Balance..................	✓	....	....	29,250	....
3	....	23	750	....	30,000	....

Prob. 4–3B   Continued

Accumulated Depreciation—Equipment   19

Date	Item	Post. Ref.	Dr.	Cr.	Balance Dr.	Balance Cr.
2006						
Mar. 1	Balance..................	✓	....	....	....	10,200
31	Adjusting...............	26	....	150	....	10,350

Accounts Payable   21

Date	Item	Post. Ref.	Dr.	Cr.	Balance Dr.	Balance Cr.
2006						
Mar. 1	Balance..................	✓	....	....	....	8,625
3	....	23	....	750	....	9,375
8	....	23	2,584	....	....	6,791
19	....	24	2,135	....	....	4,656
31	....	25	....	485	....	5,141

Wages Payable   22

Date	Item	Post. Ref.	Dr.	Cr.	Balance Dr.	Balance Cr.
2006						
Mar. 31	Adjusting...............	26	....	601	....	601

Unearned Rent   23

Date	Item	Post. Ref.	Dr.	Cr.	Balance Dr.	Balance Cr.
2006						
Mar. 1	Balance..................	✓	....	....	....	2,200
31	Adjusting...............	26	200	....	....	2,000

Natasha Morrow, Capital   31

Date	Item	Post. Ref.	Dr.	Cr.	Balance Dr.	Balance Cr.
2006						
Mar. 1	Balance..................	✓	....	....	....	52,825
4	....	23	....	5,000	....	57,825
31	Closing	27	....	18,042	....	75,867
31	Closing	27	2,000	....	....	73,867

Natasha Morrow, Drawing   32

Date	Item	Post. Ref.	Dr.	Cr.	Balance Dr.	Balance Cr.
2006						
Mar. 16	....	24	1,000	....	1,000	....
31	....	25	1,000	....	2,000	....
31	Closing	27	....	2,000	—	—

Prob. 4–3B Continued

Income Summary 33

Date	Item	Post. Ref.	Dr.	Cr.	Balance Dr.	Balance Cr.
2006						
Mar. 31	Closing	27	....	43,434	....	43,434
31	Closing	27	25,392	....	....	18,042
31	Closing	27	18,042	....	—	—

Service Revenue 41

Date	Item	Post. Ref.	Dr.	Cr.	Balance Dr.	Balance Cr.
2006						
Mar. 8	....	23	....	9,695	....	9,695
15	....	24	....	7,718	....	17,413
22	....	24	....	8,992	....	26,405
22	....	24	....	7,550	....	33,955
31	....	25	....	8,029	....	41,984
31	Adjusting	26	....	1,250	....	43,234
31	Closing	27	43,234	....	—	—

Rent Revenue 42

Date	Item	Post. Ref.	Dr.	Cr.	Balance Dr.	Balance Cr.
2006						
Mar. 1	Adjusting	26	....	200	....	200
31	Closing	27	200	....	—	—

Wages Expense 51

Date	Item	Post. Ref.	Dr.	Cr.	Balance Dr.	Balance Cr.
2006						
Mar. 12	....	24	7,319	....	7,319	....
26	....	25	7,480	....	14,799	....
31	Adjusting	26	601	....	15,400	....
31	Closing	27	....	15,400	—	—

Supplies Expense 52

Date	Item	Post. Ref.	Dr.	Cr.	Balance Dr.	Balance Cr.
2006						
Mar. 31	Adjusting	26	1,247	....	1,247	....
31	Closing	27	....	1,247	—	—

Prob. 4–3B   Continued

Rent Expense   53

Date		Item	Post. Ref.	Dr.	Cr.	Balance Dr.	Balance Cr.
2006							
Mar.	3	....	23	3,910	....	3,910	....
	31	Closing	27	....	3,910	—	—

Depreciation Expense—Building   54

Date		Item	Post. Ref.	Dr.	Cr.	Balance Dr.	Balance Cr.
2006							
Mar.	31	Adjusting	26	500	....	500	....
	31	Closing	27	....	500	—	—

Utilities Expense   55

Date		Item	Post. Ref.	Dr.	Cr.	Balance Dr.	Balance Cr.
2006							
Mar.	5	....	24	586	....	586	....
	30	....	25	456	....	1,042	....
	31	....	25	686	....	1,728	....
	31	Closing	27	....	1,728	—	—

Depreciation Expense—Equipment   56

Date		Item	Post. Ref.	Dr.	Cr.	Balance Dr.	Balance Cr.
2006							
Mar.	31	Adjusting	26	150	....	150	....
	31	Closing	27	....	150	—	—

Insurance Expense   57

Date		Item	Post. Ref.	Dr.	Cr.	Balance Dr.	Balance Cr.
2006							
Mar.	31	Adjusting	26	150	....	150	....
	31	Closing	27	....	150	—	—

Miscellaneous Expense   59

Date		Item	Post. Ref.	Dr.	Cr.	Balance Dr.	Balance Cr.
2006							
Mar.	30	....	25	1,026	....	1,026	....
	31	....	25	1,281	....	2,307	....
	31	Closing	27	....	2,307	—	—

Prob. 4–3B Concluded

5.

LITHIUM SERVICES CO.
Post-Closing Trial Balance
March 31, 2006

Cash	4,509	
Accounts Receivable	3,800	
Supplies	400	
Prepaid Insurance	1,650	
Land	20,000	
Building	55,500	
Accumulated Depreciation—Building		23,900
Equipment	30,000	
Accumulated Depreciation—Equipment		10,350
Accounts Payable		5,141
Wages Payable		601
Unearned Rent		2,000
Natasha Morrow, Capital		73,867
	115,859	115,859

Prob. 4–4B

1.

FLAMINGO COMPANY
Work Sheet
For the Year Ended July 31, 2006

	Trial Balance Dr.	Trial Balance Cr.	Adjustments Dr.	Adjustments Cr.	Adjusted Trial Balance Dr.	Adjusted Trial Balance Cr.	Income Statement Dr.	Income Statement Cr.	Balance Sheet Dr.	Balance Sheet Cr.	
Account Title											
1 Cash	4,500				4,500				4,500		1
2 Accounts Receivable	13,500		(a) 3,500		17,000				17,000		2
3 Prepaid Insurance	3,000			(b) 2,000	1,000				1,000		3
4 Supplies	1,950			(c) 1,600	350				350		4
5 Land	70,000				70,000				70,000		5
6 Building	100,500				100,500				100,500		6
7 Accum. Depr.—Bldg.		71,700		(d) 1,520		73,220				73,220	7
8 Equipment	71,400				71,400				71,400		8
9 Accum. Depr.—Equip.		60,800		(e) 2,160		62,960				62,960	9
10 Accounts Payable		4,100				4,100				4,100	10
11 Unearned Rent		1,500	(g) 1,000			500				500	11
12 Mac Copas, Capital		55,700				55,700				55,700	12
13 Mac Copas, Drawing	4,000				4,000				4,000		13
14 Fees Revenue		181,200		(a) 3,500		184,700		184,700			14
15 Sal. & Wages Expense	73,200		(f) 2,800		76,000		76,000				15
16 Advertising Expense	15,500				15,500		15,500				16
17 Utilities Expense	8,100				8,100		8,100				17
18 Repairs Expense	6,300				6,300		6,300				18
19 Misc. Expense	3,050				3,050		3,050				19
20	375,000	375,000									20
21 Insurance Expense			(b) 2,000		2,000		2,000				21
22 Supplies Expense			(c) 1,600		1,600		1,600				22
23 Depr. Exp.—Building			(d) 1,520		1,520		1,520				23
24 Depr. Exp.—Equip.			(e) 2,160		2,160		2,160				24
25 Sal. & Wages Payable				(f) 2,800		2,800				2,800	25
26 Rent Revenue				(g) 1,000		1,000		1,000			26
27			14,580	14,580	384,980	384,980	116,230	185,700	268,750	199,280	27
28 Net income							69,470			69,470	28
29							185,700	185,700	268,750	268,750	29

Prob. 4–4B Continued

2.

Accounts Receivable	3,500	
Fees Revenue		3,500
Insurance Expense	2,000	
Prepaid Insurance		2,000
Supplies Expense	1,600	
Supplies		1,600
Depreciation Expense	1,520	
Building		1,520
Depreciation Expense	2,160	
Equipment		2,160
Salaries and Wages Expense	2,800	
Salaries and Wages Payable		2,800
Unearned Rent	1,000	
Rent Revenue		1,000

3.

FLAMINGO COMPANY
Adjusted Trial Balance
July 31, 2006

Cash	4,500	
Accounts Receivable	17,000	
Prepaid Insurance	1,000	
Supplies	350	
Land	70,000	
Building	100,500	
Accumulated Depreciation—Building		73,220
Equipment	71,400	
Accumulated Depreciation—Equipment		62,960
Accounts Payable		4,100
Unearned Rent		500
Salaries and Wages Payable		2,800
Mac Copas, Capital		55,700
Mac Copas, Drawing	4,000	
Fees Revenue		184,700
Rent Revenue		1,000
Salaries and Wages Expense	76,000	
Advertising Expense	15,500	
Utilities Expense	8,100	
Repairs Expense	6,300	
Depreciation Expense—Equipment	2,160	
Insurance Expense	2,000	
Supplies Expense	1,600	
Depreciation Expense—Building	1,520	
Miscellaneous Expense	3,050	
	384,980	384,980

Prob. 4–4B   Continued

4.

FLAMINGO COMPANY
Income Statement
For the Year Ended July 31, 2006

Revenues:		
Fees revenue...	$184,700	
Rent revenue...	1,000	
Total revenues..		$185,700
Operating expenses:		
Salaries and wages expense.....................................	$ 76,000	
Advertising expense...	15,500	
Utilities expense	8,100	
Repairs expense...	6,300	
Depreciation expense—equipment...........................	2,160	
Insurance expense	2,000	
Supplies expense	1,600	
Depreciation expense—building...............................	1,520	
Miscellaneous expense..	3,050	
Total operating expenses...		116,230
Net income		$ 69,470

5.

FLAMINGO COMPANY
Statement of Owner's Equity
For the Year Ended July 31, 2006

Mac Copas, capital, August 1, 2005		$ 55,700
Net income for the year...	$69,470	
Less withdrawals...	4,000	
Increase in owner's capital...		65,470
Mac Copas, capital, July 31, 2006		$121,170

Prob. 4-4B Concluded

6.

FLAMINGO COMPANY
Balance Sheet
July 31, 2006

Assets			
Current assets:			
Cash		$ 4,500	
Accounts receivable		17,000	
Prepaid insurance		1,000	
Supplies		350	
Total current assets			$ 22,850
Property, plant, and equipment:			
Land		$70,000	
Building	$100,500		
Less accum. depreciation	73,220	27,280	
Equipment	$ 71,400		
Less accum. depreciation	62,960	8,440	
Total property, plant, and equipment			105,720
Total assets			$128,570

Liabilities		
Current liabilities:		
Accounts payable	$4,100	
Salaries and wages payable	2,800	
Unearned rent	500	
Total liabilities		$ 7,400
Owner's Equity		
Mac Copas, capital		121,170
Total liabilities and owner's equity		$128,570

7. $69,470 \div $185,700 = 37.4\%$

Prob. 4–5B

1., 3., and 6.

Cash   11

Date	Item	Post. Ref.	Dr.	Cr.	Balance Dr.	Balance Cr.
2006						
Oct. 31	Balance..................	✓	....	....	3,950	....

Supplies   13

Date	Item	Post. Ref.	Dr.	Cr.	Balance Dr.	Balance Cr.
2006						
Oct. 31	Balance..................	✓	....	....	6,295	....
31	Adjusting................	26	....	5,145	1,150	....

Prepaid Insurance   14

Date	Item	Post. Ref.	Dr.	Cr.	Balance Dr.	Balance Cr.
2006						
Oct. 31	Balance..................	✓	....	....	2,735	....
31	Adjusting................	26	....	1,800	935	....

Equipment   16

Date	Item	Post. Ref.	Dr.	Cr.	Balance Dr.	Balance Cr.
2006						
Oct. 31	Balance..................	✓	....	....	50,650	....

Accumulated Depreciation—Equipment   17

Date	Item	Post. Ref.	Dr.	Cr.	Balance Dr.	Balance Cr.
2006						
Oct. 31	Balance..................	✓	....	....	....	11,209
31	Adjusting................	26	....	3,380	....	14,589

Trucks   18

Date	Item	Post. Ref.	Dr.	Cr.	Balance Dr.	Balance Cr.
2006						
Oct. 31	Balance..................	✓	....	....	36,300	....

Accumulated Depreciation—Trucks   19

Date	Item	Post. Ref.	Dr.	Cr.	Balance Dr.	Balance Cr.
2006						
Oct. 31	Balance..................	✓	....	....	....	7,400
31	Adjusting................	26	....	4,400	....	11,800

Prob. 4–5B   Continued

Accounts Payable   21

Date	Item	Post. Ref.	Dr.	Cr.	Balance Dr.	Balance Cr.
2006						
Oct. 31	Balance..................	✓	....	....	....	4,015

Wages Payable   22

Date	Item	Post. Ref.	Dr.	Cr.	Balance Dr.	Balance Cr.
2006						
Oct. 31	Adjusting...............	26	....	1,075	....	1,075

Ernie Richt, Capital   31

Date	Item	Post. Ref.	Dr.	Cr.	Balance Dr.	Balance Cr.
2006						
Oct. 31	Balance..................	✓	....	....	....	37,426
31	Closing	27	....	30,080	....	67,506
31	Closing	27	6,000	....	....	61,506

Ernie Richt, Drawing   32

Date	Item	Post. Ref.	Dr.	Cr.	Balance Dr.	Balance Cr.
2006						
Oct. 31	Balance..................	✓	....	....	6,000	....
31	Closing	27	....	6,000	—	—

Income Summary   33

Date	Item	Post. Ref.	Dr.	Cr.	Balance Dr.	Balance Cr.
2006						
Oct. 31	Closing	27	....	89,950	....	89,950
31	Closing	27	59,870	....	....	30,080
31	Closing	27	30,080	....	—	—

Service Revenue   41

Date	Item	Post. Ref.	Dr.	Cr.	Balance Dr.	Balance Cr.
2006						
Oct. 31	Balance..................	✓	....	....	....	89,950
	Closing	27	89,950	....	—	—

Wages Expense   51

Date	Item	Post. Ref.	Dr.	Cr.	Balance Dr.	Balance Cr.
2006						
Oct. 31	Balance..................	✓	....	....	26,925	....
31	Adjusting...............	26	1,075	....	28,000	....
31	Closing	27	....	28,000	—	—

Prob. 4–5B Continued

Supplies Expense 52

Date		Item	Post. Ref.	Dr.	Cr.	Balance Dr.	Balance Cr.
2006							
Oct.	31	Adjusting	26	5,145	....	5,145	....
	31	Closing	27	....	5,145	—	—

Rent Expense 53

Date		Item	Post. Ref.	Dr.	Cr.	Balance Dr.	Balance Cr.
2006							
Oct.	31	Balance	✓	....	....	9,600	....
	31	Closing	27	....	9,600	—	—

Depreciation Expense—Equipment 54

Date		Item	Post. Ref.	Dr.	Cr.	Balance Dr.	Balance Cr.
2006							
Oct.	31	Adjusting	26	3,380	....	3,380	....
	31	Closing	27	....	3,380	—	—

Truck Expense 55

Date		Item	Post. Ref.	Dr.	Cr.	Balance Dr.	Balance Cr.
2006							
Oct.	31	Balance	✓	....	....	5,350	....
	31	Closing	27	....	5,350	—	—

Depreciation Expense—Trucks 56

Date		Item	Post. Ref.	Dr.	Cr.	Balance Dr.	Balance Cr.
2006							
Oct.	31	Adjusting	26	4,400	....	4,400	....
	31	Closing	27	....	4,400	—	—

Insurance Expense 57

Date		Item	Post. Ref.	Dr.	Cr.	Balance Dr.	Balance Cr.
2006							
Oct.	31	Adjusting	26	1,800	....	1,800	....
	31	Closing	27	....	1,800	—	—

Miscellaneous Expense 59

Date		Item	Post. Ref.	Dr.	Cr.	Balance Dr.	Balance Cr.
2006							
Oct.	31	Balance	✓	....	....	2,195	....
	31	Closing	27	....	2,195	—	—

Prob. 4–5B Continued

2.

GESUNDHEIT REPAIRS
Work Sheet
For the Year Ended October 31, 2006

	Trial Balance Dr.	Trial Balance Cr.	Adjustments Dr.	Adjustments Cr.	Adjusted Trial Balance Dr.	Adjusted Trial Balance Cr.	Income Statement Dr.	Income Statement Cr.	Balance Sheet Dr.	Balance Sheet Cr.	
Account Title											
1 Cash	3,950				3,950				3,950		1
2 Supplies	6,295			(a) 5,145	1,150				1,150		2
3 Prepaid Insurance	2,735			(b) 1,800	935				935		3
4 Equipment	50,650				50,650				50,650		4
5 Accum. Depr.—Equip.		11,209		(c) 3,380		14,589				14,589	5
6 Trucks	36,300				36,300				36,300		6
7 Accum. Depr.—Trucks		7,400		(d) 4,400		11,800				11,800	7
8 Accounts Payable		4,015				4,015				4,015	8
9 Ernie Richt, Capital		37,426				37,426				37,426	9
10 Ernie Richt, Drawing	6,000				6,000				6,000		10
11 Service Revenue		89,950				89,950		89,950			11
12 Wages Expense	26,925		(e) 1,075		28,000		28,000				12
13 Rent Expense	9,600				9,600		9,600				13
14 Truck Expense	5,350				5,350		5,350				14
15 Misc. Expense	2,195				2,195		2,195				15
16	150,000	150,000									16
17 Supplies Expense			(a) 5,145		5,145		5,145				17
18 Insurance Expense			(b) 1,800		1,800		1,800				18
19 Depr. Exp.—Equip.			(c) 3,380		3,380		3,380				19
20 Depr. Exp.—Trucks			(d) 4,400		4,400		4,400				20
21 Wages Payable				(e) 1,075		1,075				1,075	21
22			15,800	15,800	158,855	158,855	59,870	89,950	98,985	68,905	22
23 Net income							30,080			30,080	23
24							89,950	89,950	98,985	98,985	24

Prob. 4–5B   Continued

5.

GESUNDHEIT REPAIRS
Income Statement
For the Year Ended October 31, 2006

Service revenue		$89,950
Operating expenses:		
Wages expense	$28,000	
Rent expense	9,600	
Truck expense	5,350	
Supplies expense	5,145	
Depreciation expense—trucks	4,400	
Depreciation expense—equipment............................	3,380	
Insurance expense	1,800	
Miscellaneous expense..	2,195	
Total operating expenses...		59,870
Net income		$30,080

GESUNDHEIT REPAIRS
Statement of Owner's Equity
For the Year Ended October 31, 2006

Ernie Richt, capital, November 1, 2005............................		$37,426
Net income for the year..	$30,080	
Less withdrawals..	6,000	
Increase in owner's capital...		24,080
Ernie Richt, capital, October 31, 2006		$61,506

Prob. 4–5B   Continued

GESUNDHEIT REPAIRS
Balance Sheet
October 31, 2006

Assets		
Current assets:		
Cash	$ 3,950	
Supplies	1,150	
Prepaid insurance	935	
Total current assets		$ 6,035
Property, plant, and equipment:		
Equipment	$50,650	
Less accum. depreciation	14,589	$36,061
Trucks	$36,300	
Less accum. depreciation	11,800	24,500
Total property, plant, and equipment		60,561
Total assets		$66,596

Liabilities		
Current liabilities:		
Accounts payable	$4,015	
Wages payable	1,075	
Total liabilities		$ 5,090
Owner's Equity		
Ernie Richt, capital		61,506
Total liabilities and owner's equity		$66,596

Prob. 4–5B Concluded

6.

JOURNAL

Date		Post. Ref.	Debit	Credit
	Closing Entries			
2006				
Oct. 31	Service Revenue..	41	89,950	
	Income Summary..................................	33		89,950
31	Income Summary..	33	59,870	
	Wages Expense	51		28,000
	Supplies Expense.................................	52		5,145
	Rent Expense..	53		9,600
	Depreciation Expense—Equipment.....	54		3,380
	Truck Expense	55		5,350
	Depreciation Expense—Trucks............	56		4,400
	Insurance Expense...............................	57		1,800
	Miscellaneous Expense	59		2,195
31	Income Summary..	33	30,080	
	Ernie Richt, Capital..............................	31		30,080
31	Ernie Richt, Capital	31	6,000	
	Ernie Richt, Drawing.............................	32		6,000

7.

GESUNDHEIT REPAIRS
Post-Closing Trial Balance
October 31, 2006

Cash...	3,950	
Supplies..	1,150	
Prepaid Insurance	935	
Equipment...	50,650	
Accumulated Depreciation—Equipment		14,589
Trucks..	36,300	
Accumulated Depreciation—Trucks		11,800
Accounts Payable..		4,015
Wages Payable		1,075
Ernie Richt, Capital.......................................		61,506
	92,985	92,985

CONTINUING PROBLEM

DANCIN MUSIC
Work Sheet
For the Two Months Ended May 31, 2006

1.

Account Title	Trial Balance Dr.	Trial Balance Cr.	Adjustments Dr.	Adjustments Cr.	Adjusted Trial Balance Dr.	Adjusted Trial Balance Cr.	Income Statement Dr.	Income Statement Cr.	Balance Sheet Dr.	Balance Sheet Cr.	
1 Cash	7,330				7,330				7,330		1
2 Accounts Receivable	1,760		(a) 1,200		2,960				2,960		2
3 Supplies	920			(b) 750	170				170		3
4 Prepaid Insurance	3,360			(c) 140	3,220				3,220		4
5 Office Equipment	5,000				5,000				5,000		5
6 Acc. Depr.—Office Equipment				(d) 100		100				100	6
7 Accounts Payable		5,750				5,750				5,750	7
8 Wages Payable				(f) 130		130				130	8
9 Unearned Revenue		4,800	(e) 2,400			2,400				2,400	9
10 S. Burns, Capital		10,000				10,000				10,000	10
11 S. Burns, Drawing	2,250				2,250				2,250		11
12 Fees Earned		11,210		(a) 1,200		14,810		14,810			12
13				(e) 2,400							13
14 Wages Expense	2,800		(f) 130		2,930		2,930				14
15 Office Rent Expense	2,600				2,600		2,600				15
16 Equip. Rent Expense	1,150				1,150		1,150				16
17 Utilities Expense	860				860		860				17
18 Music Expense	1,780				1,780		1,780				18
19 Advertising Expense	1,300				1,300		1,300				19
20 Supplies Expense	180		(b) 750		930		930				20
21 Insurance Expense			(c) 140		140		140				21
22 Depr. Expense			(d) 100		100		100				22
23 Misc. Expense	470				470		470				23
24	31,760	31,760	4,720	4,720	33,190	33,190	12,260	14,810	20,930	18,380	24
25 Net income							2,550			2,550	25
26							14,810	14,810	20,930	20,930	26

205

Continuing Problem   Continued

Supplies   14

Date	Item	Post. Ref.	Dr.	Cr.	Balance Dr.	Balance Cr.
2006						
May 1	Balance..................	✓	....	....	170	....
18	....	2	750	....	920	....
31	Adjusting..............	3	....	750	170	....

Prepaid Insurance   15

Date	Item	Post. Ref.	Dr.	Cr.	Balance Dr.	Balance Cr.
2006						
May 1	....	1	3,360	....	3,360	....
31	Adjusting..............	3	....	140	3,220	....

Office Equipment   17

Date	Item	Post. Ref.	Dr.	Cr.	Balance Dr.	Balance Cr.
2006						
May 5	....	1	5,000	....	5,000	....

Accumulated Depreciation—Office Equipment   18

Date	Item	Post. Ref.	Dr.	Cr.	Balance Dr.	Balance Cr.
2006						
May 31	Adjusting..............	3	....	100	....	100

Accounts Payable   21

Date	Item	Post. Ref.	Dr.	Cr.	Balance Dr.	Balance Cr.
2006						
May 1	Balance..................	✓	....	....	....	250
3	....	1	250	....	—	—
5	....	1	....	5,000	....	5,000
18	....	2	....	750	....	5,750

Wages Payable   22

Date	Item	Post. Ref.	Dr.	Cr.	Balance Dr.	Balance Cr.
2006						
May 31	Adjusting..............	3	....	130	....	130

Unearned Revenue   23

Date	Item	Post. Ref.	Dr.	Cr.	Balance Dr.	Balance Cr.
2006						
May 3	....	1	....	4,800	....	4,800
31	Adjusting..............	3	2,400	....	....	2,400

Continuing Problem   Continued

Shannon Burns, Capital

31

Date	Item	Post. Ref.	Dr.	Cr.	Balance Dr.	Balance Cr.
2006						
May 1	Balance..................	✓	....	....	....	7,000
1	....	1	....	3,000	....	10,000
31	Closing	4	....	2,550	....	12,550
	Closing	4	2,250	....	....	10,300

Shannon Burns, Drawing

32

Date	Item	Post. Ref.	Dr.	Cr.	Balance Dr.	Balance Cr.
2006						
May 1	Balance..................	✓	....	....	250	....
31	....	2	2,000	....	2,250	....
31	Closing	4	....	2,250	—	—

Income Summary

33

Date	Item	Post. Ref.	Dr.	Cr.	Balance Dr.	Balance Cr.
2006						
May 31	Closing	4	....	14,810	....	14,810
31	Closing	4	12,260	....	....	2,550
31	Closing	4	2,550	....	—	—

Fees Earned

41

Date	Item	Post. Ref.	Dr.	Cr.	Balance Dr.	Balance Cr.
2006						
May 1	Balance..................	✓	....	....	....	4,750
11	....	1	....	600	....	5,350
16	....	2	....	1,100	....	6,450
23	....	2	....	1,560	....	8,010
30	....	2	....	1,200	....	9,210
31	....	2	....	2,000	....	11,210
31	Adjusting...............	3	....	1,200	....	12,410
31	Adjusting...............	3	....	2,400	....	14,810
31	Closing	4	14,810	....	—	—

Wages Expense

50

Date	Item	Post. Ref.	Dr.	Cr.	Balance Dr.	Balance Cr.
2006						
May 1	Balance..................	✓	....	....	400	....
14	....	1	1,200	....	1,600	....
28	....	2	1,200	....	2,800	....
31	Adjusting...............	3	130	....	2,930	....
31	Closing	4	....	2,930	—	—

Continuing Problem Continued

Office Rent Expense 51

Date		Item	Post. Ref.	Dr.	Cr.	Balance Dr.	Balance Cr.
2006							
May	1	Balance..................	✓	....	....	1,000	....
	1	....	1	1,600	....	2,600	....
	31	Closing	4	....	2,600	—	—

Equipment Rent Expense 52

Date		Item	Post. Ref.	Dr.	Cr.	Balance Dr.	Balance Cr.
2006							
May	1	Balance..................	✓	....	....	650	....
	13	....	1	500	....	1,150	....
	31	Closing	4	....	1,150	—	—

Utilities Expense 53

Date		Item	Post. Ref.	Dr.	Cr.	Balance Dr.	Balance Cr.
2006							
May	1	Balance..................	✓	....	....	300	....
	27	....	2	560	....	860	....
	31	Closing	4	....	860	—	—

Music Expense 54

Date		Item	Post. Ref.	Dr.	Cr.	Balance Dr.	Balance Cr.
2006							
May	1	Balance..................	✓	....	....	940	....
	21	....	2	240	....	1,180	....
	31	....	2	600	....	1,780	....
	31	Closing	4	....	1,780	—	—

Advertising Expense 55

Date		Item	Post. Ref.	Dr.	Cr.	Balance Dr.	Balance Cr.
2006							
May	1	Balance..................	✓	....	....	600	....
	8	....	1	200	....	800	....
	22	....	2	500	....	1,300	....
	31	Closing	4	....	1,300	—	—

Supplies Expense 56

Date		Item	Post. Ref.	Dr.	Cr.	Balance Dr.	Balance Cr.
2006							
May	1	Balance..................	✓	....	....	180	....
	31	Adjusting	3	750	....	930	....
	31	Closing	4	....	930	—	—

Continuing Problem   Concluded

Insurance Expense   57

Date		Item	Post. Ref.	Dr.	Cr.	Balance Dr.	Balance Cr.
2006							
May	31	Adjusting............	3	140	....	140	....
	31	Closing	4	....	140	—	—

Depreciation Expense   58

Date		Item	Post. Ref.	Dr.	Cr.	Balance Dr.	Balance Cr.
2006							
May	31	Adjusting............	3	100	....	100	....
	31	Closing	4	....	100	—	—

Miscellaneous Expense   59

Date		Item	Post. Ref.	Dr.	Cr.	Balance Dr.	Balance Cr.
2006							
May	1	Balance...............	✓	....	....	150	....
	4	....	1	150	....	300	....
	29	....	2	170	....	470	....
	31	Closing	4	....	470	—	—

4.

DANCIN MUSIC
Post-Closing Trial Balance
May 31, 2006

Cash...	7,330	
Accounts Receivable..	2,960	
Supplies..	170	
Prepaid Insurance	3,220	
Office Equipment...	5,000	
Accumulated Depreciation—Office Equipment		100
Accounts Payable..		5,750
Wages Payable		130
Unearned Revenue		2,400
Shannon Burns, Capital..		10,300
	18,680	18,680

COMPREHENSIVE PROBLEM 1

1. and 2.	JOURNAL			Pages 1 and 2

Date	Description	Post. Ref.	Debit	Credit
2006				
April 1	Cash...	11	13,100	
	Accounts Receivable	12	3,000	
	Supplies	14	1,400	
	Office Equipment..	18	12,500	
	Kelly Pitney, Capital...........................	31		30,000
1	Prepaid Rent	15	4,800	
	Cash...	11		4,800
2	Prepaid Insurance	16	1,800	
	Cash...	11		1,800
4	Cash...	11	5,000	
	Unearned Fees	23		5,000
5	Office Equipment..	18	2,000	
	Accounts Payable	21		2,000
6	Cash...	11	1,800	
	Accounts Receivable.............................	12		1,800
10	Miscellaneous Expense	59	120	
	Cash...	11		120
12	Accounts Payable..	21	1,200	
	Cash...	11		1,200
12	Accounts Receivable	12	4,200	
	Fees Earned	41		4,200
14	Salary Expense..	51	750	
	Cash...	11		750
17	Cash...	11	6,250	
	Fees Earned	41		6,250
18	Supplies	14	800	
	Cash...	11		800
20	Accounts Receivable	12	2,100	
	Fees Earned	41		2,100
24	Cash...	11	3,850	
	Fees Earned	41		3,850

Comp. Prob. 1   Continued

JOURNAL   Pages 1 and 2

Date	Description	Post. Ref.	Debit	Credit
2006				
April 26	Cash...	11	5,600	
	Accounts Receivable............................	12		5,600
27	Salary Expense...................................	51	750	
	Cash...	11		750
29	Miscellaneous Expense...........................	59	130	
	Cash...	11		130
30	Miscellaneous Expense...........................	59	200	
	Cash...	11		200
30	Cash...	11	3,050	
	Fees Earned	41		3,050
30	Accounts Receivable	12	1,500	
	Fees Earned	41		1,500
30	Kelly Pitney, Drawing.............................	32	6,000	
	Cash...	11		6,000

Comp. Prob. 1   Continued

2., 5., and 6.

Cash   11

Date		Item	Post. Ref.	Dr.	Cr.	Balance Dr.	Cr.
2006							
April	1	....	1	13,100	....	13,100	....
	1	....	1	....	4,800	8,300	....
	2	....	1	....	1,800	6,500	....
	4	....	1	5,000	....	11,500	....
	6	....	1	1,800	....	13,300	....
	10	....	1	....	120	13,180	....
	12	....	1	....	1,200	11,980	....
	14	....	1	....	750	11,230	....
	17	....	2	6,250	....	17,480	....
	18	....	2	....	800	16,680	....
	24	....	2	3,850	....	20,530	....
	26	....	2	5,600	....	26,130	....
	27	....	2	....	750	25,380	....
	29	....	2	....	130	25,250	....
	30	....	2	....	200	25,050	....
	30	....	2	3,050	....	28,100	....
	30	....	2	....	6,000	22,100	....

Accounts Receivable   12

Date		Item	Post. Ref.	Dr.	Cr.	Balance Dr.	Cr.
2006							
April	1	....	1	3,000	....	3,000	....
	6	....	1	....	1,800	1,200	....
	12	....	1	4,200	....	5,400	....
	20	....	2	2,100	....	7,500	....
	26	....	2	....	5,600	1,900	....
	30	....	2	1,500	....	3,400	....

Supplies   14

Date		Item	Post. Ref.	Dr.	Cr.	Balance Dr.	Cr.
2006							
April	1	....	1	1,400	....	1,400	....
	18	....	2	800	....	2,200	....
	30	Adjusting...............	3	....	850	1,350	....

Prepaid Rent   15

Date	Item	Post. Ref.	Dr.	Cr.	Balance Dr.	Balance Cr.
2006						
April 1	....	1	4,800	....	4,800	....
30	Adjusting...............	3	....	1,600	3,200	....

Prepaid Insurance   16

Date	Item	Post. Ref.	Dr.	Cr.	Balance Dr.	Balance Cr.
2006						
April 2	....	1	1,800	....	1,800	....
30	Adjusting...............	3	....	300	1,500	....

Office Equipment   18

Date	Item	Post. Ref.	Dr.	Cr.	Balance Dr.	Balance Cr.
2006						
April 1	....	1	12,500	....	12,500	....
5	....	1	2,000	....	14,500	....

Accumulated Depreciation   19

Date	Item	Post. Ref.	Dr.	Cr.	Balance Dr.	Balance Cr.
2006						
April 30	Adjusting...............	3	....	700	....	700

Accounts Payable   21

Date	Item	Post. Ref.	Dr.	Cr.	Balance Dr.	Balance Cr.
2006						
April 5	....	1	....	2,000	....	2,000
12	....	1	1,200	....	....	800

Salaries Payable   22

Date	Item	Post. Ref.	Dr.	Cr.	Balance Dr.	Balance Cr.
2006						
April 30	Adjusting...............	3	....	120	....	120

Unearned Fees   23

Date	Item	Post. Ref.	Dr.	Cr.	Balance Dr.	Balance Cr.
2006						
April 4	....	1	....	5,000	....	5,000
30	Adjusting...............	3	2,500	....	....	2,500

Comp. Prob. 1   Continued

Kelly Pitney, Capital   31

Date	Item	Post. Ref.	Dr.	Cr.	Balance Dr.	Balance Cr.
2006						
April 1	....	1	....	30,000	....	30,000
30	Closing	4	....	17,930	....	47,930
30	Closing	4	6,000	....	....	41,930

Kelly Pitney, Drawing   32

Date	Item	Post. Ref.	Dr.	Cr.	Balance Dr.	Balance Cr.
2006						
April 30	....	2	6,000	....	6,000	....
30	Closing	4	....	6,000	—	—

Income Summary   33

Date	Item	Post. Ref.	Dr.	Cr.	Balance Dr.	Balance Cr.
2006						
April 30	Closing	4	....	23,450	....	23,450
30	Closing	4	5,520	....	....	17,930
30	Closing	4	17,930	....	—	—

Fees Earned   41

Date	Item	Post. Ref.	Dr.	Cr.	Balance Dr.	Balance Cr.
2006						
April 12	....	1	....	4,200	....	4,200
17	....	2	....	6,250	....	10,450
20	....	2	....	2,100	....	12,550
24	....	2	....	3,850	....	16,400
30	....	2	....	3,050	....	19,450
30	....	2	....	1,500	....	20,950
30	Adjusting	3	....	2,500	....	23,450
30	Closing	4	23,450	....	—	—

Salary Expense   51

Date	Item	Post. Ref.	Dr.	Cr.	Balance Dr.	Balance Cr.
2006						
April 14	....	1	750	....	750	....
27	....	2	750	....	1,500	....
30	Adjusting	3	120	....	1,620	....
30	Closing	4	....	1,620	—	—

Comp. Prob. 1   Continued

Rent Expense 52

Date	Item	Post. Ref.	Dr.	Cr.	Balance Dr.	Balance Cr.
2006						
April 30	Adjusting..............	3	1,600	....	1,600	....
30	Closing.................	4	....	1,600	—	—

Supplies Expense 53

Date	Item	Post. Ref.	Dr.	Cr.	Balance Dr.	Balance Cr.
2006						
April 30	Adjusting..............	3	850	....	850	....
30	Closing.................	4	....	850	—	—

Depreciation Expense 54

Date	Item	Post. Ref.	Dr.	Cr.	Balance Dr.	Balance Cr.
2006						
April 30	Adjusting..............	3	700	....	700	....
30	Closing.................	4	....	700	—	—

Insurance Expense 55

Date	Item	Post. Ref.	Dr.	Cr.	Balance Dr.	Balance Cr.
2006						
April 30	Adjusting..............	3	300	....	300	....
30	Closing.................	4	....	300	—	—

Miscellaneous Expense 59

Date	Item	Post. Ref.	Dr.	Cr.	Balance Dr.	Balance Cr.
2006						
April 10	....	1	120	....	120	....
29	....	2	130	....	250	....
30	....	2	200	....	450	....
30	Closing.................	4	....	450	—	—

Comp. Prob. 1   Continued

3.

HIPPOCRATES CONSULTING
Work Sheet
For the Month Ended April 30, 2006

	Trial Balance Dr.	Cr.	Adjustments Dr.	Cr.	Adjusted Trial Balance Dr.	Cr.	Income Statement Dr.	Cr.	Balance Sheet Dr.	Cr.	
Account Title											
1 Cash	22,100				22,100				22,100		1
2 Accounts Receivable	3,400				3,400				3,400		2
3 Supplies	2,200			(b) 850	1,350				1,350		3
4 Prepaid Rent	4,800			(e) 1,600	3,200				3,200		4
5 Prepaid Insurance	1,800			(a) 300	1,500				1,500		5
6 Office Equipment	14,500				14,500				14,500		6
7 Accum. Depreciation				(c) 700		700				700	7
8 Accounts Payable		800				800				800	8
9 Salaries Payable				(d) 120		120				120	9
10 Unearned Fees		5,000	(f) 2,500			2,500				2,500	10
11 Kelly Pitney, Capital		30,000				30,000				30,000	11
12 Kelly Pitney, Drawing	6,000				6,000				6,000		12
13 Fees Earned		20,950		(f) 2,500		23,450		23,450			13
14 Salary Expense	1,500		(d) 120		1,620		1,620				14
15 Rent Expense			(e) 1,600		1,600		1,600				15
16 Supplies Expense			(b) 850		850		850				16
17 Depreciation Expense			(c) 700		700		700				17
18 Insurance Expense			(a) 300		300		300				18
19 Miscellaneous Expense	450				450		450				19
20	56,750	56,750	6,070	6,070	57,570	57,570	5,520	23,450	52,050	34,120	20
21 Net income							17,930			17,930	21
22							23,450	23,450	52,050	52,050	22

220

Comp. Prob. 1   Continued

4.

HIPPOCRATES CONSULTING
Income Statement
For the Month Ended April 30, 2006

Fees earned..		$23,450
Operating expenses:		
Salary expense	$1,620	
Rent expense..	1,600	
Supplies expense..	850	
Depreciation expense	700	
Insurance expense...	300	
Miscellaneous expense...	450	
Total operating expenses.....................................		5,520
Net income		$17,930

HIPPOCRATES CONSULTING
Statement of Owner's Equity
For the Month Ended April 30, 2006

Kelly Pitney, capital, April 1, 2006		$ 0
Additional investments during the month		30,000
Total...		$30,000
Net income for the month	$17,930	
Less withdrawals...	6,000	
Increase in owner's equity...		11,930
Kelly Pitney, capital, April 30, 2006		$41,930

Activity 4–3

1. A set of financial statements provides useful information concerning the economic condition of a company. For example, the balance sheet describes the financial condition of the company as of a given date and is useful in assessing the company's financial soundness and liquidity. The income statement describes the results of operations for a period and indicates the profitability of the company. The statement of owner's equity describes the changes in the owner's interest in the company for a period. Each of these statements is useful in evaluating whether to extend credit to the company.

2. The following adjustments might be necessary before an accurate set of financial statements could be prepared:

   - No supplies expense is shown. The supplies account should be adjusted for the supplies used during the year.

   - No depreciation expense is shown for the trucks or equipment accounts. An adjusting entry should be prepared for depreciation expense on each of these assets.

   - An inquiry should be made as to whether any accrued expenses, such as wages or utilities, exist at the end of the year.

   - An inquiry should be made as to whether any prepaid expenses, such as rent or insurance, exist at the end of the year.

   - An inquiry should be made as to whether the owner withdrew any funds from the company during the year. No drawing account is shown in the "Statement of Accounts."

   - The following items should be relabeled for greater clarity:

         Billings Due from Others—Accounts Receivable

         Amounts Owed to Others—Accounts Payable

         Investment in Business—Samantha Joyner, Capital

         Other Expenses—Miscellaneous Expense

Note to Instructors: The preceding items are not intended to include all adjustments that might exist in the Statement of Accounts. The possible adjustments listed include only items that have been covered in Chapters 1–4. For example, uncollectible accounts expense (discussed in a later chapter) is not mentioned.

Activity 4–3 Concluded

3. In general, the decision to extend a loan is based upon an assessment of the profitability and riskiness of the loan. Although the financial statements provide useful data for this purpose, other factors such as the following might also be significant:

- The due date and payment terms of the loan.
- Security for the loan. For example, whether Samantha Joyner is willing to pledge personal assets in support of the loan will affect the riskiness of the loan.
- The intended use of the loan. For example, if the loan is to purchase real estate (possibly for a future building site), the real estate could be used as security for the loan.
- The projected profitability of the company.

Activity 4–4

Note to Instructors: The purpose of this activity is to familiarize students with the information that a balance sheet provides about a company.

Activity 4–5

1. The primary factor that affects the demand for carpet is the demand for housing. Some of the factors affecting the demand for housing, and thus carpet, include the following:

   a. Periods of economic growth tend to increase the demand for housing and, thus, carpet.

   b. A growing population tends to increase the demand for housing and, thus, carpet.

   c. Increasing house sizes increases the demand for carpet.

   d. Increasing demand for vacation and second homes increases the demand for carpet.

2. The objective of this question is to make the students think strategically.

   The primary advantage for Mohawk of viewing itself as a floorcovering manufacturer is that the company will become more flexible and forward in its strategic and operational thinking. This may allow the company to more easily take advantage of floorcovering opportunities beyond carpets. For example, the current trend among consumers is to shift away from carpets to hardwood flooring, ceramic tile, vinyl, rubber, and laminated products. Without an ability or willingness to shift to other types of floorcovering, Mohawk may lose market share and profitability.

   The primary disadvantage for Mohawk of viewing itself as a floorcovering manufacturer is that the company may not have the core competencies to manufacture other types of floorcoverings. That is, Mohawk may not be able to manufacture other types of floorcoverings at competitive prices.

3. Mohawk views itself as "a leading producer of floorcovering products for residential and commercial applications." Thus, Mohawk views itself as a floorcovering manufacturer. In 2002, Mohawk acquired Dal-Tile International, a leading manufacturer and retailer of ceramic tile and natural stone flooring. In addition, Mohawk is rumored to be searching to buy manufacturers of hardwood and laminated wood flooring. Thus, Mohawk is strategically expanding its product line beyond carpets into other types of floorcoverings.

CHAPTER 5
ACCOUNTING SYSTEMS AND INTERNAL CONTROLS

CLASS DISCUSSION QUESTIONS

1. The knowledge that job rotation is practiced and that one employee may perform another's job at a later date tends to discourage deviations from prescribed procedures. Also, rotation helps to disclose any irregularities that may occur.

2. Authorizing complete control over a sequence of related operations by one individual presents opportunities for inefficiency, errors, and fraud. The control over a sequence of operations should be divided so that the work of each employee is automatically checked by another employee in the normal course of work. A system functioning in this manner helps prevent errors and inefficiency. Fraud is unlikely without collusion between two or more employees.

3. To reduce the possibility of errors and embezzlement, the functions of operations and accounting should be separated. Thus, one employee should not be responsible for handling cash receipts (operations) and maintaining the accounts receivable records (accounting).

4. No. Combining the responsibility for related operations, such as combining the functions of purchasing, receiving, and storing of supplies, increases the possibility of errors and fraud.

5. The control procedure requiring that responsibility for a sequence of related operations be divided among different persons is violated in this situation. This weakness in the internal control may permit irregularities. For example, the ticket seller, while acting as ticket taker, could admit friends without a ticket.

6. The responsibility for maintaining the accounting records should be separated from the responsibility for operations so that the accounting records can serve as an independent check on operations.

7. The individual accounts receivable ledger accounts provide business managers information on the status of individual customer accounts, which is necessary for managing collections. Managers need to know which customers owe money, how much they owe, and how long the amount owed has been outstanding.

8. The major advantages of the use of special journals are substantial savings in record-keeping expenses and a reduction of record-keeping errors.

9. a. 250
   b. None

10. a. 250
    b. 1

11. a. Sometime following the end of the current month, one of two things may happen: (1) an overdue notice will be received from Hoffman Co., and/or (2) a letter will be received from Hoffer Co., informing the buyer of the overpayment. (It is also possible that the error will be discovered at the time of making payment if the original invoice is inspected at the time the check is being written.)

    b. The schedule of accounts payable would not agree with the balance of the accounts payable account. The error might also be discovered at the time the invoice is paid.

    c. The creditor will call the attention of the debtor to the unpaid balance of $1,000.

    d. The error will become evident during the verification process at the end of the month. The total debits in the purchases journal will be less than the total credits by $2,000.

12. a. No, the error will not cause the trial balance totals to be unequal.

    b. No, the sum of the balances in the creditors ledger will not agree with the balance of the accounts payable account in the general ledger.

13. a. Cash payments journal
    b. Purchases journal
    c. Cash payments journal
    d. Purchases journal
    e. Cash payments journal

14. An electronic form is a software window that provides the inputs for a particular transaction. For example, a check form provides the

inputs (payee, amount, date) for a cash payment transaction. An electronic invoice provides the inputs (customer, amount sold, item sold) for recording revenues earned on account.

15. The use of controlling accounts to verify the accuracy of subsidiary accounts is used in a manual system. In a computerized system, it is assumed that the computer will accurately sum the individual transactions in the subsidiary accounts in determining the aggregate balance. Thus, there is no need for controlling accounts for controlling the accuracy of the individual postings.

16. For automated systems that use electronic forms the special journals are not used to record original transactions. Rather, electronic forms capture the original transaction detail from an invoice, for example, and automatically post the transaction details to the appropriate ledger accounts.

17. E-commerce can be used by a business to conduct transactions directly with customers. Thus, an order can be received directly from the customer's Internet input and cash can be received from the credit card. Many times, the cash is received prior to actually shipping the product, resulting in a faster revenue/collection cycle. Reducing paperwork throughout the cycle also improves the efficiency of the process. For example, all of the accounting transactions can be fed automatically from the initial Web-based inputs.

EXERCISES

Ex. 5–1

a. Agree. Barbara has made one employee responsible for the cash drawer in accordance with the internal control principle of assignment of responsibility.

b. Disagree. It is commendable that Barbara has given the employee a specific responsibility and is holding that employee accountable for it. However, after the cashier has counted the cash, another employee (or perhaps Barbara) should remove the cash register tape and compare the amount on the tape with the cash in the drawer. Also, Barbara's standard of no mistakes may encourage the cashiers to overcharge a few customers in order to cover any possible shortages in the cash drawer.

c. Disagree. Stealing is a serious issue. An employee who can justify taking a box of tea bags can probably justify "borrowing" cash from the cash register.

Ex. 5–2

a. The sales clerks could steal money by writing phony refunds and pocketing the cash supposedly refunded to these fictitious customers.

b. 1. Elegance by Elaine suffers from inadequate separation of responsibilities for related operations since the clerks issue refunds and restock all merchandise. In addition, there is a lack of proofs and security measures since the supervisors authorize returns two hours after they are issued.

2. A store credit for any merchandise returned without a receipt would reduce the possibility of theft of cash. In this case, a clerk could only issue a phony store credit rather than taking money from the cash register. A store credit is not as tempting as cash. In addition, sales clerks could only use a few store credits to purchase merchandise for themselves without management getting suspicious.

An advantage of issuing a store credit for returns without a receipt is that the possibility of stealing cash is reduced. The store will also lose less revenue if customers must choose other store merchandise instead of getting a cash refund. The overall level of returns/exchanges may be reduced, since customers will not return an acceptable gift simply because they need cash more than the gift. The policy will also reduce the "cash drain" during the weeks immediately following the holidays, allowing Elegance by Elaine to keep more of its money earning interest or to use that cash to purchase spring merchandise or pay creditors.

Ex. 5–6

Event Sound should not have relied on the unusual nature of the vendors and delivery frequency to uncover this fraud. The purchase and payment cycle is one of the most critical business cycles to control, because the potential for abuse is so great. Purchases should be initiated by a requisition document. This document should be countersigned by a superior so that two people agree as to what is being purchased. The requisition should initiate a purchase order to a vendor for goods or services. The vendor responds to the purchase order by delivering the goods. The goods should be formally received using a receiving document. An accounts payable clerk matches the requisition, purchase order, and invoice before any payment is made. Such "triple matching" prevents unauthorized requests and payments. In this case, the requests were unauthorized, suggesting that the employee had sole authority to make a request. Second, this employee had access to the invoices. This access allowed the employee to change critical characteristics of the invoice to hide the true nature of the goods being received. The invoice should have been delivered directly to the accounts payable clerk to avoid corrupting the document. There apparently was no receiving document (common for smaller companies); thus, only the invoice provided proof of what was received and to be paid. If there had been a receiving report, the invoice could not have been doctored and gone undetected, because it would not have matched the receiving report.

Note to Instructors: This exercise is based on an actual fraud.

Ex. 5–7

a. The most difficult frauds to detect are those that involve the senior management of a company that is in a conspiracy to commit the fraud. The senior managers have the power to access many parts of the accounting system, while the normal separation of duties is subverted by involving many people in the fraud. In addition, the authorization control is subverted because most of the authorization power resides in the senior management.

b. Overall, this type of fraud can be stopped if there is strong oversight of senior management, such as an audit committee of the board of directors. Individual "whistle blowers" in the company can make their concerns known to the independent or internal auditors who, in turn, can inform the audit committee. The audit committee should be independent of management and have the power to monitor the actions of management.

Ex. 5–8

1. General ledger accounts: (e)
2. Subsidiary ledger accounts: (a), (b), (c), (d)

Ex. 5–9

a., b., and c.

Accounts Receivable

Nov. 1 Bal. 480	
Nov. 30 6,240	
Nov. 30 Bal. 6,720	

Envirolab

Nov. 1 Bal. 480	
Nov. 27 965	
Nov. 30 Bal. 1,445	

Environmental Safety Co.

Nov. 1 2,625	
Nov. 30 Bal. 2,625	

Greenberg Co.

Nov. 10 1,050	
Nov. 30 Bal. 1,050	

Smith and Smith

Nov. 20 1,600	
Nov. 30 Bal. 1,600	

d.

DELTA CONSULTING CO.
Schedule of Accounts Receivable
November 30, 2006

Envirolab	$1,445
Environmental Safety Co.	2,625
Greenberg Co.	1,050
Smith and Smith	1,600
Total accounts receivable	$6,720

Ex. 5–10

a. Cash receipts journal

b. Cash receipts journal

c. General journal (not a revenue transaction)

d. General journal

e. Cash receipts journal

f. Cash receipts journal

g. Cash receipts journal

h. Revenue journal

i. Cash receipts journal

j. General journal

Ex. 5–11

a. Cash payments journal

b. Purchases journal

c. Cash payments journal

d. General journal

e. General journal

f. Cash payments journal

g. Purchases journal

h. Cash payments journal

i. General journal

j. General journal

k. Purchases journal

Ex. 5–12

Nov. 3 Provided service on account; posted from revenue journal.

9 Granted allowance or corrected error related to sale of November 3; posted from general journal.

13 Received cash for balance due; posted from cash receipts journal.

Ex. 5–13

Gold Coast Production Co.
Schedule of Accounts Receivable
April 30, 2006

Central States Broadcasting Co.	$2,450
Korvette Co.	975
Trask Co.	3,440
Star Media	0
Total accounts receivable	$6,865

Accounts Receivable
(Controlling)

Balance, April 1, 2006	$ 4,670
Total debits (from revenue journal)	16,165
Total credits (from cash receipts journal)	(13,970)
Balance, April 30, 2006	$ 6,865

Ex. 5–14

REVENUE JOURNAL

PAGE 8

	Date	Invoice No.	Account Debited	Post. Ref.	Accounts Rec. Dr. Fees Earned Cr.	
	2006					
1	Mar. 2	512	Conrad Co.	✓	790	1
2	8	513	Orlando Co.	✓	310	2
3	12	514	Drake Inc.	✓	580	3
4	22	515	Electronic Central, Inc.	✓	250	4
	31		Total		1,930	5

CASH RECEIPTS JOURNAL

PAGE 12

	Date	Account Credited	Post. Ref.	Fees Earned Cr.	Accts. Rec. Cr.	Cash Dr.	
	2006						
1	Mar. 4	CMI, Inc.	✓	....	240	240	1
2	19	Drake Inc.	✓	....	530	530	2
3	27	Fees Earned		70	....	70	3
4	29	Conrad Co.	✓	....	790	790	4
5	31	Fees Earned		40	....	40	5
6	31	Total		110	1,560	1,670	6

Ex. 5–15

1. General ledger account: (c), (e), (h), (j), (k), (l)
2. Subsidiary ledger account: (a), (b), (d), (f), (g), (i)
3. No posting required: (m)

Ex. 5–16

1. General ledger account: (b), (c), (d), (f), (g), (i), (k), (l)
2. Subsidiary ledger account: (a), (e), (h)
3. No posting required: (j)

Ex. 5–23   Continued

ACCOUNTS RECEIVABLE SUBSIDIARY LEDGER

D. Jeffries

Date	Item	Post. Ref.	Dr.	Cr.	Balance
2006					
June 22	....	R1	126	....	126

J. Koss

Date	Item	Post. Ref.	Dr.	Cr.	Balance
2006					
June 21	....	R1	84	....	84
26	....	R1	273	....	357

K. Lee

Date	Item	Post. Ref.	Dr.	Cr.	Balance
2006					
June 19	....	R1	126	....	126
28	....	R1	63	....	189

A. Sommerfeld

Date	Item	Post. Ref.	Dr.	Cr.	Balance
2006					
June 16	....	R1	315	....	315

Ex. 5–23   Concluded

b.

GENERAL LEDGER

Accounts Receivable _____ **12**

Date	Item	Post. Ref.	Dr.	Cr.	Balance Dr.	Balance Cr.
2006						
June 30	....	R1	987	....	987	....

Office Supplies _____ **14**

2006						
June 24	....	J1	168	....	168	....

Sales Tax Payable _____ **22**

2006						
June 24	....	J1	....	8	....	8
30	....	R1	....	47	....	55

Fees Earned _____ **41**

2006						
June 24	....	J1	....	160	....	160
30	....	R1	....	940	....	1,100

c. 1. $987 ($126 + $357 + $189 + $315)

    2. $987

Ex. 5-24

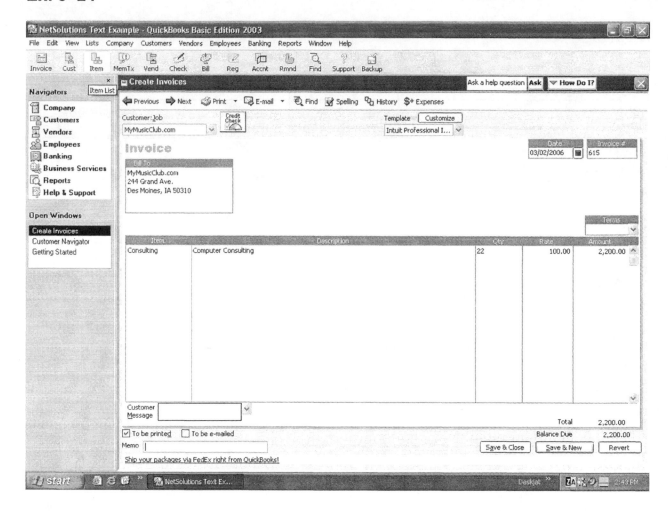

a. In the electronic invoice form from QuickBooks® shown above, typical fields for data input can be identified:

1. Customer name and address

2. Date and invoice number

3. Description of item sold

4. Amount of revenue

b. The customer accounts receivable is debited and Fees Earned is credited. A computerized accounting system does not require posting to a separate accounts receivable controlling account. In this case, the total accounts receivable reported on the balance sheet is merely the sum of the balances of the individual customer account balances.

Ex. 5–24   Concluded

c.   Controlling accounts are not posted at the end of the month in a computerized accounting system. In addition, special journals are not normally used to accumulate transactions. Transactions are recorded through data input into electronic forms (or for infrequent transactions, by an electronic general journal). Balances of affected accounts are automatically posted and updated from the information recorded on the form. If desired, the computer can provide a printout of the monthly transaction history for a particular account, which provides the same information as a journal. In addition, the controlling account is not separately posted. In a manual system, separate posting to the controlling account provides additional control by reconciling the controlling account balance against the sum of the individual customer account balances. However, in a computerized accounting system there are no separate postings to a controlling account because the computer is not going to make posting or mathematical errors. Therefore, there is no need for the additional control provided by posting a journal total to a controlling account.

PROBLEMS

Prob. 5–1A

1. and 2.

REVENUE JOURNAL

PAGE 1

	Date	Invoice No.	Account Debited	Post. Ref.	Accounts Rec. Dr. Fees Earned Cr.	
	2006					
1	Aug. 18	1	Jacob Co.	✓	920	1
2	20	2	Ro-Gain Co.	✓	650	2
3	22	3	Great Northern Co................	✓	2,480	3
4	27	4	Carson Co.	✓	1,870	4
5	28	5	Bower Co.	✓	950	5
6	30	6	Ro-Gain Co.	✓	2,860	6
7	31	7	Great Northern Co................	✓	985	7
8	31				10,715	8
9					(12) (41)	9

JOURNAL

PAGE 1

Date	Description	Post. Ref.	Debit	Credit
2006				
Aug. 28	Supplies	14	575	
	Fees Earned...	41		575

Prob. 5–1A   Continued

1.

ACCOUNTS RECEIVABLE LEDGER

Bower Co.

Date	Item	Post. Ref.	Dr.	Cr.	Balance
2006					
Aug. 28	....	R1	950	....	950

Carson Co.

Date	Item	Post. Ref.	Dr.	Cr.	Balance
2006					
Aug. 27	....	R1	1,870	....	1,870

Great Northern Co.

Date	Item	Post. Ref.	Dr.	Cr.	Balance
2006					
Aug. 22	....	R1	2,480	....	2,480
31	....	R1	985	....	3,465

Jacob Co.

Date	Item	Post. Ref.	Dr.	Cr.	Balance
2006					
Aug. 18	....	R1	920	....	920

Ro-Gain Co.

Date	Item	Post. Ref.	Dr.	Cr.	Balance
2006					
Aug. 20	....	R1	650	....	650
30	....	R1	2,860	....	3,510

Prob. 5–1A   Concluded

2.

GENERAL LEDGER

Accounts Receivable   12

Date	Item	Post. Ref.	Dr.	Cr.	Balance Dr.	Balance Cr.
2006						
Aug. 31	....	R1	10,715	....	10,715	....

Supplies   14

Date	Item	Post. Ref.	Dr.	Cr.	Balance Dr.	Balance Cr.
2006						
Aug. 28	....	J1	575	....	575	....

Fees Earned   41

Date	Item	Post. Ref.	Dr.	Cr.	Balance Dr.	Balance Cr.
2006						
Aug. 28	....	J1	....	575	....	575
31	....	R1	....	10,715	....	11,290

3. a. $10,715 ($950 + $1,870 + $3,465 + $920 + $3,510)

    b. $10,715

4. The single money column in the revenue journal can be replaced with three columns for (1) Accounts Receivable Dr., (2) Fees Earned Cr., and (3) Sales Tax Payable Cr.

Prob. 5–2A

1. and 5.

GENERAL LEDGER

Cash   11

Date	Item	Post. Ref.	Dr.	Cr.	Balance Dr.	Balance Cr.
2006						
Nov. 1	Balance	✓	....	....	18,940	....
30		CR36	30,410	....	49,350	....

Accounts Receivable   12

Date	Item	Post. Ref.	Dr.	Cr.	Balance Dr.	Balance Cr.
2006						
Nov. 1	Balance	✓	....	....	15,320	....
30		J1	....	9,000	6,320	....
30		R40	37,950	....	44,270	....
30		CR36	....	25,860	18,410	....

Office Equipment   18

Date	Item	Post. Ref.	Dr.	Cr.	Balance Dr.	Balance Cr.
2006						
Nov. 1	Balance	✓	....	....	32,600	....
30		J1	9,000	....	41,600	....

Fees Earned   41

Date	Item	Post. Ref.	Dr.	Cr.	Balance Dr.	Balance Cr.
2006						
Nov. 30		R40	....	37,950	....	37,950
30		CR36	....	4,550	....	42,500

Prob. 5–2A   Continued

2. and 4.

ACCOUNTS RECEIVABLE SUBSIDIARY LEDGER

AGI Co.

Date	Item	Post. Ref.	Dr.	Cr.	Balance
2006					
Nov. 1	Balance............................	✓	....	....	12,340
3	....	CR36	....	12,340	—
23	....	R40	8,950	....	8,950

Dover Co.

Date	Item	Post. Ref.	Dr.	Cr.	Balance
2006					
Nov. 1	Balance............................	✓	....	....	2,980
7	....	R40	4,120	....	7,100
14	....	CR36	....	2,980	4,120
16	....	R40	8,320	....	12,440
20	....	CR36	....	4,120	8,320

Ross and Son

Date	Item	Post. Ref.	Dr.	Cr.	Balance
2006					
Nov. 10	....	R40	10,140	....	10,140
30	....	J1	....	9,000	1,140

Yamura Co.

Date	Item	Post. Ref.	Dr.	Cr.	Balance
2006					
Nov. 2	....	R40	6,420	....	6,420
19	....	CR36	....	6,420	—

Prob. 5–2A   Concluded

3., 4., and 5.

	Date	Invoice No.	Account Debited	Post. Ref.	Accounts Rec. Dr. Fees Earned Cr.	
	2006					
1	Nov. 2	717	Yamura Co.	✓	6,420	1
2	7	718	Dover Co.	✓	4,120	2
3	10	719	Ross and Son	✓	10,140	3
4	16	720	Dover Co.	✓	8,320	4
5	23	721	AGI Co.	✓	8,950	5
6	30				37,950	6
7					(12) (41)	7

	Date	Account Credited	Post. Ref.	Fees Earned Cr.	Accts. Rec. Cr.	Cash Dr.	
	2006						
1	Nov. 3	AGI Co.	✓	....	12,340	12,340	1
2	14	Dover Co.	✓	....	2,980	2,980	2
3	19	Yamura Co.	✓	....	6,420	6,420	3
4	20	Dover Co.	✓	....	4,120	4,120	4
5	30	Fees Earned	✓	4,550	....	4,550	5
6	30			4,550	25,860	30,410	6
7				(41)	(12)	(11)	7

Date	Description	Post. Ref.	Debit	Credit
2006				
Nov. 30	Office Equipment...	18	9,000	
	Accounts Receivable—Ross and Son...	12/✓		9,000

The subsidiary account for Ross and Son must also be posted for a $9,000 credit.

6. The subsidiary ledger is in agreement with the controlling account. Both have balances of $18,410 ($8,950 + $8,320 + $1,140).

Prob. 5–3A

1. and 4.

GENERAL LEDGER

Field Supplies 14

Date		Item	Post. Ref.	Dr.	Cr.	Balance Dr.	Balance Cr.
2006							
May	1	Balance............................	✓	....	....	5,300	....
	31	....	P30	15,780	....	21,080	....

Office Supplies 15

2006							
May	1	Balance............................	✓	....	....	1,230	....
	31	....	P30	1,380	....	2,610	....

Office Equipment 18

2006							
May	1	Balance............................	✓	....	....	18,400	....
	19	....	P30	6,500	....	24,900	....

Accounts Payable 21

2006							
May	1	Balance............................	✓	....	....	....	3,240
	31	....	P30	....	23,660	....	26,900

Prob. 5–3A   Continued

2. and 3.

ACCOUNTS PAYABLE SUBSIDIARY LEDGER

Eskew Co.

Date		Item	Post. Ref.	Dr.	Cr.	Balance
2006						
May	1	Balance	✓	....	....	2,200
	19	....	P30	....	6,500	8,700

J-Mart Co.

2006						
May	1	Balance	✓	....	....	620
	15	....	P30	....	485	1,105
	26	....	P30	....	575	1,680

Lassiter Co.

2006						
May	1	Balance	✓	....	....	420
	3	....	P30	....	320	740

Timberland Supply

2006						
May	8	....	P30	....	2,010	2,010
	23	....	P30	....	2,450	4,460
	30	....	P30	....	5,600	10,060

Wendell Co.

2006						
May	1	....	P30	....	3,720	3,720
	12	....	P30	....	2,000	5,720

Prob. 5–4A   Continued

1. and 2.

	JOURNAL			PAGE 1

Date	Description	Post. Ref.	Debit	Credit
2006				
Mar. 31	Land...	19	13,100	
	Field Equipment	17		13,100

1., 2., and 3.

	CASH PAYMENTS JOURNAL					PAGE 1	

Date	Check No.	Account Debited	Post. Ref.	Other Accounts Dr.	Accounts Payable Dr.	Cash Cr.	
2006							
Mar. 16	1	Rent Expense.....................	71	2,400	....	2,400	1
18	2	Field Supplies	14	1,400	....	1,400	2
		Office Supplies	15	440	....	440	3
24	3	PMI Sales, Inc.	✓	....	32,400	32,400	4
26	4	Culver Supply Co..............	✓	....	12,300	12,300	5
28	5	Land...................................	19	38,000	....	38,000	6
30	6	Castle Office Supply Co....	✓	....	3,060	3,060	7
31	7	Salary Expense.................	61	21,400	....	21,400	8
31		Total...................................		63,640	47,760	111,400	9
				(✓)	(21)	(11)	10

Prob. 5–4A   Continued

1.

ACCOUNTS PAYABLE LEDGER

Castle Office Supply Co.

Date		Item	Post. Ref.	Dr.	Cr.	Balance
2006						
Mar.	20	....	P1	....	3,060	3,060
	28	....	P1	....	3,600	6,660
	30	....	CP1	3,060	....	3,600

Culver Supply Co.

Date		Item	Post. Ref.	Dr.	Cr.	Balance
2006						
Mar.	17	....	P1	....	12,300	12,300
	26	....	CP1	12,300	....	—
	30	....	P1	....	9,200	9,200

PMI Sales, Inc.

Date		Item	Post. Ref.	Dr.	Cr.	Balance
2006						
Mar.	16	....	P1	....	32,400	32,400
	24	....	CP1	32,400	....	—
	30	....	P1	....	34,900	34,900

Prob. 5–4A   Continued

2. and 3.

GENERAL LEDGER

Cash   11

Date	Item	Post. Ref.	Dr.	Cr.	Balance Dr.	Balance Cr.
2006						
Mar. 31	....	CP1	....	111,400	....	111,400

Field Supplies   14

Date	Item	Post. Ref.	Dr.	Cr.	Balance Dr.	Balance Cr.
2006						
Mar. 18	....	CP1	1,400	....	1,400	....
31	....	P1	40,000	....	41,400	....

Office Supplies   15

Date	Item	Post. Ref.	Dr.	Cr.	Balance Dr.	Balance Cr.
2006						
Mar. 18	....	CP1	440	....	440	....
31	....	P1	6,660	....	7,100	....

Field Equipment   17

Date	Item	Post. Ref.	Dr.	Cr.	Balance Dr.	Balance Cr.
2006						
Mar. 16	....	P1	32,400	....	32,400	....
31	....	J1	....	13,100	19,300	....

Office Equipment   18

Date	Item	Post. Ref.	Dr.	Cr.	Balance Dr.	Balance Cr.
2006						
Mar. 30	....	P1	16,400	....	16,400	....

Land   19

Date	Item	Post. Ref.	Dr.	Cr.	Balance Dr.	Balance Cr.
2006						
Mar. 28	....	CP1	38,000	....	38,000	....
31	....	J1	13,100	....	51,100	....

Accounts Payable   21

Date	Item	Post. Ref.	Dr.	Cr.	Balance Dr.	Balance Cr.
2006						
Mar. 31	....	P1	....	95,460	....	95,460
31	....	CP1	47,760	....	....	47,700

Prob. 5–4A   Concluded

GENERAL LEDGER

Salary Expense   61

Date	Item	Post. Ref.	Dr.	Cr.	Balance Dr.	Balance Cr.
2006						
Mar. 31	....	CP1	21,400	....	21,400	....

Rent Expense   71

Date	Item	Post. Ref.	Dr.	Cr.	Balance Dr.	Balance Cr.
2006						
Mar. 16	....	CP1	2,400	....	2,400	....

4.

BLACK GOLD EXPLORATION CO.
Schedule of Accounts Payable
March 31, 2006

Castle Office Supply Co.	$ 3,600
Culver Supply Co.	9,200
PMI Sales, Inc.	34,900
Total accounts payable	$47,700*

* The total of the schedule of accounts payable is equal to the balance of the accounts payable controlling account.

Prob. 5–5A

1., 3., and 4.

GENERAL LEDGER

Cash   11

Date		Item	Post. Ref.	Dr.	Cr.	Balance Dr.	Balance Cr.
2006							
May	1	Balance	✓	....	....	57,900	....
	31		CR31	75,095	....	132,995	....
	31		CP34	....	118,630	14,365	....

Accounts Receivable   12

Date		Item	Post. Ref.	Dr.	Cr.	Balance Dr.	Balance Cr.
2006							
May	1	Balance	✓	....	....	32,815	....
	31		R35	34,200	....	67,015	....
	31		CR31	....	40,045	26,970	....

Maintenance Supplies   14

Date		Item	Post. Ref.	Dr.	Cr.	Balance Dr.	Balance Cr.
2006							
May	1	Balance	✓	....	....	6,150	....
	20		J1	....	3,000	3,150	....
	31		P37	3,430	....	6,580	....

Office Supplies   15

Date		Item	Post. Ref.	Dr.	Cr.	Balance Dr.	Balance Cr.
2006							
May	1	Balance	✓	....	....	2,580	....
	31		P37	1,160	....	3,740	....
	31		CP34	230	....	3,970	....

Office Equipment   16

Date		Item	Post. Ref.	Dr.	Cr.	Balance Dr.	Balance Cr.
2006							
May	1	Balance	✓	....	....	14,370	....
	3		P37	4,500	....	18,870	....

Accumulated Depreciation—Office Equipment   17

Date		Item	Post. Ref.	Dr.	Cr.	Balance Dr.	Balance Cr.
2006							
May	1	Balance	✓	....	....	....	3,000

Prob. 5–5A   Continued

Vehicles   18

Date	Item	Post. Ref.	Dr.	Cr.	Balance Dr.	Balance Cr.
2006						
May 1	Balance	✓	....	....	48,000	....
2	....	P37	26,800	....	74,800	....
16	....	CP34	31,400	....	106,200	....

Accumulated Depreciation—Vehicles   19

Date	Item	Post. Ref.	Dr.	Cr.	Balance Dr.	Balance Cr.
2006						
May 1	Balance	✓	....	....	....	13,590

Accounts Payable   21

Date	Item	Post. Ref.	Dr.	Cr.	Balance Dr.	Balance Cr.
2006						
May 1	Balance	✓	....	....	....	2,790
31	....	P37	....	35,890	....	38,680
31	....	CP34	34,090	....	....	4,590

F. Melendez, Capital   31

Date	Item	Post. Ref.	Dr.	Cr.	Balance Dr.	Balance Cr.
2006						
May 1	Balance	✓	....	....	....	142,435

F. Melendez, Drawing   32

Date	Item	Post. Ref.	Dr.	Cr.	Balance Dr.	Balance Cr.
2006						
May 27	....	CP34	4,000	....	4,000	....

Fees Earned   41

Date	Item	Post. Ref.	Dr.	Cr.	Balance Dr.	Balance Cr.
2006						
May 16	....	CR31	....	14,450	....	14,450
31	....	R35	....	34,200	....	48,650
31	....	CR31	....	19,200	....	67,850

Rent Revenue   42

Date	Item	Post. Ref.	Dr.	Cr.	Balance Dr.	Balance Cr.
2006						
May 18	....	CR31	....	1,400	....	1,400

Prob. 5–5A   Continued

Driver Salaries Expense   51

Date	Item	Post. Ref.	Dr.	Cr.	Balance Dr.	Cr.
2006						
May 30	....	CP34	23,500	....	23,500	....

Maintenance Supplies Expense   52

2006						
May 20	....	J1	3,000	....	3,000	....

Fuel Expense   53

2006						
May 9	....	CP34	680	....	680	....

Office Salaries Expense   61

2006						
May 31	....	CP34	16,750	....	16,750	....

Rent Expense   62

2006						
May 1	....	CP34	900	....	900	....

Advertising Expense   63

2006						
May 20	....	CP34	6,800	....	6,800	....

Miscellaneous Administrative Expense   64

2006						
May 17	....	CP34	280	....	280	....

Prob. 5–5A   Continued

2. and 3.

		JOURNAL			PAGE 1

Date	Description	Post. Ref.	Debit	Credit
2006				
May 20	Maintenance Supplies Expense............	52	3,000	
	Maintenance Supplies	14		3,000

2. and 4.

			REVENUE JOURNAL			PAGE 35	

	Date	Invoice No.	Account Debited	Post. Ref.	Accounts Rec. Dr. Fees Earned Cr.	
	2006					
1	May 5	91	Martin Co.	✓	7,230	1
2	7	92	Trent Co.	✓	4,340	2
3	11	93	Joy Co.	✓	5,200	3
4	24	94	Sing Co.	✓	11,530	4
5	25	95	Trent Co.	✓	5,900	5
6	31		Total		34,200	6
7					(12) (41)	7

Prob. 5–5A Continued

2., 3., and 4.

PURCHASES JOURNAL
PAGE 37

Date	Account Credited	Post. Ref.	Accounts Payable Cr.	Maintenance Supplies Dr.	Office Supplies Dr.	Other Accounts Dr. — Account	Post. Ref.	Amount
2006								
May 2	McIntyre Sales Co.	✓	26,800			Vehicles	18	26,800
3	Office Mate, Inc.	✓	4,500			Office Equipment	16	4,500
18	Bastille Co.	✓	1,480	1,480				
19	Master Supply Co.	✓	2,500	1,950	550			
21	Office City	✓	610		610			
31	Total		35,890	3,430	1,160			31,300
			(21)	(14)	(15)			(✓)

CASH RECEIPTS JOURNAL
PAGE 31

Date	Account Credited	Post. Ref.	Other Accounts Cr.	Accounts Receivable Cr.	Cash Dr.
2006					
May 6	Baker Co.	✓		6,245	6,245
10	Sing Co.	✓		10,890	10,890
12	Martin Co.	✓		7,230	7,230
16	Fees Earned	41	14,450		14,450
18	Rent Revenue	42	1,400		1,400
25	Baker Co.	✓		15,680	15,680
31	Fees Earned	41	19,200		19,200
31	Total		35,050	40,045	75,095
			(✓)	(12)	(11)

264

Prob. 5–5A   Continued

2., 3., and 4.

Date	Check No.	Account Debited	Post. Ref.	Other Accounts Dr.	Accounts Payable Dr.	Cash Cr.	
2006							
May 1	205	Rent Expense.....................	62	900	....	900	1
9	206	Fuel Expense	53	680	....	680	2
10	207	Office City.........................	✓	....	510	510	3
10	208	Bastille Co........................	✓	....	2,010	2,010	4
11	209	Porter Co.	✓	....	270	270	5
13	210	McIntyre Sales Co.	✓	....	26,800	26,800	6
16	211	Vehicles...........................	18	31,400	....	31,400	7
17	212	Misc. Admin. Exp..............	64	280	....	280	8
20	213	Advertising Expense	63	6,800	....	6,800	9
26	214	Office Mate, Inc................	✓	....	4,500	4,500	10
27	215	F. Melendez, Drawing.......	32	4,000	....	4,000	11
30	216	Driver Salaries Exp.	51	23,500	....	23,500	12
31	217	Office Salaries Exp.	61	16,750	....	16,750	13
31	218	Office Supplies	15	230	....	230	14
31		Total.................................		84,540	34,090	118,630	15
				(✓)	(21)	(11)	16

Prob. 5–5A   Concluded

5.

PAUL REVERE COURIER COMPANY
Trial Balance
May 31, 2006

Cash	14,365	
Accounts Receivable	26,970	
Maintenance Supplies	6,580	
Office Supplies	3,970	
Office Equipment	18,870	
Accumulated Depreciation—Office Equipment		3,000
Vehicles	106,200	
Accumulated Depreciation—Vehicles		13,590
Accounts Payable		4,590
F. Melendez, Capital		142,435
F. Melendez, Drawing	4,000	
Fees Earned		67,850
Rent Revenue		1,400
Driver Salaries Expense	23,500	
Maintenance Supplies Expense	3,000	
Fuel Expense	680	
Office Salaries Expense	16,750	
Rent Expense	900	
Advertising Expense	6,800	
Miscellaneous Administrative Expense	280	
	232,865	232,865

6. Balance of accounts receivable controlling account, $26,970.

Balance of accounts payable controlling account, $4,590.

Prob. 5–1B

1. and 2.

			REVENUE JOURNAL		PAGE 1	

	Date	Invoice No.	Account Debited	Post. Ref.	Accounts Rec. Dr. Fees Earned Cr.	
	2006					
1	Jan. 21	1	J. Dunlop..............................	✓	70	1
2	22	2	L. Summers	✓	225	2
3	24	3	T. Morris.............................	✓	65	3
4	27	4	F. Mintz..............................	✓	190	4
5	28	5	D. Bennett..........................	✓	145	5
6	30	6	L. Summers.	✓	105	6
7	31	7	T. Morris.............................	✓	130	7
8	31				930	8
9					(12) (41)	9

		JOURNAL			PAGE 1

Date	Description	Post. Ref.	Debit	Credit
2006				
Jan. 25	Supplies	13	115	
	Fees Earned..	41		115

Prob. 5–1B   Continued

ACCOUNTS RECEIVABLE LEDGER

D. Bennett

Date	Item	Post. Ref.	Dr.	Cr.	Balance
2006					
Jan. 28	....	R1	145	....	145

J. Dunlop

Date	Item	Post. Ref.	Dr.	Cr.	Balance
2006					
Jan. 21	....	R1	70	....	70

F. Mintz

Date	Item	Post. Ref.	Dr.	Cr.	Balance
2006					
Jan. 27	....	R1	190	....	190

T. Morris

Date	Item	Post. Ref.	Dr.	Cr.	Balance
2006					
Jan. 24	....	R1	65	....	65
31	....	R1	130	....	195

L. Summers

Date	Item	Post. Ref.	Dr.	Cr.	Balance
2006					
Jan. 22	....	R1	225	....	225
30	....	R1	105	....	330

Prob. 5–1B   Concluded

2.

GENERAL LEDGER

Accounts Receivable 12

Date	Item	Post. Ref.	Dr.	Cr.	Balance Dr.	Balance Cr.
2006						
Jan. 31	....	R1	930	....	930	....

Supplies 13

Date	Item	Post. Ref.	Dr.	Cr.	Balance Dr.	Balance Cr.
2006						
Jan. 25	....	J1	115	....	115	....

Fees Earned 41

Date	Item	Post. Ref.	Dr.	Cr.	Balance Dr.	Balance Cr.
2006						
Jan. 25	....	J1	....	115	....	115
31	....	R1	....	930	....	1,045

3. a. $930 ($145 + $70 + $190 + $195 + $330)

    b. $930

4. The single money column in the revenue journal can be replaced with three columns for (1) Accounts Receivable Dr., (2) Fees Earned Cr., and (3) Sales Tax Payable Cr.

Prob. 5–2B

1. and 5.

GENERAL LEDGER

Cash   11

Date		Item	Post. Ref.	Dr.	Cr.	Balance Dr.	Balance Cr.
2006							
June	1	Balance...........................	✓	....	....	12,150	....
	30	....	CR36	39,040	....	51,190	....

Accounts Receivable   12

Date		Item	Post. Ref.	Dr.	Cr.	Balance Dr.	Balance Cr.
2006							
June	1	Balance...........................	✓	....	....	18,880	....
	25	....	J1	....	4,400	14,480	....
	30	....	R40	26,080	....	40,560	....
	30	....	CR36	....	28,160	12,400	....

Notes Receivable   14

Date		Item	Post. Ref.	Dr.	Cr.	Balance Dr.	Balance Cr.
2006							
June	1	Balance...........................	✓	....	....	5,000	....
	25	....	J1	4,400	....	9,400	....

Fees Earned   41

Date		Item	Post. Ref.	Dr.	Cr.	Balance Dr.	Balance Cr.
2006							
June	30	....	R40	....	26,080	....	26,080
	30	....	CR36	....	10,880	....	36,960

Prob. 5–2B   Continued

2. and 4.

ACCOUNTS RECEIVABLE SUBSIDIARY LEDGER

Mendez Co.

Date	Item	Post. Ref.	Dr.	Cr.	Balance
2006					
June 1	Balance	✓	....	....	10,670
5	....	CR36	....	10,670	—
22	....	R40	7,150	....	7,150

Morton Co.

Date	Item	Post. Ref.	Dr.	Cr.	Balance
2006					
June 2	....	R40	7,300	....	7,300
19	....	CR36	....	7,300	—

Ping Co.

Date	Item	Post. Ref.	Dr.	Cr.	Balance
2006					
June 13	....	R40	5,050	....	5,050
25	....	J1	....	4,400	650

Quest Co.

Date	Item	Post. Ref.	Dr.	Cr.	Balance
2006					
June 1	Balance	✓	....	....	8,210
6	....	R40	1,980	....	10,190
15	....	CR36	....	8,210	1,980
16	....	R40	4,600	....	6,580
20	....	CR36	....	1,980	4,600

Prob. 5–2B   Concluded

3., 4., and 5.

REVENUE JOURNAL
PAGE 40

	Date	Invoice No.	Account Debited	Post. Ref.	Accounts Rec. Dr. Fees Earned Cr.	
	2006					
1	June 2	793	Morton Co.	✓	7,300	1
2	6	794	Quest Co.	✓	1,980	2
3	13	795	Ping Co.	✓	5,050	3
4	16	796	Quest Co.	✓	4,600	4
5	22	797	Mendez Co.	✓	7,150	5
6	30				26,080	6
7					(12) (41)	7

CASH RECEIPTS JOURNAL
PAGE 36

	Date	Account Credited	Post. Ref.	Fees Earned Cr.	Accts. Rec. Cr.	Cash Dr.	
	2006						
1	June 5	Mendez Co.	✓	....	10,670	10,670	1
2	15	Quest Co.	✓	....	8,210	8,210	2
3	19	Morton Co.	✓	....	7,300	7,300	3
4	20	Quest Co.	✓	....	1,980	1,980	4
5	30	Fees Earned	✓	10,880	....	10,880	5
6	30			10,880	28,160	39,040	6
7				(41)	(12)	(11)	7

JOURNAL
PAGE 1

Date	Description	Post. Ref.	Debit	Credit
2006				
June 25	Notes Receivable....................................	14	4,400	
	Accounts Receivable—Ping Co.	12/✓		4,400

The subsidiary account of Ping Co. must also be posted for a $4,400 credit.

6. The subsidiary ledger is in agreement with the controlling account. Both have balances of $12,400 ($7,150 + $650 + $4,600).

Prob. 5–3B

1. and 4.

GENERAL LEDGER

Field Supplies   **14**

		Post.			Balance	
Date	Item	Ref.	Dr.	Cr.	Dr.	Cr.
2006						
July 1	Balance............................	✓	....	....	5,820	....
31	....	P30	9,915	....	15,735	....

Office Supplies   **15**

2006						
July 1	Balance............................	✓	....	....	830	....
31	....	P30	1,610	....	2,440	....

Office Equipment   **18**

2006						
July 1	Balance............................	✓	....	....	14,300	....
5	....	P30	4,500	....	18,800	....

Accounts Payable   **21**

2006						
July 1	Balance............................	✓	....	....	....	1,055
31	....	P30	....	16,025	....	17,080

Prob. 5–3B   Continued

2. and 3.

ACCOUNTS PAYABLE SUBSIDIARY LEDGER

Executive Office Supply Co.

Date		Item	Post. Ref.	Dr.	Cr.	Balance
2006						
July	1	Balance............................	✓	....	....	365
	9	....	P30	....	265	630
	29	....	P30	....	295	925

Lapp Co.

Date		Item	Post. Ref.	Dr.	Cr.	Balance
2006						
July	1	Balance............................	✓	....	....	690
	2	....	P30	....	1,050	1,740

Nelson Co.

Date		Item	Post. Ref.	Dr.	Cr.	Balance
2006						
July	14	....	P30	....	3,610	3,610
	24	....	P30	....	2,975	6,585
	31	....	P30	....	1,005	7,590

Peach Computers Co.

Date		Item	Post. Ref.	Dr.	Cr.	Balance
2006						
July	5	....	P30	....	4,500	4,500

Yin Co.

Date		Item	Post. Ref.	Dr.	Cr.	Balance
2006						
July	13	....	P30	....	980	980
	17	....	P30	....	1,345	2,325

Prob. 5–3B   Concluded

3. and 4.

PURCHASES JOURNAL

			Accounts	Field	Office	Other Accounts Dr.		
Date	Account Credited	Post. Ref.	Payable Cr.	Supplies Dr.	Supplies Dr.	Account	Post. Ref.	Amount
2006								
July 2	Lapp Co.	✓	1,050	....	1,050	....		....
5	Peach Computers Co.	✓	4,500	....	....	Office Equipment	18	4,500
9	Executive Office Supply Co.	✓	265	....	265	....		....
13	Yin Co.	✓	980	980	....	....		....
14	Nelson Co.	✓	3,610	3,610	....	....		....
17	Yin Co.	✓	1,345	1,345	....	....		....
24	Nelson Co.	✓	2,975	2,975	....	....		....
29	Executive Office Supply Co.	✓	295	....	295	....		....
31	Nelson Co.	✓	1,005	1,005	....	....		....
31			16,025	9,915	1,610			4,500
			(21)	(14)	(15)			(✓)

5. a. $17,080 ($925 + $1,740 + $7,590 + $4,500 + $2,325)

    b. $17,080

Prob. 5–4B

1., 2., and 3.

PURCHASES JOURNAL

Date	Account Credited	Post. Ref.	Accounts Payable Cr.	Field Supplies Dr.	Office Supplies Dr.	Other Accounts Dr. Account	Post. Ref.	Amount	
2006									
June 16	Heath Supply Co.	✓	3,920	3,920	....	....			1
16	Test-Rite Equipment Co.	✓	12,200	....	....	Field Equipment.	17	12,200	2
17	Aztec Supply Co.	✓	415	....	415	....			3
23	Aztec Supply Co.	✓	545	....	545	....			4
30	Heath Supply Co.	✓	5,300	5,300	....	....			5
30	Test-Rite Equipment Co.	✓	4,100	900	....	Field Equipment	17	3,200	6
30			26,480	10,120	960			15,400	7
			(21)	(14)	(15)			(✓)	8

276

Prob. 5–4B   Continued

Date	Check No.		Account Debited	Post. Ref.	Other Accounts Dr.	Accounts Payable Dr.	Cash Cr.	
2006								
June 16	1		Rent Expense....................	71	1,200	....	1,200	1
19	2		Field Supplies...................	14	2,050	....	2,050	2
			Office Supplies	15	250	....	250	3
23	3		Land................................	19	35,000	....	35,000	4
24	4		Heath Supply Co..............	✓	....	3,920	3,920	5
26	5		Test-Rite Equipment Co...	✓	....	12,200	12,200	6
30	6		Aztec Supply Co.	✓	....	415	415	7
30	7		Salary Expense................	61	16,900	....	16,900	8
30			Total..................................		55,400	16,535	71,935	9
					(✓)	(21)	(11)	10

1. and 2.

Date	Description	Post. Ref.	Debit	Credit
2006				
June 30	Land..	19	7,500	
	Field Equipment	17		7,500

Prob. 5–4B   Continued

1.

ACCOUNTS PAYABLE SUBSIDIARY LEDGER

Aztec Supply Co.

Date		Item	Post. Ref.	Dr.	Cr.	Balance
2006						
June	17	....	P1	....	415	415
	23	....	P1	....	545	960
	30	....	CP1	415	....	545

Heath Supply Co.

Date		Item	Post. Ref.	Dr.	Cr.	Balance
2006						
June	16	....	P1	....	3,920	3,920
	24	....	CP1	3,920	....	—
	30	....	P1	....	5,300	5,300

Test-Rite Equipment Co.

Date		Item	Post. Ref.	Dr.	Cr.	Balance
2006						
June	16	....	P1	....	12,200	12,200
	26	....	CP1	12,200	....	—
	30	....	P1	....	4,100	4,100

Prob. 5–4B   Continued

2. and 3.

GENERAL LEDGER

Cash   11

Date	Item	Post. Ref.	Dr.	Cr.	Balance Dr.	Balance Cr.
2006						
June 30	....	CP1	....	71,935	....	71,935

Field Supplies   14

Date	Item	Post. Ref.	Dr.	Cr.	Balance Dr.	Balance Cr.
2006						
June 19	....	CP1	2,050	....	2,050	....
30	....	P1	10,120	....	12,170	....

Office Supplies   15

Date	Item	Post. Ref.	Dr.	Cr.	Balance Dr.	Balance Cr.
2006						
June 19	....	CP1	250	....	250	....
30	....	P1	960	....	1,210	....

Field Equipment   17

Date	Item	Post. Ref.	Dr.	Cr.	Balance Dr.	Balance Cr.
2006						
June 16	....	P1	12,200	....	12,200	....
30	....	P1	3,200	....	15,400	....
30	....	J1	....	7,500	7,900	....

Land   19

Date	Item	Post. Ref.	Dr.	Cr.	Balance Dr.	Balance Cr.
2006						
June 23	....	CP1	35,000	....	35,000	....
30	....	J1	7,500	....	42,500	....

Accounts Payable   21

Date	Item	Post. Ref.	Dr.	Cr.	Balance Dr.	Balance Cr.
2006						
June 30	....	P1	....	26,480	....	26,480
30	....	CP1	16,535	....	....	9,945

Prob. 5–4B   Concluded

Salary Expense   61

Date	Item	Post. Ref.	Dr.	Cr.	Balance Dr.	Balance Cr.
2006						
June 30	....	CP1	16,900	....	16,900	....

Rent Expense   71

Date	Item	Post. Ref.	Dr.	Cr.	Balance Dr.	Balance Cr.
2006						
June 16	....	CP1	1,200	....	1,200	....

4.

ARCTIC SPRINGS WATER TESTING SERVICE
Schedule of Accounts Payable
June 30, 2006

Aztec Supply Co.	$ 545
Heath Supply Co.	5,300
Test-Rite Equipment Co.	4,100
Total accounts payable	$9,945*

* The total of the schedule of accounts payable is equal to the balance of the accounts payable controlling account.

Prob. 5–5B

1., 3., and 4.

GENERAL LEDGER

Cash   **11**

Date		Item	Post. Ref.	Dr.	Cr.	Balance Dr.	Balance Cr.
2006							
July	1	Balance............................	✓	....	....	56,800	....
	31	....	CR31	51,390	....	108,190	....
	31	....	CP34	....	102,860	5,330	....

Accounts Receivable   **12**

Date		Item	Post. Ref.	Dr.	Cr.	Balance Dr.	Balance Cr.
2006							
July	1	Balance............................	✓	....	....	15,330	....
	31	....	R35	20,420	....	35,750	....
	31	....	CR31	....	18,310	17,440	....

Maintenance Supplies   **14**

Date		Item	Post. Ref.	Dr.	Cr.	Balance Dr.	Balance Cr.
2006							
July	1	Balance............................	✓	....	....	9,300	....
	20	....	J1	....	3,800	5,500	....
	31	....	P37	4,360	....	9,860	....

Office Supplies   **15**

Date		Item	Post. Ref.	Dr.	Cr.	Balance Dr.	Balance Cr.
2006							
July	1	Balance............................	✓	....	....	4,500	....
	31	....	CP34	900	....	5,400	....
	31	....	P37	1,245	....	6,645	....

Office Equipment   **16**

Date		Item	Post. Ref.	Dr.	Cr.	Balance Dr.	Balance Cr.
2006							
July	1	Balance............................	✓	....	....	24,300	....
	6	....	P37	4,200	....	28,500	....

Accumulated Depreciation—Office Equipment   **17**

Date		Item	Post. Ref.	Dr.	Cr.	Balance Dr.	Balance Cr.
2006							
July	1	Balance............................	✓	....	....	....	4,500

Prob. 5–5B   Continued

GENERAL LEDGER

Vehicles   18

Date		Item	Post. Ref.	Dr.	Cr.	Balance Dr.	Balance Cr.
2006							
July	1	Balance..............................	✓	....	....	84,600	....
	5	....	P37	31,600	....	116,200	....
	16	....	CP34	27,900	....	144,100	....

Accumulated Depreciation—Vehicles   19

Date		Item	Post. Ref.	Dr.	Cr.	Balance Dr.	Balance Cr.
2006							
July	1	Balance..............................	✓	....	....	....	12,300

Accounts Payable   21

Date		Item	Post. Ref.	Dr.	Cr.	Balance Dr.	Balance Cr.
2006							
July	1	Balance..............................	✓	....	....	....	5,080
	31	....	P37	....	41,405	....	46,485
	31	....	CP34	40,880	....	....	5,605

K. Huss, Capital   31

Date		Item	Post. Ref.	Dr.	Cr.	Balance Dr.	Balance Cr.
2006							
July	1	Balance..............................	✓	....	....	....	172,950

K. Huss, Drawing   32

Date		Item	Post. Ref.	Dr.	Cr.	Balance Dr.	Balance Cr.
2006							
July	24	....	CP34	2,000	....	2,000	....

Fees Earned   41

Date		Item	Post. Ref.	Dr.	Cr.	Balance Dr.	Balance Cr.
2006							
July	16	....	CR31	....	15,900	....	15,900
	31	....	CR31	....	17,180	....	33,080
	31	....	R35	....	20,420	....	53,500

Prob. 5–5B   Continued

GENERAL LEDGER

Driver Salaries Expense 51

Date	Item	Post. Ref.	Dr.	Cr.	Balance Dr.	Balance Cr.
2006						
July 30	....	CP34	15,400	....	15,400	....

Maintenance Supplies Expense 52

Date	Item	Post. Ref.	Dr.	Cr.	Balance Dr.	Balance Cr.
2006						
July 20	....	J1	3,800	....	3,800	....

Fuel Expense 53

Date	Item	Post. Ref.	Dr.	Cr.	Balance Dr.	Balance Cr.
2006						
July 9	....	CP34	850	....	850	....

Office Salaries Expense 61

Date	Item	Post. Ref.	Dr.	Cr.	Balance Dr.	Balance Cr.
2006						
July 30	....	CP34	7,500	....	7,500	....

Rent Expense 62

Date	Item	Post. Ref.	Dr.	Cr.	Balance Dr.	Balance Cr.
2006						
July 1	....	CP34	5,500	....	5,500	....

Advertising Expense 63

Date	Item	Post. Ref.	Dr.	Cr.	Balance Dr.	Balance Cr.
2006						
July 20	....	CP34	1,500	....	1,500	....

Miscellaneous Administrative Expense 64

Date	Item	Post. Ref.	Dr.	Cr.	Balance Dr.	Balance Cr.
2006						
July 17	....	CP34	430	....	430	....

2., 3., and 4.

PURCHASES JOURNAL

PAGE 37

Date	Account Credited	Post. Ref.	Accounts Payable Cr.	Maintenance Supplies Dr.	Office Supplies Dr.	Other Accounts Dr. Account	Post. Ref.	Amount	
2006									
July 5	Browning Trans.	✓	31,600	......	......	Vehicles	18	31,600	1
6	Bell Computer Co.	✓	4,200	......	......	Office Equipment	16	4,200	2
18	Crowne Supply Co.	✓	2,445	2,445	......	......			3
19	McClain Co.	✓	2,460	1,915	545	......			4
23	Office To Go, Inc.	✓	700	......	700	......			5
31			41,405	4,360	1,245			35,800	6
			(21)	(14)	(15)			(✓)	7

CASH RECEIPTS JOURNAL

PAGE 31

Date	Account Credited	Post. Ref.	Other Accounts Cr.	Accounts Receivable Cr.	Cash Dr.	
2006						
July 3	Pease Co.	✓	......	5,400	5,400	1
10	Sokol Co.	✓	......	5,980	5,980	2
12	Capps Co.	✓	......	2,980	2,980	3
16	Fees Earned	41	15,900	......	15,900	4
25	Pease Co.	✓	......	3,950	3,950	5
31	Fees Earned	41	17,180	......	17,180	6
31	Total		33,080	18,310	51,390	7
			(✓)	(12)	(11)	8

Prob. 5–5B   Continued

2. and 4.

REVENUE JOURNAL

Date		Invoice No.	Account Debited	Post. Ref.	Accounts Rec. Dr. Fees Earned Cr.	
2006						
1	July	2	940	Capps Co.	✓	2,980	1
2		6	941	Collins Co.	✓	6,210	2
3		10	942	Joy Co.	✓	2,470	3
4		24	943	Sokol Co.	✓	4,090	4
5		25	944	Collins Co.	✓	4,670	5
6		31				20,420	6
7						(12) (41)	7

2., 3., and 4.

CASH PAYMENTS JOURNAL

Date	Check No.	Account Debited	Post. Ref.	Other Accounts Dr.	Accounts Payable Dr.	Cash Cr.	
2006							
1 July	1 610	Rent Expense....................	62	5,500	....	5,500	1
2	9 611	Fuel Expense	53	850	....	850	2
3	10 612	Office To Go, Inc...............	✓	....	1,140	1,140	3
4	11 613	Crowne Supply Co............	✓	....	2,980	2,980	4
5	11 614	Porter Co.	✓	....	960	960	5
6	13 615	Browning Trans.	✓	....	31,600	31,600	6
7	16 616	Vehicles...........................	18	27,900	....	27,900	7
8	17 617	Misc. Admin. Exp.............	64	430	....	430	8
9	20 618	Advertising Exp.	63	1,500	....	1,500	9
10	24 619	K. Huss, Drawing.............	32	2,000	....	2,000	10
11	26 620	Bell Computer Co.	✓	....	4,200	4,200	11
12	30 621	Driver Salaries Exp...........	51	15,400	....	15,400	12
13		Office Salaries Exp...........	61	7,500	....	7,500	13
14	31 622	Office Supplies	15	900	....	900	14
15	31			61,980	40,880	102,860	15
16				(✓)	(21)	(11)	16

Prob. 5–5B   Concluded

2. and 3.

<table>
<tr><td colspan="5" align="center">JOURNAL</td><td align="right">PAGE 1</td></tr>
<tr><td></td><td></td><td>Post.</td><td></td><td></td></tr>
<tr><td>Date</td><td>Description</td><td>Ref.</td><td>Debit</td><td>Credit</td></tr>
<tr><td>2006</td><td></td><td></td><td></td><td></td></tr>
<tr><td>July 20</td><td>Maintenance Supplies Expense............</td><td>52</td><td>3,800</td><td></td></tr>
<tr><td></td><td>Maintenance Supplies ....</td><td>14</td><td></td><td>3,800</td></tr>
</table>

5.

NEXT DAY DELIVERY COMPANY
Trial Balance
July 31, 2006

Cash...	5,330	
Accounts Receivable...	17,440	
Maintenance Supplies..	9,860	
Office Supplies	6,645	
Office Equipment...	28,500	
Accumulated Depreciation—Office Equipment		4,500
Vehicles..	144,100	
Accumulated Depreciation—Vehicles		12,300
Accounts Payable..		5,605
K. Huss, Capital		172,950
K. Huss, Drawing...	2,000	
Fees Earned		53,500
Driver Salaries Expense..	15,400	
Maintenance Supplies Expense	3,800	
Fuel Expense	850	
Office Salaries Expense..	7,500	
Rent Expense..	5,500	
Advertising Expense	1,500	
Miscellaneous Administrative Expense............................	430	
	248,855	248,855

6.   Balance of accounts receivable controlling account, $17,440.

   Balance of accounts payable controlling account, $5,605.

SPECIAL ACTIVITIES

Activity 5–1

a. Based on Garrett's knowledge of the situation, Garrett was not acting in the best interests of his employer but was acting in his own short-term best interests. Thus, Garrett was not acting in an ethical manner. Garrett could still have had the sale by insisting on cash up front, rather than performing the service on account. Moreover, this contract may come back to haunt Garrett in the long term, once the company determines that the account cannot be collected after the security system has been installed. Garrett may have to answer for this decision.

b. Guardsman management has placed Garrett in a short-term dilemma by requiring him to act contrary to his own short-term best interests. Guardsman Security Co. could avoid this scenario by establishing a separate credit department. All potential contracts could be referred from the field salesperson to the credit office. If credit is approved, then the sale is credited to the salesperson for purposes of quota determination. If credit is not approved, then a contract is not signed. This is an example of separation of duties (sales are separated from credit authorization). Another approach would be to determine the quota on the basis of collections, rather than sales. In this way, the salesperson would be more concerned about the eventual collection of a sale.

Activity 5–2

a. Employees are responsible for their own decisions, even if they are "following orders." A "following orders" defense will not be successful in a criminal court proceeding. Often prosecutors will offer plea agreements to mid-level managers in return for cooperation and testimony against superiors. Such pleas do not remove legal jeopardy but can reduce the penalty at sentencing.

b. An employee facing pressure to conduct unethical or illegal requests from superiors has very few options. Going along with these requests will not remove legal jeopardy (see a.). Employees facing such pressure may:

   (1) quit and find another job.
   (2) refuse to cooperate with the requests, thereby risking their jobs and career advancement.
   (3) report the behavior or issues to an oversight authority, such as the audit committee of the board of directors or other ombudsmen office established within the company for such reports.
   (4) report the behavior or issues to the CEO (unless the CEO is approving these actions).

Activity 5–3

Kelly is missing some of the principal benefits of the computerized system. There are three primary advantages of a computerized system. First, the computerized system is much more efficient and accurate at transaction processing. In the computerized system, once the transaction data have been input, the information is simultaneously recorded in the electronic journal (file) and posted to the subsidiary and controlling ledger accounts. This saves a significant amount of time in recording and posting transactions. Second, the computerized environment is less prone to mathematical, posting, and recording errors. The computer does not make these types of mistakes. Thus, the computerized environment should require less time correcting errors. Third, the computerized system provides more timely information to management because account balances are always kept current. Under the manual system, ledger accounts will only be as current as the latest posting date, but the computerized system posts every transaction when it is journalized or recorded on a form. Thus, management has more current information with which to make decisions.

As an additional note, Kelly may be reacting out of some fear of the unknown. This is a common reaction to change. Thus, Kelly may be overreacting to the new computer environment because it will require significant change in the way the job is done as compared to the manual approach.

Activity 5–4

One of the major reasons businesses have transactions "on account" is because of internal control. The cash of the business does not belong to the employees. Thus, with good internal control, the cash transaction is separated from the decision to purchase or sell. This provides for separation of duties between the sale (or purchase) event and the cash receipt (or payment) event. This prevents possible embezzlement and fraud by employees. As an example, if an employee selling the service also received the cash, then it would be possible to hide the sale event by not reporting it and then pocketing the cash. However, with a sale on account, the person providing the service bills the customer. The customer then remits payment to a different function in the firm according to the terms of the bill. In this case, there is very little possibility that a single person would be able to defraud Falcon Company. These control issues do not arise with individuals because the person controlling the cash also owns the cash in the checking account. Thus, there is no internal control problem because it is not possible to embezzle cash from oneself.

Activity 5–5

a. Cisco uses Internet technology to link its accounting information continually to its underlying business events. As a result, Cisco practices what is termed a "virtual close." A virtual close continually updates the financial records as transactions are completed. Under more typical scenarios, the computer systems are like a set of leaky pipes. At the end of each period, the financial "leaks" must be cleaned up and reconciled, causing a delay in the close cycle. Using Internet technology, Cisco has tightened up the financial "pipeline," so that there are few information leaks and minimal corrections required.

b. A virtual close means that the financial records are available for management decision making on a real-time basis. No more does Cisco management need to wait until the end of an accounting period and closing cycle to receive financial information for decision making. Day-by-day financial information is accumulated and summarized for management so that managers are able to plan and react to business conditions as required. Cisco uses database technology so that its corporate data may be sorted and queried on demand by management's need of the moment.

Activity 5–6

1. Special journals are used to reduce the processing time and expense to record transactions. A special journal is usually created when a specific type of transaction occurs frequently enough so that the use of the traditional two-column journal becomes cumbersome. The frequency of transactions for CMG would probably justify the following special journals:

> Purchases Journal
>
> Cash Payments Journal
>
> Revenue Journal
>
> Cash Receipts Journal

Note to Instructors: The number and nature of the special journals to be established for CMG involve judgment. Differences of opinion may exist as to whether all the preceding special journals are necessary or cost-efficient. You may wish to use this time to comment further on the costs of establishing special journals and the potential benefits of reducing the processing time to record transactions.

Activity 5–6   Concluded

2.

PURCHASES JOURNAL

| | | | | | | Other Accounts Dr. | | |
Date	Account Credited	Post. Ref.	Accounts Payable Cr.	Medical Supplies Dr.	Office Supplies Dr.	Account	Post. Ref.	Amount

REVENUE JOURNAL

Date	Invoice No.	Account Debited	Post. Ref.	Accounts Receivable Dr.	Fees Earned Cr.	Sales Tax Payable Cr.

Note: The Sales Tax Payable column is included because fees earned are subject to a sales tax, which is collected by the business. The sales tax must then be periodically remitted to the state or local government. Many states do not charge sales tax on services.

3. The business should maintain subsidiary ledgers for customer accounts receivable, supplier accounts payable, and medical equipment.

Activity 5–7

MEMORANDUM

To: Senior Management

From: Student

Re: Web-based accounting software

A new approach to automating our accounting processing is now available. It is called Web-based accounting. Rather than purchasing our accounting software and loading it on our own computers, Web-based accounting software is rented and resides on the provider's computers. Our data, along with the accounting software, stays with the provider. There are several advantages to this approach:

1. We don't need to administer the application or data on our own computers. This becomes the job of the service provider, thus saving us computer system personnel costs. All we need is a desktop computer and browser to use the software.

2. Our people can work with our data anytime or anyplace. We don't need to rely on our own internal computer network for accounting-related work. Instead, the Web-based product is available on the Internet. This means that we can enter transactions and access our accounting data from anywhere in the world, rather than having to be plugged into our corporate network. This also will save us network support costs.

3. We never need to purchase and load software upgrades. All upgrades are provided on the provider's server when they are available. Thus, we are always using the latest version.

4. Providers promise a highly secure environment for our data.

5. An Internet-based accounting system should help us when passing data, such as orders, between ourselves and our customers and suppliers.

There are also a number of disadvantages we need to consider:

1. The cost of the software is recurring. Thus, we are trading off the recurring costs of maintaining our system infrastructure for the recurring cost of the service. A financial analysis should be conducted to determine if the service is cost effective.

2. The Internet can be slow. During busy times, we may experience slow response times.

3. Our data physically resides with the service provider. Thus, we don't control the security of our own data; the provider does. Our data is our lifeblood, so confidence in the provider's controls is paramount.

4. Once we begin, we will become "locked in" to the provider. It will be hard to change our mind at a later date. However, this is also true for purchased software to some extent.

Activity 5–8

Note to Instructors: While the list of functions can be quite large, the key functions are identified below. The purpose of these functions will be fairly advanced for most students. The activity asks for a listing rather than an explanation because most students would have very limited experience by which to provide much explanation. Use this case to demonstrate the scope and basic nature of these application tools.

Manugistic's Supply Chain Management Solution

- Collaborate with customers, distribution partners, transportation providers, and suppliers in order to plan, order, move, and receive materials from suppliers and deliver finished goods to customers.
- Provide trading platforms for conducting Internet auctions.
- Design optimal supply chain networks (finding the optimal location for plants and warehouses).
- Optimize manufacturing planning and scheduling for a given set of demand and capacity constraints.
- Support sales and operations planning (which is a process for coordinating the demand plan with the plant capacity).
- Optimize inventory levels across the supply chain.

Siebel Systems Customer Relationship Management Solution

- Provide the sales force with real-time information about all customer contacts with the firm in order to improve the effectiveness of the sales call.
- Provide real-time forecast estimation and accumulation tools.
- Support promotion plans and integrate the plans with forecasting and manufacturing.
- Decision tools for evaluating marketing campaign effectiveness.
- Tools to support call center responsiveness.

CHAPTER 6
ACCOUNTING FOR MERCHANDISING BUSINESSES

CLASS DISCUSSION QUESTIONS

1. Merchandising businesses acquire merchandise for resale to customers. It is the selling of merchandise, instead of a service, that makes the activities of a merchandising business different from the activities of a service business.

2. Yes. Gross profit is the excess of (net) sales over cost of merchandise sold. A net loss arises when operating expenses exceed gross profit. Therefore, a business can earn a gross profit but incur operating expenses in excess of this gross profit and end up with a net loss.

3. **a.** Increase   **c.** Decrease
   b. Increase   **d.** Decrease

4. Under the **periodic method**, the inventory records do not show the amount available for sale or the amount sold during the period. In contrast, under the **perpetual method** of accounting for merchandise inventory, each purchase and sale of merchandise is recorded in the inventory and the cost of merchandise sold accounts. As a result, the amount of merchandise available for sale and the amount sold are continuously (perpetually) disclosed in the inventory records.

5. The multiple-step form of income statement contains conventional groupings for revenues and expenses, with intermediate balances, before concluding with the net income balance. In the single-step form, the total of all expenses is deducted from the total of all revenues, without intermediate balances.

6. The major advantages of the single-step form of income statement are its simplicity and its emphasis on total revenues and total expenses as the determinants of net income. The major objection to the form is that such relationships as gross profit to sales and income from operations to sales are not as readily determinable as when the multiple-step form is used.

7. Revenues from sources other than the principal activity of the business are classified as other income.

8. Sales to customers who use bank credit cards are generally treated as cash sales. The credit card invoices representing these sales are deposited by the seller directly into the bank, along with the currency and checks received from customers. Sales made by the use of nonbank credit cards generally must be reported periodically to the card company before cash is received. Therefore, such sales create a receivable with the card company. In both cases, any service or collection fees charged by the bank or card company are debited to expense accounts.

9. The date of sale as shown by the date of the invoice or bill.

10. **a.** 2% discount allowed if paid within ten days of date of invoice; entire amount of invoice due within 60 days of date of invoice.
    b. Payment due within 30 days of date of invoice.
    c. Payment due by the end of the month in which the sale was made.

11. **a.** A credit memorandum issued by the seller of merchandise indicates the amount for which the buyer's account is to be credited (credit to Accounts Receivable) and the reason for the sales return or allowance.
    b. A debit memorandum issued by the buyer of merchandise indicates the amount for which the seller's account is to be debited (debit to Accounts Payable) and the reason for the purchases return or allowance.

12. **a.** The buyer
    b. The seller

13. Examples of such accounts include the following: Sales, Sales Discounts, Sales Returns and Allowances, Cost of Merchandise Sold, Merchandise Inventory.

14. Cost of Merchandise Sold would be debited; Merchandise Inventory would be credited.

15. Loss From Merchandise Inventory Shrinkage would be debited.

EXERCISES

Ex. 6–1

a. $490,000 ($250,000 + $975,000 − $735,000)

b. 40% ($490,000 ÷ $1,225,000)

c. No. If operating expenses are less than gross profit, there will be a net income. On the other hand, if operating expenses exceed gross profit, there will be a net loss.

Ex. 6–2

$15,710 million ($20,946 million − $5,236 million)

Ex. 6–3

a. Purchases discounts, purchases returns and allowances
b. Transportation in
c. Merchandise available for sale
d. Merchandise inventory (ending)

Ex. 6–4

a. Cost of merchandise sold:

Merchandise inventory, May 1, 2005			$ 121,200
Purchases		$985,000	
Less: Purchases returns and allowances	$23,500		
Purchases discounts	21,000	44,500	
Net purchases		$940,500	
Add transportation in		11,300	
Cost of merchandise purchased			951,800
Merchandise available for sale			$1,073,000
Less merchandise inventory, April 30, 2006			142,000
Cost of merchandise sold			$ 931,000

b. $489,000 ($1,420,000 − $931,000)

Ex. 6–5

1. The schedule should begin with the January 1, not the December 31, merchandise inventory.

2. Purchases returns and allowances and purchases discounts should be deducted from (not added to) purchases.

3. The result of subtracting purchases returns and allowances and purchases discounts from purchases should be labeled "net purchases."

4. Transportation in should be added to net purchases to yield cost of merchandise purchased.

5. The merchandise inventory at December 31 should be deducted from merchandise available for sale to yield cost of merchandise sold.

A correct cost of merchandise sold section is as follows:

Cost of merchandise sold:

Merchandise inventory, January 1, 2006..			$132,000
Purchases		$600,000	
Less: Purchases returns and allowances	$14,000		
Purchases discounts	6,000	20,000	
Net purchases		$580,000	
Add transportation in		7,500	
Cost of merchandise purchased			587,500
Merchandise available for sale			$719,500
Less merchandise inventory,			
December 31, 2006			120,000
Cost of merchandise sold			$599,500

Ex. 6–6

Net sales: $3,010,000 ($3,570,000 – $320,000 – $240,000)

Gross profit: $868,000 ($3,010,000 – $2,142,000)

Ex. 6–7

a. Selling expense, (1), (3), (8)

b. Administrative expense, (2), (5), (6), (7)

c. Other expense, (4)

Ex. 6–8

THE MERIDEN COMPANY
Income Statement
For the Year Ended June 30, 2006

Revenues:		
Net sales...		$5,400,000
Rent revenue..		30,000
Total revenues..		$5,430,000
Expenses:		
Cost of merchandise sold...	$3,240,000	
Selling expenses	480,000	
Administrative expenses	300,000	
Interest expense	47,500	
Total expenses...		4,067,500
Net income		$1,362,500

Ex. 6–9

1. Sales returns and allowances and sales discounts should be deducted from (not added to) sales.

2. Sales returns and allowances and sales discounts should be deducted from sales to yield "net sales" (not gross sales).

3. Deducting the cost of merchandise sold from net sales yields gross profit.

4. Deducting the total operating expenses from gross profit would yield income from operations (or operating income).

5. Interest revenue should be reported under the caption "Other income" and should be added to Income from operations to arrive at Net income.

6. The final amount on the income statement should be labeled Net income, not Gross profit.

A correct income statement would be as follows:

THE PLAUTUS COMPANY
Income Statement
For the Year Ended October 31, 2006

Revenue from sales:			
Sales..		$4,200,000	
Less: Sales returns and allowances	$81,200		
Sales discounts	20,300	101,500	
Net sales			$4,098,500
Cost of merchandise sold............................			2,093,000
Gross profit..			$2,005,500
Operating expenses:			
Selling expenses		$ 203,000	
Transportation out		7,500	
Administrative expenses		122,000	
Total operating expenses....................			332,500
Income from operations...............................			$1,673,000
Other income:			
Interest revenue			66,500
Net income			$1,739,500

Ex. 6–10

a. $25,000

b. $210,000

c. $477,000

d. $192,000

e. $40,000

f. $520,000

g. $757,500

h. $690,000

Ex. 6–11

a.

CALLOWAY COMPANY
Income Statement
For the Year Ended January 31, 2006

Revenue from sales:			
Sales..			$925,000
Less: Sales returns and allowances........	$60,000		
Sales discounts..............................	20,000	80,000	
Net sales...			$845,000
Cost of merchandise sold............................			560,000
Gross profit...			$285,000
Operating expenses:			
Selling expenses...		$120,000	
Administrative expenses		80,000	
Total operating expenses.....................			200,000
Income from operations...............................			$ 85,000
Other expense:			
Interest expense...			7,500
Net income			$ 77,500

b. The major advantage of the multiple-step form of income statement is that relationships such as gross profit to sales are indicated. The major disadvantages are that it is more complex and the total revenues and expenses are not indicated, as is the case in the single-step income statement.

Ex. 6–12

a.	Cash..	6,900	
	Sales...		6,900
	Cost of Merchandise Sold	4,830	
	Merchandise Inventory		4,830
b.	Accounts Receivable..	7,500	
	Sales...		7,500
	Cost of Merchandise Sold	5,625	
	Merchandise Inventory		5,625
c.	Cash..	10,200	
	Sales...		10,200
	Cost of Merchandise Sold	6,630	
	Merchandise Inventory		6,630
d.	Accounts Receivable—American Express.................	7,200	
	Sales...		7,200
	Cost of Merchandise Sold	5,040	
	Merchandise Inventory		5,040
e.	Credit Card Expense	675	
	Cash		675
f.	Cash..	6,875	
	Credit Card Expense	325	
	Accounts Receivable—American Express		7,200

Ex. 6–13

It was acceptable to debit Sales for the $235,750. However, using Sales Returns and Allowances assists management in monitoring the amount of returns so that quick action can be taken if returns become excessive.

Accounts Receivable should also have been credited for $235,750. In addition, Cost of Merchandise Sold should only have been credited for the cost of the merchandise sold, not the selling price. Merchandise Inventory should also have been debited for the cost of the merchandise returned. The entries to correctly record the returns would have been as follows:

Sales (or Sales Returns and Allowances)..................	235,750	
Accounts Receivable		235,750
Merchandise Inventory..	141,450	
Cost of Merchandise Sold		141,450

Ex. 6–14

a. $7,350 [$7,500 – $150 ($7,500 × 2%)]

b. Sales Returns and Allowances	7,500	
Sales Discounts		150
Cash		7,350
Merchandise Inventory...	4,500	
Cost of Merchandise Sold		4,500

Ex. 6–15

(1) Sold merchandise on account, $12,000.

(2) Recorded the cost of the merchandise sold and reduced the merchandise inventory account, $7,800.

(3) Accepted a return of merchandise and granted an allowance, $2,500.

(4) Updated the merchandise inventory account for the cost of the merchandise returned, $1,625.

(5) Received the balance due within the discount period, $9,405. [Sale of $12,000, less return of $2,500, less discount of $95 (1% × $9,500).]

Ex. 6–16

a. $18,000

b. $18,375

c. $540 (3% × $18,000)

d. $17,835

Ex. 6–17

a. $7,546 [Purchase of $8,500, less return of $800, less discount of $154 ($7,700 × 2%)]

b. Merchandise Inventory

Ex. 6–18

Offer A is lower than offer B. Details are as follows:

	A	B
List price	$40,000	$40,300
Less discount	800	403
	$39,200	$39,897
Transportation	625	
	$39,825	$39,897

Ex. 6–19

(1) Purchased merchandise on account at a net cost of $8,000.

(2) Paid transportation costs, $175.

(3) An allowance or return of merchandise was granted by the creditor, $1,000.

(4) Paid the balance due within the discount period: debited Accounts Payable, $7,000, and credited Merchandise Inventory for the amount of the discount, $140, and Cash, $6,860.

Ex. 6–20

a.	Merchandise Inventory	7,500	
	Accounts Payable		7,500
b.	Accounts Payable	1,200	
	Merchandise Inventory		1,200
c.	Accounts Payable	6,300	
	Cash		6,174
	Merchandise Inventory		126

Ex. 6–21

a.	Merchandise Inventory..	12,000	
	Accounts Payable—Loew Co.		12,000
b.	Accounts Payable—Loew Co.	12,000	
	Cash		11,760
	Merchandise Inventory		240
c.	Accounts Payable*—Loew Co....................................	2,940	
	Merchandise Inventory		2,940
d.	Merchandise Inventory..	2,000	
	Accounts Payable—Loew Co.		2,000
e.	Cash...	940	
	Accounts Payable—Loew Co.		940

Note: The debit of $2,940 to Accounts Payable in entry (c) is the amount of cash refund due from Loew Co. It is computed as the amount that was paid for the returned merchandise, $3,000, less the purchase discount of $60 ($3,000 × 2%). The credit to Accounts Payable of $2,000 in entry (d) reduces the debit balance in the account to $940, which is the amount of the cash refund in entry (e). The alternative entries below yield the same final results.

c.	Accounts Receivable—Loew Co.	2,940	
	Merchandise Inventory		2,940
d.	Merchandise Inventory..	2,000	
	Accounts Payable—Loew Co.		2,000
e.	Cash...	940	
	Accounts Payable—Loew Co.	2,000	
	Accounts Receivable—Loew Co.............................		2,940

Ex. 6–22

a. $10,500

b. $4,160 [($4,500 – $500) × 0.99] + $200

c. $4,900

d. $3,960

e. $834 [($1,500 – $700) × 0.98] + $50

Ex. 6–23

a. At the time of sale
b. $4,000
c. $4,280
d. Sales Tax Payable

Ex. 6–24

a.	Accounts Receivable..	9,720	
	Sales...		9,000
	Sales Tax Payable		720
	Cost of Merchandise Sold	6,300	
	Merchandise Inventory		6,300
b.	Sales Tax Payable	9,175	
	Cash		9,175

Ex. 6–25

a.	Accounts Receivable—Beta Co.	11,500	
	Sales...		11,500
	Cost of Merchandise Sold	6,900	
	Merchandise Inventory		6,900
b.	Sales Returns and Allowances	900	
	Accounts Receivable—Beta Co.		900
	Merchandise Inventory...	540	
	Cost of Merchandise Sold		540
c.	Cash..	10,388	
	Sales Discounts..	212	
	Accounts Receivable—Beta Co.		10,600

Ex. 6–26

a.	Merchandise Inventory...	11,500	
	Accounts Payable—Superior Co.		11,500
b.	Accounts Payable—Superior Co................................	900	
	Merchandise Inventory		900
c.	Accounts Payable—Superior Co................................	10,600	
	Cash		10,388
	Merchandise Inventory		212

Ex. 6–27

a. debit

b. debit

c. credit

d. debit

e. debit

f. debit

Ex. 6–28

Cost of Merchandise Sold	11,550	
Merchandise Inventory		11,550

Ex. 6–29

(b) Cost of Merchandise Sold

(d) Sales

(e) Sales Discounts

(f) Sales Returns and Allowances

(g) Salaries Expense

(j) Supplies Expense

Ex. 6–30

Balance Sheet Accounts

100 Assets
- 110 Cash
- 112 Accounts Receivable
- 114 Merchandise Inventory
- 115 Store Supplies
- 116 Office Supplies
- 117 Prepaid Insurance
- 120 Land
- 123 Store Equipment
- 124 Accumulated Depreciation— Store Equipment
- 125 Office Equipment
- 126 Accumulated Depreciation— Office Equipment

200 Liabilities
- 210 Accounts Payable
- 211 Salaries Payable
- 212 Notes Payable (Short-Term)

300 Owner's Equity
- 310 Kimberly Skilling, Capital
- 311 Kimberly Skilling, Drawing
- 312 Income Summary

Income Statement Accounts

400 Revenues
- 410 Sales
- 411 Sales Returns and Allowances
- 412 Sales Discounts

500 Expenses
- 510 Cost of Merchandise Sold
- 520 Sales Salaries Expense
- 521 Advertising Expense
- 522 Depreciation Expense— Store Equipment
- 523 Store Supplies Expense
- 524 Transportation Out
- 529 Miscellaneous Selling Expense
- 530 Office Salaries Expense
- 531 Rent Expense
- 532 Depreciation Expense— Office Equipment
- 533 Insurance Expense
- 534 Office Supplies Expense
- 539 Miscellaneous Administrative Expense

600 Other Expense
- 610 Interest Expense

Note: The order of some of the accounts within subclassifications is somewhat arbitrary, as in accounts 115–117 and accounts 521–524. In a new business, the order of magnitude of balances in such accounts is not determinable in advance. The magnitude may also vary from period to period.

Ex. 6–31

a. 2003:   2.07 [$58,247,000,000 ÷ ($30,011,000,000 + $26,394,000,000)/2]

    2002:   2.24 [$53,553,000,000 ÷ ($26,394,000,000 + $21,385,000,000)/2]

b. These analyses indicate a decrease in the effectiveness in the use of the as-
    sets to generate profits. This decrease is probably due to the slowdown in the
    U.S. economy during 2002–2003. However, a comparison with similar compa-
    nies or industry averages would be helpful in making a more definitive state-
    ment on the effectiveness of the use of the assets.

Ex. 6–32

a. 4.13 [$12,334,353,000 ÷ ($2,937,578,000 + $3,041,670,000)/2]

b. Although Winn-Dixie and Zales are both retail stores, Zales sells jewelry at a
    much slower velocity than Winn-Dixie sells groceries. Thus, Winn-Dixie is
    able to generate $4.13 of sales for every dollar of assets. Zales, however, is
    only able to generate $1.53 in sales per dollar of assets. This makes sense
    when one considers the sales rate for jewelry and the relative cost of holding
    jewelry inventory, relative to groceries. Fortunately, Zales is able to counter
    its slow sales velocity, relative to groceries, with higher gross profits, relative
    to groceries.

Appendix 1—Ex. 6–33

a. and c.

SALES JOURNAL

Date	Invoice No.	Account Debited	Post. Ref.	Accts. Rec. Dr. Sales Cr.	Cost of Merchandise Sold Dr. Merchandise Inventory Cr.
2006					
Aug. 3	80	Adrienne Richt...............	✓	12,000	4,000
8	81	K. Smith.........................	✓	10,000	5,500
19	82	L. Lao.............................	✓	9,000	4,000
26	83	Cheryl Pugh	✓	14,000	6,500
				45,000	20,000
				(11)(41)	(51)(12)

b. and c.

PURCHASES JOURNAL

Date	Account Credited	Post Ref.	Accounts Payable Cr.	Merchandise Inventory Dr.	Other Accounts Dr.	Post. Ref.	Amount
2006							
Aug. 10	Draco Rug Importers.............	✓	8,000	8,000			
12	Draco Rug Importers.............	✓	3,500	3,500			
21	Draco Rug Importers.............	✓	19,500	19,500			
			31,000	31,000			
			(21)	(12)			

d.

Merchandise inventory, August 1	$19,000
Plus: August purchases......................................	31,000
Less: Cost of merchandise sold	(20,000)
Merchandise inventory, August 31	$30,000

OR

Quantity	Rug Style	Cost
2	10 by 6 Chinese*	$ 7,500
1	8 by 10 Persian	5,500
1	8 by 10 Indian	4,000
2	10 by 12 Persian	13,000
		$30,000

*($4,000 + $3,500)

Appendix 2—Ex. 6–34

Sales	925,000	
Income Summary		925,000
Income Summary..	847,500	
Sales Discounts		20,000
Sales Returns and Allowances		60,000
Cost of Merchandise Sold		560,000
Selling Expenses..		120,000
Administrative Expenses..		80,000
Interest Expense		7,500
Income Summary..	77,500	
Mark Donovan, Capital..		77,500
Mark Donovan, Capital..	25,000	
Mark Donovan, Drawing		25,000

PROBLEMS

Prob. 6–1A

1.

SOMBRERO CO.
Income Statement
For the Year Ended November 30, 2006

Revenue from sales:			
Sales..		$1,802,400	
Less: Sales returns and allowances........	$ 25,200		
Sales discounts	13,200	38,400	
Net sales			$1,764,000
Cost of merchandise sold.............................			1,284,000
Gross profit..			$ 480,000
Operating expenses:			
Selling expenses:			
Sales salaries expense.........................	$252,000		
Advertising expense............................	33,960		
Depreciation expense—store			
equipment	5,520		
Miscellaneous selling expense............	1,320		
Total selling expenses		$ 292,800	
Administrative expenses:			
Office salaries expense	$ 49,200		
Rent expense...	26,580		
Insurance expense....................................	15,300		
Depreciation expense—office			
equipment	10,800		
Office supplies expense	1,080		
Miscellaneous administrative expense	1,440		
Total administrative expenses.............		104,400	
Total operating expenses.........................			397,200
Income from operations................................			$ 82,800
Other expense:			
Interest expense.......................................			1,200
Net income			$ 81,600

Prob. 6–1A   Continued

2.

SOMBRERO CO.
Statement of Owner's Equity
For the Year Ended November 30, 2006

Hector Rodrique, capital, December 1, 2005....................		$321,600
Net income for the year..	$81,600	
Less withdrawals..	30,000	
Increase in owner's equity...		51,600
Hector Rodrique, capital, November 30, 2006.................		$373,200

Prob. 6–1A   Continued

3.

SOMBRERO CO.
Balance Sheet
November 30, 2006

Assets

Current assets:

Cash	$ 91,800	
Accounts receivable	74,400	
Merchandise inventory	120,000	
Office supplies	3,120	
Prepaid insurance	8,160	
Total current assets		$297,480

Property, plant, and equipment:

Office equipment...	$ 76,800		
Less accumulated depreciation	12,960	$ 63,840	
Store equipment..	$141,000		
Less accumulated depreciation	58,320	82,680	
Total property, plant, and equipment..			146,520
Total assets..			$444,000

Liabilities

Current liabilities:

Accounts payable...	$ 32,400	
Note payable (current portion)..................	3,000	
Salaries payable	2,400	
Total current liabilities		$ 37,800

Long-term liabilities:

Note payable (final payment due 2016)		33,000
Total liabilities..		$ 70,800

Owner's Equity

Hector Rodrique, capital		373,200
Total liabilities and owner's equity		$444,000

Prob. 6–1A   Concluded

4.   a.   The multiple-step form of income statement contains various sections for revenues and expenses, with intermediate balances, and concludes with net income. In the single-step form, the total of all expenses is deducted from the total of all revenues. There are no intermediate balances.

      b.   In the report form of balance sheet, the assets, liabilities, and owner's equity are presented in that order in a downward sequence. In the account form, the assets are listed on the left-hand side, and the liabilities and owner's equity are listed on the right-hand side.

Prob. 6–2A

1.

SOMBRERO CO.
Income Statement
For the Year Ended November 30, 2006

Revenues:		
Net sales...		$1,764,000
Expenses:		
Cost of merchandise sold...	$1,284,000	
Selling expenses	292,800	
Administrative expenses	104,400	
Interest expense	1,200	
Total expenses..		1,682,400
Net income		$ 81,600

2.

SOMBRERO CO.
Statement of Owner's Equity
For the Year Ended November 30, 2006

Hector Rodrique, capital, December 1, 2005...................		$321,600
Net income for the year..	$81,600	
Less withdrawals...	30,000	
Increase in owner's equity...		51,600
Hector Rodrique, capital, November 30, 2006.................		$373,200

Prob. 6–2A   Concluded

3.

SOMBRERO CO.
Balance Sheet
November 30, 2006

Assets

Current assets:

Cash		$ 91,800
Accounts receivable		74,400
Merchandise inventory		120,000
Office supplies		3,120
Prepaid insurance		8,160
Total current assets		$297,480

Property, plant, and equipment:

Office equipment	$ 76,800		
Less accum. depreciation	12,960	$ 63,840	
Store equipment	$141,000		
Less accum. depreciation	58,320	82,680	
Total property, plant, and equipment			146,520
Total assets			$444,000

Liabilities

Current liabilities:

Accounts payable	$32,400	
Note payable (current portion)	3,000	
Salaries payable	2,400	
Total current liabilities		$ 37,800

Long-term liabilities:

Note payable (final payment due 2016)		33,000
Total liabilities		$ 70,800

Owner's Equity

Hector Rodrique, capital	373,200
Total liabilities and owner's equity	$444,000

Prob. 6–3A

Mar.	1	Accounts Receivable—Babcock Co.	7,500	
		Sales...		7,500
	1	Cost of Merchandise Sold	4,500	
		Merchandise Inventory		4,500
	2	Cash..	8,480	
		Sales...		8,000
		Sales Tax Payable..................................		480
	2	Cost of Merchandise Sold	4,750	
		Merchandise Inventory		4,750
	5	Accounts Receivable—North Star Company	16,000	
		Sales...		16,000
	5	Cost of Merchandise Sold	10,500	
		Merchandise Inventory		10,500
	8	Cash..	6,519	
		Sales...		6,150
		Sales Tax Payable..................................		369
	8	Cost of Merchandise Sold	3,700	
		Merchandise Inventory		3,700
	13	Accounts Receivable—American Express........	6,500	
		Sales...		6,500
	13	Cost of Merchandise Sold	3,600	
		Merchandise Inventory		3,600
	14	Accounts Receivable—Blech Co.	7,500	
		Sales...		7,500
	14	Cost of Merchandise Sold	4,000	
		Merchandise Inventory		4,000
	15	Cash..	15,840	
		Sales Discounts..	160	
		Accounts Receivable—North Star		
		Company		16,000

Prob. 6–3A   Continued

Mar.	16	Sales Returns and Allowances	800	
		Accounts Receivable—Blech Co.		800
	16	Merchandise Inventory	360	
		Cost of Merchandise Sold		360
	18	Accounts Receivable—Westech Company	6,850	
		Sales..		6,850
	18	Accounts Receivable—Westech Company	210	
		Cash		210
	18	Cost of Merchandise Sold	4,100	
		Merchandise Inventory		4,100
	24	Cash..	6,633	
		Sales Discounts...	67	
		Accounts Receivable—Blech Co.		6,700
	27	Cash..	7,680	
		Credit Card Expense	320	
		Accounts Receivable—American Express ..		8,000
	28	Cash..	6,923	
		Sales Discounts...	137	
		Accounts Receivable—Westech Company..		7,060
	31	Transportation Out..	1,275	
		Cash		1,275
	31	Cash..	7,500	
		Accounts Receivable—Babcock Co.............		7,500
April	3	Credit Card Expense	725	
		Cash		725
	10	Sales Tax Payable	2,800	
		Cash		2,800

Prob. 6–3A Concluded

This solution is applicable only if the P.A.S.S. Software that accompanies the text is used.

INTERSTATE SUPPLIES CO.
Trial Balance
April 10, 20—

110	Cash	88,315	
111	Notes Receivable	120,000	
112	Accounts Receivable	117,500	
115	Merchandise Inventory	140,210	
116	Office Supplies	5,600	
117	Prepaid Insurance	3,400	
120	Office Equipment	85,000	
121	Accum. Depreciation—Office Equipment		12,800
210	Accounts Payable		55,600
212	Salaries Payable		2,400
220	Notes Payable		48,500
310	Oscar Beamer, Capital		349,999
311	Oscar Beamer, Drawing	29,500	
410	Sales		1,333,500
411	Sales Returns and Allowance	23,900	
412	Sales Discounts	22,264	
510	Cost of Merchandise Sold	809,790	
520	Sales Salaries Expense	173,200	
521	Advertising Expense	43,800	
522	Depreciation Expense—Store Equipment	6,400	
523	Credit Card Expense	1,045	
524	Transportation Out	1,275	
529	Miscellaneous Selling Expense	1,600	
530	Office Salaries Expense	84,150	
531	Rent Expense	31,350	
532	Depreciation Expense—Office Equipment	12,700	
533	Insurance Expense	3,900	
534	Office Supplies Expense	1,300	
539	Miscellaneous Administrative Expense	1,600	
610	Interest Revenue		11,000
710	Interest Expense	6,000	
	Totals	1,813,799	1,813,799

Prob. 6–4A

Aug.	1	Merchandise Inventory	8,750	
		Accounts Payable—Fisher Co.		8,750
	5	Merchandise Inventory	10,400	
		Accounts Payable—Byrd Co.		10,400
	10	Accounts Payable—Fisher Co............................	8,750	
		Cash		8,580
		Merchandise Inventory		170
	13	Merchandise Inventory	7,500	
		Accounts Payable—Mickle Co.		7,500
	14	Accounts Payable—Mickle Co.	2,500	
		Merchandise Inventory		2,500
	18	Merchandise Inventory	10,000	
		Accounts Payable—Lanning Company........		10,000
	18	Merchandise Inventory	150	
		Cash		150
	19	Merchandise Inventory	7,500	
		Accounts Payable—Hatcher Co....................		7,500
	23	Accounts Payable—Mickle Co.	5,000	
		Cash		4,950
		Merchandise Inventory		50
	29	Accounts Payable—Hatcher Co.	7,500	
		Cash		7,350
		Merchandise Inventory		150
	31	Accounts Payable—Lanning Company	10,000	
		Cash		10,000
	31	Accounts Payable—Byrd Co.	10,400	
		Cash		10,400

Prob. 6–4A Concluded

This solution is applicable only if the P.A.S.S. Software that accompanies the text is used.

PETUNIA CO.
Trial Balance
August 31, 20—

110	Cash	42,320	
111	Notes Receivable	120,000	
112	Accounts Receivable	121,000	
115	Merchandise Inventory	216,430	
116	Office Supplies	5,600	
117	Prepaid Insurance	3,400	
120	Office Equipment	85,000	
121	Accumulated Depreciation—Office Equipment		12,800
122	Store Equipment	153,000	
123	Accumulated Depreciation—Store Equipment		34,200
210	Accounts Payable		55,600
212	Salaries Payable		2,400
220	Notes Payable		56,000
310	Esther O'Malley, Capital		520,750
311	Esther O'Malley, Drawing	35,000	
410	Sales		1,275,000
411	Sales Returns and Allowance	23,100	
412	Sales Discounts	21,900	
510	Cost of Merchandise Sold	775,000	
520	Sales Salaries Expense	173,200	
521	Advertising Expense	43,800	
522	Depreciation Expense—Store Equipment	6,400	
529	Miscellaneous Selling Expense	1,600	
530	Office Salaries Expense	84,150	
531	Rent Expense	31,350	
532	Depreciation Expense—Office Equipment	12,700	
533	Insurance Expense	3,900	
534	Office Supplies Expense	1,300	
539	Miscellaneous Administrative Expense	1,600	
610	Interest Revenue		11,000
710	Interest Expense	6,000	
	Totals	1,967,750	1,967,750

Prob. 6–5A

Jan.	3	Merchandise Inventory	10,720	
		Accounts Payable—Pynn Co.		10,720
		[$16,000 – ($16,000 × 35%)] = $10,400		
		$10,400 + $320 = $10,720		
	5	Merchandise Inventory	8,000	
		Accounts Payable—Wilhelm Co.		8,000
	6	Accounts Receivable—Sievert Co.	7,500	
		Sales..		7,500
	6	Cost of Merchandise Sold	4,500	
		Merchandise Inventory		4,500
	7	Accounts Payable—Wilhelm Co.........................	1,800	
		Merchandise Inventory		1,800
	13	Accounts Payable—Pynn Co.............................	10,720	
		Cash		10,512
		Merchandise Inventory		208
	15	Accounts Payable—Wilhelm Co.........................	6,200	
		Cash		6,138
		Merchandise Inventory		62
	16	Cash..	7,350	
		Sales Discounts..	150	
		Accounts Receivable—Sievert Co.		7,500
	19	Accounts Receivable—American Express........	6,450	
		Sales..		6,450
	19	Cost of Merchandise Sold	3,950	
		Merchandise Inventory		3,950
	22	Accounts Receivable—Elk River Co..................	3,480	
		Sales..		3,480
	22	Cost of Merchandise Sold	1,400	
		Merchandise Inventory		1,400
	23	Cash..	9,350	
		Sales..		9,350

Prob. 6–5A   Continued

Jan.	23	Cost of Merchandise Sold	5,750	
		Merchandise Inventory		5,750
	25	Sales Returns and Allowances	1,480	
		Accounts Receivable—Elk River Co.		1,480
	25	Merchandise Inventory	600	
		Cost of Merchandise Sold		600
	31	Cash..	6,225	
		Credit Card Expense	225	
		Accounts Receivable—American Express ..		6,450

Prob. 6–5A   Concluded

This solution is applicable only if the P.A.S.S. Software that accompanies the text is used.

INGRESS COMPANY
Trial Balance
January 31, 20—

110	Cash	23,819	
111	Accounts Receivable	11,500	
115	Merchandise Inventory	77,745	
116	Prepaid Insurance	3,200	
117	Office Supplies	1,000	
210	Accounts Payable		12,000
310	E. Montoya, Capital		84,660
311	E. Montoya, Drawing	16,000	
410	Sales		104,080
411	Sales Returns and Allowance	6,980	
412	Sales Discounts	816	
510	Cost of Merchandise Sold	31,245	
520	Sales Salaries Expense	10,500	
521	Advertising Expense	5,000	
522	Credit Card Expense	485	
529	Miscellaneous Selling Expense	250	
530	Office Salaries Expense	6,500	
531	Rent Expense	5,500	
539	Miscellaneous Administrative Expense	200	
	Totals	200,740	200,740

Prob. 6–6A

1.

June	2	Accounts Receivable—Brandy Company	14,000	
		Sales		14,000
	2	Accounts Receivable—Brandy Company	350	
		Cash		350
	2	Cost of Merchandise Sold	8,000	
		Merchandise Inventory		8,000
	8	Accounts Receivable—Brandy Company	12,500	
		Sales		12,500
	8	Cost of Merchandise Sold	7,500	
		Merchandise Inventory		7,500
	8	Transportation Out	550	
		Cash		550
	12	Sales Returns and Allowances	3,000	
		Accounts Receivable—Brandy Company		3,000
	12	Merchandise Inventory	1,800	
		Cost of Merchandise Sold		1,800
	12	Cash	14,070	
		Sales Discounts	280	
		Accounts Receivable—Brandy Company		14,350
	23	Cash	9,405	
		Sales Discounts	95	
		Accounts Receivable—Brandy Company		9,500
	24	Accounts Receivable—Brandy Company	10,000	
		Sales		10,000
	24	Cost of Merchandise Sold	6,000	
		Merchandise Inventory		6,000
	30	Cash	10,000	
		Accounts Receivable—Brandy Company		10,000

Prob. 6–6A   Concluded

2.

June	2	Merchandise Inventory	14,350	
		Accounts Payable—Schnaps Company........		14,350
		$14,000 + $350 = $14,350		
	8	Merchandise Inventory	12,500	
		Accounts Payable—Schnaps Company........		12,500
	12	Accounts Payable—Schnaps Company............	3,000	
		Merchandise Inventory		3,000
	12	Accounts Payable—Schnaps Company............	14,350	
		Cash		14,070
		Merchandise Inventory		280
	23	Accounts Payable—Schnaps Company............	9,500	
		Cash		9,405
		Merchandise Inventory		95
	24	Merchandise Inventory	10,000	
		Accounts Payable—Schnaps Company........		10,000
	26	Merchandise Inventory	310	
		Cash		310
	30	Accounts Payable—Schnaps Company............	10,000	
		Cash		10,000

Appendix 2—Prob. 6–7A

1.

GLYCOL CO.
Work Sheet
For the Year Ended December 31, 2006

Account Title	Trial Balance Dr.	Trial Balance Cr.	Adjustments Dr.	Adjustments Cr.	Adjusted Trial Balance Dr.	Adjusted Trial Balance Cr.	Income Statement Dr.	Income Statement Cr.	Balance Sheet Dr.	Balance Sheet Cr.
1 Cash	11,165				11,165				11,165	
2 Accounts Receivable	86,100				86,100				86,100	
3 Merchandise Inventory	235,000			(a) 6,400	228,600				228,600	
4 Prepaid Insurance	10,600			(b) 5,000	5,600				5,600	
5 Store Supplies	3,750			(c) 2,550	1,200				1,200	
6 Office Supplies	1,700			(d) 800	900				900	
7 Store Equipment	225,000				225,000				225,000	
8 Acc. Depr.—Store Equip.		40,300		(e) 8,500		48,800				48,800
9 Office Equipment	72,000				72,000				72,000	
10 Acc. Depr.—Office Equip.		17,200		(f) 4,500		21,700				21,700
11 Accounts Payable		56,700				56,700				56,700
12 Salaries Payable				(g) 2,200		2,200				2,200
13 Unearned Rent		1,200	(h) 800			400				400
14 Note Payable (final										
15 payment due 2016)		185,000				185,000				185,000
16 Doug Easterly, Capital		282,100				282,100				282,100
17 Doug Easterly, Drawing	40,000				40,000				40,000	
18 Sales		847,500				847,500		847,500		
19 Sales Returns and Allow.	15,500				15,500		15,500			
20 Sales Discounts	6,000				6,000		6,000			
21 Cost of Merch. Sold	501,200		(a) 6,400		507,600		507,600			
22 Sales Salaries Expense	86,400		(g) 1,450		87,850		87,850			
23 Advertising Expense	29,450				29,450		29,450			
24 Depr. Exp.—Store Equip.			(e) 8,500		8,500		8,500			
25 Store Supplies Expense			(c) 2,550		2,550		2,550			
26 Misc. Selling Expense	1,885				1,885		1,885			
27 Office Salaries Expense	60,000		(g) 750		60,750		60,750			
28 Rent Expense	30,000				30,000		30,000			
29 Insurance Expense			(b) 5,000		5,000		5,000			
30 Depr. Exp.—Office Equip.			(f) 4,500		4,500		4,500			
31 Office Supplies Expense			(d) 800		800		800			
32 Misc. Admin. Expense	1,650				1,650		1,650			
33 Rent Revenue				(h) 800		800		800		
34 Interest Expense	12,600				12,600		12,600			
35	1,430,000	1,430,000	30,750	30,750	1,445,200	1,445,200	774,635	848,300	670,565	596,900
36 Net income							73,665			73,665
37							848,300	848,300	670,565	670,565

325

2.

GLYCOL CO.
Income Statement
For the Year Ended December 31, 2006

Revenue from sales:			
Sales		$847,500	
Less: Sales returns and allowances	$15,500		
Sales discounts	6,000	21,500	
Net sales			$826,000
Cost of merchandise sold			507,600
Gross profit			$318,400
Operating expenses:			
Selling expenses:			
Sales salaries expense	$87,850		
Advertising expense	29,450		
Depreciation expense—store equip.	8,500		
Store supplies expense	2,550		
Miscellaneous selling expense	1,885		
Total selling expenses		$130,235	
Administrative expenses:			
Office salaries expense	$60,750		
Rent expense	30,000		
Insurance expense	5,000		
Depreciation expense—office equip.	4,500		
Office supplies expense	800		
Miscellaneous admin. expense	1,650		
Total administrative expenses		102,700	
Total operating expenses			232,935
Income from operations			$ 85,465
Other income and expense:			
Rent revenue		$ 800	
Interest expense		(12,600)	(11,800)
Net income			$ 73,665

Appendix 2—Prob. 6–7A   Continued

3.

GLYCOL CO.
Statement of Owner's Equity
For the Year Ended December 31, 2006

Doug Easterly, capital, January 1, 2006		$282,100
Net income for the year...	$73,665	
Less withdrawals...	40,000	
Increase in owner's equity...		33,665
Doug Easterly, capital, December 31, 2006.....................		$315,765

6.

Sales	847,500	
Rent Revenue..	800	
Income Summary		848,300
Income Summary...	774,635	
Sales Returns and Allowances		15,500
Sales Discounts		6,000
Cost of Merchandise Sold		507,600
Sales Salaries Expense		87,850
Advertising Expense..		29,450
Depreciation Expense—Store Equipment		8,500
Store Supplies Expense		2,550
Miscellaneous Selling Expense		1,885
Office Salaries Expense		60,750
Rent Expense		30,000
Insurance Expense		5,000
Depreciation Expense—Office Equipment		4,500
Office Supplies Expense		800
Miscellaneous Administrative Expense		1,650
Interest Expense		12,600
Income Summary...	73,665	
Doug Easterly, Capital		73,665
Doug Easterly, Capital..	40,000	
Doug Easterly, Drawing		40,000

Prob. 6–1B

1.

SCIATIC CO.
Income Statement
For the Year Ended July 31, 2006

Revenue from sales:			
Sales...		$1,028,000	
Less: Sales returns and allowances........	$ 18,480		
Sales discounts...............................	17,520	36,000	
Net sales..			$ 992,000
Cost of merchandise sold..............................			620,000
Gross profit...			$ 372,000
Operating expenses:			
Selling expenses:			
Sales salaries expense.........................	$138,560		
Advertising expense.............................	35,040		
Depreciation expense—store			
equipment.......................................	5,120		
Miscellaneous selling expense............	1,280		
Total selling expenses.....................		$ 180,000	
Administrative expenses:			
Office salaries expense........................	$ 67,320		
Rent expense.......................................	25,080		
Depreciation expense—office			
equipment.......................................	10,160		
Insurance expense..............................	3,120		
Office supplies expense.......................	1,040		
Miscellaneous administrative			
expense...	1,280		
Total administrative expenses.......		108,000	
Total operating expenses..........................			288,000
Income from operations................................			$ 84,000
Other expense:			
Interest expense..			4,000
Net income...			$ 80,000

Prob. 6–1B   Continued

2.

SCIATIC CO.
Statement of Owner's Equity
For the Year Ended July 31, 2006

Gary McNiven, capital, August 1, 2005		$376,600
Net income for the year..	$80,000	
Less withdrawals..	28,000	
Increase in owner's equity...		52,000
Gary McNiven, capital, July 31, 2006		$428,600

Prob. 6–1B   Continued

3.

SCIATIC CO.
Balance Sheet
July 31, 2006

Assets

Current assets:			
Cash		$123,000	
Accounts receivable		96,800	
Merchandise inventory		140,000	
Office supplies		4,480	
Prepaid insurance......................................		2,720	
Total current assets			$367,000
Property, plant, and equipment:			
Office equipment...	$ 68,000		
Less accumulated depreciation	10,240	$ 57,760	
Store equipment..	$122,400		
Less accumulated depreciation	27,360	95,040	
Total property, plant, and equipment			152,800
Total assets...			$519,800

Liabilities

Current liabilities:			
Accounts payable.......................................		$ 44,480	
Note payable (current portion).................		6,000	
Salaries payable		1,920	
Total current liabilities			$ 52,400
Long-term liabilities:			
Note payable (final payment due 2016)			38,800
Total liabilities..			$ 91,200

Owner's Equity

Gary McNiven, capital	428,600
Total liabilities and owner's equity	$519,800

Prob. 6–1B   Concluded

4.   a.   The multiple-step form of income statement contains various sections for revenues and expenses, with intermediate balances, and concludes with net income. In the single-step form, the total of all expenses is deducted from the total of all revenues. There are no intermediate balances.

   b.   In the report form of balance sheet, the assets, liabilities, and owner's equity are presented in that order in a downward sequence. In the account form, the assets are listed on the left-hand side, and the liabilities and owner's equity are listed on the right-hand side.

Prob. 6–2B

1.

SCIATIC CO.
Income Statement
For the Year Ended July 31, 2006

Revenues:		
Net sales..		$992,000
Expenses:		
Cost of merchandise sold...	$620,000	
Selling expenses	180,000	
Administrative expenses	108,000	
Interest expense	4,000	
Total expenses..		912,000
Net income		$ 80,000

2.

SCIATIC CO.
Statement of Owner's Equity
For the Year Ended July 31, 2006

Gary McNiven, capital, August 1, 2005		$376,600
Net income for the year...	$80,000	
Less withdrawals..	28,000	
Increase in owner's equity...		52,000
Gary McNiven, capital, July 31, 2006		$428,600

3.

SCIATIC CO.
Balance Sheet
July 31, 2006

Assets

Current assets:

Cash	$123,000	
Accounts receivable	96,800	
Merchandise inventory	140,000	
Office supplies	4,480	
Prepaid insurance	2,720	
Total current assets		$367,000

Property, plant, and equipment:

Office equipment	$ 68,000		
Less accumulated depreciation	10,240	$ 57,760	
Store equipment	$122,400		
Less accumulated depreciation	27,360	95,040	
Total property, plant, and equipment			152,800
Total assets			$519,800

Liabilities

Current liabilities:

Accounts payable	$44,480	
Note payable (current portion)	6,000	
Salaries payable	1,920	
Total current liabilities		$ 52,400

Long-term liabilities:

Note payable (final payment due 2016)		38,800
Total liabilities		$ 91,200

Owner's Equity

Gary McNiven, capital	428,600
Total liabilities and owner's equity	$519,800

336

Prob. 6–3B

Aug.	2	Accounts Receivable—Runyan Co.	12,800	
		Sales...		12,800
	2	Cost of Merchandise Sold	7,600	
		Merchandise Inventory		7,600
	3	Cash...	5,350	
		Sales...		5,000
		Sales Tax Payable		350
	3	Cost of Merchandise Sold	3,000	
		Merchandise Inventory		3,000
	4	Accounts Receivable—McNutt Co.	2,800	
		Sales...		2,800
	4	Cost of Merchandise Sold	1,800	
		Merchandise Inventory		1,800
	5	Cash...	4,708	
		Sales...		4,400
		Sales Tax Payable		308
	5	Cost of Merchandise Sold	2,500	
		Merchandise Inventory		2,500
	12	Cash...	12,544	
		Sales Discounts..	256	
		Accounts Receivable—Runyan Co.		12,800
	14	Accounts Receivable—American Express........	15,000	
		Sales...		15,000
	14	Cost of Merchandise Sold	9,200	
		Merchandise Inventory		9,200
	16	Accounts Receivable—Westpark Co.	12,000	
		Sales...		12,000
	16	Cost of Merchandise Sold	7,200	
		Merchandise Inventory		7,200
	18	Sales Returns and Allowances	3,000	
		Accounts Receivable—Westpark Co............		3,000
	18	Merchandise Inventory	1,800	
		Cost of Merchandise Sold		1,800

Prob. 6–3B   Continued

Aug.	19	Accounts Receivable—DeGroot Co..................	9,500	
		Sales..		9,500
	19	Accounts Receivable—DeGroot Co..................	200	
		Cash		200
	19	Cost of Merchandise Sold	5,700	
		Merchandise Inventory		5,700
	26	Cash...	8,910	
		Sales Discounts..	90	
		Accounts Receivable—Westpark Co............		9,000
	27	Cash...	7,680	
		Credit Card Expense	320	
		Accounts Receivable—American Express ..		8,000
	28	Cash...	9,605	
		Sales Discounts..	95	
		Accounts Receivable—DeGroot Co.		9,700
	31	Cash...	2,800	
		Accounts Receivable—McNutt Co...............		2,800
	31	Transportation Out...	1,050	
		Cash		1,050
Sept.	3	Credit Card Expense	850	
		Cash		850
	15	Sales Tax Payable	4,100	
		Cash		4,100

Prob. 6–3B Concluded

This solution is applicable only if the P.A.S.S. Software that accompanies the text is used.

HOLISTIC SUPPLY CO.
Trial Balance
September 15, 20—

110	Cash	71,897	
112	Accounts Receivable	67,600	
115	Merchandise Inventory	64,800	
116	Office Supplies	2,600	
117	Prepaid Insurance	6,800	
120	Office Equipment	64,000	
121	Accumulated Depreciation—Office Equipment		10,800
210	Accounts Payable		27,000
212	Salaries Payable		2,000
220	Notes Payable		30,000
310	Miles Wren, Capital		149,258
311	Miles Wren, Drawing	25,000	
410	Sales		1,561,500
411	Sales Returns and Allowance	24,000	
412	Sales Discounts	11,441	
510	Cost of Merchandise Sold	1,105,200	
520	Sales Salaries Expense	210,000	
521	Advertising Expense	28,300	
522	Depreciation Expense—Store Equipment	4,600	
523	Credit Card Expense	1,170	
524	Transportation Out	1,050	
529	Miscellaneous Selling Expense	1,100	
530	Office Salaries Expense	41,000	
531	Rent Expense	22,150	
532	Insurance Expense	12,750	
533	Depreciation Expense—Office Equipment	9,000	
534	Office Supplies Expense	900	
539	Miscellaneous Administrative Expense	1,200	
710	Interest Expense	4,000	
	Totals	1,780,558	1,780,558

Prob. 6–4B

Mar.	1	Merchandise Inventory	16,000	
		Accounts Payable—Fastow Co.		16,000
	3	Merchandise Inventory	9,150	
		Accounts Payable—Moss Co.		9,150
	4	Merchandise Inventory	7,500	
		Accounts Payable—Picadilly Co.		7,500
	6	Accounts Payable—Picadilly Co.	1,000	
		Merchandise Inventory		1,000
	13	Accounts Payable—Moss Co.	9,150	
		Cash		8,970
		Merchandise Inventory		180
	14	Accounts Payable—Picadilly Co.	6,500	
		Cash		6,370
		Merchandise Inventory		130
	19	Merchandise Inventory	12,000	
		Accounts Payable—Reardon Co.		12,000
	19	Merchandise Inventory	500	
		Cash		500
	20	Merchandise Inventory	8,000	
		Accounts Payable—Hatcher Co.		8,000
	30	Accounts Payable—Hatcher Co.	8,000	
		Cash		7,920
		Merchandise Inventory		80
	31	Accounts Payable—Fastow Co.	16,000	
		Cash		16,000
	31	Accounts Payable—Reardon Co.	12,000	
		Cash		12,000

Prob. 6–4B   Concluded

This solution is applicable only if the P.A.S.S. Software that accompanies the text is used.

DAFFODIL COMPANY
Trial Balance
March 31, 20—

110	Cash	34,740	
111	Notes Receivable	50,000	
112	Accounts Receivable	62,000	
115	Merchandise Inventory	151,760	
116	Office Supplies	2,600	
117	Prepaid Insurance	6,800	
120	Office Equipment	64,000	
121	Accumulated Depreciation—Office Equipment		10,800
210	Accounts Payable		27,000
212	Salaries Payable		2,000
220	Notes Payable		30,000
310	Susan Mosteller, Capital		264,100
311	Susan Mosteller, Drawing	25,000	
410	Sales		1,500,000
411	Sales Returns and Allowance	21,000	
412	Sales Discounts	11,000	
510	Cost of Merchandise Sold	1,070,000	
520	Sales Salaries Expense	210,000	
521	Advertising Expense	28,300	
522	Depreciation Expense—Store Equipment	4,600	
529	Miscellaneous Selling Expense	1,100	
530	Office Salaries Expense	41,000	
531	Rent Expense	22,150	
532	Insurance Expense	12,750	
533	Depreciation Expense—Office Equipment	9,000	
534	Office Supplies Expense	900	
539	Miscellaneous Administrative Expense	1,200	
710	Interest Expense	4,000	
	Totals	1,833,900	1,833,900

Prob. 6–5B

Nov.				
3	Merchandise Inventory	20,000	
	Accounts Payable—Whiting Co.		20,000
	[$25,000 – ($25,000 × 20%)] = $20,000		
4	Cash..	7,100	
	Sales..		7,100
4	Cost of Merchandise Sold	4,150	
	Merchandise Inventory		4,150
5	Merchandise Inventory	10,800	
	Accounts Payable—Alamosa Co.		10,800
6	Accounts Payable—Whiting Co.	5,000	
	Merchandise Inventory		5,000
11	Accounts Receivable—Bowles Co.....................	1,800	
	Sales..		1,800
	[$2,250 – ($2,250 × 20%)] = $1,800		
11	Cost of Merchandise Sold	1,050	
	Merchandise Inventory		1,050
13	Accounts Payable—Whiting Co.	15,000	
	Cash		14,700
	Merchandise Inventory		300
14	Accounts Receivable—American Express........	9,850	
	Sales..		9,850
14	Cost of Merchandise Sold	5,900	
	Merchandise Inventory		5,900
15	Accounts Payable—Alamosa Co.......................	10,800	
	Cash		10,590
	Merchandise Inventory		210
21	Cash..	1,782	
	Sales Discounts...	18	
	Accounts Receivable—Bowles Co.		1,800
24	Accounts Receivable—Kapinos Co.	4,200	
	Sales..		4,200

Prob. 6–5B   Continued

Nov.	24	Cost of Merchandise Sold	1,850	
		Merchandise Inventory		1,850
	28	Cash..	9,410	
		Credit Card Expense	440	
		Accounts Receivable—American Express ..		9,850
	30	Sales Returns and Allowances	1,100	
		Accounts Receivable—Kapinos Co..............		1,100
	30	Merchandise Inventory	600	
		Cost of Merchandise Sold		600

Prob. 6–6B   Concluded

2.

Mar.	1	Merchandise Inventory	12,750	
		Accounts Payable—Snyder Company..........		12,750
	5	Merchandise Inventory	18,500	
		Accounts Payable—Snyder Company..........		18,500
	6	Accounts Payable—Snyder Company...............	2,000	
		Merchandise Inventory		2,000
	9	Merchandise Inventory	180	
		Cash		180
	15	Merchandise Inventory	21,750	
		Accounts Payable—Snyder Company..........		21,750
		$20,000 + $1,750 = $21,750		
	16	Accounts Payable—Snyder Company...............	10,750	
		Cash		10,535
		Merchandise Inventory		215
	25	Accounts Payable—Snyder Company...............	21,750	
		Cash		21,550
		Merchandise Inventory		200
	31	Accounts Payable—Snyder Company...............	18,500	
		Cash		18,500

Appendix 2—Prob. 6–7B

1.

VIADUCT CO.
Work Sheet
For the Year Ended December 31, 2006

#	Account Title	Trial Balance Dr.	Trial Balance Cr.	Adjustments Dr.	Adjustments Cr.	Adjusted Trial Balance Dr.	Adjusted Trial Balance Cr.	Income Statement Dr.	Income Statement Cr.	Balance Sheet Dr.	Balance Sheet Cr.
1	Cash	18,000				18,000				18,000	
2	Accounts Receivable	82,500				82,500				82,500	
3	Merchandise Inventory	165,000			(a) 7,500	157,500				157,500	
4	Prepaid Insurance	9,700			(b) 4,000	5,700				5,700	
5	Store Supplies	4,250			(c) 3,150	1,100				1,100	
6	Office Supplies	2,100			(d) 1,500	600				600	
7	Store Equipment	157,000				157,000				157,000	
8	Acc. Depr.—Store Equip.		40,300		(e) 4,500		44,800				44,800
9	Office Equipment	50,000				50,000				50,000	
10	Acc. Depr.—Office Equip.		17,200		(f) 2,800		20,000				20,000
11	Accounts Payable		66,700				66,700				66,700
12	Salaries Payable				(g) 3,650		3,650				3,650
13	Unearned Rent		1,200	(h) 800			400				400
14	Note Payable (final										
15	payment due 2016)		105,000				105,000				105,000
16	Robbin Jaeger, Capital		134,600				134,600				134,600
17	Robbin Jaeger, Drawing	30,000				30,000				30,000	
18	Sales		815,000				815,000		815,000		
19	Sales Returns and Allow.	11,900				11,900		11,900			
20	Sales Discounts	7,100				7,100		7,100			
21	Cost of Merch. Sold	476,200		(a) 7,500		483,700		483,700			
22	Sales Salaries Expense	76,400		(g) 2,850		79,250		79,250			
23	Advertising Expense	25,000				25,000		25,000			
24	Depr. Exp.—Store Equip.			(e) 4,500		4,500		4,500			
25	Store Supplies Expense			(c) 3,150		3,150		3,150			
26	Misc. Selling Expense	1,600				1,600		1,600			
27	Office Salaries Expense	34,000		(g) 800		34,800		34,800			
28	Rent Expense	16,000				16,000		16,000			
29	Insurance Expense			(b) 4,000		4,000		4,000			
30	Depr. Exp.—Office Equip.			(f) 2,800		2,800		2,800			
31	Office Supplies Expense			(d) 1,500		1,500		1,500			
32	Misc. Admin. Expense	1,650				1,650		1,650			
33	Rent Revenue				(h) 800		800		800		
34	Interest Expense	11,600				11,600		11,600			
35		1,180,000	1,180,000	27,900	27,900	1,190,950	1,190,950	688,550	815,800	502,400	375,150
36	Net Income							127,250			127,250
37								815,800	815,800	502,400	502,400

347

2.

VIADUCT CO.
Income Statement
For the Year Ended December 31, 2006

Revenue from sales:			
Sales		$815,000	
Less: Sales returns and allowances	$11,900		
Sales discounts	7,100	19,000	
Net sales			$796,000
Cost of merchandise sold			483,700
Gross profit			$312,300
Operating expenses:			
Selling expenses:			
Sales salaries expense	$79,250		
Advertising expense	25,000		
Depreciation expense—store equipment	4,500		
Store supplies expense	3,150		
Miscellaneous selling expense	1,600		
Total selling expenses		$113,500	
Administrative expenses:			
Office salaries expense	$34,800		
Rent expense	16,000		
Insurance expense	4,000		
Depreciation expense—office equipment	2,800		
Office supplies expense	1,500		
Miscellaneous administrative expense	1,650		
Total administrative expenses		60,750	
Total operating expenses			174,250
Income from operations			$138,050
Other income and expense:			
Rent revenue		$ 800	
Interest expense		(11,600)	(10,800)
Net income			$127,250

3.

VIADUCT CO.
Statement of Owner's Equity
For the Year Ended December 31, 2006

Robbin Jaeger, capital, January 1, 2006..........................		$134,600
Net income for the year..	$127,250	
Less withdrawals..	30,000	
Increase in owner's equity..		97,250
Robbin Jaeger, capital, December 31, 2006....................		$231,850

6.

Sales	815,000	
Rent Revenue	800	
Income Summary		815,800
Income Summary	688,550	
Sales Returns and Allowances		11,900
Sales Discounts		7,100
Cost of Merchandise Sold		483,700
Sales Salaries Expense		79,250
Advertising Expense		25,000
Depreciation Expense—Store Equipment		4,500
Store Supplies Expense		3,150
Miscellaneous Selling Expense		1,600
Office Salaries Expense		34,800
Rent Expense		16,000
Insurance Expense		4,000
Depreciation Expense—Office Equipment		2,800
Office Supplies Expense		1,500
Miscellaneous Administrative Expense		1,650
Interest Expense		11,600
Income Summary	127,250	
Robbin Jaeger, Capital		127,250
Robbin Jaeger, Capital	30,000	
Robbin Jaeger, Drawing		30,000

COMPREHENSIVE PROBLEM 2

1., alt. 1, 3., alt. 3., 4., 6., alt. 6., and alt. 7.

Cash   110

Date	Item	Post. Ref.	Dr.	Cr.	Balance Dr.	Balance Cr.
2006						
Aug. 1	Balance............	✓	....	....	14,160	....
1	....	20	....	1,600	....	....
4	....	20	....	400	....	....
7	....	20	7,500	....	....	....
10	....	20	18,300	....	....	....
13	....	20	....	14,700	....	....
15	....	20	....	1,500	....	....
16	....	20	6,860	....	....	....
19	....	20	....	8,100	....	....
19	....	20	....	6,100	....	....
21	....	21	....	600	....	....
21	....	21	11,750	....	....	....
26	....	21	....	720	....	....
28	....	21	....	2,700	....	....
29	....	21	....	550	....	....
30	....	21	16,440	....	....	....
31	....	21	....	11,385	26,655	....

Accounts Receivable   112

Date	Item	Post. Ref.	Dr.	Cr.	Balance Dr.	Balance Cr.
2006						
Aug. 1	Balance............	✓	....	....	34,220	....
6	....	20	8,500	....	....	....
7	....	20	....	7,500	....	....
14	....	20	....	1,500	....	....
16	....	20	....	7,000	....	....
20	....	21	16,000	....	....	....
21	....	21	600	....	....	....
21	....	21	....	11,750	....	....
30	....	21	18,750	....	....	....
30	....	21	....	16,600	33,720	....

Comp. Prob. 2   Continued

Merchandise Inventory   115

Date		Item	Post. Ref.	Dr.	Cr.	Balance Dr.	Balance Cr.
2006							
Aug.	1	Balance...................	✓	....	....	133,900	....
	3	....	20	15,000	....	....	....
	4	....	20	400	....	....	....
	6	....	20	....	5,000	....	....
	10	....	20	....	11,000	....	....
	13	....	20	....	300	....	....
	14	....	20	900	....	....	....
	19	....	20	8,100	....	....	....
	20	....	21	....	9,600	....	....
	21	....	21	15,000	....	....	....
	24	....	21	....	3,500	....	....
	26	....	21	380	....	....	....
	30	....	21	....	11,250	....	....
	31	....	21	....	115	132,915	....
	31	Adjusting................	22	....	8,800	124,115	....

Prepaid Insurance   116

Date		Item	Post. Ref.	Dr.	Cr.	Balance Dr.	Balance Cr.
2006							
Aug.	1	Balance..................	✓	....	....	3,750	....
	31	Adjusting................	22	....	1,250	2,500	....

Store Supplies   117

Date		Item	Post. Ref.	Dr.	Cr.	Balance Dr.	Balance Cr.
2006							
Aug.	1	Balance..................	✓	....	....	2,550	....
	29	....	21	550	....	3,100	....
	31	Adjusting................	22	....	2,125	975	....

Store Equipment   123

Date		Item	Post. Ref.	Dr.	Cr.	Balance Dr.	Balance Cr.
2006							
Aug.	1	Balance..................	✓	....	....	104,300	....

Comp. Prob. 2   Continued

Accumulated Depreciation—Store Equipment 124

Date	Item	Post. Ref.	Dr.	Cr.	Balance Dr.	Balance Cr.
2006						
Aug. 1	Balance.................	✓	....	....	....	12,600
31	Adjusting................	22	....	7,400	....	20,000

Accounts Payable 210

Date	Item	Post. Ref.	Dr.	Cr.	Balance Dr.	Balance Cr.
2006						
Aug. 1	Balance.................	✓	....	....	....	21,450
3	....	20	....	15,000	....	....
13	....	20	15,000	....	....	....
19	....	20	6,100	....	....	....
21	....	21	....	15,000	....	....
24	....	21	3,500	....	....	....
31	....	21	11,500	....	....	15,350

Salaries Payable 211

Date	Item	Post. Ref.	Dr.	Cr.	Balance Dr.	Balance Cr.
2006						
Aug. 31	Adjusting................	22	....	530	....	530

Kevin Wilcox, Capital 310

Date	Item	Post. Ref.	Dr.	Cr.	Balance Dr.	Balance Cr.
2005						
Sept. 1	Balance.................	✓	....	....	....	103,280
2006						
Aug. 31	Closing	23	....	163,105	....	....
31	Closing	23	10,000	....	....	256,385

Kevin Wilcox, Drawing 311

Date	Item	Post. Ref.	Dr.	Cr.	Balance Dr.	Balance Cr.
2006						
Aug. 1	Balance.................	✓	....	....	10,000	....
31	Closing	23	....	10,000	—	—

Comp. Prob. 2   Continued

Income Summary   312

Date	Item	Post. Ref.	Dr.	Cr.	Balance Dr.	Balance Cr.
2006						
Aug. 31	Closing	23	....	777,350	....	....
31	Closing	23	614,245	....	....	....
31	Closing	23	163,105	....	—	—

Sales   410

Date	Item	Post. Ref.	Dr.	Cr.	Balance Dr.	Balance Cr.
2006						
Aug. 1	Balance..................	✓	....	....	....	715,800
6	....	20	....	8,500	....	....
10	....	20	....	18,300	....	....
20	....	21	....	16,000	....	....
30	....	21	....	18,750	....	777,350
31	Closing	23	777,350	....	—	—

Sales Returns and Allowances   411

Date	Item	Post. Ref.	Dr.	Cr.	Balance Dr.	Balance Cr.
2006						
Aug. 1	Balance..................	✓	....	....	20,600	....
14	....	20	1,500	....	....	....
26	....	21	720	....	22,820	....
31	Closing	23	....	22,820	—	—

Sales Discounts   412

Date	Item	Post. Ref.	Dr.	Cr.	Balance Dr.	Balance Cr.
2006						
Aug. 1	Balance..................	✓	....	....	13,200	....
16	....	20	140	....	....	....
30	....	21	160	....	13,500	....
31	Closing	23	....	13,500	—	—

Comp. Prob. 2   Continued

Cost of Merchandise Sold 510

Date		Item	Post. Ref.	Dr.	Cr.	Balance Dr.	Balance Cr.
2006							
Aug.	1	Balance....................	✓	....	....	360,500	....
	6	....	20	5,000	....	....	....
	10	....	20	11,000	....	....	....
	14	....	20	....	900	....	....
	20	....	21	9,600	....	....	....
	26	....	21	....	380	....	....
	30	....	21	11,250	....	396,070	....
	31	Adjusting................	22	8,800	....	404,870	....
	31	Closing	23	....	404,870	—	—

Sales Salaries Expense 520

Date		Item	Post. Ref.	Dr.	Cr.	Balance Dr.	Balance Cr.
2006							
Aug.	1	Balance....................	✓	....	....	74,400	....
	28	....	21	1,750	....	76,150	....
	31	Adjusting................	22	350	....	76,500	....
	31	Closing	23	....	76,500	—	—

Advertising Expense 521

Date		Item	Post. Ref.	Dr.	Cr.	Balance Dr.	Balance Cr.
2006							
Aug.	1	Balance....................	✓	....	....	18,000	....
	15	....	20	1,500	....	19,500	....
	31	Closing	23	....	19,500	—	—

Depreciation Expense 522

Date		Item	Post. Ref.	Dr.	Cr.	Balance Dr.	Balance Cr.
2006							
Aug.	31	Adjusting................	22	7,400	....	7,400	....
	31	Closing	23	....	7,400	—	—

Store Supplies Expense 523

Date		Item	Post. Ref.	Dr.	Cr.	Balance Dr.	Balance Cr.
2006							
Aug.	31	Adjusting................	22	2,125	....	2,125	....
	31	Closing	23	....	2,125	—	—

Comp. Prob. 2   Continued

Miscellaneous Selling Expense 529

Date	Item	Post. Ref.	Dr.	Cr.	Balance Dr.	Balance Cr.
2006						
Aug. 1	Balance..................	✓	....	....	2,800	....
31	Closing	23	....	2,800	—	—

Office Salaries Expense 530

Date	Item	Post. Ref.	Dr.	Cr.	Balance Dr.	Balance Cr.
2006						
Aug. 1	Balance..................	✓	....	....	40,500	....
28	....	21	950	....	41,450	....
31	Adjusting................	22	180	....	41,630	....
31	Closing	23	....	41,630	—	—

Rent Expense 531

Date	Item	Post. Ref.	Dr.	Cr.	Balance Dr.	Balance Cr.
2006						
Aug. 1	Balance..................	✓	....	....	18,600	....
1	....	20	1,600	....	20,200	....
31	Closing	23	....	20,200	—	—

Insurance Expense 532

Date	Item	Post. Ref.	Dr.	Cr.	Balance Dr.	Balance Cr.
2006						
Aug. 31	Adjusting................	22	1,250	....	1,250	....
31	Closing	23	....	1,250	—	—

Miscellaneous Administrative Expense 539

Date	Item	Post. Ref.	Dr.	Cr.	Balance Dr.	Balance Cr.
2006						
Aug. 1	Balance..................	✓	....	....	1,650	....
31	Closing	23	....	1,650	—	—

Comp. Prob. 2　Continued

2., alt 2.　　　　　　　　　　　　　　JOURNAL　　　　　　　　　　　

Date		Description	Post. Ref.	Debit	Credit
2006					
Aug.	1	Rent Expense	531	1,600	
		Cash	110		1,600
	3	Merchandise Inventory	115	15,000	
		Accounts Payable—Biathlon Co.	210		15,000
	4	Merchandise Inventory	115	400	
		Cash	110		400
	6	Accounts Receivable—Hillcrest Co.	112	8,500	
		Sales	410		8,500
	6	Cost of Merchandise Sold	510	5,000	
		Merchandise Inventory	115		5,000
	7	Cash	110	7,500	
		Accounts Receivable—Aaberg Co.	112		7,500
	10	Cash	110	18,300	
		Sales	410		18,300
	10	Cost of Merchandise Sold	510	11,000	
		Merchandise Inventory	115		11,000
	13	Accounts Payable—Biathlon Co.	210	15,000	
		Cash	110		14,700
		Merchandise Inventory	115		300
	14	Sales Returns and Allowances	411	1,500	
		Accounts Receivable—Hillcrest Co.	112		1,500
	14	Merchandise Inventory	115	900	
		Cost of Merchandise Sold	510		900
	15	Advertising Expense	521	1,500	
		Cash	110		1,500
	16	Cash	110	6,860	
		Sales Discounts	412	140	
		Accounts Receivable—Hillcrest Co.	112		7,000
	19	Merchandise Inventory	115	8,100	
		Cash	110		8,100
	19	Accounts Payable—Ramler Co.	210	6,100	
		Cash	110		6,100

JOURNAL

Date		Description	Post. Ref.	Debit	Credit
2006					
Aug.	20	Accounts Receivable—Petroski Co.	112	16,000	
		Sales	410		16,000
	20	Cost of Merchandise Sold......................	510	9,600	
		Merchandise Inventory......................	115		9,600
	21	Accounts Receivable—Petroski Co.	112	600	
		Cash..	110		600
	21	Cash..	110	11,750	
		Accounts Receivable—Phillips Co.	112		11,750
	21	Merchandise Inventory..........................	115	15,000	
		Accounts Payable—Walden Co.	210		15,000
	24	Accounts Payable—Walden Co.	210	3,500	
		Merchandise Inventory......................	115		3,500
	26	Sales Returns and Allowances..............	411	720	
		Cash..	110		720
	26	Merchandise Inventory..........................	115	380	
		Cost of Merchandise Sold	510		380
	28	Sales Salaries Expense........................	520	1,750	
		Office Salaries Expense	530	950	
		Cash..	110		2,700
	29	Store Supplies.......................................	117	550	
		Cash..	110		550
	30	Accounts Receivable—Whitetail Co......	112	18,750	
		Sales	410		18,750
	30	Cost of Merchandise Sold......................	510	11,250	
		Merchandise Inventory......................	115		11,250
	30	Cash..	110	16,440	
		Sales Discounts	412	160	
		Accounts Receivable—Petroski Co.	112		16,600
	31	Accounts Payable—Walden Co.	210	11,500	
		Cash..	110		11,385
		Merchandise Inventory......................	115		115

Comp. Prob. 2   Continued

JOURNAL

Date	Description	Post. Ref.	Debit	Credit
	Adjusting Entries			
2006				
Aug. 31	Cost of Merchandise Sold......................	510	8,800	
	Merchandise Inventory......................	115		8,800
31	Insurance Expense	532	1,250	
	Prepaid Insurance	116		1,250
31	Store Supplies Expense.........................	523	2,125	
	Store Supplies	117		2,125
31	Depreciation Expense	522	7,400	
	Accumulated Depreciation—Store Equipment...	124		7,400
31	Sales Salaries Expense.........................	520	350	
	Office Salaries Expense	530	180	
	Salaries Payable	211		530

Comp. Prob. 2   Continued

Date	Description	Post. Ref.	Debit	Credit
	Closing Entries			
2006				
Aug. 31	Sales	410	777,350	
	Income Summary.............................	312		777,350
31	Income Summary	312	614,245	
	Sales Returns and Allowances	411		22,820
	Sales Discounts.............................	412		13,500
	Cost of Merchandise Sold	510		404,870
	Sales Salaries Expense	520		76,500
	Advertising Expense	521		19,500
	Depreciation Expense.......................	522		7,400
	Store Supplies Expense...................	523		2,125
	Miscellaneous Selling Expense	529		2,800
	Office Salaries Expense...................	530		41,630
	Rent Expense....................................	531		20,200
	Insurance Expense...........................	532		1,250
	Miscellaneous Administrative Exp...	539		1,650
31	Income Summary..................................	312	163,105	
	Kevin Wilcox, Capital	310		163,105
31	Kevin Wilcox, Capital.............................	310	10,000	
	Kevin Wilcox, Drawing	311		10,000

Comp. Prob. 2   Continued

5., alt. 5

LYRE CO.
Income Statement
For the Year Ended August 31, 2006

Revenue from sales:			
Sales...		$777,350	
Less: Sales returns and allowances........	$22,820		
Sales discounts	13,500	36,320	
Net sales..			$741,030
Cost of merchandise sold..............................			404,870
Gross profit..			$336,160
Operating expenses:			
Selling expenses:			
Sales salaries expense.........................	$76,500		
Advertising expense.............................	19,500		
Depreciation expense...........................	7,400		
Store supplies expense.........................	2,125		
Miscellaneous selling expense............	2,800		
Total selling expenses		$108,325	
Administrative expenses:			
Office salaries expense.........................	$41,630		
Rent expense	20,200		
Insurance expense	1,250		
Miscellaneous administrative expense	1,650		
Total administrative expenses		64,730	
Total operating expenses...........................			173,055
Net income			$163,105

LYRE CO.
Statement of Owner's Equity
For the Year Ended August 31, 2006

Kevin Wilcox, capital, September 1, 2005		$103,280
Net income for the year..	$163,105	
Less withdrawals..	10,000	
Increase in owner's equity..		153,105
Kevin Wilcox, capital, August 31, 2006............................		$256,385

LYRE CO.
Balance Sheet
August 31, 2006

Assets

Current assets:

Cash	$ 26,655	
Accounts receivable	33,720	
Merchandise inventory	124,115	
Prepaid insurance	2,500	
Store supplies	975	
Total current assets		$187,965

Property, plant, and equipment:

Store equipment	$104,300	
Less accumulated depreciation	20,000	
Total property, plant, and equipment		84,300
Total assets		$272,265

Liabilities

Current liabilities:

Accounts payable	$ 15,350	
Salaries payable	530	
Total liabilities		$ 15,880

Owner's Equity

Kevin Wilcox, capital	256,385
Total liabilities and owner's equity	$272,265

Comp. Prob. 2   Continued

7. and alt. 8.

LYRE CO.
Post-Closing Trial Balance
August 31, 2006

Cash	26,655	
Accounts Receivable	33,720	
Merchandise Inventory	124,115	
Prepaid Insurance	2,500	
Store Supplies	975	
Store Equipment	104,300	
Accumulated Depreciation		20,000
Accounts Payable		15,350
Salaries Payable		530
Kevin Wilcox, Capital		256,385
Total	292,265	292,265

Comp. Prob. 2 Concluded

This solution is applicable only if the work sheet is used.

alt. 4.

LYRE CO.
Work Sheet
For the Year Ended August 31, 2006

Account Title	Trial Balance Dr.	Trial Balance Cr.	Adjustments Dr.	Adjustments Cr.	Adjusted Trial Balance Dr.	Adjusted Trial Balance Cr.	Income Statement Dr.	Income Statement Cr.	Balance Sheet Dr.	Balance Sheet Cr.
1 Cash	26,655				26,655				26,655	
3 Accounts Receivable	33,720				33,720				33,720	
4 Merchandise Inventory	132,915			(a) 8,800	124,115				124,115	
5 Prepaid Insurance	3,750			(b) 1,250	2,500				2,500	
6 Store Supplies	3,100			(c) 2,125	975				975	
7 Store Equipment	104,300				104,300				104,300	
8 Accum. Depreciation—										
9 Store Equipment		12,600		(d) 7,400		20,000				20,000
10 Accounts Payable		15,350				15,350				15,350
11 Salaries Payable				(e) 530		530				530
12 Kevin Wilcox, Capital		103,280				103,280				103,280
13 Kevin Wilcox, Drawing	10,000				10,000				10,000	
14 Sales		777,350				777,350		777,350		
15 Sales Returns and Allow.	22,820				22,820		22,820			
16 Sales Discounts	13,500				13,500		13,500			
17 Cost of Merch. Sold	396,070		(a) 8,800		404,870		404,870			
18 Sales Salaries Expense	76,150		(e) 350		76,500		76,500			
19 Advertising Expense	19,500				19,500		19,500			
20 Depreciation Expense			(d) 7,400		7,400		7,400			
21 Store Supplies Expense			(c) 2,125		2,125		2,125			
22 Misc. Selling Expense	2,800				2,800		2,800			
23 Office Salaries Expense	41,450		(e) 180		41,630		41,630			
24 Rent Expense	20,200				20,200		20,200			
25 Insurance Expense			(b) 1,250		1,250		1,250			
26 Misc. Admin. Expense	1,650				1,650		1,650			
28	908,580	908,580	20,105	20,105	916,510	916,510	614,245	777,350	302,265	139,160
29 Net income							163,105			163,105
30							777,350	777,350	302,265	302,265

366

SPECIAL ACTIVITIES

Activity 6–1

Standards of Ethical Conduct for Management Accountants requires management accountants to perform in a competent manner and to comply with relevant laws, regulations, and technical standards. If Sandi Kurtz intentionally subtracted the discount with knowledge that the discount period had expired, she would have behaved in an unprofessional manner. Such behavior could eventually jeopardize Cardinal Company's buyer/supplier relationship with Iowa Farm Co.

Activity 6–2

Todd Shovic is correct. The accounts payable due suppliers could be included on the balance sheet at an amount of $88,200. This is the amount that will be expected to be paid to satisfy the obligation (liability) to suppliers. However, this is proper only if The Video Store Co. has a history of taking all purchases discounts, has a properly designed accounting system to identify available discounts, and has sufficient liquidity (cash) to pay the accounts payable within the discount period. In this case, The Video Store Co. apparently meets these criteria, since it has a history of taking all available discounts, as indicated by Susan Mastin. Thus, The Video Store Co. could report total accounts payable of $108,200 ($88,200 + $20,000) on its balance sheet. Merchandise Inventory would also need to be reduced by the discount of $1,800 in order to maintain consistency in approach.

Activity 6–3

1. If Brad doesn't need the stereo immediately (by the next day), Audio Pro Electronics offers the best buy, as shown below.

   Audio Pro Electronics:

List price...	$399.99
Shipping and handling (not including next-day air)	12.50
Total	$412.49

   Radiant Sound:

List price...	$395.00
Sales tax (6%)...	23.70
Total	$418.70

   Even if the 1% cash discount offered by Radiant Sound is considered, Audio Pro Electronics still offers the best buy, as shown below.

List price...	$395.00
Less 1% cash discount	3.95
Subtotal	$391.05
Sales tax (6%)...	23.46
Total	$414.51

   If Brad needs the stereo immediately (the next day), then Radiant Sound has the best price. This is because a shipping and handling charge of $25 would be added to the Audio Pro Electronics price, as shown below.

Audio Pro Electronics list price..	$399.99
Next-day freight charge..	25.00
Total	$424.99

   Since both Audio Pro Electronics and Radiant Sound will accept Brad's MasterCard, the ability to use a credit card would not affect the buying decision. Radiant Sound will, however, allow Brad to pay his bill in three installments (the first due immediately). This would allow Brad to save some interest charges on his MasterCard for two months. If we assume that Brad would have otherwise used his MasterCard and that Brad's MasterCard carries an interest of 1.5% per month on the unpaid balance, the potential interest savings would be calculated as follows:

Activity 6–3 Concluded

Radiant Sound price (see previous page)	$418.70
Less first installment (down payment)................................	139.57
Remaining balance	$279.13
Interest for first month at 1.5%	$ 4.19
($279.13 × 1.5%)	
Remaining balance ($279.13 + $4.19).................................	$283.32
Less second installment	139.57
Remaining balance	$143.75
Interest for second month at 1.5%	$ 2.16
($143.75 × 1.5%)	

The total interest savings would be $6.35 ($4.19 + $2.16). This interest savings would be enough to just offset the price advantage of Audio Pro Electronics, as shown below, resulting in a $0.14 price advantage ($412.49 − $412.35) to Radiant Sound.

Radiant Sound price (see above)	$418.70
Less interest savings	6.35
Total	$412.35

2. Other considerations in buying the stereo include the ability to have the stereo repaired locally by Radiant Sound. In addition, Radiant Sound employees would presumably be available to answer questions on the operation and installation of the stereo. In addition, if Brad purchased the stereo from Radiant Sound, he would have the stereo the same day rather than the next day, which is the earliest that Audio Pro Electronics could deliver the stereo.

Activity 6–4

1.

CALLENDER PARTS COMPANY
Projected Income Statement
For the Year Ended March 31, 2007

Revenues:		
Net sales (a)		$1,056,000
Interest revenue		8,000
Total revenues		$1,064,000
Expenses:		
Cost of merchandise sold (b)	$739,200	
Selling expenses (c)	74,480	
Administrative expenses (d)	54,848	
Interest expense	16,000	
Total expenses		884,528
Net income		$ 179,472

Notes:

(a) Projected net sales		
[$960,000 + (10% × $960,000)]		$1,056,000
(b) Projected cost of merchandise sold		
($1,056,000 × 70%)		$ 739,200
(c) Total selling expenses for year ended		
March 31, 2006		$ 105,600
Add: Increase in store supplies expense		
($8,000 × 10%)	$800	
Increase in miscellaneous selling expense		
($3,200 × 10%)	320	1,120
Less transportation-out expenses		(32,240)
Projected total selling expenses		$ 74,480
(d) Total administrative expenses for year ended		
March 31, 2006		$ 54,400
Add: Increase in office supplies expense		
($1,600 × 10%)	$160	
Increase in miscellaneous administrative		
expense ($2,880 × 10%)	288	448
Projected total administrative expenses		$ 54,848

Activity 6–4 Concluded

2. a. Yes. The proposed change will increase net income from $120,000 to $179,472, a change of $59,472.

    b. Possible concerns related to the proposed changes include the following:

    The primary concern is with the accuracy of the estimates used for projecting the effects of the proposed changes. If the increase in sales does not materialize, Callender Parts Company could incur significant costs of carrying excess inventory stocked in anticipation of increasing sales. At the same time it is incurring these additional inventory costs, cash collections from customers will be reduced by the amount of the discounts. This could create a liquidity problem for Callender Parts Company.

    Another concern arises from the proposed change in shipping terms so as to eliminate all shipments of merchandise FOB destination, thereby eliminating transportation-out expenses. Callender Parts Company assumes that this change will have no effect on sales. However, some (perhaps a significant number) customers may object to this change and may seek other vendors with more favorable shipping terms. Hence, an unanticipated decline in sales could occur because of this change.

    As with any business decision, risks (concerns) such as those mentioned above must be thoroughly considered before final action is taken.

Activity 6–5

Note to Instructors: The purpose of this activity is to familiarize students with the variety of possible purchase prices for a fairly common household item. Students should report several alternative prices when they consider the source of the purchase and the other factors that affect the purchase, e.g., delivery, financing, warranties, etc.

CHAPTER 7
CASH

CLASS DISCUSSION QUESTIONS

1. Many transactions affect cash, and it is the asset most susceptible to improper diversion and use because of its high value in relation to its mass and its ease of transfer among parties. For these reasons, the control of cash often warrants special attention.

2. a. Cash Short and Over
   b. Cash shortages are debited to this account.

3. Other income section

4. The three documents supporting the liability are vendor's invoice, purchase order, and receiving report. The invoice should be compared with the receiving report to determine that the items billed have been received and with the purchase order to verify quantities, prices, and terms.

5. A voucher is recorded after it has been approved for payment.

6. The prenumbering of checks and the paying of all obligations by check are desirable elements of internal control. The fundamental weakness in internal control is the failure to separate the responsibility for the maintenance of the accounting records (bookkeeping) from the responsibility for operations (payment of obligations).

7. a. In the unpaid voucher file, the vouchers should be filed by the due dates so that each voucher can be paid when due.
   b. In the paid voucher file, the vouchers should be filed in numerical order so that they can be easily located when needed.

8. The Cash balance and the bank statement balance are likely to differ because of (1) a delay by bank or depositor in recording transactions (such as checks or deposits) or (2) errors by bank or depositor in recording transactions.

9. The purpose of a bank reconciliation is to determine the reasons for the difference between the balance according to the depositor's records and the balance according to the bank statement, and to correct those items representing errors in recording that may have been made by the bank or by the depositor.

10. Additions made by the bank to the depositor's balance

11. Accounts Receivable should be debited and Cash should be credited.

12. Payments of small amounts by check often result in delay, annoyance, and excessive expense of maintaining records and processing the payments. For these reasons, small cash payments are made from a petty cash fund.

13. a. Petty Cash
    b. Various expense and asset accounts as indicated by a summary of expenditures

14. The fund should be replenished as of the last day of the period. It is the simplest means of recording the $690 of expenditures in the appropriate accounts and restoring the amount of the petty cash to the amount shown in the ledger account.

15. Cash and cash equivalents are usually reported as one amount in the Current Assets section of the balance sheet.

16. The details of a compensating balance are reported in notes to the financial statements.

EXERCISES

Ex. 7–1

a. The sales clerks should not have access to the cash register tapes.

b. The cash register tapes should be locked in the cash register and the key retained by the cashier. An employee of the cashier's office should remove the cash register tape, record the total on the memorandum form, and note discrepancies.

Ex. 7–2

Awesome Burgers suffers from a failure to separate responsibilities for related operations.

Awesome Burgers could stop this theft by limiting the drive-through clerk to taking customer orders, entering them on the cash register, accepting the customers' payments, returning customers' change, and handing customers their orders that another employee has assembled. By making another employee responsible for assembling orders, the drive-through clerk must enter the orders on the cash register. This will produce a printed receipt or an entry on a computer screen at the food bin area, specifying the items that must be assembled to fill each order. Once the drive-through clerk has entered the sale on the cash register, the clerk cannot steal the customer's payment because the clerk's cash drawer will not balance at the end of the shift. This change also makes the drive-through more efficient and could reduce the time it takes to service a drive-through customer.

If another employee cannot be added, the weakness in internal control could be improved with more thorough supervision. The restaurant manager should be directed to keep a watchful eye on the drive-through area in order to detect when a clerk takes an order without ringing up the sale.

Ex. 7–3

a. The remittance advices should not be sent to the cashier.

b. The remittance advices should be sent directly to the Accounting Department by the mailroom.

Ex. 7–4

Cash	17,572.40	
Cash Short and Over	17.25	
Sales		17,589.65

Ex. 7–5

Cash	6,973.60	
Sales		6,932.15
Cash Short and Over		41.45

Ex. 7–6

The use of the voucher system is appropriate, the essentials of which are outlined below. (Although invoices could be used instead of vouchers, the latter more satisfactorily provide for account distribution, signatures, and other significant data.)

1. Each voucher should be approved for payment by a designated official only after completion of the following verifications: (a) that prices, quantities, terms, etc., on the invoice are in accordance with the provisions of the purchase order, (b) that all quantities billed have been received in good condition, as indicated on a receiving report, and (c) that all arithmetic details are correct.

2. The file for unpaid vouchers should be composed of 31 compartments, one for each day of the month. Each voucher should be filed in the compartment representing the last day of the discount period or the due date if the invoice is not subject to a cash discount.

3. Each day, the vouchers should be removed from the appropriate section of the file and checks issued by the disbursing official. If the bank balance is insufficient to pay all of the vouchers, those that remain unpaid should be refiled according to the date when payment should next be considered.

4. At the time of payment, all vouchers and supporting documents should be stamped or perforated "Paid" to prevent their resubmission for payment. They should then be filed in numerical sequence for future reference.

Ex. 7–14

1. The heading should be for April 30, 2006, and not For the Month Ended April 30, 2006.

2. The outstanding checks should be deducted from the balance per bank.

3. The deposit of April 30, not recorded by the bank, should be added to the balance per bank.

4. In deducting the deposit of April 30, not recorded by the bank, the adjusted balance of $9,637.50 is mathematically incorrect. It should be $10,637.50.

5. Service charges should be deducted from the balance per depositor's records.

6. The error in recording the April 10 deposit of $4,850 as $4,580 should be added to the balance per depositor's records.

A correct bank reconciliation would be as follows:

IMAGING SERVICES CO.
Bank Reconciliation
April 30, 2006

Cash balance according to bank statement..			$ 9,767.76
Add deposit of April 30, not recorded by bank			1,010.06
			$10,777.82
Deduct outstanding checks:			
No. 821		$ 345.95	
839		272.75	
843		759.60	
844		501.50	1,879.80
Adjusted balance			$ 8,898.02
Cash balance according to depositor's			
records			$ 1,118.32
Add: Proceeds of note collected by bank:			
Principal	$8,000.00		
Interest	280.00	$8,280.00	
Error in recording April 10 deposit as			
$4,580 instead of $4,850		270.00	8,550.00
			$ 9,668.32
Deduct: Check returned because			
of insufficient funds		$ 752.30	
Service charges		18.00	770.30
Adjusted balance			$ 8,898.02

Ex. 7–15

a. The amount of cash receipts stolen by the sales clerk can be determined by attempting to reconcile the bank account. The bank reconciliation will not reconcile by the amount of cash receipts stolen. The amount stolen by the sales clerk is $6,207.18, determined as shown below.

PROMETHEUS CO.
Bank Reconciliation
April 30, 2006

Cash balance according to bank statement.................................	$13,271.14
Deduct: Outstanding checks...	1,750.20
Adjusted balance...	$11,520.94
Cash balance according to depositor's records	$12,573.22
Add: Note collected by bank, including interest...........................	5,200.00
	$17,773.22
Deduct: Bank service charges	45.10
Adjusted balance...	$17,728.12

Amount stolen: $6,207.18 ($17,728.12 – $11,520.94)

b. The theft of the cash receipts might have been prevented by having more than one person make the daily deposit. Collusion between two individuals would then have been necessary to steal cash receipts. In addition, two employees making the daily cash deposits would tend to discourage theft of the cash receipts from the employees on the way to the bank.

   Daily reconciliation of the amount of cash receipts, comparing the cash register tapes to a receipt from the bank as to the amount deposited (a duplicate deposit ticket), would also discourage theft of the cash receipts. In this latter case, if the reconciliation were prepared by an employee independent of the cash function, any theft of cash receipts from the daily deposit would be discovered immediately. That is, the daily deposit would not reconcile against the daily cash receipts.

Prob. 7–2A

2006				
June	1	Petty Cash..	600.00	
		Cash		600.00
	6	Cash	8,008.15	
		Cash Short and Over		9.65
		Sales..		7,998.50
	30	Store Supplies	30.75	
		Merchandise Inventory	166.25	
		Office Supplies	161.50	
		Miscellaneous Administrative Expense	179.50	
		Cash Short and Over	11.25	
		Cash		549.25
	30	Cash	8,988.35	
		Cash Short and Over	21.15	
		Sales..		9,009.50
	30	Cash	150.00	
		Petty Cash..		150.00

Prob. 7–3A

1.

SHOWTIME SYSTEMS
Bank Reconciliation
February 28, 2006

Cash balance according to bank statement......................		$31,391.40
Add deposit of February 28, not recorded by bank........		6,215.50
		$37,606.90
Deduct: Outstanding checks..	$11,021.50	
Bank error in charging check as $585 instead of $855...	270.00	11,291.50
Adjusted balance...		$26,315.40
Cash balance according to depositor's records............		$19,144.15
Add: Proceeds of note collected by bank, including $300 interest..	$ 6,300.00	
Error in recording check.......................................	900.00	7,200.00
		$26,344.15
Deduct bank service charges..		28.75
Adjusted balance...		$26,315.40

2.	Cash...	7,200.00	
	Notes Receivable...		6,000.00
	Interest Revenue...		300.00
	Accounts Payable—Wilson Co.		900.00
	Miscellaneous Administrative Expense......................	28.75	
	Cash..		28.75

Prob. 7–4A

1.

ALPINE SPORTS CO.
Bank Reconciliation
April 30, 2006

Balance per bank statement..		$18,880.45
Add deposit of April 30, not recorded by bank		3,481.70
		$22,362.15
Deduct: Outstanding checks	$ 5,180.27	
Bank error in charging check as $260		
instead of $620	360.00	5,540.27
Adjusted balance		$16,821.88
Balance per depositor's records....................................		$14,284.88*
Add: Proceeds of note collected by bank,		
including $224 interest....................................	$ 3,424.00	
Error in recording check	18.00	3,442.00
		$17,726.88
Deduct: Check returned because of insufficient funds	$ 880.00	
Bank service charges...	25.00	905.00
Adjusted balance		$16,821.88
*Cash balance, April 1......................................	$16,911.95	
Plus cash deposited in April.....................................	65,500.40	
Less checks written in April	(68,127.47)	
Balance per depositor's records, April 30...............	$14,284.88	

2. Cash	3,442.00	
Notes Receivable...		3,200.00
Interest Revenue...		224.00
Accounts Payable—Bray & Son		18.00
Accounts Receivable—Shuler Co.	880.00	
Miscellaneous Administrative Expense.......................	25.00	
Cash...		905.00

Prob. 7–5A

1.

ROCKY MOUNTAIN INTERIORS
Bank Reconciliation
May 31, 20—

Cash balance according to bank statement....................		$14,145.54
Add deposit of May 31, not recorded by bank		1,325.05
		$15,470.59
Deduct outstanding checks:		
No. 602	$ 85.50	
628	837.70	
634	303.30	1,226.50
Adjusted balance		$14,244.09
Cash balance according to depositor's records		$ 8,531.99*
Add proceeds of note collected by bank:		
Principal	$ 5,000.00	
Interest	400.00	
Add error in recording Check No. 632	561.60	5,961.60
		$14,493.59
Deduct: Check returned because of insufficient funds .	$ 225.40	
Service charges	24.10	249.50
Adjusted balance		$14,244.09
*Balance per cash in bank account, May 1	$10,578.00	
Add May receipts	6,630.60	
Deduct May disbursements	(8,676.61)	
Balance per cash in bank account, May 31..............	$ 8,531.99	

2. Cash..	5,961.60	
Notes Receivable...		5,000.00
Interest Revenue...		400.00
Accounts Payable...		561.60
Accounts Receivable...	225.40	
Miscellaneous Administrative Expense......................	24.10	
Cash..		249.50

3. $14,244.09

4.   The error of $360 in the canceled check should be added to the "balance according to bank statement" on the bank reconciliation. The canceled check should be presented to the bank, with a request that the bank balance be corrected.

Prob. 7–1B

Strengths: a, e, g, and h

Weaknesses:

b. The bank reconciliation should be prepared by someone not involved with the handling or recording of cash.

c. Requiring cash register clerks to make up any cash shortages from their own funds gives the clerks an incentive to short-change customers. That is, the clerks will want to make sure that they don't have a shortage at the end of the day. In addition, one might also assume that the clerks can keep any overages. This would again encourage clerks to short-change customers. The short-changing of customers will create customer complaints, etc. The best policy is to report any cash shortages or overages at the end of each day. If a clerk is consistently short or over, then corrective action (training, removal, etc.) could be taken.

d. Employees should not be allowed to use the petty cash fund to cash personal checks. In any case, post-dated checks should not be accepted. In effect, post-dated checks represent a receivable from the employees.

f. The mail clerk should prepare an initial listing of cash remittances before forwarding the cash receipts to the cashier. This establishes initial accountability for the cash receipts. The mail clerk should forward a copy of the listing of remittances to the accounts receivable clerk for recording in the accounts.

Prob. 7–2B

2006

Mar.	1	Petty Cash...	850.00	
		Cash		850.00
	18	Cash	12,007.50	
		Cash Short and Over		36.90
		Sales...		11,970.60
	31	Store Supplies	198.10	
		Transportation Out......................................	245.00	
		Office Supplies	178.20	
		Miscellaneous Administrative Expense	190.00	
		Cash Short and Over....................................	18.52	
		Cash		829.82
	31	Cash	9,010.25	
		Cash Short and Over....................................	45.25	
		Sales...		9,055.50
	31	Petty Cash...	100.00	
		Cash		100.00

Prob. 7–3B

1.

PICKRON CO.
Bank Reconciliation
April 30, 2006

Cash balance according to bank statement....................		$18,016.30
Add: Deposit of April 30, not recorded by bank............	$5,189.40	
Bank error in charging check as $1,860 instead		
of $1,680	180.00	5,369.40
		$23,385.70
Deduct outstanding checks...		7,169.75
Adjusted balance		$16,215.95
Cash balance according to depositor's records		$13,290.95
Add proceeds of note collected by bank, including		
$240 interest		3,240.00
		$16,530.95
Deduct: Error in recording check.................................	$ 270.00	
Bank service charges...................................	45.00	315.00
Adjusted balance		$16,215.95

2. Cash...	3,240.00	
Notes Receivable...		3,000.00
Interest Revenue..		240.00
Accounts Payable—Jones Co.	270.00	
Miscellaneous Administrative Expense........................	45.00	
Cash...		315.00

Prob. 7–4B

1.

SEAL-TEK CO.
Bank Reconciliation
December 31, 2006

Balance per bank statement..		$5,465.50
Add: Deposit of December 31 not recorded by bank....	$ 2,148.21	
Bank error in charging check as $1,200 instead		
of $120	1,080.00	3,228.21
		$8,693.71
Deduct outstanding checks...		3,003.84
Adjusted balance..		$5,689.87
Balance per depositor's records..		$4,627.87*
Add proceeds of note collected by bank,		
including $108 interest...		1,908.00
		$6,535.87
Deduct: Check returned because of insufficient funds	$ 636.00	
Bank service charges..	30.00	
Error in recording check.......................................	180.00	846.00
Adjusted balance..		$5,689.87

*Cash balance, December 1	$ 3,945.90	
Plus cash deposited in December...........................	31,077.75	
Less checks written in December	(30,395.78)	
Balance per depositor's books, December 31	$ 4,627.87	

2. Cash...	1,908.00	
Notes Receivable..		1,800.00
Interest Revenue...		108.00
Accounts Payable—Kenyon Co.	180.00	
Accounts Receivable—Fontana Co.............................	636.00	
Miscellaneous Administrative Expense.......................	30.00	
Cash...		846.00

SPECIAL ACTIVITIES

Activity 7–1

Acceptable business and professional conduct requires Chris Renees to notify the bank of the error. *Note to Instructors:* Individuals may be criminally prosecuted for knowingly using funds that are erroneously credited to their bank accounts.

Activity 7–2

Several control procedures could be implemented to prevent or detect the theft of cash from fictitious returns.

One procedure would be to establish a policy of "no cash refunds." That is, returns could only be exchanged for other merchandise. However, such a policy might not be popular with customers, and Reboot Electronics might lose sales from customers who would shop at other stores with a more liberal return policy.

Another procedure would be to allow returns only through a centralized location, such as a customer service desk. The customer service desk clerk would issue an approved refund slip, which the customer could then take to a cash register to receive a cash refund. Since the customer service clerk does not have access to cash, the customer service clerk could not steal cash through fictitious returns.

Yet another procedure would be to allow returns at the individual cash registers but require that all returns be approved by a supervisor. In this way, cash could be stolen through fictitious returns only with collusion of the supervisor and the cash register clerk.

Activity 7–3

Several possible procedures for preventing or detecting the theft of grocery items by failing to scan their prices include the following:

a. Most scanning systems are designed so that an audible beep is heard each time an item is rung up on the cash register. This is intended to alert the cashier that the item has been properly rung up. Thus, observing whether a cashier is ringing up all merchandise can be accomplished by standing near the cash register and listening for the beeps. Such observations might be done on a periodic, surprise basis by supervisors.

b. Some grocery stores have their cash registers networked so that a monitor in a centralized office, usually high above the floor, can monitor any cash register's activity. In this way, a supervisor could monitor cash register activity on a periodic basis.

c. Although this detection procedure would probably not be used in a grocery store, it is used by Sam's Clubs to detect this activity. Specifically, an employee is stationed at the exit to the store and checks each cash register receipt against the items with which the customer is leaving the store. This would not work well for a grocery store because of the large number of items that are usually placed in grocery bags at the checkout counter.

Activity 7–4

Kerri is clearly behaving in an unprofessional manner in intentionally short-changing her customers.

At this point, Tim is in a difficult position. He is apparently adhering to Frontier Markets' policy of making up shortages out of his own pocket, but he is obviously upset about it. If Tim accepts Kerri's advice, he will be engaging in unprofessional behavior. Tim is also faced with the dilemma of whether he should report Kerri's behavior. If Tim continues to work for Frontier Markets, his best course of action is simply to try to do the best job possible in not making errors in ringing up sales and providing customers change.

One could argue that Rostad is also acting in an unprofessional manner. First, allowing Kerri to keep overages will simply encourage her to continue to short-change customers. Second, since Kerri has had no shortages in over a year, it should be obvious to Rostad that Kerri is short-changing customers. Therefore, as store manager, Rostad should take action to stop Kerri's behavior. Better yet, Rostad should consider revising Frontier Markets' control policy on shortages and overages. The cash register clerks should be required to report all shortages and overages without having to make up shortages from their own pockets. The cash register clerks could then be monitored for their effectiveness in making change for customers. Unusual amounts or trends could be investigated and corrective action taken, such as training, reassigning employees to other duties, etc. In any case, employees should not be allowed to keep overages at the end of each day.

Activity 7–5

1. There are several methods that could be used to determine how much the cashier has stolen. The method described below is based on preparing a bank reconciliation as illustrated in this chapter. Because of the theft of the undeposited receipts, the bank reconciliation adjusted balances will not agree. The difference between the adjusted balances is the estimate of the amount stolen by the cashier.

LUMBERJACK COMPANY
Bank Reconciliation
July 31, 20—

Balance according to bank statement............................		$ 6,004.95
Add undeposited cash receipts on hand.........................		5,000.00
		$11,004.95
Deduct outstanding checks:		
No. 670	$781.20	
679	610.00	
690	716.50	
1996	127.40	
1997	520.00	
1999	851.50	3,606.60
Adjusted balance		$ 7,398.35
Balance according to depositor's records........................		$ 9,806.05
Add note collected by bank, with interest.......................		4,240.00
Adjusted balance		$14,046.05
Adjusted balance according to depositor's records		$14,046.05
Adjusted balance according to bank statement		7,398.35
Amount stolen by cashier...		$ 6,647.70

Note to Instructors: The amount stolen by the cashier could also be computed directly from the cashier-prepared bank reconciliation as follows:

Outstanding checks omitted from the bank reconciliation prepared by the cashier:		
No. 670	$781.20	
679	610.00	
690	716.50	$ 2,107.70
Unrecorded note plus interest incorrectly recorded on the bank reconciliation prepared by the cashier.....		4,240.00
Addition error in the total of the outstanding checks in the bank reconciliation prepared by the cashier*....		300.00
		$ 6,647.70

Note: The cashier has altered the adding machine tape so that the total is not correct.

CHAPTER 8
RECEIVABLES

CLASS DISCUSSION QUESTIONS

1. Receivables are normally classified as (1) accounts receivable, (2) notes receivable, or (3) other receivables.
2. Transactions in which merchandise is sold or services are provided on credit generate accounts receivable.
3. **a.** Current assets
   b. Investments
4. Examples of other receivables include interest receivable, taxes receivable, and receivables from officers or employees.
5. The principle of separation of operations and accounting is violated. (*Note to Instructors:* This weakness in internal control may permit embezzlement. For example, the accounts receivable clerk may misappropriate cash receipts and cover the misappropriation by a process called lapping. In lapping, the cash receipts from one account are taken and the cash received on a subsequent account is used to cover the shortage. The receipts on another account are then used to cover the shortage in this latter customer's account, etc. This lapping generally continues until the records are falsified to correct for the shortage, the cash is returned by the clerk, or the embezzlement is discovered.)
6. The allowance method
7. Contra asset, credit balance
8. The accounts receivable and allowance for doubtful accounts may be reported at a net amount of $759,900 ($883,150 − $123,250) in the Current Assets section of the balance sheet. In this case, the amount of the allowance for doubtful accounts should be shown separately in a note to the financial statements or in parentheses on the balance sheet. Alternatively, the accounts receivable may be shown at the gross amount of $883,150 less the amount of the allowance for doubtful accounts of $123,250, thus yielding net accounts receivable of $759,900.

9. **1.** The percentage rate used is excessive in relationship to the volume of accounts written off as uncollectible; hence, the balance in the allowance is excessive.
   2. A substantial volume of old uncollectible accounts is still being carried in the accounts receivable account.
10. An estimate based on analysis of receivables provides the most accurate estimate of the current net realizable value.
11. The advantages of a claim evidenced by a note are (1) the debt is acknowledged, (2) the payment terms are specified, (3) it is a stronger claim in the event of court action, and (4) it is usually more readily transfer to a creditor in settlement of a debt or bank for cash.
12. **a.** Ellsworth Company
    b. Notes Receivable
13. The interest will amount to $6,300 only if the note is payable one year from the date it was created. The usual practice is to state the interest rate in terms of an annual rate, rather than in terms of the period covered by the note.
14. Debit Accounts Receivable
    Credit Notes Receivable
    Credit Interest Revenue
15. Cash............................ 20,806
       Accounts Receivable   20,600
       Interest Revenue......   206
    ($20,600 × 30/360 × 12% = $206)
16. Current assets

EXERCISES

Ex. 8–1

a. **Inappropriate.** Since Fridley has a large number of credit sales supported by promissory notes, a notes receivable ledger should be maintained. Failure to maintain a subsidiary ledger when there are a significant number of notes receivable transactions violates the internal control procedure that mandates proofs and security. Maintaining a notes receivable ledger will allow Fridley to operate more efficiently and will increase the chance that Fridley will detect accounting errors related to the notes receivable. (The total of the accounts in the notes receivable ledger must match the balance of notes receivable in the general ledger.)

b. **Inappropriate.** The procedure of proper separation of duties is violated. The accounts receivable clerk is responsible for too many related operations. The clerk also has both custody of assets (cash receipts) and accounting responsibilities for those assets.

c. **Appropriate.** The functions of maintaining the accounts receivable account in the general ledger should be performed by someone other than the accounts receivable clerk.

d. **Appropriate.** Salespersons should not be responsible for approving credit.

e. **Appropriate.** A promissory note is a formal credit instrument that is frequently used for credit periods over 45 days.

Ex. 8–2

a. Hotel accounts and notes receivable:
   $3,256,000 \div \$75,796,000 = 4.3\%$

b. Casino accounts receivable:
   $6,654,000 \div \$26,334,000 = 25.3\%$

c. Casino operations experience greater bad debt risk than do hotel operations, since it is difficult to control the creditworthiness of customers entering the casino. In addition, individuals who may have adequate creditworthiness may overextend themselves and lose more than they can afford if they get caught up in the excitement of gambling.

Ex. 8–3

Account	Due Date	Number of Days Past Due
Bear Creek Body Shop	June 8	53 (22 + 31)
First Auto	July 3	28
Kaiser Repair	March 20	133 (11 + 30 + 31 + 30 + 31)
Master's Auto Repair	May 15	77 (16 + 30 + 31)
Richter Auto	June 18	43 (12 + 31)
Sabol's	April 12	110 (18 + 31 + 30 + 31)
Uptown Auto	May 8	84 (23 + 30 + 31)
Westside Repair & Tow	May 31	61 (30 + 31)

Ex. 8–4

a.

Customer	Due Date	Number of Days Past Due
Janzen Industries	August 29	93 days (2 + 30 + 31 + 30)
Kuehn Company	September 3	88 days (27 + 31 + 30)
Mauer Inc.	October 21	40 days (10 + 30)
Pollack Company	November 23	7 days
Simrill Company	December 3	Not past due

b.

Aging of Accounts Receivable
November 30

Customer	Balance	Not Past Due	Days Past Due 1–30	31–60	61–90	Over 90
Aaker Brothers Inc.	2,000	2,000				
Aitken Company	1,500		1,500			
~~	~~~~~	~~~~~	~~~~~	~~~~~	~~~~~	~~~~~
Zollo Company	5,000			5,000		
Subtotals	972,500	640,000	180,000	78,500	42,300	31,700
Janzen Industries	40,000					40,000
Keuhn Company	8,500				8,500	
Mauer Inc.	18,000			18,000		
Pollack Company	6,500		6,500			
Simrill Company	7,500	7,500				
Totals	1,053,000	647,500	186,500	96,500	50,800	71,700

Ex. 8–5

	Balance	Not Past Due	Days Past Due			
			1–30	31–60	61–90	Over 90
Total receivables	$1,053,000	$647,500	$186,500	$96,500	$50,800	$71,700
Percentage Uncollectible		1%	4%	8%	20%	40%
Allowances for Doubtful Accounts	$60,495	$6,475	$7,460	$7,720	$10,160	$28,680

Ex. 8–6

Nov. 30	Uncollectible Accounts Expense........................	53,315*	
	Allowances for Doubtful Accounts		53,315

*$60,495 – $7,180 = $53,315

Ex. 8–7

		Estimated Uncollectible Accounts	
Age Interval	Balance	Percent	Amount
Not past due................................	$450,000	2%	$ 9,000
1–30 days past due....................	110,000	4	4,400
31–60 days past due..................	51,000	6	3,060
61–90 days past due..................	12,500	20	2,500
91–180 days past due................	7,500	60	4,500
Over 180 days past due.............	5,500	80	4,400
Total..	$636,500		$27,860

Ex. 8–8

2006

Dec. 31	Uncollectible Accounts Expense........................	29,435*	
	Allowance for Doubtful Accounts		29,435

*$27,860 + $1,575 = $29,435

Ex. 8–9

a. $17,875   c. $35,750
b. $13,600   d. $41,450

Ex. 8–10

a.   Allowance for Doubtful Accounts 7,130
         Accounts Receivable... 7,130

b.   Uncollectible Accounts Expense................................. 7,130
         Accounts Receivable... 7,130

Ex. 8–11

Feb. 20	Accounts Receivable—Darlene Brogan	12,100	
	Sales		12,100
20	Cost of Merchandise Sold	7,260	
	Merchandise Inventory....................................		7,260
May 30	Cash	6,000	
	Accounts Receivable—Darlene Brogan		6,000
30	Allowance for Doubtful Accounts......................	6,100	
	Accounts Receivable—Darlene Brogan		6,100
Aug. 3	Accounts Receivable—Darlene Brogan	6,100	
	Allowance for Doubtful Accounts		6,100
3	Cash	6,100	
	Accounts Receivable—Darlene Brogan		6,100

Ex. 8–12

July	6	Accounts Receivable—Dr. Jerry Jagers	18,500	
		Sales		18,500
	6	Cost of Merchandise Sold	11,100	
		Merchandise Inventory		11,100
Sept.	12	Cash	9,000	
		Accounts Receivable—Dr. Jerry Jagers.....		9,000
	12	Uncollectible Accounts Expense	9,500	
		Accounts Receivable—Dr. Jerry Jagers.....		9,500
Dec.	20	Accounts Receivable—Dr. Jerry Jagers	9,500	
		Uncollectible Accounts Expense		9,500
	20	Cash	9,500	
		Accounts Receivable—Dr. Jerry Jagers.....		9,500

Ex. 8–13

$223,900 [$212,800 + $112,350 − ($4,050,000 × 2 1/2%)]

Ex. 8–14

a. $257,100 [$262,300 + $114,800 − ($4,800,000 × 2 1/2%)]

b. $5,900 Dr. [($101,250 − $112,350) + ($120,000 − $114,800)]

Ex. 8–15

	Due Date	Interest
a.	Aug. 31	$120
b.	Dec. 28	480
c.	Nov. 30	250
d.	May 5	150
e.	July 19	100

Ex. 8–16

a. August 8

b. $24,480

c. (1) Notes Receivable.. 24,000

          Accounts Rec.—Magpie Interior Decorators   24,000

   (2) Cash... 24,480

          Notes Receivable   24,000

          Interest Revenue   480

Ex. 8–17

1. Sale on account.
2. Cost of merchandise sold for the sale on account.
3. A sales return or allowance.
4. Cost of merchandise returned.
5. Note received from customer on account.
6. Note dishonored and charged maturity value of note to customer's account receivable.
7. Payment received from customer for dishonored note plus interest earned after due date.

Ex. 8–18

2005

Dec.	13	Notes Receivable	25,000	
		Accounts Receivable—Visage Co...............		25,000
	31	Interest Receivable	75*	
		Interest Revenue...		75
	31	Interest Revenue	75	
		Income Summary...		75

2006

Apr.	12	Cash	25,500	
		Notes Receivable..		25,000
		Interest Receivable.....................................		75
		Interest Revenue..		425

*$25,000 \times 0.06 \times 18/360 = \$75$

Ex. 8–19

July	8	Notes Receivable	30,000.00	
		Accounts Receivable—Pennington Co.......		30,000.00
Oct.	6	Accounts Receivable—Pennington Co.	30,600.00	
		Notes Receivable..		30,000.00
		Interest Revenue..		600.00
Nov.	5	Cash	30,855.00	
		Accounts Receivable—Pennington Co.......		30,600.00
		Interest Revenue..		255.00*

*$30,600 \times 0.10 \times 30/360 = \$255.00$

Ex. 8–20

Mar.	1	Notes Receivable	15,000	
		Accounts Receivable—Absaroka Co.		15,000
	18	Notes Receivable	12,000	
		Accounts Receivable—Sturgis Co.		12,000
Apr.	30	Accounts Receivable—Absaroka Co.	15,125	
		Notes Receivable		15,000
		Interest Revenue		125
June	16	Accounts Receivable—Sturgis Co.	12,270	
		Notes Receivable		12,000
		Interest Revenue		270
July	11	Cash	15,367	
		Accounts Receivable—Absaroka Co.		15,125
		Interest Revenue		242*

*$15,125 × 0.08 × 72/360 = $242

Oct.	12	Allowance for Doubtful Accounts	12,270	
		Accounts Receivable—Sturgis Co.		12,270

Ex. 8–21

1. The interest receivable should be reported separately as a current asset. It should not be deducted from notes receivable.

2. The allowance for doubtful accounts should be deducted from accounts receivable.

A corrected partial balance sheet would be as follows:

PEMBROKE COMPANY
Balance Sheet
July 31, 2006

Assets

Current assets:		
Cash...		$ 43,750
Notes receivable..		300,000
Accounts receivable..	$576,180	
Less allowance for doubtful accounts..............	71,200	504,980
Interest receivable...		18,000

Ex. 8–22

a. 2003:   53.0 {$9,953,530 ÷ [($216,200 + $159,477) ÷ 2]}
   2002:   44.8 {$9,518,231 ÷ [($159,477 + $265,515) ÷ 2]}

b. The accounts receivable turnover indicates an increase in the efficiency of collecting accounts receivable by increasing from 44.8 to 53.0, a favorable trend. Before reaching a more definitive conclusion, the ratios should be compared with industry averages and similar firms.

Ex. 8–23

a. 2003:   7.9 days [$216,200 ÷ ($9,953,530 ÷ 365)]
   2002:   6.1 days [$159,477 ÷ ($9,518,231 ÷ 365)]

b. The number of days' sales in receivables indicates a decrease in the efficiency of collecting accounts receivable by increasing from 6.1 days to 7.9 days, an unfavorable trend. Before reaching a more definitive conclusion, the ratios should be compared with industry averages and similar firms.

Ex. 8–24

a. 2002:   108.2 {$9,363,000 ÷ [($79,000 + $94,000) ÷ 2]}
   2001:   99.6 {$10,105,000 ÷ [($94,000 + $109,000) ÷ 2]}

b. 2002:   3.1 days [$79,000 ÷ ($9,363,000 ÷ 365)]
   2001:   3.4 days [$94,000 ÷ ($10,105,000 ÷ 365)]

c. The accounts receivable turnover indicates a slight increase in the efficiency of collecting accounts receivable by increasing from 99.6 to 108.2, a favorable trend. The number of days' sales in receivables decreased from 3.4 days to 3.1 days, also indicating a favorable trend in collections of receivables. Before reaching a more definitive conclusion, both ratios should be compared with those of past years, industry averages, and similar firms.

Note to Instructors: The high accounts receivable turnover and low number of days' sales in receivables suggests that most of The Limited's sales are cash sales, such as those from MasterCard and VISA.

Appendix Ex. 8–25

a. $20,300

b. 60 days

c. $271 ($20,300 × 0.08 × 60/360)

d. $20,029 ($20,300 – $271)

e. Cash 20,029
    Interest Revenue 29
    Notes Receivable 20,000

Appendix Ex. 8–26

June 1   Notes Receivable 60,000
          Accounts Receivable—Rhodes Co. 60,000

July 1   Cash 60,344*
          Notes Receivable 60,000
          Interest Revenue 344
      *$60,800 – ($60,800 × 0.09 × 30/360) = $60,344

    31   Accounts Receivable—Rhodes Co. 61,000
          Cash 61,000

Aug. 30   Cash 61,610*
          Accounts Receivable—Rhodes Co. 61,000
          Interest Revenue 610
      *$61,000 + ($61,000 × 0.12 × 30/360) = $61,610

PROBLEMS

Prob. 8–1A

2.

2006

			Debit	Credit
Mar.	15	Cash	11,100	
		Accounts Receivable—Bimba Co.		11,100
	15	Allowance for Doubtful Accounts	7,400	
		Accounts Receivable—Bimba Co.		7,400
Apr.	16	Accounts Receivable—Tom Miner	5,782	
		Allowance for Doubtful Accounts		5,782
	16	Cash	5,782	
		Accounts Receivable—Tom Miner		5,782
July	20	Allowance for Doubtful Accounts	5,500	
		Accounts Receivable—Martz Co.		5,500
Oct.	31	Accounts Receivable—Two Bit Saloon Co.	6,100	
		Allowance for Doubtful Accounts		6,100
	31	Cash	6,100	
		Accounts Receivable—Two Bit Saloon Co.		6,100
Dec.	31	Allowance for Doubtful Accounts	9,250	
		Accounts Receivable—Asche Co.		950
		Dorsch Co.		4,600
		Krebs Distributors		2,500
		J. J. Levi		1,200
	31	Uncollectible Accounts Expense	11,918	
		Allowance for Doubtful Accounts		11,918
	31	Income Summary	11,918	
		Uncollectible Accounts Expense		11,918

Prob. 8–1A   Concluded

1. and 2.

Allowance for Doubtful Accounts   **115**

Date	Item	Dr.	Cr.	Balance Dr.	Balance Cr.
2006					
Jan. 1	Balance.................	....	....	....	12,050
Mar. 15	....	7,400	....	....	4,650
Apr. 16	....	....	5,782	....	10,432
July 20	....	5,500	....	....	4,932
Oct. 31	....	....	6,100	....	11,032
Dec. 31	....	9,250	....	....	1,782
31	....	....	11,918	....	13,700

Income Summary   **313**

Date	Item	Dr.	Cr.	Balance Dr.	Balance Cr.
2006					
Dec. 31	....	11,918	....	11,918	....

Uncollectible Accounts Expense   **718**

Date	Item	Dr.	Cr.	Balance Dr.	Balance Cr.
2006					
Dec. 31	....	11,918	....	11,918	....
31	....	....	11,918	—	—

3. $522,050 ($535,750 – $13,700)

4. a. $15,500 ($3,100,000 × 0.005)

   b. $17,282 ($15,500 + $1,782)

   c. $518,468 ($535,750 – $17,282)

Prob. 8–2A

1.

Customer	Due Date	Number of Days Past Due
Able Sports & Flies	June 15, 2006	199 days (15 + 31 + 31 + 30 + 31 + 30 + 31)
Red Tag Sporting Goods	July 28, 2006	156 days (3 + 31 + 30 + 31 + 30 + 31)
Highlite Flies	Sept. 11, 2006	111 days (19 + 31 + 30 + 31)
Midge Co.	Sept. 30, 2006	92 days (31 + 30 + 31)
Snake River Outfitters	Oct. 7, 2006	85 days (24 + 30 + 31)
Pheasant Tail Sports	Oct. 27, 2006	65 days (4 + 30 + 31)
Big Sky Sports	Oct. 30, 2006	62 days (1 + 30 + 31)
Ross Sports	Nov. 18, 2006	43 days (12 + 31)
Sawyer's Pheasant Tail	Nov. 26, 2006	35 days (4 + 31)
Tent Caddis Outfitters	Nov. 29, 2006	32 days
Wulff Company	Dec. 10, 2006	21 days
Zug Bug Sports	Jan. 6, 2007	Not past due

Prob. 8–2A Concluded

2. and 3.

Aging of Accounts Receivable
December 31, 2006

Customer	Balance	Not Past Due	Days Past Due				
			1–30	31–60	61–90	91–120	Over 120
Alpha Fishery	5,000	5,000					
Brown Trout Sports	6,400			6,400			
~~							
Zinger Sports	2,900		2,900				
Subtotals	580,000	248,600	147,250	98,750	33,300	29,950	22,150
Able Sports & Flies	3,500						3,500
Red Tag Sporting Goods	4,000						4,000
Highlite Flies	2,500					2,500	
Midge Co.	3,100					3,100	
Snake River Outfitters	4,500				4,500		
Pheasant Tail Sports	1,600				1,600		
Big Sky Sports	2,000				2,000		
Ross Sports	500			500			
Sawyer's Pheasant Tail	2,800			2,800			
Tent Caddis Outfitters	3,500			3,500			
Wulff Company	1,000		1,000				
Zug Bug Sports	6,200	6,200					
Totals	615,200	254,800	148,250	105,550	41,400	35,550	29,650
Percentage Uncollectible		1%	4%	8%	25%	40%	80%
Estimate of Doubtful Accounts	65,212	2,548	5,930	8,444	10,350	14,220	23,720

4. Uncollectible Accounts Expense.................................. 68,012*
   Allowance for Doubtful Accounts 68,012

   *$65,212 + $2,800

Prob. 8–3A

1.

| | Uncollectible Accounts Expense | | | Balance of |
Year	Expense Actually Reported	Expense Based on Estimate	Increase (Decrease) in Amount of Expense	Allowance Account, End of Year
1st	$3,500	$ 6,375	$2,875	$ 2,875
2nd	3,250	7,200	3,950	6,825
3rd	6,300	9,000	2,700	9,525
4th	8,400	13,500	5,100	14,625

2. Yes. The actual write-offs of accounts originating in the first two years are reasonably close to the expense that would have been charged to those years on the basis of 3/4% of sales. The total write-off of receivables originating in the first year amounted to $6,200 ($3,500 + $1,900 + $800), as compared with uncollectible accounts expense, based on the percentage of sales, of $6,375. For the second year, the comparable amounts were $7,650 ($1,350 + $4,500 + $1,800) and $7,200.

Prob. 8–4A

1.

Note	(a) Due Date	(b) Interest Due at Maturity
(1)	May 6	$240
(2)	July 18	126
(3)	Dec. 28	204
(4)	Dec. 30	405
(5)	Jan. 18	120
(6)	Jan. 22	120

2.

Dec. 28	Accounts Receivable	10,404	
	Notes Receivable......................................		10,200
	Interest Revenue.......................................		204

3.

Dec. 31	Interest Receivable	116	
	Interest Revenue.......................................		116

$12,000 × 0.06 × 42/360 = $ 84
$16,000 × 0.09 × 8/360 = 32
Total $116

4.

Jan. 18	Cash	12,120	
	Notes Receivable......................................		12,000
	Interest Receivable...................................		84
	Interest Revenue.......................................		36
22	Cash	16,120	
	Notes Receivable......................................		16,000
	Interest Receivable...................................		32
	Interest Revenue.......................................		88

Prob. 8–5A

June 4	Notes Receivable	18,800	
	Accounts Receivable		18,800
July 15	Notes Receivable	27,000	
	Accounts Receivable		27,000
Aug. 3	Cash	19,082	
	Notes Receivable.......................................		18,800
	Interest Revenue.......................................		282
Sept. 1	Notes Receivable	24,000	
	Accounts Receivable		24,000
Oct. 31	Cash	24,360	
	Notes Receivable.......................................		24,000
	Interest Revenue.......................................		360
Nov. 5	Notes Receivable	9,600	
	Accounts Receivable		9,600
12	Cash	27,900	
	Notes Receivable.......................................		27,000
	Interest Revenue.......................................		900
30	Notes Receivable	15,000	
	Accounts Receivable		15,000
Dec. 5	Cash	9,656	
	Notes Receivable.......................................		9,600
	Interest Revenue.......................................		56
30	Cash	15,125	
	Notes Receivable.......................................		15,000
	Interest Revenue.......................................		125

Prob. 8–6A

Jan.	10	Notes Receivable	12,000	
		Cash..		12,000
Feb.	4	Accounts Receivable—Emerson and Son	24,000	
		Sales		24,000
	4	Cost of Merchandise Sold	14,400	
		Merchandise Inventory.................................		14,400
	12	Accounts Receivable—Gwyn Co.	25,000	
		Sales		25,000
	12	Cost of Merchandise Sold	15,000	
		Merchandise Inventory.................................		15,000
Mar.	6	Notes Receivable	24,000	
		Accounts Receivable—Emerson and Son .		24,000
	14	Notes Receivable	25,000	
		Accounts Receivable—Gwyn Co.		25,000
Apr.	10	Notes Receivable	12,000	
		Cash	240	
		Notes Receivable...		12,000
		Interest Revenue...		240
May	5	Cash	24,240	
		Notes Receivable...		24,000
		Interest Revenue...		240
	13	Accounts Receivable—Gwyn Co.	25,500	
		Notes Receivable...		25,000
		Interest Revenue...		500
June	12	Cash	25,755	
		Accounts Receivable—Gwyn Co.		25,500
		Interest Revenue...		255
		($25,500 × 0.12 × 30/360 = $255)		
July	9	Cash	12,270	
		Notes Receivable...		12,000
		Interest Revenue...		270

Prob. 8–6A   Continued

Aug. 24	Accounts Receivable—Haggerty Co.	10,200	
	Sales		10,200
24	Cost of Merchandise Sold	6,000	
	Merchandise Inventory...............................		6,000
Sept. 3	Cash	10,098	
	Sales Discounts	102	
	Accounts Receivable—Haggerty Co...........		10,200

Prob. 8–6A   Continued

This solution is applicable only if the P.A.S.S. Software that accompanies the text is used.

RIMROCK CO.
Income Statement
For the Year Ended December 31, 20—

Operating revenue:			
Sales	$219,200		105.44
Less: Sales returns and allowance	(10,000)		(4.81)
Sales discounts	(1,302)		(0.63)
Net sales		$207,898	100.00
Cost of merchandise sold		84,413	40.60
Gross profit		$123,485	59.40
Operating expenses:			
Sales salaries expense	$ 40,500		19.48
Advertising expense	8,000		3.85
Miscellaneous selling expense	500		0.24
Office salaries expense	16,500		7.94
Rent expense	12,250		5.89
Miscellaneous administrative expense	200		0.10
Total operating expenses		77,950	37.49
Net income from operations		$ 45,535	21.90
Other revenue:			
Interest revenue		1,505	0.72
Net income		$ 47,040	22.63

Prob. 8–1B Concluded

1. and 2.

Allowance for Doubtful Accounts   115

Date	Item	Dr.	Cr.	Balance Dr.	Balance Cr.
2006					
Jan. 1	Balance....................	....	....	....	28,500
Feb. 24	....	....	1,025	....	29,525
Mar. 29	....	7,500	....	....	22,025
July 10	....	7,200	....	....	14,825
Sept. 8	....	....	1,200	....	16,025
Dec. 31	....	20,905	....	4,880	....
31	....	....	35,380	....	30,500

Income Summary   313

Date	Item	Dr.	Cr.	Balance Dr.	Balance Cr.
2006					
Dec. 31	....	35,380	....	35,380	....

Uncollectible Accounts Expense   718

Date	Item	Dr.	Cr.	Balance Dr.	Balance Cr.
2006					
Dec. 31	....	35,380	....	35,380	....
31	....	....	35,380	—	—

3. $857,050 ($887,550 − $30,500)

4. a. $31,875 ($12,750,000 × 0.0025)
   b. $26,995 ($31,875 − $4,880)
   c. $860,555 ($887,550 − $26,995)

Prob. 8–2B

1.

Customer	Due Date	Number of Days Past Due
Allison's Uniquely Yours	July 6, 2006	178 days (25 + 31 + 30 + 31 + 30 + 31)
Western Designs	Aug. 10, 2006	143 days (21 + 30 + 31 + 30 + 31)
Treat's	Sept. 6, 2006	116 days (24 + 31 + 30 + 31)
Nicole's Beauty Store	Sept. 29, 2006	93 days (1 + 31 + 30 + 31)
Ginburg Supreme	Oct. 10, 2006	82 days (21 + 30 + 31)
Jeremy's Hair Products	Oct. 20, 2006	72 days (11 + 30 + 31)
Hairy's Hair Care	Oct. 31, 2006	61 days (30 + 31)
Southern Images	Nov. 18, 2006	43 days (12 + 31)
Lopez's Blond Bombs	Nov. 23, 2006	38 days (7 + 31)
Josset Ritz	Nov. 30, 2006	31 days
Cool Designs	Dec. 4, 2006	27 days
Buttram Images	Jan. 3, 2007	Not past due

Prob. 8–2B Concluded

2. and 3.

Aging of Accounts Receivable
December 31, 2006

Customer	Balance	Not Past Due	1–30	31–60	61–90	91–120	Over 120
Adams Beauty	8,000	8,000					
Barkell Wigs	7,500			7,500			
~~							
Zimmer's Beauty	2,900		2,900				
Subtotals	880,000	498,600	197,250	88,750	43,300	29,950	22,150
Allison's Uniquely Yours	1,000						1,000
Western Designs	2,500						2,500
Treat's	1,800					1,800	
Nicole's Beauty Store	4,000					4,000	
Ginburg Supreme	1,500				1,500		
Jeremy's Hair Products	600				600		
Hairy's Hair Care	2,000				2,000		
Southern Images	1,200			1,200			
Lopez's Blond Bombs	1,800			1,800			
Josset Ritz	3,500			3,500			
Cool Designs	1,000		1,000				
Buttram Images	5,200	5,200					
Totals	906,100	503,800	198,250	95,250	47,400	35,750	25,650
Percentage Uncollectible		1%	4%	6%	15%	30%	70%
Estimate of Doubtful Accounts	54,473	5,038	7,930	5,715	7,110	10,725	17,955

4.			
Uncollectible Accounts Expense		46,123*	
Allowance for Doubtful Accounts			46,123

*$54,473 – $8,350

428

Prob. 8–3B

1.

	Uncollectible Accounts Expense			
Year	Expense Actually Reported	Expense Based on Estimate	Increase (Decrease) in Amount of Expense	Balance of Allowance Account, End of Year
1st	$1,000	$ 3,250	$2,250	$2,250
2nd	2,650	4,600	1,950	4,200
3rd	6,200	5,250	(950)	3,250
4th	9,150	11,250	2,100	5,350

2. Yes. The actual write-offs of accounts originating in the first two years are reasonably close to the expense that would have been charged to those years on the basis of 1/2% of sales. The total write-off of receivables originating in the first year amounted to $3,550 ($1,000 + $750 + $1,800), as compared with uncollectible accounts expense, based on the percentage of sales, of $3,250. For the second year, the comparable amounts were $5,200 ($1,900 + $1,400 + $1,900) and $4,600.

Prob. 8–6B

20—

Jan.	6	Accounts Receivable—Alta Co.	10,500	
		Sales		10,500
	6	Cost of Merchandise Sold	6,300	
		Merchandise Inventory		6,300
Mar.	9	Notes Receivable	10,500	
		Accounts Receivable—Alta Co.		10,500
May	8	Cash	10,640	
		Notes Receivable		10,500
		Interest Revenue		140
June	1	Accounts Receivable—Witmer's	8,000	
		Sales		8,000
	1	Cost of Merchandise Sold	4,800	
		Merchandise Inventory		4,800
	5	Notes Receivable	11,000	
		Cash		11,000
	11	Cash	7,840	
		Sales Discounts	160	
		Accounts Receivable—Witmer's		8,000
July	5	Notes Receivable	11,000	
		Cash	55	
		Notes Receivable		11,000
		Interest Revenue		55
Sept.	3	Cash	11,165	
		Notes Receivable		11,000
		Interest Revenue		165
	8	Accounts Receivable—Rochin Co.	10,000	
		Sales		10,000
	8	Cost of Merchandise Sold	6,000	
		Merchandise Inventory		6,000

Prob. 8–6B   Continued

Oct.	8	Notes Receivable	10,000	
		Accounts Receivable—Rochin Co.		10,000
Dec.	7	Accounts Receivable—Rochin Co.	10,100	
		Notes Receivable...		10,000
		Interest Revenue..		100
	28	Cash	10,153	
		Accounts Receivable—Rochin Co.		10,100
		Interest Revenue..		53
		($10,100 × 0.09 × 21/360 = $53)		

Prob. 8–6B   Continued

This solution is applicable only if the P.A.S.S. Software that accompanies the text is used.

WESTPHAL CO.
Income Statement
For the Year Ended December 31, 20—

Operating revenue:			
Sales	$203,025		100.08
Less: Sales discounts	(160.00)		(0.08)
Net sales		$202,865	100.00
Cost of merchandise sold		54,100	26.67
Gross profit		$148,765	73.33
Operating expenses:			
Sales salaries expense	$ 45,500		22.43
Advertising expense	7,500		3.70
Miscellaneous selling expense	1,250		0.62
Office salaries expense	26,500		13.06
Rent expense	25,500		12.57
Miscellaneous administrative expense	225		0.11
Total operating expenses		106,475	52.49
Net income from operations		$ 42,290	20.85
Other revenue:			
Interest revenue		513	0.25
Net income		$ 42,803	21.10

Prob. 8–6B Concluded

This solution is applicable only if the P.A.S.S. Software that accompanies the text is used.

WESTPHAL CO.
Statement of Owner's Equity
For the Year Ended December 31, 20—

Andrea Young, capital (beg. of year)		$ 75,779
Net income	$42,803	
Less: Withdrawals	31,000	
Increase in capital		11,803
Andrea Young, capital (end of year)		$ 87,582

WESTPHAL CO.
Balance Sheet
December 31, 20—

Assets

Cash..	$77,182
Accounts receivable...	9,500
Merchandise inventory...	10,900
Total assets...	$97,582

Liabilities

Accounts payable	$10,000

Owner's Equity

Andrea Young, capital..	87,582
Total liabilities and equity..	$97,582

SPECIAL ACTIVITIES

Activity 8–1

By computing interest using a 365-day year for depository accounts (payables), Precilla is minimizing interest expense to the bank. By computing interest using a 360-day year for loans (receivables), Precilla is maximizing interest revenue to the bank. However, federal legislation (Truth in Lending Act) requires banks to compute interest on a 365-day year. Hence, Precilla is behaving in an unprofessional manner.

Activity 8–2

Because of the size and number of customers' accounts, it is probably unreasonable for Stonecipher to not allow credit to contractors and to require cash or credit card payment. To do so, as Bruce points out, would probably cost Stonecipher most of its contractor customers. Thus, Stonecipher is faced with having to allow credit to its contracting customers.

Many building contractors obtain construction loans from local financial institutions. They are then allowed to draw upon (withdraw) these funds as portions of the construction are completed. Most of the time, a representative of the financial institution granting the construction loan must approve the disbursement based upon an observation of the work to verify that it was actually performed. Building contractors are, of course, charged interest on the balances withdrawn from their construction loans. Thus, building contractors have an incentive to delay payment of construction bills as long as possible. At the same time, it is unreasonable to expect payment from the contractors until the representative of the financial institution has approved payment. Thus, it is probably reasonable to expect that accounts will remain open for 30–45 days after the contractor has received the materials.

The primary problem that Stonecipher is facing is that some contractors are apparently abusing Stonecipher's liberal credit policy. One alternative would be for Stonecipher to allow a discount for payment within 30 days. For example, Stonecipher might allow a 2% discount if the bill is paid within 30 days. Credit then might be discontinued for any contractor with a bill outstanding more than 60 days. This would provide the contractors an incentive to pay their bills early. That is, a 2% discount for payment 30 days early (the bill must be paid within 60 days) is equivalent to an annual interest rate of 24% (2% × 360/30). This discount

Activity 8–2 Concluded

rate would easily exceed most interest rates on construction loans. Such a payment policy would give contractors a "positive" incentive to pay early. Before initiating such a policy, Stonecipher should consider its effect on profits. That is, does the discount offered compensate for the reduction in the uncollectible accounts expense? Also, earlier payments would allow Stonecipher to earn interest (profit) on the monies received from the contractors.

An alternative approach would be to charge contractors interest on past-due accounts. For example, Stonecipher might charge accounts over 60 days past due interest at 1 1/2% per month (equivalent to approximately 18% per year). This approach would be more of a "negative" approach to motivating contractors to pay earlier.

Finally, yet another approach would be to stop extending credit to contractors who routinely abuse Stonecipher's liberal credit policy. However, this approach is more extreme than the preceding two approaches. It might be more appropriate for contractors who continue to abuse the credit policy after one of the preceding approaches has been implemented.

Regardless of the approach chosen, exceptions probably should be allowed for good customers who suffer unusual situations. For example, a contractor's bill might be past due because of unforeseen construction problems, such as bad weather, disagreement on contract specifications, etc.

Activity 8–3

Pam's first suggestion of recording only $42,000 of uncollectible accounts expense to increase the allowance for doubtful accounts to $60,000 is acceptable. Accounting standards allow for recording the minimum estimate for the allowance account if a range of estimates is provided, with no one estimate within the range better than any other.

Pam's second suggestion of paying $50,000 of her receivable to decrease it to $20,000 so that it can be reported as part of accounts receivable is improper. Pam's receivable is $70,000 as of December 31, 2005, and therefore a payment in January 2006 will not decrease the amount of the receivable as of December 31, 2005.

A more difficult issue is whether the receivable should be reported as a current asset. Pam made no payments during 2005. Instead, the amount of the receivable actually increased by $50,000. This would suggest that the receivable is a noncurrent asset. However, the fact that Pam agrees to pay $50,000 next week would suggest that the receivable is current.

Eric should probably respond to Pam by arguing that (1) the receivable has to be reported as $70,000 on the December 31, 2005 balance sheet; (2) the receivable is too large to be reported as an account receivable but must be reported as an "other receivable" or "officer receivable"; and (3) the receivable can be reported as a current receivable as long as Pam commits to a payment schedule that will pay off the receivable within the next year. Pam may resist these suggestions. In this case, Eric should point out that the bank will be receiving the financial statements, and to distort or file false statements with the bank is fraudulent. That is, Pam has no other choice in this matter. If Pam refuses, then Eric should disassociate himself from the financial statements and probably resign from the company.

Note to Instructors: Consider pointing out to students that if Eric agreed with Pam's treatment of the receivable, he could be considered an accomplice to fraud.

Activity 8–4

1.

Year	a. Addition to Allowance for Doubtful Accounts	b. Accounts Written Off During Year
2003	$17,000	$ 9,900 ($17,000 – $7,100)
2004	17,500	11,400 ($7,100 + $17,500 – $13,200)
2005	17,750	12,050 ($13,200 + $17,750 – $18,900)
2006	18,125	9,675 ($18,900 + $18,125 – $27,350)

2. a. The estimate of 1/4 of 1% of credit sales may be too large, since the allowance for doubtful accounts has steadily increased each year. The increasing balance of the allowance for doubtful accounts may also be due to the failure to write off a large number of uncollectible accounts. These possibilities could be evaluated by examining the accounts in the subsidiary ledger for collectibility and comparing the result with the balance in the allowance for doubtful accounts.

Note to Instructors: Since the amount of credit sales has been fairly uniform over the years, the increase cannot be explained by an expanding volume of sales.

    b. The balance of Allowance for Doubtful Accounts that should exist at December 31, 2006, can only be determined after all attempts have been made to collect the receivables on hand at December 31, 2006. However, the account balances at December 31, 2006, could be analyzed, perhaps using an aging schedule, to determine a reasonable amount of allowance and to determine accounts that should be written off. Also, past write-offs of uncollectible accounts could be analyzed in depth in order to develop a reasonable percentage for future adjusting entries, based on past history. Caution, however, must be exercised in using historical percentages. Specifically, inquiries should be made to determine whether any significant changes between prior years and the current year may have occurred, which might reduce the accuracy of the historical data. For example, a recent change in credit-granting policies or changes in the general economy (entering a recessionary period, for example) could reduce the usefulness of analyzing historical data.

Based on the preceding analyses, a recommendation to decrease the annual rate charged as an expense may be in order (perhaps Filet Co. is experiencing a lower rate of uncollectibles than is the industry average), or perhaps a change to the "estimate based on analysis of receivables" method may be appropriate.

Activity 8–5

Note to Instructors: The purpose of this activity is to familiarize students with the factors that a bank or a business uses in deciding to grant credit to a customer.

Activity 8–6

Note to Instructors: The purpose of this activity is to familiarize students with the financial information that is available online and to calculate and compare the accounts receivable turnover for two real companies, based on that information.

Activity 8–7

1. 2002: 25.7 {$1,357,421 ÷ [($59,014 + $46,736) ÷ 2]}
   2001: 23.5 {$1,244,928 ÷ [($46,736 + $59,211) ÷ 2]}

2. 2002: 15.9 days [$59,014 ÷ ($1,357,421 ÷ 365)]
   2001: 13.7 days [$46,736 ÷ ($1,244,928 ÷ 365)]

3. The accounts receivable turnover indicates an increase in the efficiency of collecting accounts receivable by increasing from 23.5 to 25.7, a favorable trend. However, the days' sales in receivables also increased from 13.7 days to 15.9 days, an unfavorable trend. Before reaching a more definitive conclusion, the ratios should be compared with industry averages and similar firms.

4. Earthlink's accounts receivable turnover would normally be higher than that of a typical manufacturing company such as Boeing or Kellogg. This is because Earthlink is an Internet Service Provider (ISP) that bills its customers monthly for Internet service access fees. The monthly bills are normally charged to customers' MasterCard, VISA, or American Express cards. In contrast, the customers of Boeing and Kellogg are other businesses who pay their accounts receivable on a less timely basis. For a recent year, the accounts receivable turnover ratios for Kellogg and Boeing were 10.2 and 10.4, respectively.

Activity 8–8

1. *Note to Instructors:* The turnover ratios will vary over time. For a recent year, the various turnover ratios (rounded to one decimal place) were as follows:

Alcoa	8.9
AutoZone	251.8
Barnes & Noble	60.6
Coca-Cola	10.7
Delta Air Lines	37.7
Gillette	6.1
Home Depot	58.7
IBM	9.4
Kroger	66.3
Maytag Corporation	7.0
Wal-Mart	109.3
Whirlpool	7.1

2. Based upon (1), the companies can be categorized as follows:

Accounts Receivable Turnover Ratio

Below 15	Above 15
Alcoa	AutoZone
Coca-Cola	Barnes & Noble
Gillette	Delta Air Lines
IBM	Home Depot
Maytag Corporation	Kroger
Whirlpool	Wal-Mart

3. The companies with accounts receivable turnover ratios above 15 are all companies selling directly to individual consumers. In contrast, companies with turnover ratios below 15 all sell to other businesses. Generally, we would expect companies selling directly to consumers to have higher turnover ratios since many customers will charge their purchases on credit cards that will be collected within a month. In contrast, companies selling to other businesses normally allow a credit period of at least 30 days or longer.

CHAPTER 9
INVENTORIES

CLASS DISCUSSION QUESTIONS

1. To protect inventory from customer theft, retailers use two-way mirrors, cameras, security guards, locked display cabinets, and inventory tags that set off an alarm if the inventory is removed from the store.

2. Perpetual. The perpetual inventory system provides the more effective means of controlling inventories, since the inventory account is updated for each purchase and sale. This also assists managers in determining when to reorder inventory items.

3. The receiving report should be reconciled to the initial purchase order and the vendor's invoice before recording or paying for inventory purchases. This procedure will verify that the inventory received matches the type and quantity of inventory ordered. It also verifies that the vendor's invoice is charging the company for the actual quantity of inventory received at the agreed-upon price.

4. An employee should present a requisition form signed by an authorized manager before receiving inventory items from the company's warehouse.

5. A physical inventory should be taken periodically to test the accuracy of the perpetual records.

6. a. Gross profit for the year was overstated by $18,500.
   b. Merchandise inventory and owner's equity were overstated by $18,500.

7. Fess Company. Since the merchandise was shipped FOB shipping point, title passed to Fess Company when it was shipped and should be reported in Fess Company's financial statements at December 31, the end of the fiscal year.

8. Manufacturer's

9. No, they are not techniques for determining physical quantities. The terms refer to cost flow assumptions, which affect the determination of the cost prices assigned to items in the inventory.

10. No, the term refers to the flow of costs rather than the items remaining in the inventory. The inventory cost is composed of the earliest acquisitions costs rather than the most recent acquisitions costs.

11. a. Fifo   c. Fifo
    b. Lifo   d. Lifo

12. Fifo

13. Lifo. In periods of rising prices, the use of lifo will result in the lowest net income and thus the lowest income tax expense.

14. Yes. The inventory method may be changed for a valid reason. The effect of any change in method and the reason for the change should be fully disclosed in the financial statements for the period in which the change occurred.

15. Net realizable value (estimated selling price less any direct cost of disposition, such as sales commissions).

16. By a notation next to "merchandise inventory" on the balance sheet or in a footnote to the financial statements.

17. Inventories estimated by the gross profit method are useful in preparing interim statements and in establishing an estimate of the cost of merchandise destroyed by fire or other disasters.

EXERCISES

Ex. 9–1

Switching to a perpetual inventory system will strengthen Onsite Hardware's internal controls over inventory, since the store managers will be able to keep track of how much of each item is on hand. This should minimize shortages of good-selling items and excess inventories of poor-selling items.

On the other hand, switching to a perpetual inventory system will not eliminate the need to take a physical inventory count. A physical inventory must be taken to verify the accuracy of the inventory records in a perpetual inventory system. In addition, a physical inventory count is needed to detect shortages of inventory due to damage or theft.

Ex. 9–2

a. Inappropriate. Good internal controls include a receiving report, prepared after all inventory items received have been counted and inspected. Inventory purchased should only be recorded and paid for after reconciling the receiving report, the initial purchase order, and the vendor's invoice.

b. Appropriate. The inventory tags will protect the inventory from customer theft.

c. Inappropriate. The internal control procedure of using security measures to protect the inventory is violated if the stockroom is not locked.

Ex. 9–3

Include in inventory: c, e, g, i
Exclude from inventory: a, b, d, f, h

Ex. 9–4

a.

	Balance Sheet
Merchandise inventory	$1,950 understated
Current assets	$1,950 understated
Total assets	$1,950 understated
Owner's equity	$1,950 understated

b.

	Income Statement
Cost of merchandise sold	$1,950 overstated
Gross profit	$1,950 understated
Net income	$1,950 understated

Ex. 9–5

a.

	Balance Sheet
Merchandise inventory	$4,150 overstated
Current assets	$4,150 overstated
Total assets	$4,150 overstated
Owner's equity	$4,150 overstated

b.

	Income Statement
Cost of merchandise sold	$4,150 understated
Gross profit	$4,150 overstated
Net income	$4,150 overstated

Ex. 9–6

When an error is discovered affecting the prior period, it should be corrected. In this case, the merchandise inventory account should be debited and the owner's capital account credited for $12,800.

Failure to correct the error for 2005 and purposely misstating the inventory and the cost of merchandise sold in 2006 would cause the balance sheets and the income statements for the two years to not be comparable.

Ex. 9–7

Portable CD Players

Date	Purchases			Cost of Merchandise Sold			Inventory		
	Quantity	Unit Cost	Total Cost	Quantity	Unit Cost	Total Cost	Quantity	Unit Cost	Total Cost
April 1							35	50	1,750
5				26	50	1,300	9	50	450
11	15	53	795				9	50	450
							15	53	795
21				9	50	450	12	53	636
				3	53	159			
28				4	53	212	8	53	424
30	7	54	378				8	53	424
							7	54	378
						2,121			

Total cost of merchandise sold 2,121

Inventory, April 30: $802 ($424 + $378)

446

Ex. 9–8

Portable CD Players

Date	Purchases			Cost of Merchandise Sold			Inventory		
	Quantity	Unit Cost	Total Cost	Quantity	Unit Cost	Total Cost	Quantity	Unit Cost	Total Cost
April 1							35	50	1,750
5				26	50	1,300	9	50	450
11	15	53	795				9	50	450
							15	53	795
21				12	53	636	9	50	450
							3	53	159
28				3	53	159	8	50	400
				1	50	50			
30	7	54	378				8	50	400
							7	54	378
						2,145			

Total cost of merchandise sold..............................

Inventory, April 30: $778 ($400 + $378)

447

Ex. 9–9

Cell Phones

Date	Purchases Quantity	Purchases Unit Cost	Purchases Total Cost	Cost of Merchandise Sold Quantity	Cost of Merchandise Sold Unit Cost	Cost of Merchandise Sold Total Cost	Inventory Quantity	Inventory Unit Cost	Inventory Total Cost
Mar. 1							25	90	2,250
5	20	94	1,880				25	90	2,250
							20	94	1,880
9				18	94	1,692	25	90	2,250
							2	94	188
13				2	94	188	7	90	630
				18	90	1,620			
21	15	95	1,425				7	90	630
							15	95	1,425
31				8	95	760	7	90	630
							7	95	665

Total cost of merchandise sold............................ 4,260

Inventory, March 31: $1,295 ($630 + $665)

Cell Phones

Date	Purchases Quantity	Purchases Unit Cost	Purchases Total Cost	Cost of Merchandise Sold Quantity	Cost of Merchandise Sold Unit Cost	Cost of Merchandise Sold Total Cost	Inventory Quantity	Inventory Unit Cost	Inventory Total Cost
Mar. 1							25	90	2,250
5	20	94	1,880				25	90	2,250
							20	94	1,880
9				18	90	1,620	7	90	630
							20	94	1,880
13				7	90	630			
				13	94	1,222	7	94	658
21	15	95	1,425				7	94	658
							15	95	1,425
31				7	94	658			
				1	95	95	14	95	1,330
						4,225			

Total cost of merchandise sold... 4,225

Inventory, March 31: $1,330

449

Ex. 9–11

a. $700 ($50 × 14 units)

b. $663 [($45 × 5 units) + ($47 × 4 units) + ($50 × 5 units)]

Ex. 9–12

a. $360 (8 units at $33 plus 3 units at $32)

b. $318 (6 units at $28 plus 5 units at $30)

c. $341 (11 units at $31; $1,240 ÷ 40 units = $31)

Cost of merchandise available for sale:

6 units at $28	$ 168
12 units at $30	360
14 units at $32	448
8 units at $33	264
40 units (at average cost of $31).............................	$1,240

Ex. 9–13

| | | Cost | |
	Inventory Method	Merchandise Inventory	Merchandise Sold
a.	Fifo	$5,016	$14,484
b.	Lifo	4,320	15,180
c.	Average cost	4,680	14,820

Cost of merchandise available for sale:

42 units at $120	$ 5,040
58 units at $130	7,540
20 units at $136	2,720
30 units at $140	4,200
150 units (at average cost of $130)...........................	$19,500

a. First-in, first-out:

Merchandise inventory:

30 units at $140	$4,200
6 units at $136	816
36 units	$5,016

Merchandise sold:

$19,500 – $5,016	$14,484

b. Last-in, first-out:

Merchandise inventory:

36 units at $120	$4,320

Merchandise sold:

$19,500 – $4,320	$15,180

c. Average cost:

Merchandise inventory:

36 units at $130 ($19,500 ÷ 150 units)	$4,680

Merchandise sold:

$19,500 – $4,680	$14,820

Ex. 9–14

1. a. LIFO inventory   < (less than)   FIFO inventory
    b. LIFO cost of goods sold   > (greater than)   FIFO cost of goods sold
    c. LIFO net income   < (less than)   FIFO net income
    d. LIFO income tax   < (less than)   FIFO income tax

2. Under the lifo conformity rule a company selecting lifo for tax purposes must also use lifo for financial reporting purposes. Thus, in periods of rising prices the reported net income would be lower than would be the case under fifo. However, the lower reported income would also be shown on the corporation's tax return; thus, there is a tax advantage from using lifo. Firms electing to use lifo believe the tax advantage from using lifo outweighs any negative impact from reporting a lower earnings number to shareholders. Lifo is supported because the tax impact is a real cash flow benefit, while a lower lifo earnings number (compared to fifo) is merely the result of a reporting assumption.

Ex. 9–15

Commodity	Inventory Quantity	Unit Cost Price	Unit Market Price	Total Cost	Total Market	Lower of C or M
M76	8	$150	$160	$1,200	$1,280	$1,200
T53	20	75	70	1,500	1,400	1,400
A19	10	275	260	2,750	2,600	2,600
J81	15	50	40	750	600	600
K10	25	101	105	2,525	2,625	2,525
Total...............				$8,725	$8,505	$8,325

Ex. 9–16

The merchandise inventory would appear in the Current Assets section, as follows:

Merchandise inventory—at lower of cost, fifo, or market............ $8,325

Alternatively, the details of the method of determining cost and the method of valuation could be presented in a note.

Ex. 9–17

$495,450 ($825,750 × 60%)

Ex. 9–18

	Cost	Retail
Merchandise inventory, June 1	$160,000	$ 180,000
Purchases in June (net)	680,000	1,020,000
Merchandise available for sale	$840,000	$1,200,000

Ratio of cost to retail price:

$$\frac{\$\ 840,000}{\$1,200,000} = 70\%$$

Sales for June (net)		875,000
Merchandise inventory, June 30, at retail price		$ 325,000
Merchandise inventory, June 30, at estimated cost ($325,000 × 70%)		$ 227,500

Ex. 9–19

a.

Merchandise inventory, Jan. 1		$180,000
Purchases (net), Jan. 1–May 17		750,000
Merchandise available for sale		$930,000
Sales (net), Jan. 1–May 17	$1,250,000	
Less estimated gross profit ($1,250,000 × 35%)	437,500	
Estimated cost of merchandise sold		812,500
Estimated merchandise inventory, May 17		$117,500

b. The gross profit method is useful for estimating inventories for monthly or quarterly financial statements. It is also useful in estimating the cost of merchandise destroyed by fire or other disasters.

Ex. 9–20

a. Apple: 147.8 {$4,139,000,000 ÷ [($45,000,000 + $11,000,000) ÷ 2]}

American Greetings: 3.1 {$881,771,000 ÷ [($278,807,000 + $290,804,000) ÷ 2]}

b. Lower. Although American Greetings' business is seasonal in nature, with most of its revenue generated during the major holidays, much of its nonholiday inventory may turn over very slowly. Apple, on the other hand, turns its inventory over very fast because it maintains a low inventory, which allows it to respond quickly to customer needs. Additionally, Apple's computer products can quickly become obsolete, so it cannot risk building large inventories.

Ex. 9–21

a. $$\text{Number of days' sales in inventory} = \frac{\text{Inventory, end of period}}{\text{Cost of goods sold/365}}$$

Albertson's, $\dfrac{\$2,973}{\$25,242/365}$ = 43 days

Kroger, $\dfrac{\$4,175}{\$37,810/365}$ = 40 days

Safeway, $\dfrac{\$2,558}{\$22,303/365}$ = 42 days

$$\text{Inventory turnover} = \frac{\text{Cost of goods sold}}{\text{Average inventory}}$$

Albertson's, $\dfrac{\$25,242}{(\$2,973 \ + \$3,196)/2}$ = 8.2

Kroger, $\dfrac{\$37,810}{(\$4,175 \ + \$4,178)/2}$ = 9.1

Safeway, $\dfrac{\$22,303}{(\$2,558 \ + \$2,437)/2}$ = 8.9

b. The number of days' sale in inventory and inventory turnover ratios are consistent. Albertson's has slightly more inventory than does Safeway. Kroger has relatively less inventory (2–3 days) than does Albertson's and Safeway.

Ex. 9–21   Concluded

c. If Albertson's matched Kroger's days' sales in inventory, then its hypothetical ending inventory would be determined as follows,

$$\text{Number of days' sales in inventory} = \frac{\text{Inventory, end of period}}{\text{Cost of goods sold}/365}$$

$$40 \text{ days} = \frac{X}{\$25{,}242/365}$$

$$X = 40 \times (\$25{,}242/365)$$

$$X = \$2{,}766$$

Thus, the additional cash flow that would have been generated is the difference between the actual ending inventory and the hypothetical ending inventory, as follows:

Actual ending inventory	$ 2,973 million
Hypothetical ending inventory.................	2,766
Positive cash flow potential.....................	$ 207 million

That is, a lower ending inventory amount would have required less cash than actually was required.

1.

Drift Boats

Date	Purchases			Cost of Merchandise Sold			Inventory		
	Quantity	Unit Cost	Total Cost	Quantity	Unit Cost	Total Cost	Quantity	Unit Cost	Total Cost
Aug. 1							22	2,200	48,400
8	18	2,250	40,500				22	2,200	48,400
							18	2,250	40,500
11				12	2,250	27,000	22	2,200	48,400
							6	2,250	13,500
22				6	2,250	13,500	17	2,200	37,400
				5	2,200	11,000			
Sept. 3	16	2,300	36,800				17	2,200	37,400
							16	2,300	36,800
10				10	2,300	23,000	17	2,200	37,400
							6	2,300	13,800
21				5	2,300	11,500	17	2,200	37,400
							1	2,300	2,300
30	20	2,350	47,000				17	2,200	37,400
							1	2,300	2,300
							20	2,350	47,000

Continued

Prob. 9–2A   Concluded

Drift Boats

Date	Purchases			Cost of Merchandise Sold			Inventory		
	Quantity	Unit Cost	Total Cost	Quantity	Unit Cost	Total Cost	Quantity	Unit Cost	Total Cost
Oct. 5				20	2,350	47,000	17	2,200	37,400
							1	2,300	2,300
13				1	2,300	2,300	6	2,200	13,200
				11	2,200	24,200			
21	30	2,400	72,000				6	2,200	13,200
							30	2,400	72,000
28				15	2,400	36,000	6	2,200	13,200
							15	2,400	36,000

Total cost of merchandise sold............................... 195,500

2. Total sales $434,400
Total cost of merchandise sold 195,500
Gross profit $238,900

3. $49,200 ($13,200 + $36,000)

459

Prob. 9–3A

1. First-In, First-Out Method

Model	Quantity	Unit Cost	Total Cost
231T	4	$225	$ 900
	2	213	426
673W	2	535	1,070
	2	530	1,060
193Q	6	542	3,252
	1	549	549
144Z	6	225	1,350
	5	222	1,110
160M	4	317	1,268
	1	316	316
180X	2	232	464
971K	6	156	936
Total			$12,701

2. Last-In, First-Out Method

Model	Quantity	Unit Cost	Total Cost
231T	3	$208	$ 624
	3	212	636
673W	2	520	1,040
	2	527	1,054
193Q	6	520	3,120
	1	531	531
144Z	9	213	1,917
	2	215	430
160M	5	305	1,525
180X	2	222	444
971K	4	140	560
	2	144	288
Total			$12,169

Prob. 9–3A   Concluded

3. Average Cost Method

Model	Quantity	Unit Cost	Total Cost
231T	6	$215*	$ 1,290
673W	4	528	2,112
193Q	7	534	3,738
144Z	11	218	2,398
160M	5	311	1,555
180X	2	227	454
971K	6	148	888
Total			$12,435

* $215 = [(3 × $208) + (3 × $212) + (5 × $213) + (4 × $225)] ÷ (3 + 3 + 5 + 4)

4. a. During periods of rising prices, the lifo method will result in a lesser amount of inventory, a greater amount of the cost of merchandise sold, and a lesser amount of net income than the other two methods. For Henning Appliances, the lifo method would be preferred for the current year, since it would result in a lesser amount of income tax.

   b. During periods of declining prices, the fifo method will result in a lesser amount of net income and would be preferred for income tax purposes.

Prob. 9–4A

Inventory Sheet
December 31, 2006

Description	Inventory Quantity		Unit Cost Price	Unit Market Price	Total Cost	Total Market	Lower of C or M
A90	~~35~~	25	$ 59	$ 57	$ 1,475	$ 1,425	
		10	58		580	570	
					2,055	1,995	$ 1,995
C18	16		188	200	3,008	3,200	3,008
D41	~~24~~	16	145	140	2,320	2,240	
		8	142		1,136	1,120	
					3,456	3,360	3,360
E34	125		25	26	3,125	3,250	3,125
F17	~~18~~	6	550	550	3,300	3,300	
		12	540		6,480	6,600	
					9,780	9,900	9,780
G68	60		14	15	840	900	840
K41	5		400	390	2,000	1,950	1,950
Q79	375		6	6	2,250	2,250	2,250
R72	~~100~~	70	18	17	1,260	1,190	
		30	16		480	510	
					1,740	1,700	1,700
S60	~~6~~	5	250	235	1,250	1,175	
		1	260		260	235	
					1,510	1,410	1,410
W21	~~140~~	120	20	18	2,400	2,160	
		20	17		340	360	
					2,740	2,520	2,520
Z35	~~9~~	8	701	700	5,608	5,600	
		1	699		699	700	
					6,307	6,300	6,300
							$38,238

Prob. 9–5A

1.

BOZEMAN CO.

	Cost	Retail
Merchandise inventory, February 1	$ 210,000	$ 300,000
Net purchases...	1,135,500	1,650,000
Merchandise available for sale..	$ 1,345,500	$ 1,950,000

Ratio of cost to retail price:

$$\frac{\$1,345,500}{\$1,950,000} = 69\%$$

Sales	$ 1,800,000	
Less sales returns and allowances	40,000	
Net sales...		1,760,000
Merchandise inventory, February 28, at retail.................		$ 190,000
Merchandise inventory, at estimated cost ($190,000 × 69%)		$ 131,100

2. a.

GALLATIN CO.

Merchandise inventory, March 1		$ 250,000
Net purchases		1,385,000
Merchandise available for sale		$ 1,635,000
Sales	$ 2,510,000	
Less sales returns and allowances..........................	110,000	
Net sales	$ 2,400,000	
Less estimated gross profit ($2,400,000 × 36%)	864,000	
Estimated cost of merchandise sold		1,536,000
Estimated merchandise inventory, April 30..............		$ 99,000

b.

Estimated merchandise inventory, April 30..............		$ 99,000
Physical inventory count, April 30...........................		88,125
Estimated loss due to theft or damage, March 1–April 30..		$ 10,875

Prob. 9–1B

1.

Floor Mats

Date	Purchases			Cost of Merchandise Sold			Inventory		
	Quantity	Unit Cost	Total Cost	Quantity	Unit Cost	Total Cost	Quantity	Unit Cost	Total Cost
Apr. 1							200	2.10	420
8	800	2.20	1,760				200	2.10	420
							800	2.20	1,760
20				200	2.10	420	650	2.20	1,430
				150	2.20	330			
30				450	2.20	990	200	2.20	440
May 8				50	2.20	110	150	2.20	330
10	500	2.30	1,150				150	2.20	330
							500	2.30	1,150
27				150	2.20	330	300	2.30	690
				200	2.30	460			
31				200	2.30	460	100	2.30	230
June 5	750	2.40	1,800				100	2.30	230
							750	2.40	1,800
13				100	2.30	230	500	2.40	1,200
				250	2.40	600			
23	400	2.60	1,040				500	2.40	1,200
							400	2.60	1,040
30				500	2.40	1,200	400	2.60	1,040

Total cost of merchandise sold................. <u>5,130</u>

Prob. 9–1B   Concluded

2.	Accounts Receivable	10,025	
	Sales		10,025
	Cost of Merchandise Sold	5,130	
	Merchandise Inventory		5,130

3. $4,895 ($10,025 – $5,130)

4. $1,040

Prob. 9–2B

1.

Floor Mats

Date	Purchases Quantity	Purchases Unit Cost	Purchases Total Cost	Cost of Merchandise Sold Quantity	Cost of Merchandise Sold Unit Cost	Cost of Merchandise Sold Total Cost	Inventory Quantity	Inventory Unit Cost	Inventory Total Cost
Apr. 1							200	2.10	420
8	800	2.20	1,760				200	2.10	420
							800	2.20	1,760
20				350	2.20	770	200	2.10	420
							450	2.20	990
30				450	2.20	990	200	2.10	420
May 8				50	2.10	105	150	2.10	315
10	500	2.30	1,150				150	2.10	315
							500	2.30	1,150
27				350	2.30	805	150	2.10	315
							150	2.30	345
31				150	2.30	345	100	2.10	210
				50	2.10	105			
June 5	750	2.40	1,800				100	2.10	210
							750	2.40	1,800
13				350	2.40	840	100	2.10	210
							400	2.40	960
23	400	2.60	1,040				100	2.10	210
							400	2.40	960
							400	2.60	1,040
30				400	2.60	1,040	100	2.10	210
				100	2.40	240	300	2.40	720

Total cost of merchandise sold............... 5,240

Prob. 9–2B   Concluded

2. Total sales.. $10,025
    Total cost of merchandise sold 5,240
    Gross profit.. $ 4,785

3. $930 ($210 + $720)

Prob. 9–3B

1. First-In, First-Out Method

Model	Quantity	Unit Cost	Total Cost
AC54	4	$272	$1,088
	2	271	542
BH43	6	90	540
GI13	3	130	390
	2	128	256
K243	6	92	552
	2	85	170
PM18	8	259	2,072
Q661	7	180	1,260
	1	175	175
W490	4	202	808
	1	200	200
Total			$8,053

2. Last-In, First-Out Method

Model	Quantity	Unit Cost	Total Cost
AC54	2	$250	$ 500
	2	260	520
	2	271	542
BH43	6	80	480
GI13	2	108	216
	2	110	220
	1	128	128
K243	8	88	704
PM18	7	242	1,694
	1	250	250
Q661	5	160	800
	3	170	510
W490	4	150	600
	1	200	200
Total			$7,364

Prob. 9–3B   Concluded

3. Average Cost Method

Model	Quantity	Unit Cost	Total Cost
AC54	6	$266*	$1,596
BH43	6	86	516
GI13	5	121	605
K243	8	87	696
PM18	8	253	2,024
Q661	8	172	1,376
W490	5	184	920
Total			$7,733

*$266 = [(2 × $250) + (2 × $260) + (4 × $271) + (4 × $272)] ÷ (2 + 2 + 4 + 4)

4.   a.   During periods of rising prices, the lifo method will result in a lesser amount of inventory, a greater amount of the cost of merchandise sold, and a lesser amount of net income than the other two methods. For Three Forks Appliances, the lifo method would be preferred for the current year, since it would result in a lesser amount of income tax.

      b.   During periods of declining prices, the fifo method will result in a lesser amount of net income and would be preferred for income tax purposes.

Prob. 9–4B

Inventory Sheet
December 31, 2006

Description	Inventory Quantity		Unit Cost Price	Unit Market Price	Total Cost	Total Market	Lower of C or M
A90	~~35~~	25	$ 59	$ 57	$ 1,475	$ 1,425	
		10	58		580	570	
					2,055	1,995	$ 1,995
C18	16		206	200	3,296	3,200	3,200
D41	~~24~~	10	144	140	1,440	1,400	
		14	142		1,988	1,960	
					3,428	3,360	3,360
E34	125		25	26	3,125	3,250	3,125
F17	~~18~~	10	565	550	5,650	5,500	
		8	560		4,480	4,400	
					10,130	9,900	9,900
G68	60		15	15	900	900	900
K41	5		385	390	1,925	1,950	1,925
Q79	375		6	6	2,250	2,250	2,250
R72	~~100~~	80	20	17	1,600	1,360	
		20	18		360	340	
					1,960	1,700	1,700
S60	~~6~~	5	250	235	1,250	1,175	
		1	260		260	235	
					1,510	1,410	1,410
W21	~~140~~	100	20	18	2,000	1,800	
		40	19		760	720	
					2,760	2,520	2,520
Z35	~~9~~	7	701	700	4,907	4,900	
		2	699		1,398	1,400	
					6,305	6,300	6,300
							$38,585

Prob. 9–5B

1.

AVALANCHE CO.

	Cost	Retail
Merchandise inventory, October 1	$ 98,000	$ 140,000
Net purchases..	813,200	1,200,000
Merchandise available for sale.......................................	$ 911,200	$ 1,340,000

Ratio of cost to retail price:

$$\frac{\$911,200}{\$1,340,000} = 68\%$$

Sales	$ 1,080,000	
Less sales returns and allowances	40,000	
Net sales...		1,040,000
Merchandise inventory, October 31, at retail		$ 300,000
Merchandise inventory, at estimated cost		
($300,000 × 68%)		$ 204,000

2.   a.

BRIDGER CO.

Merchandise inventory, August 1...............................		$ 150,000
Net purchases		1,375,000
Merchandise available for sale		$ 1,525,000
Sales	$ 1,800,000	
Less sales returns and allowances...........................	100,000	
Net sales	$ 1,700,000	
Less estimated gross profit ($1,700,000 × 35%)	595,000	
Estimated cost of merchandise sold..........................		1,105,000
Estimated merchandise inventory, September 30 ...		$ 420,000

b.

Estimated merchandise inventory, September 30 ...		$ 420,000
Physical inventory count, September 30		402,600
Estimated loss due to theft or damage,		
August 1–September 30..		$ 17,400

SPECIAL ACTIVITIES

Activity 9–1

Since the title to merchandise shipped FOB shipping point passes to the buyer when the merchandise is shipped, the shipments made before midnight, December 31, 2006, should properly be recorded as sales for the fiscal year ending December 31, 2006. Hence, Preston Shipley is behaving in a professional manner. However, Preston should realize that recording these sales in 2006 precludes them from being recognized as sales in 2007. Thus, accelerating the shipment of orders to increase sales of one period will have the effect of decreasing sales of the next period.

Activity 9–2

a. $4,338,700,000 ($3,645,200,000 + $693,500,000)

b. $1,693,200,000 ($1,637,300,000 + $693,500,000 – $637,600,000)

Activity 9–3

In developing a response to Jaime's concerns, you should probably first emphasize the practical need for an assumption concerning the flow of cost of goods purchased and sold. That is, when identical goods are frequently purchased, it may not be practical to specifically identify each item of inventory. If all the identical goods were purchased at the same price, it wouldn't make any difference for financial reporting purposes which goods we assumed were sold first, second, etc. However, in most cases, goods are purchased over time at different prices, and hence, a need arises to determine which goods are sold so that the price (cost) of those goods can be matched against the revenues to determine operating income.

Next, you should emphasize that accounting principles allow for the fact that the physical flow of the goods may differ from the flow of costs. Specifically, accounting principles allow for three cost flow assumptions: first-in, first-out; last-in, first-out; and average. Each of these methods has advantages and disadvantages. One primary advantage of the last-in, first-out method is that it better matches current costs (the cost of goods purchased last) with current revenues. Therefore, the reported operating income is more reflective of current operations and what might be expected in the future. Another reason that the last-in, first-out method is often used is that it tends to minimize taxes during periods of price increases. Since for most businesses prices tend to increase, the lifo method will generate lower taxes than will the alternative cost flow methods.

The preceding explanation should help Jaime better understand lifo and its impact on the financial statements and taxes.

Activity 9–4

Note to Instructors: The purpose of this activity is to familiarize students with internal controls over inventory and how those controls differ according to the inventory. Students should be able to observe safeguarding controls for inventory assets.

Activity 9–5

1. **a.** First-in, first-out method:

2,000 units at $32.00	$ 64,000
2,000 units at $29.90	59,800
3,200 units at $29.00	92,800
800 units at $28.50	22,800
8,000 units	$239,400

b. Last-in, first-out method:

7,750 units at $24.40	$189,100
250 units at $26.00	6,500
8,000 units	$195,600

c. Average cost method:

8,000 units at $27.16*	$217,280

*($1,358,000 ÷ 50,000) = $27.16

2.

	Fifo	Lifo	Average Cost
Sales	$ 1,300,000	$ 1,300,000	$ 1,300,000
Cost of merchandise sold*	1,118,600	1,162,400	1,140,720
Gross profit	$ 181,400	$ 137,600	$ 159,280
*Cost of merchandise available for sale	$ 1,358,000	$ 1,358,000	$ 1,358,000
Less ending inventory	239,400	195,600	217,280
Cost of merchandise sold	$ 1,118,600	$ 1,162,400	$ 1,140,720

3. **a.** The lifo method is often viewed as the best basis for reflecting income from operations. This is because the lifo method matches the most current cost of merchandise purchases against current sales. The matching of current costs with current sales results in a gross profit amount that many consider to best reflect the results of current operations. For Feedbag Company, the gross profit of $137,600 reflects the matching of the most current costs of the product of $1,162,400 against the current period sales of $1,300,000. This matching of current costs with current sales also tends to minimize the effects of price trends on the results of operations.

The lifo method will not match current sales and the current cost of merchandise sold if the current period quantity of sales exceeds the current period quantity of purchases. In this case, the cost of merchandise sold will include a portion of the cost of the beginning inventory, which may have a unit cost from purchases made several years prior to the current period. The results of operations may then be distorted in the sense of the current matching concept. This situation occurs rarely in most businesses because of consistently increasing quantities of year-end inventory from year to year.

While the lifo method is often viewed as the best method for matching revenues and expenses, the fifo method is often in harmony with the physical movement of merchandise in a business, since most businesses tend to dispose of commodities in the order of their acquisition. To the extent that this is the case, the fifo method approximates the results that will be attained by a specific identification of costs.

The average cost method is, in a sense, a compromise between lifo and fifo. The effect of price trends is averaged, both in determining net income and in determining inventory cost.

Which inventory costing method best reflects the results of operations for Feedbag Company depends upon whether one emphasizes the importance of matching revenues and expenses (the lifo method) or whether one emphasizes the physical flow of merchandise (the fifo method). The average cost method might be considered best if one emphasizes the matching and physical flow of goods concepts equally.

b. The fifo method provides the best reflection of the replacement cost of the ending inventory for the balance sheet. This is because the amount reported on the balance sheet for merchandise inventory will be assigned costs from the most recent purchases. For most businesses, these costs will reflect purchases made near the end of the period. For example, Feedbag Company's ending inventory on December 31, 2005, is assigned costs totaling $239,400 under the fifo method. These costs represent purchases made during the period of August through December. This fifo inventory amount ($239,400) more closely approximates the replacement cost of the ending inventory than either the lifo ($195,600) or the average cost ($217,280) figures.

c. During periods of rising prices, such as shown for Feedbag Company, the lifo method will result in a lesser amount of net income than the other two methods. Hence, for Feedbag Company, the lifo method would be preferred for the current year, since it would result in a lesser amount of income tax.

During periods of declining prices, the fifo method will result in a lesser amount of net income and would be preferred for income tax purposes.

Activity 9–5   Concluded

d. The advantages of the perpetual inventory system include the following:

1. A perpetual inventory system provides an effective means of control over inventory. A comparison of the amount of inventory on hand with the balance of the subsidiary account can be used to determine the existence and seriousness of any inventory shortages.

2. A perpetual inventory system provides an accurate method for determining inventories used in the preparation of interim statements.

3. A perpetual inventory system provides an aid for maintaining inventories at optimum levels. Frequent review of the perpetual inventory records helps management in the timely reordering of merchandise, so that loss of sales and excessive accumulation of inventory are avoided. An analysis of Feedbag Company's purchases and sales, as shown below, indicates that the company may have accumulated excess inventory from May through August because the amount of month-end inventory increased materially, while sales remained relatively constant for the period.

Month	Purchases	Sales	Increase (Decrease) in Inventory	Inventory at End of Month	Next Month's Sales
April	7,750 units	4,000 units	3,750 units	3,750 units	4,000 units
May	8,250	4,000	4,250	8,000	5,000
June	10,000	5,000	5,000	13,000	6,000
July	10,000	6,000	4,000	17,000	7,000
August	6,800	7,000	(200)	16,800	7,000
September	—	7,000	(7,000)	9,800	4,500
October	3,200	4,500	(1,300)	8,500	2,500
November	2,000	2,500	(500)	8,000	2,000
December	2,000	2,000	0	8,000	—

It appears that during April through July, the company ordered inventory without regard to the accumulation of excess inventory. A perpetual inventory system might have prevented this excess accumulation from occurring.

The primary disadvantage of the perpetual inventory system is the cost of maintaining the necessary inventory records. However, computers may be used to reduce this cost.

CHAPTER 10
FIXED ASSETS AND INTANGIBLE ASSETS

CLASS DISCUSSION QUESTIONS

1. **a.** Tangible
   b. Capable of repeated use in the operations of the business
   e. Long-lived
2. **a.** Property, plant, and equipment
   b. Current assets (merchandise inventory)
3. Real estate acquired as speculation should be listed in the balance sheet under the caption "Investments," below the Current Assets section.
4. $375,000
5. Ordinarily not; if the book values closely approximate the market values of fixed assets, it is coincidental.
6. **a.** No, it does not provide a special cash fund for the replacement of assets. Unlike most expenses, however, depreciation expense does not require an equivalent outlay of cash in the period to which the expense is allocated.
   b. Depreciation is the cost of fixed assets periodically charged to revenue over their expected useful lives.
7. 12 years
8. **a.** No
   b. No
9. **a.** An accelerated depreciation method is most appropriate for situations in which the decline in productivity or earning power of the asset is proportionately greater in the early years of use than in later years, and the repairs tend to increase with the age of the asset.
   b. An accelerated depreciation method reduces income tax payable to the IRS in the earlier periods of an asset's life. Thus, cash is freed up in the earlier periods to be used for other business purposes.
   c. MACRS was enacted by the Tax Reform Act of 1986 and provides for depreciation for fixed assets acquired after 1986.
10. No. Accounting Principles Board Opinion No. 20, *Accounting Changes*, is quite specific about the treatment of changes in depreciable assets' estimated service lives. Such changes should be reflected in the amounts for depreciation expense in the current and future periods. The amounts recorded for depreciation expense in the past are not affected.
11. Capital expenditures are recorded as assets and include the cost of acquiring fixed assets, adding a component, or replacing a component of fixed assets. Revenue expenditures are recorded as expenses and are costs that benefit only the current period and are incurred for normal maintenance and repairs of fixed assets.
12. Capital expenditure (component replacement)
13. **a.** No, the accumulated depreciation for an asset cannot exceed the cost of the asset. To do so would create a negative book value, which is meaningless.
   b. The cost and accumulated depreciation should be removed from the accounts when the asset is no longer useful and is removed from service. Presumably, the asset will then be sold, traded in, or discarded.
14. **a.** All purchases of fixed assets should be approved by an appropriate level of management. In addition, competitive bids should be solicited to ensure that the company is acquiring the assets at the lowest possible price.
   b. A physical count of fixed assets will verify the accuracy of accounting records. It will also detect missing fixed assets that should be removed from the records and obsolete or idle fixed assets that should be disposed of.
15. **a.** Over the years of its expected usefulness
   b. Expense as incurred
   c. Goodwill should not be amortized, but written down when impaired.

Activity 9–6

a. Saks uses the LIFO method for determining cost; however, market was less than this amount. Inventories must be recorded at the lower of cost or market. This is an example of the conservatism principle. Recording at lower of cost or market causes inventory obsolescence losses to be recorded on the income statement in the period of the market decline, rather than the period of sale. In the case of Saks, market may be less than cost due to fashion obsolescence, as evidenced by the markdowns.

b. Consigned goods are held for sale on a commission basis. That is, Saks earns a commission upon selling the goods, but does not actually own the goods. As a result, the value of the goods should not be included in the inventory. Saks could not pledge these goods for a loan because it has no claim on these goods, nor does it assume obsolescence risk with these goods. If the goods do not sell, Saks simply returns the goods to the owner.

Activity 9–7

a. Inventory turnover = $\dfrac{\text{Cost of goods sold}}{\text{Average inventory}}$

Number of days' sales in inventory = $\dfrac{\text{Inventory, end of period}}{\text{Cost of goods sold/365}}$

Dell Computer

Inventory turnover: $\dfrac{\$29,055}{(\$278 + \$306)/2} = 99.5$

Days' sales in inventory: $\dfrac{\$306}{\$29,055/365} = 3.84$ days

Hewlett-Packard

Inventory turnover : $\dfrac{\$34,573}{(\$5,204 + \$5,797)/2} = 6.29$

Days' sales in inventory: $\dfrac{\$5,797}{\$34,573/365} = 61.20$ days

b. Dell builds its computers to a customer order, called a build-to-order strategy. That is, Dell doesn't make a computer until it has an order from a customer. Customers place their orders on the Internet. Dell then builds and delivers the computer, usually in a matter of days. HP, in contrast, builds computers before actual orders are received. This is called a build-to-stock strategy. HP must forecast the type of computers customers want before it receives the orders. This strategy results in greater inventory for HP, since the computers are built before there is a sale. HP has significant finished goods inventory, while Dell has little finished goods. This difference in strategy is why you see HP computers at a retail store, but not a Dell computer. It also explains the difference in their inventory efficiency ratios.

Activity 9–8

Note to Instructors: The purpose of this activity is to familiarize students with the cost flow assumptions that an actual retailing company would use.

EXERCISES

Ex. 10–1

a. New printing press: 1, 2, 3, 4, 5

b. Secondhand printing press: 8, 9, 10, 12

Ex. 10–2

a. Yes. All expenditures incurred for the purpose of making the land suitable for its intended use should be debited to the land account.

b. No. Land is not depreciated.

Ex. 10–3

Initial cost of land ($35,000 + $125,000).....................		$160,000
Plus: Legal fees	$ 1,100	
Delinquent taxes	12,500	
Demolition of building	18,000	31,600
		$191,600
Less: Salvage of materials		3,600
Cost of land..		$188,000

Ex. 10–4

a. No. The $859,600 represents the original cost of the equipment. Its replacement cost, which may be more or less than $859,600, is not reported in the financial statements.

b. No. The $317,500 is the accumulation of the past depreciation charges on the equipment. The recognition of depreciation expense has no relationship to the cash account or accumulation of cash funds.

Ex. 10–5

(a) 5%, (b) 4%, (c) 2½%, (d) 25%, (e) 20%, (f) 10%, (g) 2%

Ex. 10–6

$18,000 [($312,000 – $42,000) ÷ 15]

Ex. 10–7

$$\frac{\$345,000 \ - \ \$18,000}{75,000 \text{ hours}} = \$4.36 \text{ depreciation per hour}$$

1,250 hours at $4.36 = $5,450 depreciation for July

Ex. 10–8

a.

Truck No.	Rate per Mile	Miles Operated	Credit to Accumulated Depreciation
1	20.0 cents	40,000	$ 8,000
2	21.0	12,000	2,100*
3	17.5	36,000	6,300
4	20.0	21,000	4,200
Total..			$20,600

* Mileage depreciation of $2,520 (21 cents × 12,000) is limited to $2,100, which reduces the book value of the truck to $6,600, its residual value.

b.   Depreciation Expense—Trucks   20,600
       Accumulated Depreciation—Trucks   20,600

Ex. 10–9

First Year	Second Year
a. 8 1/3% of $84,000 = $7,000	8 1/3% of $84,000 = $7,000
b. 16 2/3% of $84,000 = $14,000	16 2/3% of $70,000* = $11,667
	*$84,000 – $14,000

Ex. 10–10

a. 10% of ($98,500 – $7,500) = $9,100

b. Year 1: 20% of $98,500 = $19,700
    Year 2: 20% of ($98,500 – $19,700) = $15,760

Ex. 10–11

a. Year 1: 9/12 × [($54,000 – $10,800) ÷ 12] = $2,700
    Year 2: ($54,000 – $10,800) ÷ 12 = $3,600

b. Year 1: 9/12 × 16 2/3% of $54,000 = $6,750
    Year 2: 16 2/3% of ($54,000 – $6,750) = $7,875

Ex. 10–12

a. $15,000 [($800,000 – $200,000) ÷ 40]

b. $500,000 [$800,000 – ($15,000 × 20 yrs.)]

c. $14,000 [($500,000 – $150,000) ÷ 25 yrs.]

Ex. 10–13

a.

	Current Year	Preceding Year
Land and buildings	$ 426,322,000	$ 418,928,000
Machinery and equipment	1,051,861,000	1,038,323,000
Total cost	$1,478,183,000	$1,457,251,000
Accumulated depreciation	633,178,000	582,941,000
Book value	$ 845,005,000	$ 874,310,000

A comparison of the book values of the current and preceding years indicates that they decreased. A comparison of the total cost and accumulated depreciation reveals that Interstate Bakeries purchased $20,932,000 ($1,478,183,000 − $1,457,251,000) of additional fixed assets, which was offset by the additional depreciation expense of $50,237,000 ($633,178,000 − $582,941,000) taken during the current year.

b. The book value of fixed assets should normally increase during the year. Although additional depreciation expense will reduce the book value, most companies invest in new assets in an amount that is at least equal to the depreciation expense. However, during periods of economic downturn, companies purchase fewer fixed assets, and the book value of their fixed assets may decline. This is apparently the case with Interstate Bakeries.

Ex. 10–14

Capital expenditures:

New component: 4, 6, 7
Replacement component: 1, 2, 9, 10

Revenue expenditures: 3, 5, 8

Ex. 10–15

Capital expenditures:

New component: 4, 6, 7
Replacement component: 2, 5, 8, 9, 10

Revenue expenditures: 1, 3

Ex. 10–16

a. Mar. 15 Removal Expense.. 1,500
                    Cash 1,500

b. Mar. 15 Depreciation Expense.................................. 6,000
                    Accumulated Depreciation...................... 6,000

      15 Accumulated Depreciation 18,000
                    Carpet... 18,000

      30 Carpet... 45,000
                    Cash 45,000

c. Dec. 31 Depreciation Expense.................................. 2,250*
                    Accumulated Depreciation...................... 2,250

    *($45,000 ÷ 15 years) × 9/12

Ex. 10–17

a. Initial cost of old alarm system...................................... $50,000
Accumulated depreciation from old system................. 35,000*
Book value of old system charged to
    depreciation expense $15,000
2006 depreciation expense on new component........... 12,000
Total depreciation expense... $27,000

    * ($50,000/10 years) × 7 years

b. Total depreciation expense (from [a]) $27,000
Removal expense... 2,000
Total expense for 2006 .... $29,000

Ex. 10–18

a. Cost of equipment $240,000
Accumulated depreciation at December 31, 2006
   (4 years at $22,500* per year) 90,000
Book value at December 31, 2006 .... $150,000
*($240,000 – $15,000) ÷ 10 = $22,500

b. 1. Depreciation Expense—Equipment........................ 11,250
     Accumulated Depreciation—Equipment........... 11,250

   2. Cash.. 135,000
     Accumulated Depreciation—Equipment 101,250
     Loss on Disposal of Fixed Assets 3,750
     Equipment.. 240,000

Ex. 10–19

a. 2003 depreciation expense: $15,000 [($96,000 – $6,000) ÷ 6]

   2004 depreciation expense: $15,000

   2005 depreciation expense: $15,000

b. $51,000 ($96,000 – $45,000)

c. Cash 38,000
Accumulated Depreciation—Equipment...................... 45,000
Loss on Disposal of Fixed Assets............................... 13,000
   Equipment... 96,000

d. Cash 53,000
Accumulated Depreciation—Equipment...................... 45,000
   Equipment... 96,000
   Gain on Disposal of Fixed Assets.......................... 2,000

Ex. 10–20

a. $205,000 ($315,000 – $110,000)

b. $303,750 [$315,000 – ($110,000 – $98,750)], or
   $303,750 ($205,000 + $98,750)

Ex. 10–21

a. $205,000 ($315,000 – $110,000)

b. $315,000. The new printing press's cost cannot exceed $315,000 on a similar exchange. The $18,500 loss on disposal ($128,500 book value – $110,000 trade-in allowance) must be recognized.

Ex. 10–22

a.	Depreciation Expense—Equipment	8,000	
	Accumulated Depreciation—Equipment		8,000
b.	Accumulated Depreciation—Equipment	152,000	
	Equipment	385,000	
	Loss on Disposal of Fixed Assets	28,000	
	Equipment		280,000
	Cash		35,000
	Notes Payable		250,000*

*$385,000 – $100,000 – $35,000

Ex. 10–23

a.	Depreciation Expense—Trucks	1,500	
	Accumulated Depreciation—Trucks		1,500
b.	Accumulated Depreciation—Trucks	37,500	
	Trucks	76,000	
	Trucks		62,500
	Cash		11,000
	Notes Payable		40,000*

*$80,000 – $29,000 – $11,000

Ex. 10–24

a. $55,000. The new truck's cost cannot exceed $55,000 in a similar exchange.

b. $54,000 ($55,000 – $1,000) or
   $54,000 ($30,000 + $24,000)

Ex. 10–25

The managers at MarketNet Co. are not required to obtain approval before disposing of fixed assets. Managers may be disposing of assets that are in good working order and that are needed at another location within the company. Alternatively, managers may be persuaded to sell used assets to employees and replace them with new assets, even though the older items are still in good working order. This weakness in the internal control system could be minimized by establishing policies regarding the disposition of common assets, such as office equipment and vehicles. For example, a policy might state that vehicles must have over 80,000 miles before disposal is permitted.

Ex. 10–26

a. $80,000,000 ÷ 100,000,000 tons = $0.80 depletion per ton

   15,500,000 × $0.80 = $12,400,000 depletion expense

b.   Depletion Expense... 12,400,000

   Accumulated Depletion... 12,400,000

Ex. 10–27

a.   ($472,500 ÷ 15) + ($75,000 ÷ 12) = $37,750 total patent expense

b.   Amortization Expense—Patents.................................... 37,750

   Patents 37,750

Ex. 10–28

1.   Fixed assets should be reported at cost and not replacement cost.

2.   Land does not depreciate.

3.   Patents and goodwill are intangible assets that should be listed in a separate section following the fixed assets section. Patents should be reported at their net book values (cost less amortization to date). Goodwill should not be amortized, but should be only written down upon impairment.

Ex. 10–29

a. Current year: Ratio of fixed assets to long-term liabilities (debt) =
$181,758,000/$14,610,000 = 12.4

Preceding year: Ratio of fixed assets to long-term liabilities (debt) =
$174,659,000/$12,150,000 = 14.4

b. The ratio of fixed assets to long-term liabilities has declined from 14.4 in the preceding year to 12.4 in the current year. This indicates a decrease in the margin of safety for long-term creditors. However, the ratio of fixed assets to long-term liabilities is large enough that Intuit will be able to borrow with relative ease.

Ex. 10–30

a. Current year: Ratio of fixed assets to long-term liabilities (debt) =
$17,168,000,000/$1,321,000,000 = 13.0

Preceding year: Ratio of fixed assets to long-term liabilities (debt) =
$15,375,000,000/$1,250,000,000 = 12.3

b. The ratio of fixed assets to long-term liabilities has increased from 12.3 in the preceding year to 13.0 in the current year. This indicates an increase in the margin of safety for long-term creditors. Home Depot can borrow on a long-term basis with relative ease, since it has few long-term liabilities.

Appendix Ex. 10–31

First year: 12/78 × $84,000 = $12,923
Second year: 11/78 × $84,000 = $11,846

Appendix Ex. 10–32

First year: 10/55 × $91,000 = $16,545
Second year: 9/55 × $91,000 = $14,891

Appendix Ex. 10–33

First year: 9/12 × 12/78 × $43,200 = $4,985
Second year: (3/12 × 12/78 × $43,200) + (9/12 × 11/78 × $43,200) = $6,231

PROBLEMS

Prob. 10–1A

1.

Item	Land	Land Improvements	Building	Other Accounts
a.	$ 5,000			
b.	160,000			
c.	3,500			
d.	17,500			
e.	16,250			
f.	12,500			
g.	(4,500)*			
h.	11,000			
i.			$ 7,200	
j.			50,000	
k.				$ 2,500
l.				1,800
m.		$12,000		
n.		18,500		
o.				(4,000)*
p.			65,000	
q.				(1,000,000)*
r.			1,250,000	
s.			(1,200)*	
2.	$221,250	$30,500	$1,371,000	

*Receipt

3. Since land used as a plant site does not lose its ability to provide services, it is not depreciated. However, land improvements do lose their ability to provide services as time passes and are therefore depreciated.

Prob. 10–2A

Depreciation Expense

Year	a. Straight-Line Method	b. Units-of-Production Method	c. Declining-Balance Method
2005	$ 50,000	$ 68,800	$107,000
2006	50,000	60,800	53,500
2007	50,000	38,400	26,750
2008	50,000	32,000	12,750
Total	$200,000	$200,000	$200,000

Calculations:

Straight-line method:

($214,000 – $14,000) ÷ 4 = $50,000 each year

Units-of-production method:

($214,000 – $14,000) ÷ 31,250 hours = $6.40 per hour

2005: 10,750 hours @ $6.40 = $68,800
2006: 9,500 hours @ $6.40 = $60,800
2007: 6,000 hours @ $6.40 = $38,400
2008: 5,000 hours @ $6.40 = $32,000

Declining-balance method:

2005: $214,000 × 50% = $107,000
2006: ($214,000 – $107,000) × 50% = $53,500
2007: ($214,000 – $107,000 – $53,500) × 50% = $26,750
2008: ($214,000 – $107,000 – $53,500 – $26,750 – $14,000*) = $12,750

*Book value should not be reduced below the residual value of $14,000.

Prob. 10–3A

a. **Straight-line method:**

2005: [($194,400 – $10,800) ÷ 3] × 1/2	$30,600
2006: ($194,400 – $10,800) ÷ 3...	61,200
2007: ($194,400 – $10,800) ÷ 3...	61,200
2008: [($194,400 – $10,800) ÷ 3] × 1/2	30,600

b. **Units-of-production method:**

2005: 4,650 hours @ $8*	$37,200
2006: 7,500 hours @ $8..	60,000
2007: 7,350 hours @ $8..	58,800
2008: 3,450 hours @ $8..	27,600

*($194,400 – $10,800) ÷ 22,950 hours = $8 per hour

c. **Declining-balance method:**

2005: $194,400 × 2/3 × 1/2...	$64,800
2006: ($194,400 – $64,800) × 2/3...	86,400
2007: ($194,400 – $64,800 – $86,400) × 2/3..................................	28,800
2008: ($194,400 – $64,800 – $86,400 – $28,800 – $10,800*)	3,600

*Book value should not be reduced below $10,800, the residual value.

Prob. 10–4A

1.

	Year	Depreciation Expense	Accumulated Depreciation, End of Year	Book Value, End of Year
a.	1	$36,000	$ 36,000	$124,000
	2	36,000	72,000	88,000
	3	36,000	108,000	52,000
	4	36,000	144,000	16,000
b.	1	$80,000	$ 80,000	$ 80,000
	2	40,000	120,000	40,000
	3	20,000	140,000	20,000
	4	4,000	144,000	16,000

2. Book value of old equipment... $ 20,000
Boot given (cash and notes payable)................................. 176,000
Cost of new equipment $196,000

or

Price of new equipment.. $200,000
Less unrecognized gain on exchange 4,000
Cost of new equipment $196,000

3. Accumulated Depreciation—Equipment...................... 140,000
Equipment 196,000
    Equipment.. 160,000
    Cash.. 16,000
    Notes Payable 160,000

4. Accumulated Depreciation—Equipment...................... 140,000
Equipment 200,000
Loss on Disposal of Fixed Assets 7,200
    Equipment.. 160,000
    Cash.. 16,000
    Notes Payable 171,200

Prob. 10–5A

2005

Jan.	2	Delivery Equipment	37,000	
		Cash..		37,000
	5	Depreciation Expense—Delivery Equipment	2,000	
		Accumulated Depreciation—Delivery Equipment		2,000
	5	Delivery Equipment	5,000	
		Cash..		5,000
	5	Accumulated Depreciation—Delivery Equipment......	2,000	
		Delivery Equipment		2,000
Apr.	7	Truck Repair Expense	125	
		Cash..		125
Dec.	31	Depreciation Expense—Delivery Equipment	10,000	
		Accumulated Depreciation—Delivery Equipment [25% × ($37,000 − $2,000 + $5,000)]....		10,000

2006

Jan.	1	Delivery Equipment	80,000	
		Cash..		80,000
Mar.	13	Truck Repair Expense	180	
		Cash..		180

Prob. 10–1B

1.

Item	Land	Land Improvements	Building	Other Accounts
a.	$ 2,500			
b.	190,000			
c.	13,750			
d.	4,800			
e.	10,200			
f.	(5,000)*			
g.	29,700			
h.			$ 6,600	
i.				$ 3,500
j.		$12,500		
k.		7,000		
l.			75,000	
m.				1,600
n.			30,000	
o.		8,500		
p.				(500,000)*
q.			750,000	
r.				(4,000)*
s.			(550)*	
2.	$245,950	$28,000	$861,050	

*Receipt

3. Since land used as a plant site does not lose its ability to provide services, it is not depreciated. However, land improvements do lose their ability to provide services as time passes and are therefore depreciated.

Prob. 10–2B

	Depreciation Expense		
Year	a. Straight-Line Method	b. Units-of Production Method	c. Declining-Balance Method
2005	$ 55,800	$ 93,750	$120,000
2006	55,800	45,000	40,000
2007	55,800	28,650	7,400
Total	$167,400	$167,400	$167,400

Calculations:

Straight-line method:

($180,000 – $12,600) ÷ 3 = $55,800 each year

Units-of-production method:

($180,000 – $12,600) ÷ 22,320 hours = $7.50 per hour

2005: 12,500 hours @ $7.50 = $93,750
2006: 6,000 hours @ $7.50 = $45,000
2007: 3,820 hours @ $7.50 = $28,650

Declining-balance method:

2005: $180,000 × 2/3 = $120,000
2006: ($180,000 – $120,000) × 2/3 = $40,000
2007: ($180,000 – $120,000 – $40,000 – $12,600*) = $7,400

*Book value should not be reduced below the residual value of $12,600.

Prob. 10–3B

a. Straight-line method:

2005:	[($174,000 – $5,700) ÷ 3] × 1/2	$28,050
2006:	($174,000 – $5,700) ÷ 3	56,100
2007:	($174,000 – $5,700) ÷ 3	56,100
2008:	[($174,000 – $5,700) ÷ 3] × 1/2	28,050

b. Units-of-production method:

2005:	2,500 hours @ $12*	$30,000
2006:	5,500 hours @ $12	66,000
2007:	4,025 hours @ $12	48,300
2008:	2,000 hours @ $12	24,000

*($174,000 – $5,700) ÷ 14,025 hours = $12 per hour

c. Declining-balance method:

2005:	$174,000 × 2/3 × 1/2	$58,000
2006:	($174,000 – $58,000) × 2/3	77,333
2007:	($174,000 – $58,000 – $77,333) × 2/3	25,778
2008:	($174,000 – $58,000 – $77,333 – $25,778 – $5,700*)	7,189

*Book value should not be reduced below $5,700, the residual value.

Prob. 10–4B

1.

	Year	Depreciation Expense	Accumulated Depreciation, End of Year	Book Value, End of Year
a.	1	$18,400	$18,400	$81,600
	2	18,400	36,800	63,200
	3	18,400	55,200	44,800
	4	18,400	73,600	26,400
	5	18,400	92,000	8,000
b.	1	$40,000	$40,000	$60,000
	2	24,000	64,000	36,000
	3	14,400	78,400	21,600
	4	8,640	87,040	12,960
	5	4,960	92,000	8,000

2. Book value of old equipment... $ 12,960
   Boot given (cash and notes payable)... 104,000
   Cost of new equipment $116,960

or

Price of new equipment... $120,000
Less unrecognized gain on exchange 3,040
Cost of new equipment $116,960

3. Accumulated Depreciation—Equipment...................... 87,040
   Equipment 116,960
      Equipment... 100,000
      Cash... 24,000
      Notes Payable 80,000

4. Accumulated Depreciation—Equipment...................... 87,040
   Equipment 120,000
   Loss on Disposal of Fixed Assets................................ 960
      Equipment... 100,000
      Cash... 24,000
      Notes Payable 84,000

Prob. 10–5B

2005

Jan.	3	Delivery Equipment	26,500	
		Cash...		26,500
	5	Depreciation Expense—Delivery Equipment	500	
		Accumulated Depreciation—		
		Delivery Equipment		500
	5	Delivery Equipment	4,000	
		Cash...		4,000
	5	Accumulated Depreciation—Delivery Equipment......	500	
		Delivery Equipment		500
Aug.	16	Truck Repair Expense	285	
		Cash...		285
Dec.	31	Depreciation Expense—Delivery Equipment	15,000	
		Accumulated Depreciation—Delivery		
		Equipment [50% × ($26,500 – $500 + $4,000)].......		15,000

2006

Jan.	1	Delivery Equipment	65,000	
		Cash...		65,000
June	30	Depreciation Expense—Delivery Equipment	3,750	
		Accumulated Depreciation—Delivery		
		Equipment [50% × ($30,000 – $15,000) × 6/12]......		3,750

Prob. 10–5B   Concluded

2006

June	30	Accumulated Depreciation—Delivery Equipment......	18,750		
		Cash...	12,000		
		Delivery Equipment			30,500
		Gain on Disposal of Fixed Assets...........................			250
Aug.	10	Truck Repair Expense	175		
		Cash...			175
Dec.	31	Depreciation Expense—Delivery Equipment	26,000		
		Accumulated Depreciation—Delivery			
		Equipment (40% × $65,000)			26,000

2007

July	1	Delivery Equipment	84,000		
		Cash...			84,000
Oct.	1	Depreciation Expense—Delivery Equipment	11,700		
		Accumulated Depreciation—Delivery			
		Equipment [9/12 × 40% × ($65,000 – $26,000)]......			11,700
	1	Cash..	26,750		
		Accumulated Depreciation—Delivery Equipment......	37,700		
		Loss on Disposal of Fixed Assets.............................	550		
		Delivery Equipment			65,000
Dec.	31	Depreciation Expense—Delivery Equipment	10,500		
		Accumulated Depreciation—Delivery			
		Equipment (1/2 × 25% × $84,000)			10,500

Prob. 10–6B

1. a. $720,000 \div 2,250,000$ board feet = $0.32 per board foot; 600,000 board feet × $0.32 per board foot = $192,000

    b.   Goodwill is not amortized.

    c. $420,000 \div 10$ years = $42,000; 1/4 of $42,000 = $10,500

2. a.   Depletion Expense   192,000
           Accumulated Depletion   192,000

    b.   No entry for goodwill amortization.

    c.   Amortization Expense—Patents   10,500
           Patents   10,500

SPECIAL ACTIVITIES

Activity 10–1

It is considered unprofessional for employees to use company assets for personal reasons, because such use reduces the useful life of the assets for normal business purposes. Thus, it is unethical for Lizzie Paulk to use Insignia Co.'s computers and laser printers to service her part-time accounting business, even on an after-hours basis. In addition, it is improper for Lizzie's clients to call her during regular working hours. Such calls may interrupt or interfere with Lizzie's ability to carry out her assigned duties for Insignia Co.

Activity 10–2

You should explain to Hal and Jody that it is acceptable to maintain two sets of records for tax and financial reporting purposes. This can happen when a company uses one method for financial statement purposes, such as straight-line depreciation, and another method for tax purposes, such as MACRS depreciation. This should not be surprising, since the methods for taxes and financial statements are established by two different groups with different objectives. That is, tax laws and related accounting methods are established by Congress. The Internal Revenue Service then applies the laws and, in some cases, issues interpretations of the law and Congressional intent. The primary objective of the tax laws is to generate revenue in an equitable manner for government use. Generally accepted accounting principles, on the other hand, are established primarily by the Financial Accounting Standards Board. The objective of generally accepted accounting principles is the preparation and reporting of true economic conditions and results of operations of business entities.

You might note, however, that companies are required in their tax returns to reconcile differences in accounting methods. For example, income reported on the company's financial statements must be reconciled with taxable income.

Finally, you might also indicate to Hal and Jody that even generally accepted accounting principles allow for alternative methods of accounting for the same transactions or economic events. For example, a company could use straight-line depreciation for some assets and double-declining-balance depreciation for other assets.

Activity 10–3

1. a. **Straight-line method:**

2004: ($120,000 ÷ 5) × 1/2	$12,000
2005: ($120,000 ÷ 5)	24,000
2006: ($120,000 ÷ 5)	24,000
2007: ($120,000 ÷ 5)	24,000
2008: ($120,000 ÷ 5)	24,000
2009: ($120,000 ÷ 5) × 1/2	12,000

b. **MACRS:**

2004: ($120,000 × 20%)	$24,000
2005: ($120,000 × 32%)	38,400
2006: ($120,000 × 19.2%)	23,040
2007: ($120,000 × 11.5%)	13,800
2008: ($120,000 × 11.5%)	13,800
2009: ($120,000 × 5.8%)	6,960

Activity 10–3   Continued

2.

a. Straight-line method

			Year			
	2004	2005	2006	2007	2008	2009
Income before depreciation	$200,000	$200,000	$200,000	$200,000	$200,000	$200,000
Depreciation expense	12,000	24,000	24,000	24,000	24,000	12,000
Income before income tax	$188,000	$176,000	$176,000	$176,000	$176,000	$188,000
Income tax	56,400	52,800	52,800	52,800	52,800	56,400
Net income	$131,600	$123,200	$123,200	$123,200	$123,200	$131,600

b. MACRS

			Year			
	2004	2005	2006	2007	2008	2009
Income before depreciation	$200,000	$200,000	$200,000	$200,000	$200,000	$200,000
Depreciation expense	24,000	38,400	23,040	13,800	13,800	6,960
Income before income tax	$176,000	$161,600	$176,960	$186,200	$186,200	$193,040
Income tax	52,800	48,480	53,088	55,860	55,860	57,912
Net income	$123,200	$113,120	$123,872	$130,340	$130,340	$135,128

Activity 10–3   Concluded

3. For financial reporting purposes, Sharon should select the method that provides the net income figure that best represents the results of operations. (*Note to Instructors:* The concept of matching revenues and expenses is discussed in Chapter 3.) However, for income tax purposes, Sharon should consider selecting the method that will minimize taxes. Based upon the analyses in (2), both methods of depreciation will yield the same total amount of taxes over the useful life of the equipment. MACRS results in fewer taxes paid in the early years of useful life and more in the later years. For example, in 2004 the MACRS amount is less than the straight-line amount. Five Points Co. can invest such differences in the early years and earn income.

    In some situations, it may be more beneficial for a taxpayer not to choose MACRS. These situations usually occur when a taxpayer is expected to be subject to a low tax rate in the early years of use of an asset and a higher tax rate in the later years of the asset's useful life. In this case, the taxpayer may be better off to defer the larger deductions to offset the higher tax rate.

Activity 10–4

Note to Instructors: The purpose of this activity is to familiarize students with the differences in cost and other factors in leasing and buying a business vehicle.

Activity 10–5

Note to Instructors: The purpose of this activity is to familiarize students with the procedures involved in acquiring a patent, a copyright, and a trademark.

CHAPTER 11
CURRENT LIABILITIES

CLASS DISCUSSION QUESTIONS

1. To match revenues and expenses properly, the liability to cover product warranties should be recorded in the period during which the sale of the product is made.

2. When the defective product is repaired, the repair costs would be recorded by debiting Product Warranty Payable and crediting Cash, Supplies, or another appropriate account.

3. Yes. Since the $5,000 is payable within one year, Company A should present it as a current liability at September 30.

4. a. Income or withholding taxes, social security, and Medicare
   b. Employees Income Tax Payable, Social Security Tax Payable, and Medicare Tax Payable

5. There is a ceiling on (a) the social security portion of the FICA tax and (d) federal unemployment compensation tax.

6. The deductions from employee earnings are for amounts owed (liabilities) to others for such items as federal taxes, state and local income taxes, and contributions to pension plans.

7. Yes. Unemployment compensation taxes are paid by the employer on the first $7,000 of annual earnings for each employee. Therefore, hiring two employees, each earning $12,500 per year, would require the payment of twice the unemployment tax than if only one employee, earning $25,000, was hired.

8. 1. c
   2. c
   3. a
   4. b
   5. b

9. The use of special payroll checks relieves the treasurer or other executives of the task of signing a large number of regular checks each payday. Another advantage of this system is that reconciling the regular bank statement is simplified. The paid payroll checks are returned by the bank separately from regular checks and are accompanied by a statement of the special bank account. Any balance shown on the bank's statement will correspond to the sum of the payroll checks outstanding because the amount of each deposit is exactly the same as the total amount of checks drawn.

10. a. Input data that remain relatively unchanged from period to period (and therefore do not need to be reintroduced into the system frequently) are called *constants*.
    b. Input data that differ from period to period are called *variables*.

11. a. If employees' attendance records are kept and their preparation supervised in such a manner as to prevent errors and abuses, then one can be assured that wages paid are based on hours actually worked. The use of "In" and "Out" cards, whereby employees indicate by punching a time clock their time of arrival and departure, is especially useful. Employee identification cards or badges can be very helpful in giving additional assurance.
    b. The requirement that the addition of names on the payroll be supported by written authorizations from the Personnel Department can help ensure that payroll checks are not being issued to fictitious persons. Endorsements on payroll checks can be compared with other samples of employees' signatures.

12. If the vacation payment is probable and can be reasonably estimated, the vacation pay expense should be recorded during the period in which the vacation privilege is earned.

13. Employee life expectancies, expected employee retirement dates, employee turnover, employee compensation levels, and investment income on pension contributions are factors that influence the future pension obligation of an employer.

EXERCISES

Ex. 11–1

Current liabilities:

Federal income taxes payable	$ 42,000[1]
Advances on magazine subscriptions	155,250[2]
Total current liabilities	$197,250

[1]$120,000 × 35%
[2]6,900 × $30 × 9/12 = $155,250

The nine months of unfilled subscriptions are a current liability because Web World received payment prior to providing the magazines.

Ex. 11–2

a.	1.	Merchandise Inventory	196,000	
		Interest Expense	4,000[1]	
		Notes Payable		200,000
	2.	Notes Payable	200,000	
		Cash		200,000
b.	1.	Notes Receivable	200,000	
		Sales		196,000
		Interest Revenue		4,000
	2.	Cash	200,000	
		Notes Receivable		200,000

[1]$200,000 × 8% × 90/360

Ex. 11–3

a. $90,000 \times 6\% \times 90/360 = \$1,350$ for each alternative.

b. (1) $90,000 simple-interest note: $90,000 proceeds
    (2) $90,000 discounted note: $90,000 – $1,350 interest = $88,650 proceeds

c. Alternative (1) is more favorable to the borrower. This can be verified by comparing the effective interest rates for each loan as follows:

> Situation (1): 6% effective interest rate
> ($1,350 × 360/90) ÷ $90,000 = 6%
> Situation (2): 6.09% effective interest rate
> ($1,350 × 360/90) ÷ $88,650 = 6.09%

The effective interest rate is higher for the second loan because the creditor lent only $88,650 in return for $1,350 interest over 90 days. In the simple-interest loan, the creditor must lend $90,000 for 90 days to earn the same $1,350 interest.

Ex. 11–4

a.	Accounts Payable	9,000	
	Notes Payable		9,000
b.	Notes Payable	9,000	
	Interest Expense	75*	
	Cash		9,075

*$9,000 × 5% × 60/360 = $75

Ex. 11–5

a.	June	30	Building	730,000	
			Land	250,000	
			Note Payable		800,000
			Cash		180,000
b.	Dec.	31	Note Payable	40,000	
			Interest Expense ($800,000 × 8% × 1/2)	32,000	
			Cash		72,000
c.	June	30	Note Payable	40,000	
			Interest Expense ($760,000 × 8% × 1/2)	30,400	
			Cash		70,400

Ex. 11–6

a. $4,650,000, or the amount disclosed as the current portion of long-term debt.

b. By the end of 2002, the bank credit line was reduced to $299,000; thus, the bank credit line was nearly paid off in 2002. The difference between the $34,783,000 that would be due in the coming period and the $4,650,000 disclosed as the current portion must have been funded (i.e., replaced) by long-term notes payable. Indeed, of the $50 million increase in the term loans ($95 million – $45 million), around $35 million must have been used to eliminate the bank credit line.

c. The current liabilities declined by $4,351,000 ($4,650,000 – $299,000).

Ex. 11–7

a. Product Warranty Expense (2% × $750,000)................   15,000

    Product Warranty Payable   15,000

b. Product Warranty Payable   960

    Wages Payable   570

    Supplies   390

Ex. 11–8

a. The warranty liability represents estimated outstanding automobile warranty claims. Of these claims, $14,166 million is estimated to be due during 2003, while the remainder ($9,125 million) is expected to be paid after 2003. The distinction between short-term and long-term liabilities is important to creditors in order to accurately evaluate the near-term cash demands on the business, relative to the quick assets and other longer-term demands.

b. Product Warranty Expense 14,355,000,000
    Product Warranty Payable   14,355,000,000

$20,410 + X – $12,000 = $23,291
X   = $23,291 – $20,410 + $12,000
X   = $14,881 million

c. The liability might have grown for a number of possible reasons. Often the estimated warranty liability will increase if the underlying product sales are also increasing, as was the case for Ford during this time. Alternatively, Ford's actual claims experience might be declining. If the percent of sales estimate remained unchanged, this would cause the liability to potentially increase. This partially explains the increase, since only $12,000 million in claims were assumed to be paid, while the current estimated claims payable was $13,605 million at December 31, 2001. Lastly, Ford could be increasing its estimated warranty claims expense as a percent of current period sales.

Ex. 11–9

a. Damage Awards and Fines 670,000
    EPA Fines Payable   390,000
    Litigation Claims Payable   280,000

Note to Instructors: The "damage awards and fines" would be disclosed on the income statement under "other expenses."

b. The company experienced a hazardous materials spill at one of its plants during the previous period. This spill has resulted in a number of lawsuits to which the company is a party. The Environmental Protection Agency (EPA) has fined the company $390,000, which the company is contesting in court. Although the company does not admit fault, legal counsel believes that the fine payment is probable. In addition, an employee has sued the company. A $280,000 out-of-court settlement has been reached with the employee. The EPA fine and out-of-court settlement have been accrued. There is one other outstanding lawsuit related to this incident. Counsel does not believe that the lawsuit has merit. Other lawsuits and unknown liabilities may arise from this incident.

Ex. 11–10

a. Adjusting entry to accrue litigation contingency, 12/31/01:

Litigation Expenses and Losses 219,100,000
   Contingent Product and Tort Claims Payable...   219,100,000

Note to Instructors: The actual titles in the accounts may vary from those illustrated in this answer and, in practice, will vary according to the nature of the contingency.

b. Summary journal entry to pay claims in 2002:

Contingent Product and Tort Claims Payable 75,000,000
   Cash   75,000,000

c. A liability must be recognized if the contingency is both estimable and probable. The note makes it clear that the claims have been ongoing across thousands of cases. This means it is possible to reasonably estimate the losses from the historical litigation experience. That is, the average loss per case could be determined and applied to the outstanding cases. In addition, a portion of the claim losses are known to be probable, again based upon past experience.

Ex. 11–11

a.

Regular pay (40 hrs. × $18)		$720
Overtime pay (10 hrs. × $27)		270
Gross pay		$990

b.

Gross pay		$990.00
Less: Social security tax (6.0% × $990)	$ 59.40	
Medicare tax (1.5% × $990)	14.85	
Federal withholding	185.00	259.25
Net pay		$730.75

Ex. 11–12

	Consultant	Computer Programmer	Administrator
Regular earnings	$2,500.00	$1,600.00	$ 800.00
Overtime earnings		360.00	120.00
Gross pay	$2,500.00	$1,960.00	$ 920.00
Less: Social security tax	$ 0.00[1]	$ 66.00[2]	$ 55.20[3]
Medicare tax	37.50	29.40	13.80
Federal income tax withheld[4] ...	570.15	435.64	111.64
	$ 607.65	$ 531.04	$ 180.64
Net pay	$1,892.35	$1,428.96	$ 739.36

[1] Gross pay exceeds $100,000, so there is no social security tax withheld.

[2] [($100,000 − $98,900) × 6%] = $66.00

[3] $920 × 6.0% = $55.20

[4] The federal income tax withheld is determined from applying the calculation procedure associated with Exhibit 3, as follows:

Withholding calculations:	Consultant	Computer Programmer	Administrator
	$ 2,500.00	$1,960.00	$ 920.00
	− 463.76	− 404.14	− 473.46
	$ 2,036.24	$1,555.86	$ 446.54
	× 28%	× 28%	× 25%
	$ 570.15	$ 435.64	$ 111.64

Ex. 11–13

a. Summary: (1) $224,800; (3) $269,000; (8) $4,460; (12) $75,800

   Details:

Net amount paid		$189,000
Total deductions		80,000
(3) Total earnings		$269,000
Overtime		44,200
(1) Regular		$224,800
Total deductions		$ 80,000
Social security tax	$ 15,730	
Medicare tax	4,035	
Income tax withheld	47,915	
Medical insurance	7,860	75,540
(8) Union dues		$ 4,460
Total earnings		$269,000
Factory wages	$135,400	
Office salaries	57,800	193,200
(12) Sales salaries		$ 75,800

b.

Factory Wages Expense	135,400	
Sales Salaries Expense	75,800	
Office Salaries Expense	57,800	
Social Security Tax Payable		15,730
Medicare Tax Payable		4,035
Employees Income Tax Payable		47,915
Medical Insurance Payable		7,860
Union Dues Payable		4,460
Salaries Payable		189,000

c.

Salaries Payable	189,000	
Cash		189,000

d. The amount of social security tax withheld, $15,730, is $410 less than 6.0% of the total earnings of $269,000. This indicates that the cumulative earnings of some employees exceed $100,000. Therefore, it is unlikely that this payroll was paid during the first few weeks of the calendar year.

Ex. 11–14

Opry Sounds does have an internal control procedure that should detect the payroll error. Before funds are transferred from the regular bank account to the payroll account, the owner authorizes a voucher for the total amount of the week's payroll. The owner should catch the error, since the extra 360 hours will cause the weekly payroll to be substantially higher than usual.

Ex. 11–15

a. Inappropriate. Access to the check-signing machine should be restricted.

b. Appropriate. The use of a special payroll account assists in preventing fraud and makes it easier to reconcile the company's bank accounts.

c. Appropriate. All changes to the payroll system, including wage rate increases, should be authorized by someone outside the Payroll Department.

d. Inappropriate. Payroll should be informed when any employee is terminated. A supervisor or other individual could continue to clock in and out for the terminated employee and collect the extra paycheck.

e. Inappropriate. Each employee should record his or her own time out for lunch. Under the current procedures, one employee could clock in several employees who are still out to lunch. The company would be paying employees for more time than they actually worked.

Ex. 11–16

a.
Social security tax (6% × $480,000)	$28,800
Medicare tax (1.5% × $540,000)	8,100
State unemployment (4.3% × $12,000)	516
Federal unemployment (0.8% × $12,000)	96
	$37,512

b.
Payroll Taxes Expense	37,512	
Social Security Tax Payable		28,800
Medicare Tax Payable		8,100
State Unemployment Tax Payable		516
Federal Unemployment Tax Payable		96

Ex. 11–17

Tip Top Stores Inc. should not compute and report payroll taxes according to its fiscal year. Rather, employers are required to compute and report all payroll taxes on the calendar-year basis, regardless of the fiscal year they may use for financial reporting purposes. Thus, social security and FUTA maximum earnings limitations apply to the calendar-year payroll.

Ex. 11–18

Vacation Pay Expense..	13,760	
Vacation Pay Payable ($165,120 × 1/12)		13,760

Ex. 11–19

a.	Dec.	31	Pension Expense..	315,000	
			Unfunded Pension Liability....................		315,000
b.	Jan.	15	Unfunded Pension Liability	315,000	
			Cash		315,000

Ex. 11–20

The $1,032 million unfunded pension liability is the approximate amount of the pension obligation that exceeds the value of the accumulated net assets of the pension plan. Apparently, Procter & Gamble has underfunded its plan relative to the actuarial obligation that has accrued over time. This can occur when the company contributes less to the plan than the annual pension cost.

The obligation grows yearly by the amount of the periodic pension cost. Thus, the periodic pension cost is an actuarial measure of the amount of pension earned by employees during the year. The annual pension cost is determined by making actuarial assumptions about employee life expectancies, employee turnover, expected compensation levels, and interest.

Ex. 11–21

a. Quick Ratio = $\dfrac{\text{Quick Assets}}{\text{Current Liabilities}}$

    December 31, 2005: $\dfrac{\$530,000 + \$350,000}{\$800,000} = 1.10$

    December 31, 2006: $\dfrac{\$356,000 + \$400,000}{\$900,000} = 0.84$

b. The quick ratio has been decreased between the two balance sheet dates. The major reason is a significant increase in inventory. Cash also declined, possibly to purchase the inventory. As a result, quick assets actually declined, while the current liabilities increased. While the quick ratio for December 31, 2006, is below 1.0, it is not yet at an alarming level. However, the trend suggests that the firm's current asset (working capital) management should be watched closely.

Ex. 11–22

a.

	Apple Computer Inc.	Dell Computer Corp.
Quick Ratio	2.96	0.81

$$\text{Quick Ratio} = \frac{\text{Quick Assets}}{\text{Current Liabilities}}$$

Apple Computer Inc.:

$$\text{Quick ratio} = \frac{\$5,388 - \$45 - \$441}{\$1,658} = 2.96$$

Dell Computer Corp.:

$$\text{Quick ratio} = \frac{\$8,924 - \$306 - \$1,394}{\$8,933} = 0.81$$

b. It is clear that Apple Computer's short-term liquidity is stronger than Dell's. Apple's quick ratio is 215% higher. Apple has a much stronger relative cash and short-term investment position than does Dell. Apple's cash and short-term investments are 80% of total current assets (261% of current liabilities), compared to Dell's 52% of total current assets (52% of current liabilities). In addition, Dell's relative accounts payable position is larger than Apple's, indicating the possibility that Dell has longer supplier payment terms than does Apple. A quick ratio of 2.96 for Apple suggests ample flexibility to make strategic investments with its excess cash, while a quick ratio of 0.81 for Dell indicates an efficient but tight quick asset management policy.

PROBLEMS

Prob. 11–1A

1.

Feb.	15	Merchandise Inventory..	30,000	
		Accounts Payable—Ranier Co.		30,000
Mar.	17	Accounts Payable—Ranier Co.	30,000	
		Notes Payable..		30,000
Apr.	16	Notes Payable	30,000	
		Interest Expense ($30,000 × 30/360 × 5%)	125	
		Cash		30,125
July	15	Cash...	40,000	
		Notes Payable..		40,000
	25	Tools..	43,950	
		Interest Expense ($45,000 × 120/360 × 7%)	1,050	
		Notes Payable..		45,000
Oct.	13	Notes Payable	40,000	
		Interest Expense ($40,000 × 90/360 × 6%)	600	
		Notes Payable..		40,000
		Cash		600
Nov.	12	Notes Payable	40,000	
		Interest Expense ($40,000 × 30/360 × 9%)	300	
		Cash		40,300
	22	Notes Payable	45,000	
		Cash		45,000
Dec.	1	Office Equipment...	80,000	
		Notes Payable..		60,000
		Cash		20,000
	17	Litigation Loss...	41,000	
		Litigation Claims Payable.............................		41,000
	31	Notes Payable	6,000	
		Interest Expense ($6,000 × 8% × 30/360)	40	
		Cash		6,040

Prob. 11–3A

1.

Employee	Gross Earnings	Federal Income Tax Withheld	Social Security Tax Withheld	Medicare Tax Withheld
Alvarez	$124,200	$31,050	$ 6,000*	$1,863
Carver	6,000	900	360	90
Felix	40,800	6,528	2,448	612
Lydall	22,000	3,850	1,320	330
Porter	102,000	24,480	6,000*	1,530
Song	36,000	6,480	2,160	540
Walker	58,800	11,172	3,528	882
			$21,816	$5,847

*$100,000 maximum × 6%

2.

a. Social security tax paid by employer... $21,816

b. Medicare tax paid by employer 5,847

c. Earnings subject to unemployment compensation tax, $7,000 for all employees except Carver, who has only $6,000 in gross earnings. Thus, total earnings subject to SUTA and FUTA are [(6 × $7,000) + $6,000].
State unemployment compensation tax: $48,000 × 4.2% 2,016

d. Federal unemployment compensation tax: $48,000 × 0.8% 384

e. Total payroll taxes expense... $30,063

Prob. 11–4A

1. 2006

Dec. 12 Sales Salaries Expense 3,366.50
Office Salaries Expense.............................. 2,900.00
Delivery Salaries Expense 1,959.00
    Social Security Tax Payable.................... 493.53
    Medicare Tax Payable............................ 123.38
    Employees Income Tax Payable 1,402.06
    Medical Insurance Payable 469.20
    Salaries Payable...................................... 5,737.33

2. Dec. 12 Salaries Payable 5,737.33
    Cash 5,737.33

3. Dec. 12 Payroll Taxes Expense................................. 671.91
    Social Security Tax Payable.................... 493.53
    Medicare Tax Payable............................ 123.38
    State Unemployment Tax Payable 45.00
    Federal Unemployment Tax Payable..... 10.00

4. Dec. 15 Employees Income Tax Payable 1,402.06
Social Security Tax Payable 987.06
Medicare Tax Payable 246.76
    Cash 2,635.88

Prob. 11–5A

1.

PAYROLL FOR WEEK ENDING December 7, 2006

		Earnings			Deductions					Paid		Accounts Debited	
Name	Total Hours	Regular	Overtime	Total	Social Security Tax	Medicare Tax	Federal Income Tax	U.S. Savings Bonds	Total	Net Amount	Ck. No.	Sales Salaries Expense	Office Salaries Expense
M	45.00	1,120.00	210.00	1,330.00	79.80	19.95	292.60	35.00	427.35	902.65	818	1,330.00	
N	25.00	550.00		550.00	33.00	8.25	82.50		123.75	426.25	819	550.00	
O				2,350.00	0.00	35.25	564.00	50.00	649.25	1,700.75	820		2,350.00
P	40.00	720.00		720.00	43.20	10.80	144.00	15.00	213.00	507.00	821	720.00	
Q	40.00	800.00		800.00	48.00	12.00	168.00	10.00	238.00	562.00	822	800.00	
R	46.00	740.00	166.50	906.50	54.39	13.60	190.37		258.36	648.14	823	906.50	
S	40.00	640.00		640.00	38.40	9.60	121.60	15.00	184.60	455.40	824	640.00	
T				1,000.00	60.00	15.00	215.00		290.00	710.00	825		1,000.00
U	50.00	1,440.00	540.00	1,980.00	118.80	29.70	455.40	40.00	643.90	1,336.10	826	1,980.00	
		6,010.00	916.50	10,276.50	475.59	154.15	2,233.47	165.00	3,028.21	7,248.29		6,926.50	3,350.00

2.

Sales Salaries Expense	6,926.50	
Office Salaries Expense	3,350.00	
Social Security Tax Payable		475.59
Medicare Tax Payable		154.15
Employees Federal Income Tax Payable		2,233.47
Bond Deductions Payable		165.00
Salaries Payable		7,248.29

Prob. 11-6A

1.

Dec.	2	Bond Deductions Payable	2,400	
		Cash		2,400
	3	Social Security Tax Payable	8,276	
		Medicare Tax Payable	2,178	
		Employees Federal Income Tax Payable	13,431	
		Cash		23,885
	14	Operations Salaries Expense	42,500	
		Officers Salaries Expense	18,500	
		Office Salaries Expense	11,000	
		Social Security Tax Payable		3,960
		Medicare Tax Payable		1,080
		Employees Federal Income Tax Payable		12,816
		Employees State Income Tax Payable		3,240
		Bond Deductions Payable		1,200
		Medical Insurance Payable		1,500
		Salaries Payable		48,204
	14	Salaries Payable	48,204	
		Cash		48,204
	14	Payroll Taxes Expense	5,396	
		Social Security Tax Payable		3,960
		Medicare Tax Payable		1,080
		State Unemployment Tax Payable		285
		Federal Unemployment Tax Payable		71
	17	Social Security Tax Payable	7,920	
		Medicare Tax Payable	2,160	
		Employees Federal Income Tax Payable	12,816	
		Cash		22,896
	18	Medical Insurance Payable	9,000	
		Cash		9,000

BROWNIE POINTS GIFTS INC.
Statement of Owner's Equity
For the Period Ended December 31, 20—

Marco Woo, capital (beginning of period)		$715,759
Net loss	$ 65,769	
Plus withdrawals	150,000	
Decrease in capital		215,769
Marco Woo, capital (end of period)		$499,990

Prob. 11–6A   Concluded

BROWNIE POINTS GIFTS INC.
Balance Sheet
December 31, 20—

Assets

Cash	$ 30,074	
Accounts receivable	188,203	
Merchandise inventory	281,627	
Prepaid insurance	4,050	
Store supplies	7,825	
Total current assets		$ 511,779
Store equipment	$ 162,300	
Accumulated depreciation—store equipment	(44,980)	
Total plant assets		117,320
Total assets		$ 629,099

Liabilities

Accounts payable	$ 78,061	
Salaries payable	7,280	
Social security tax payable	7,862	
Medicare tax payable	2,184	
Employees federal income tax payable	12,958	
State unemployment tax payable	1,651	
Federal unemployment tax payable	413	
Medical insurance payable	1,500	
Unfunded pension liability	4,000	
Vacation pay payable	13,200	
Total liabilities		$ 129,109

Owner's Equity

Marco Woo, capital		499,990
Total liabilities and equity		$ 629,099

Prob. 11–1B

1.

Apr.	7	Cash...	20,000	
		Notes Payable...		20,000
May	10	Equipment..	87,600	
		Interest Expense ($90,000 × 120/360 × 8%)........	2,400	
		Notes Payable...		90,000
June	6	Notes Payable...	20,000	
		Interest Expense ($20,000 × 60/360 × 6%)..........	200	
		Notes Payable...		20,000
		Cash		200
July	6	Notes Payable...	20,000	
		Interest Expense ($20,000 × 30/360 × 9%)..........	150	
		Cash		20,150
Aug.	3	Merchandise Inventory.......................................	18,000	
		Accounts Payable—Hamilton Co....................		18,000
Sept.	2	Accounts Payable—Hamilton Co.	18,000	
		Notes Payable...		18,000
	7	Notes Payable...	90,000	
		Cash		90,000
Nov.	1	Notes Payable...	18,000	
		Interest Expense ($18,000 × 60/360 × 7.5%).......	225	
		Cash		18,225
	15	Store Equipment..	100,000	
		Notes Payable...		63,000
		Cash		37,000
Dec.	15	Notes Payable...	9,000	
		Interest Expense ($9,000 × 6% × 30/360)............	45	
		Cash		9,045
	21	Litigation Loss...	45,000	
		Litigation Claims Payable...............................		45,000

Prob. 11–1B   Concluded

2.   a.   **Product Warranty Expense**..................................... **13,900**
       Product Warranty Payable................................. **13,900**

   b.   **Interest Expense**.. **414**
       Interest Payable... **414**
       ($9,000 × 6% × 46/360 × 6 = $414)

Prob. 11–2B

1. a. Dec. 30

Sales Salaries Expense	436,000	
Warehouse Salaries Expense	93,400	
Office Salaries Expense	178,600	
Employees Income Tax Payable		127,440
Social Security Tax Payable		40,002
Medicare Tax Payable		10,620
Bond Deductions Payable		24,780
Group Insurance Payable		40,356
Salaries Payable		464,802

b. Dec. 30

Payroll Taxes Expense	51,450	
Social Security Tax Payable		40,002
Medicare Tax Payable		10,620
State Unemployment Tax Payable		684[1]
Federal Unemployment Tax Payable		144[2]

[1] $18,000 × 3.8%
[2] $18,000 × 0.8%

2. a. Dec. 30

Sales Salaries Expense	436,000	
Warehouse Salaries Expense	93,400	
Office Salaries Expense	178,600	
Employees Income Tax Payable		127,440
Social Security Tax Payable		42,480[3]
Medicare Tax Payable		10,620[4]
Bond Deductions Payable		24,780
Group Insurance Payable		40,356
Salaries Payable		462,324

[3] $708,000 × 6%
[4] $708,000 × 1.5%

b. Jan. 4

Payroll Taxes Expense	85,668	
Social Security Tax Payable		42,480
Medicare Tax Payable		10,620
State Unemployment Tax Payable		26,904[5]
Federal Unemployment Tax Payable		5,664[6]

[5] $708,000 × 3.8%
[6] $708,000 × 0.8%

Prob. 11–3B

1.

Employee	Gross Earnings	Federal Income Tax Withheld	Social Security Tax Withheld	Medicare Tax Withheld
Albright	$ 46,200	$10,164	$ 2,772	$ 693
Charles	102,000	24,888	6,000*	1,530
Given	53,000	10,070	3,180	795
Nelson	43,200	7,776	2,592	648
Quinn	6,000	1,110	360	90
Ramirez	27,200	4,760	1,632	408
Wu	115,000	28,520	6,000*	1,725
			$22,536	$5,889

*$100,000 maximum × 6%

2. a. Social security tax paid by employer $22,536

b. Medicare tax paid by employer 5,889

c. Earnings subject to unemployment compensation tax, $7,000 for all employees except Quinn, who has only $6,000 in gross earnings. Thus, total earnings subject to SUTA and FUTA are $48,000 [(6 × $7,000) + $6,000]. State unemployment compensation tax: $48,000 × 3.8%...... 1,824

d. Federal unemployment compensation tax: $48,000 × 0.8%.. 384

e. Total payroll taxes expense $30,633

Prob. 11–4B

1. 2006

Dec.	12	Sales Salaries Expense	3,366.50	
		Office Salaries Expense.................................	2,900.00	
		Delivery Salaries Expense	1,959.00	
		Social Security Tax Payable....................		493.53
		Medicare Tax Payable.............................		123.38
		Employees Income Tax Payable		1,402.06
		Medical Insurance Payable		469.20
		Salaries Payable.......................................		5,737.33

2. Dec.	12	Salaries Payable	5,737.33	
		Cash		5,737.33

3. Dec.	12	Payroll Taxes Expense..................................	646.91	
		Social Security Tax Payable....................		493.53
		Medicare Tax Payable.............................		123.38
		State Unemployment Tax Payable.........		24.00
		Federal Unemployment Tax Payable.....		6.00

4. Dec.	15	Employees Income Tax Payable	1,402.06	
		Social Security Tax Payable	987.06	
		Medicare Tax Payable	246.76	
		Cash		2,635.88

Prob. 11–5B

1.

PAYROLL FOR WEEK ENDING December 7, 2006

	Total	Earnings			Deductions					Paid		Accounts Debited	
Name	Hours	Regular	Overtime	Total	Social Security Tax	Medicare Tax	Federal Income Tax	U.S. Savings Bonds	Total	Net Amount	Ck. No.	Sales Salaries Expense	Office Salaries Expense
A	50.00	1,120.00	420.00	1,540.00	92.40	23.10	354.20	15.00	484.70	1,055.30	981	1,540.00	
B	42.00	880.00	66.00	946.00	56.76	14.19	189.20	0.00	260.15	685.85	982	946.00	
C				2,150.00	0.00	32.25	537.50	70.00	639.75	1,510.25	983		2,150.00
D	46.00	720.00	162.00	882.00	52.92	13.23	176.40	10.00	252.55	629.45	984	882.00	
E	40.00	600.00		600.00	36.00	9.00	108.00	0.00	153.00	447.00	985	600.00	
F	45.00	900.00	168.75	1,068.75	64.13	16.03	224.44	20.00	324.60	744.15	986	1,068.75	
G	40.00	640.00		640.00	38.40	9.60	108.80	25.00	181.80	458.20	987	640.00	
H				1,100.00	66.00	16.50	242.00	0.00	324.50	775.50	988		1,100.00
I	30.00	360.00		360.00	21.60	5.40	43.20	15.00	85.20	274.80	989	360.00	
		5,220.00	816.75	9,286.75	428.21	139.30	1,983.74	155.00	2,706.25	6,580.50		6,036.75	3,250.00

2.

Sales Salaries Expense	6,036.75	
Office Salaries Expense	3,250.00	
Social Security Tax Payable		428.21
Medicare Tax Payable		139.30
Employees Federal Income Tax Payable		1,983.74
Bond Deductions Payable		155.00
Salaries Payable		6,580.50

Prob. 11–6B

1.

Dec.	1	Medical Insurance Payable	4,200	
		Cash		4,200
	2	Social Security Tax Payable	6,236	
		Medicare Tax Payable	1,641	
		Employees Federal Income Tax Payable	10,120	
		Cash		17,997
	3	Bond Deductions Payable	1,500	
		Cash		1,500
	14	Sales Salaries Expense	33,000	
		Officers Salaries Expense	15,600	
		Office Salaries Expense	5,000	
		Social Security Tax Payable		2,948
		Medicare Tax Payable		804
		Employees Federal Income Tax Payable		9,541
		Employees State Income Tax Payable		2,412
		Bond Deductions Payable		750
		Medical Insurance Payable		700
		Salaries Payable		36,445
	14	Salaries Payable	36,445	
		Cash		36,445
	14	Payroll Taxes Expense	4,077	
		Social Security Tax Payable		2,948
		Medicare Tax Payable		804
		State Unemployment Tax Payable		260
		Federal Unemployment Tax Payable		65
	17	Social Security Tax Payable	5,896	
		Medicare Tax Payable	1,608	
		Employees Federal Income Tax Payable	9,541	
		Cash		17,045

Prob. 11–6B   Continued

Dec.	28	Sales Salaries Expense	33,600	
		Officers Salaries Expense	16,000	
		Office Salaries Expense	5,200	
		Social Security Tax Payable		2,959
		Medicare Tax Payable		822
		Employees Federal Income Tax Payable		9,754
		Employees State Income Tax Payable		2,466
		Bond Deductions Payable		750
		Salaries Payable		38,049
	28	Salaries Payable	38,049	
		Cash		38,049
	28	Payroll Taxes Expense	3,981	
		Social Security Tax Payable		2,959
		Medicare Tax Payable		822
		State Unemployment Tax Payable		160
		Federal Unemployment Tax Payable		40
	30	Employees State Income Tax Payable	14,724	
		Cash		14,724
	30	Bond Deductions Payable	1,500	
		Cash		1,500
	31	Pension Expense	65,000	
		Cash		59,500
		Unfunded Pension Liability		5,500

2.

Dec.	31	Sales Salaries Expense	3,360	
		Officers Salaries Expense	1,600	
		Office Salaries Expense	520	
		Salaries Payable		5,480
	31	Vacation Pay Expense	13,600	
		Vacation Pay Payable		13,600

Prob. 11–6B Continued

This solution is applicable only if the P.A.S.S. Software that accompanies the text is used.

ACADIA OUTDOOR EQUIPMENT COMPANY
Income Statement
For the Period Ended December 31, 20—

Sales	$ 3,387,200	100.00
Cost of merchandise sold	1,580,000	46.65
Gross profit	$ 1,807,200	53.35
Operating expenses:		
Selling expenses:		
Sales salaries expense	$ 815,760	24.08
Advertising expense	47,400	1.40
Depreciation expense—store equipment	13,662	0.40
Store supplies expense	35,850	1.06
Miscellaneous selling expense	8,250	0.24
Total selling expenses	$ 920,922	27.19
Administrative expenses:		
Officers salaries expense	$ 380,800	11.24
Office salaries expense	120,720	3.56
Rent expense	72,000	2.13
Heating and lighting expense	28,980	0.86
Insurance expense	26,921	0.79
Miscellaneous administrative expense	6,420	0.19
Payroll taxes expense	102,265	3.02
Pension expense	65,000	1.92
Vacation pay expense	13,600	0.40
Total administrative expenses	$ 816,706	24.11
Total operating expenses	$ 1,737,628	51.30
Net income	$ 69,572	2.05

Prob. 11–6B   Continued

ACADIA OUTDOOR EQUIPMENT COMPANY
Statement of Owner's Equity
For the Period Ended December 31, 20—

Merle Fiorvante, capital (beginning of period)..............		$646,210
Net income	$ 69,572	
Less withdrawals...	(110,000)	
Decrease in owner's equity		(40,428)
Merle Fiorvante, capital (end of period).........................		$605,782

ACADIA OUTDOOR EQUIPMENT COMPANY
Balance Sheet
December 31, 20—

Assets

Cash	$ 149,138	
Accounts receivable	192,300	
Merchandise inventory	261,450	
Prepaid insurance	4,250	
Store supplies	7,980	
Total current assets		$ 615,118
Store equipment	$ 161,100	
Accumulated depreciation—store equipment	(45,540)	
Total plant assets		115,560
Total assets		$ 730,678

Liabilities

Accounts payable	$ 80,400	
Salaries payable	5,480	
Social security tax payable	5,918	
Medicare tax payable	1,644	
Employees federal income tax payable	9,754	
State unemployment tax payable	1,520	
Federal unemployment tax payable	380	
Medical insurance payable	700	
Unfunded pension liability	5,500	
Vacation pay payable	13,600	
Total liabilities		$ 124,896

Owner's Equity

Merle Fiorvante, capital	605,782
Total liabilities and equity	$ 730,678

COMPREHENSIVE PROBLEM 3

1.

Jan.	2	Petty Cash	800	
		Cash		800
Mar.	1	Office Supplies	265	
		Miscellaneous Selling Expense	304	
		Miscellaneous Administrative Expense	158	
		Cash		727
Apr.	5	Merchandise Inventory.................................	10,000	
		Accounts Payable		10,000
May	5	Accounts Payable.......................................	10,000	
		Cash		10,000
	10	Cash...	8,480	
		Cash Short and Over...................................	10	
		Sales...		8,490
June	2	Notes Receivable.......................................	50,000	
		Accounts Receivable		50,000
Aug.	1	Cash...	50,600	
		Notes Receivable		50,000
		Interest Revenue		600*

*$50,000 × 7.2% × 60/360 = $600

	3	Cash...	1,400	
		Allowance for Doubtful Accounts	600	
		Accounts Receivable		2,000
	28	Accounts Receivable....................................	600	
		Allowance for Doubtful Accounts...................		600
	28	Cash...	600	
		Accounts Receivable		600

Sept.	2	Land..	118,200	
		Interest Expense..	1,800	
		Notes Payable...		120,000
Oct.	2	Office Equipment..	130,000	
		Accumulated Depreciation—Office Equipment.	35,000	
		Office Equipment		96,000
		Notes Payable...		69,000
Nov.	30	Sales Salaries Expense	42,500	
		Office Salaries Expense.....................................	22,500	
		Employees Federal Income Tax Payable		13,650
		Social Security Tax Payable...........................		3,770
		Medicare Tax Payable...................................		975
		Salaries Payable..		46,605
	30	Payroll Taxes Expense......................................	4,791	
		Social Security Tax Payable...........................		3,770
		Medicare Tax Payable...................................		975
		State Unemployment Tax Payable.................		38
		Federal Unemployment Tax Payable.............		8
Dec.	1	Notes Payable..	120,000	
		Cash		120,000
	30	Pension Expense..	65,000	
		Cash		61,300
		Unfunded Pension Liability		3,700

Comp. Prob. 3   Continued

2.

CALICO INTERIORS, INC.
Bank Reconciliation
December 31, 2006

Balance according to bank statement...............................		$105,700
Add deposit in transit, not recorded by bank.................		10,400
		$116,100
Deduct outstanding checks...		22,680
Adjusted balance		$ 93,420
Balance according to depositor's records		$ 93,600
Deduct:		
Bank service charges...	$ 80	
Error in recording check...	100	180
Adjusted balance		$ 93,420

3. Miscellaneous Administrative Expense........................	80	
Accounts Payable	100	
Cash..		180

4.   a.   Uncollectible Accounts Expense   6,480
             Allowance for Doubtful Accounts......................   6,480

      b.   Cost of Merchandise Sold   1,260
             Merchandise Inventory   1,260

      c.   Insurance Expense..   14,300
             Prepaid Insurance   14,300

      d.   Office Supplies Expense..   5,680
             Office Supplies   5,680

      e.   Depreciation Expense—Buildings   6,400
             Depreciation Expense—Office Equipment.............   5,800
             Depreciation Expense—Store Equipment..............   10,500
                 Accumulated Depreciation—Buildings   6,400
                 Accumulated Depreciation—Office Equipment   5,800
                 Accumulated Depreciation—Store Equipment.   10,500

             Computations:
                 Buildings ($320,000 × 2%)   6,400
                 Office Equipment
                 [1/4 × 20% × ($130,000 – $14,000)].....   5,800
                 Store Equipment ($42,000 × 25%)......   10,500

      f.   Amortization Expense—Patents ($42,900 ÷ 6)   7,150
             Patents   7,150

      g.   Depletion Expense   15,000
             Accumulated Depletion   15,000
                 [($105,000 ÷ 42,000 tons) × 6,000 tons]

      h.   Vacation Pay Expense   11,400
             Vacation Pay Payable   11,400

      i.   Product Warranty Expense ($568,000 × 2.5%)   14,200
             Product Warranty Payable....................................   14,200

      j.   Interest Expense ($69,000 × 9% × 90/360)   1,553
             Interest Payable...   1,553

Comp. Prob. 3   Continued

5.

CALICO INTERIORS, INC.
Balance Sheet
December 31, 2006

Assets

Current assets:

Petty cash		$ 800
Cash		93,420
Notes receivable..		40,000
Accounts receivable	$202,300	
Less allowance for doubtful accounts	5,980	196,320
Merchandise inventory—at cost		
(last-in, first-out)		140,600
Prepaid insurance		28,600
Office supplies		7,100
Total current assets.............................		$ 506,840

Property, plant, and equipment:

	Cost	Accumulated Depreciation (Depletion)	Book Value	
Land..	$118,200		$118,200	
Buildings...................................	320,000	$ 6,400	313,600	
Office equipment........................	130,000	5,800	124,200	
Store equipment.........................	42,000	10,500	31,500	
Mineral rights............................	105,000	15,000	90,000	
Total property, plant, and equipment............................	$715,200	$37,700		677,500

Intangible assets:

Patents	35,750
Total assets...	$1,220,090

Comp. Prob. 3   Continued

Liabilities

Current liabilities:

Social security tax payable	$ 7,772	
Medicare tax payable	2,010	
Employees federal income tax payable	14,070	
State unemployment tax payable	33	
Federal unemployment tax payable	6	
Salaries payable	67,000	
Accounts payable......................................	125,300	
Interest payable..	1,553	
Product warranty payable	14,200	
Vacation pay payable................................	10,000	
Notes payable (current portion).................	69,000	
Total current liabilities..........................		$ 310,944

Long-term liabilities:

Vacation pay payable................................	$ 1,400	
Unfunded pension liability	3,700	
Notes payable...	26,000	
Total long-term liabilities		31,100
Total liabilities...		$ 342,044

Owner's Equity

B. Joiner, capital......................................		878,046
Total liabilities and owner's equity		$1,220,090

Comp. Prob. 3   Concluded

6. The merchandise inventory destroyed was $129,320, determined as follows:

Merchandise inventory, January 1		$140,600
Purchases, January 1–February 7		246,720
Merchandise available for sale		$387,320
Sales, January 1–February 7	$430,000	
Less estimated gross profit ($430,000 × 40%)	172,000	
Estimated cost of merchandise sold		258,000
Estimated merchandise inventory destroyed		$129,320

SPECIAL ACTIVITIES

Activity 11–1

The firm has no implicit or explicit contract to pay any bonus. The bonus is discretionary, even if the firm paid a two-week bonus for ten straight years. The firm is not behaving unethically for reducing the bonus to one week—regardless of the reason. Sarah Lindsay, on the other hand, has taken things into her own hands. Sensing that she is being cheated, she tries to rectify the situation to her own advantage by working overtime that isn't required. This behavior could be considered fraudulent, even though Sarah is actually present on the job during the overtime hours. The point is that the overtime is not required by the firm. Sarah is incorrect in thinking that her behavior is justified because she did not receive the full two-week bonus. In fact, this behavior would not be justified even if she had a legitimate claim against the company. If she had a claim or grievance against the firm, then it should be handled by other procedural or legal means.

Activity 11–2

Connie's interpretation of the pension issue is correct. The employee earns the pension during the working years. The pension is part of the employee's compensation that is deferred until retirement. Thus, Horizon should record an expense equal to the amount of pension benefit earned by the employee for the period. This gives rise to the rather complex issue of estimating the amount of the pension expense. Peter indicates that the complexity of this calculation makes determining the annual pension expense impossible. This is not so. There are a number of mathematical and statistical approaches (termed "actuarial" approaches) that can reliably estimate the amount of benefits earned by the workforce for a given year.

As a side note, Peter's perspective can be summarized as "pay as you go." In his interpretation, there is no expense until a pension is paid to the retiree. Failing to account for pension promises when they are earned is not considered sound accounting.

Activity 11–3

The CEO may have requested the two changes because they would reduce the amount of depreciation expense and increase the amount of reported earnings recorded in a particular year. Thus, the CEO's bonus would be higher due to the larger reported earnings. Straight-line depreciation recognizes lower depreciation expense in the earlier years of a truck's life. As long as the company is replacing trucks, straight-line depreciation will result in a lower depreciation expense and hence a higher income number. Adding 50% to the useful lives of trucks (such as increasing the life from 6 to 9 years) would spread the recognition of depreciation expense over a longer life. Thus, depreciation expense would be lower and income higher in any particular year.

The CEO may request a change from one generally accepted accounting principle to another. Changing from double-declining-balance to straight-line depreciation is such a change. Though the CEO may be suggesting the change in order to influence the bonus, the change is acceptable, if Cary Trucking Company's auditors agree with the change. The increase in the useful lives of the plant and equipment is another matter. The useful lives of trucks should be based on objective analysis. An arbitrary increase in useful lives for all the trucks cannot be supported. Such a change could be viewed as a violation of generally accepted accounting principles.

Activity 11–4

a. The so-called "underground economy" hides transactions from IRS scrutiny by conducting business with cash (not check or credit card, which leaves an audit trail). The intent in many such transactions is to evade income tax illegally. However, just because a transaction is in cash does not exempt it from taxation. Cross also appears to perform landscaping services on a cash basis to evade reporting income while paying employees with cash to avoid paying social security and Medicare payroll taxes. The IRS reports that nearly 86% of the persons convicted of evading employment taxes were sentenced to an average of 17 months in prison and ordered to make restitution to the government for the taxes evaded, plus interest and penalties.

b. Carl should respond that he would rather receive a payroll check as a normal employee does. Receiving cash as an employee, rather than a payroll check, subverts the U.S. tax system. That is, such cash payments do not include deductions for payroll taxes, as required by law. That is why, for example, cash tips must be formally reported to the IRS and subjected to payroll tax deductions by the employer. In addition, if Carl followed Kevin's advice, Carl not only would be avoiding payroll taxes, but would also be underreporting income. This would subject Carl to potential fines and possible criminal prosecution for underreporting income.

Activity 11–5

The purpose of this activity is to familiarize students with the on-line job placement and career guidance information that is available. An example of the salary information from *cfstaffing.com* is as follows:

2001 Salary Guide

National Averages:

CFO	$138,750
Controller	93,250
Assistant Controller	69,200

Accounting Manager (7–9 years):

	7th Year	8th Year	9th Year
Public	$62,400	$68,200	$75,200
General	52,600	58,100	66,600
Internal Audit	64,700	68,200	73,900
Tax	66,500	75,100	82,700
Cost	57,300	60,200	62,800

Accounting Senior (4–6 years):

	4th Year	5th Year	6th Year
Public	$46,500	$51,400	$54,800
General	41,800	46,200	49,400
Internal Audit	48,900	53,400	58,500
Tax	48,400	56,900	59,300
Cost	44,600	47,300	51,000

Staff Accountant (1–3 years):

	1st Year	2nd Year	3rd Year
Public	$39,200	$40,200	$46,200
General	34,900	37,600	41,700
Internal Audit	40,100	44,100	48,100
Tax	39,700	44,200	46,400
Cost	36,500	40,000	44,400

Staff Accountant (0–1 years):

	1st Year
Public	$38,600
General	34,500
Internal Audit	38,500
Tax	39,700
Cost	35,400

A/P, A/R, P/R Manager	$44,300
Full Charge Bookkeeper	$39,600
Accounting Clerk	$30,600

Credit:

Manager	$55,100
Senior	43,100
Staff	33,700

Form 940

Form **940**	**Employer's Annual Federal**	OMB No. 1545-0028

Unemployment (FUTA) Tax Return

Department of the Treasury
Internal Revenue Service (99)

▶ See separate instructions for Form 940 for information on completing this form.

2002

		T	
Name (as distinguished from trade name)	Calendar year	FF	
Audit-Proof Tax Services		FD	
Trade name, if any		FP	
Audit-Proof Tax Services		I	
Address and ZIP code	Employer identification number	T	
2234 Franklin Avenue	62 : 2222222		
Ramsey, NJ 07446			

A Are you required to pay unemployment contributions to only one state? (If "No," skip questions B and C.) .... [x] Yes [ ] No

B Did you pay all state unemployment contributions by January 31, 2003? ((1) If you deposited your total FUTA tax when due, check "Yes" if you paid all state unemployment contributions by February 10, 2003. (2) If a 0% experience rate is granted, check "Yes." (3) If "No," skip question C.) .... [ ] Yes [x] No

C Were all wages that were taxable for FUTA tax also taxable for your state's unemployment tax? .... [ ] Yes [x] No

If you answered "No" to any of these questions, you must file Form 940. If you answered "Yes" to all the questions, you may file Form 940-EZ, which is a simplified version of Form 940. (Successor employers see **Special credit for successor employers** on page 3 of the instructions.) You can get Form 940-EZ by calling 1-800-TAX-FORM (1-800-829-3676) or from the IRS's Internet Web Site at **www.irs.gov.**

If you will not have to file returns in the future, check here (see **Who Must File** in separate instructions), **and complete and sign the return** .... ▶ [ ]

If this is an Amended Return, check here .... ▶ [ ]

Part I	**Computation of Taxable Wages**

1	Total payments (including payments shown on lines 2 and 3) during the calendar year for services of employees		**1**	12,000	00
2	Exempt payments. (Explain all exempt payments, attaching additional sheets if necessary.) ▶	**2** 0 00			
3	Payments of more than $7,000 for services. Enter only amounts over the first $7,000 paid to each employee. Do not include any exempt payments from line 2. The $7,000 amount is the Federal wage base. Your state wage base may be different. **Do not use your state wage limitation.**	**3** 0 00			
4	Total exempt payments (add lines 2 and 3)		**4**	0	00
5	**Total taxable wages** (subtract line 4 from line 1) .... ▶		**5**	12,000	00

Be sure to complete both sides of this form, and sign in the space provided on the back.

For Privacy Act and Paperwork Reduction Act Notice, see separate instructions.   Cat. No. 112340   Form **940** (2002)

Activity 11–6   Continued

Form 940

Part II   **Tax Due or Refund**

1	Gross FUTA tax. Multiply the wages in Part 1, line 5, by .062........................	**1**		**744**	**00**
2	Maximum credit. Multiply the wages in Part 1, line 5, by .054	**2**	**648**	**00**		

3   Computation of tentative credit (**Note:** *All taxpayers must complete the applicable columns.*)

(a) Name of state	(b) State reporting number(s) as shown on employer's state contribution returns	(c) Taxable payroll (as defined in state act)	(d) State experience rate period From	To	(e) State experience rate	(f) Contributions if rate had been 5.4% (col. (c) × .054)	(g) Contributions payable at experience rate (col. (c) × col. (e))	(h) Additional credit (col. (f) minus col. (g)). If 0 or less, enter -0-.	(i) Contributions paid to state by 940 due date

3a	Totals .... ▸	**0.00**						**0.00**	**0.00**
3b	**Total tentative credit** (add line 3a, columns (h) and (i) only—for late payments also see the instructions for Part II, line 6) .... ▸	**3b**		**0**	**00**
4					
5					
6	**Credit:** Enter the smaller of the amount from Part II, line 2 or line 3b; or amount from the worksheet in the Part II, line 6 instructions	**6**		**0**	**00**
7	**Total FUTA tax** (subtract line 6 from line 1). If the result is over $100, also complete Part III	**7**		**744**	**00**
8	Total FUTA tax deposited for the year, including any overpayment applied from a prior year	**8**		**0**	**00**
9	**Balance due** (subtract line 8 from line 7). Pay to the "United States Treasury". If you owe more than $100, see **Depositing FUTA Tax** on page 3 of the separate instructions .... ▸	**9**		**744**	**00**
10	**Overpayment** (subtract line 7 from line 8). Check if it is to be: ☐ **Applied to next return** or ☐ **Refunded** .... ▸	**10**		**0**	**00**

Part III   **Record of Quarterly Federal Unemployment Tax Liability** (Do not include state liability.) **Complete only if line 7 is over $100.** See page 6 of the separate instructions.

Quarter	First (Jan. 1–Mar. 31)	Second (Apr. 1–June 30)	Third (July 1–Sept. 30)	Fourth (Oct. 1–Dec. 31)	Total for year
Liability for quarter	**0.00**	**0.00**	**0.00**	**744.00**	**744.00**

Under penalties of perjury, I declare that I have examined this return, including accompanying schedules and statements, and, to the best of my knowledge and belief, it is true, correct, and complete, and that no part of any payment made to a state unemployment fund claimed as a credit was, or is to be, deducted from the payments to employees.

Signature ▸   Title (Owner, etc.) ▸   Date ▸

Form **940** (2002)

Form **941**
(Rev. January 2003)
Department of the Treasury
Internal Revenue Service

Employer's Quarterly Federal Tax Return

▶ See separate instructions for information on completing this return.
Please type or print.

Enter state code for state in which deposits were made ONLY if different from state in address to the right ▶ ☐ (see page 2 of instructions).

Name (as distinguished from trade name)	Date quarter ended	
Audit-Proof Tax Services	**12/31**	OMB No. 1545-0029

Trade name, if any	Employer identification number
Audit-Proof Tax Services	**62-2222222**

Address (number and street)	City, state, and ZIP code
2234 Franklin Avenue	**Ramsey, NJ** **07446**

T	
FF	
FD	
FP	
I	
T	

If address is different from prior return. check here ▶ ☐

IRS Use

1 1 1 1 1 1 1 1 1 1	2	3 3 3 3 3 3 3	4 4 4	5 5 5
6 7 8 8 8 8 8 8 8		9 9 9 9 9	10 10 10 10	10 10 10 10 10

If you do not have to file returns in the future, check here ▶ ☐ and enter date final wages paid ▶

If you are a seasonal employer, see **Seasonal employers** on page 1 of the instructions and check here ▶ ☐

1	Number of employees in the pay. period that includes March 12th. ▶	1	0.00	
2	Total wages and tips, plus other compensation.........................	**2**	12,000	00
3	Total income tax withheld from wages, tips, and sick pay............	**3**	1,404	00
4	Adjustment of withheld income tax for preceding quarters of calendar year............	**4**	0	00
5	Adjusted total of income tax withheld (line 3 as adjusted by line 4-see instructions).............	**5**	1,404	00

6	Taxable social security wages................	6a	12,000	00	× 12.4% (.124) =	6b	1,488	00
	Taxable social security tips...................	6c	0	00	× 12.4% (.124) =	6d	0	00
7	Taxable Medicare wages and tips.........	7a	12,000	00	× 2.9% (.029) =	7b	348	00

8	Total social security and Medicare taxes (add lines 6b, 6d, and 7b). Check here if wages are not subject to social security and/or Medicare tax .... ▶ ☐	**8**	1,836	00
9	Adjustment of social security and Medicare taxes (see instructions for required explanation) Sick Pay $ _0.00_ ± Fractions of Cents $ _0.00_ ± Other $ _0.00_ =	**9**	0	00
10	Adjusted total of social security and Medicare taxes (line 8 as adjusted by line 9–see instructions)..................	**10**	1,836	00
11	**Total taxes** (add lines 5 and 10).................	**11**	3,240	00
12	Advance earned income credit (EIC) payments made to employees................	**12**	0	00
13	Net taxes (subtract line 12 from line 11). **If $1,000 or more, this must equal line 17, column (d) below (or line D of Schedule B (Form 941))**	**13**	3,240	00
14	Total deposits for quarter, including overpayment applied from a prior quarter............	**14**	0	00
15	**Balance due** (subtract line 14 from line 13). See instructions..............	**15**	3,240	00

16 **Overpayment.** If line 14 is more than line 13, enter excess here ▶ $ _0.00_
and check if to be: ☐ Applied to next return **OR** ☐ Refunded.

• **All filers:** If line 13 is less than $1,000, you need not complete line 17 or Schedule B (Form 941).

• **Semiweekly schedule depositors:** Complete Schedule B (Form 941) and check here .... ▶ ☐

• **Monthly schedule depositors:** Complete line 17, columns (a) through (d), and check here .... ▶ ☐

17 Monthly Summary of Federal Tax Liability. Do not complete if you were a semiweekly schedule depositor.

(a) First month liability	(b) Second month liability	(c) Third month liability	(d) Total liability for quarter
0.00	1,620.00	1,620.00	3,240.00

Sign Here

Under penalties of perjury, I declare that I have examined this return, including accompanying schedules and statements, and to the best of my knowledge and belief, it is true, correct, and complete.

Signature ▶   Print your Name and Title ▶   Date ▶

For Privacy Act and Paperwork Reduction Act Notice, see back of Payment. Voucher.

Cat. No. 17001Z   Form **941** (Rev. 1-2003)

CHAPTER 12
CORPORATIONS: ORGANIZATION, CAPITAL STOCK TRANSACTIONS, AND DIVIDENDS

CLASS DISCUSSION QUESTIONS

1. Each stockholder's liability for corporation debts is limited to the amount invested in the corporation. A corporation is responsible for its own obligations, and therefore, its creditors may not look beyond the assets of the corporation for satisfaction of their claims.

2. The large investments needed by large businesses are usually obtainable only through the pooling of the resources of many people. The corporation also has the advantages over proprietorships and partnerships of transferable shares of ownership, and thus the continuity of existence, and limited liability of its owners (stockholders).

3. No. Common stock with a higher par is not necessarily a better investment than common stock with a lower par because par is an amount assigned to the shares.

4. The broker is not correct. Corporations are not legally liable to pay dividends until the dividends are declared. If the company that issued the cumulative preferred stock has operating losses, it could omit dividends, first, on its common stock and, later, on its preferred stock.

5. Factors influencing the market price of a corporation's stock include the following:
   a. Financial condition, earnings record, and dividend record of the corporation.
   b. Its potential earning power.
   c. General business and economic conditions and prospects.

6. No. Premium on stock is additional paid-in capital.

7. a. Unissued stock has never been issued, but treasury stock has been issued as fully paid and has subsequently been reacquired.
   b. As a deduction from the total of other stockholders' equity accounts.

8. a. It has no effect on revenue or expense.
   b. It reduces stockholders' equity by $420,000.

9. a. It has no effect on revenue.
   b. It increases stockholders' equity by $500,000.

10. The primary purpose of a stock split is to bring about a reduction in the market price per share and thus to encourage more investors to buy the company's shares.

11. a. Sufficient retained earnings, sufficient cash, and formal action by the board of directors.
    b. July 1, declaration date; August 15, record date; and September 1, payment date.

12. The company may not have had enough cash on hand to pay a dividend on the common stock, or resources may be needed for plant expansion, replacement of facilities, payment of liabilities, etc.

13. a. No change.
    b. Total equity is the same.

14. a. Current liability
    b. Stockholders' equity

15. The primary advantage of the combined income and retained earnings statement is that it emphasizes net income as the connecting link between the income statement and the retained earnings portion of stockholders' equity.

16. The three classifications of appropriations are legal, contractual, and discretionary. Appropriations are normally reported in the notes to the financial statements.

17. Such prior period adjustments should be reported as an adjustment to the beginning balance of retained earnings.

EXERCISES

Ex. 12–1

	1st Year	2nd Year	3rd Year	4th Year	5th Year
a. Total dividend declared	$ —	$ 40,000	$ 80,000	$ 120,000	$ 140,000
Preferred dividend (current)	$25,000	$ 25,000	$ 25,000	$ 25,000	$ 25,000
Preferred dividend in arrears (from year 1)		15,000	10,000	—	—
b. Total preferred dividends		$ 40,000	$ 35,000	$ 25,000	$ 25,000
Preferred shares outstanding		÷ 25,000	÷ 25,000	÷ 25,000	÷ 25,000
Preferred dividend per share		$ 1.60	$ 1.40	$ 1.00	$ 1.00
Dividend for common shares (a. – b.)		$ —	$ 45,000	$ 95,000	$ 115,000
Common shares outstanding			÷ 250,000	÷ 250,000	÷ 250,000
Common dividend per share			$ 0.18	$ 0.38	$ 0.46

Ex. 12–2

	1st Year	2nd Year	3rd Year	4th Year	5th Year
a. Total dividend declared	$ —	$ 45,000	$ 110,000	$ 130,000	$ 180,000
Preferred dividend (current)	$40,000	$ 40,000	$ 40,000	$ 40,000	$ 40,000
Preferred dividend in arrears (from year 1)		5,000	35,000	—	—
b. Total preferred dividends		$ 45,000	$ 75,000	$ 40,000	$ 40,000
Preferred shares outstanding		÷ 100,000	÷ 100,000	÷ 100,000	÷ 100,000
Preferred dividend per share		$ 0.45	$ 0.75	$ 0.40	$ 0.40
Dividend for common shares (a. – b.)		$ —	$ 35,000	$ 90,000	$ 140,000
Common shares outstanding			÷ 50,000	÷ 50,000	÷ 50,000
Common dividend per share			$ 0.70	$ 1.80	$ 2.80

Ex. 12–3

a. July   7 Cash.. 1,600,000

                        Common Stock... 1,000,000

                        Paid-In Capital in Excess of Par—

                        Common Stock... 600,000

   Oct.   20 Cash.. 1,800,000

                        Preferred Stock 1,500,000

                        Paid-In Capital in Excess of Par—

                        Preferred Stock 300,000

b. $3,400,000 ($1,600,000 + $1,800,000)

Ex. 12–4

a. Feb.   20 Cash.. 1,500,000

                        Common Stock... 1,000,000

                        Paid-In Capital in Excess of

                        Stated Value 500,000

   Apr.   30 Cash.. 120,000

                        Preferred Stock 100,000

                        Paid-In Capital in Excess of Par—

                        Preferred Stock 20,000

b. $1,620,000 ($1,500,000 + $120,000)

Ex. 12–5

Aug. 29 Land.. 280,000

                      Common Stock... 150,000

                      Paid-In Capital in Excess of Par 130,000

Ex. 12–6

a.	Cash	50,000	
	Common Stock		50,000
b.	Organizational Expenses	2,000	
	Common Stock		2,000
	Cash	12,000	
	Common Stock		12,000
c.	Land	60,000	
	Building	200,000	
	Interest Payable*		900
	Mortgage Note Payable		180,000
	Common Stock		79,100

*An acceptable alternative would be to credit Interest Expense.

Ex. 12–7

Buildings	80,000	
Land	45,000	
Preferred Stock		100,000
Paid-In Capital in Excess of Par—		
Preferred Stock		25,000
Cash	475,000	
Common Stock		400,000
Paid-In Capital in Excess of Par—		
Common Stock		75,000

Ex. 12–8

Jan.	5	Cash..	1,000,000	
		Common Stock..		1,000,000
	18	Organizational Expenses.........................	10,000	
		Common Stock..		10,000
Feb.	13	Land..	50,000	
		Buildings	280,000	
		Equipment..	120,000	
		Common Stock..		425,000
		Paid-In Capital in Excess of Par—		
		Common Stock..		25,000
Apr.	1	Cash..	182,000	
		Preferred Stock		175,000
		Paid-In Capital in Excess of Par—		
		Preferred Stock		7,000

Ex. 12–9

a.	June	1	Treasury Stock..............................	150,000	
			Cash		150,000
	July	8	Cash...	97,500	
			Treasury Stock		90,000
			Paid-In Capital from Sale of		
			Treasury Stock		7,500
	Nov.	2	Cash...	58,000	
			Paid-In Capital from Sale of		
			Treasury Stock............................	2,000	
			Treasury Stock		60,000

b. $5,500 credit

c. Crystal Springs may have purchased the stock to support the market price of the stock, to provide shares for resale to employees, or for reissuance to employees as a bonus according to stock purchase agreements.

Ex. 12–10

a.

Mar.	3	Treasury Stock....................................	900,000	
		Cash		900,000
Aug.	11	Cash..	520,000	
		Treasury Stock		480,000
		Paid-In Capital from Sale		
		of Treasury Stock.....................		40,000
Oct.	3	Cash..	310,000	
		Treasury Stock		300,000
		Paid-In Capital from Sale		
		of Treasury Stock.....................		10,000

b. $50,000 credit

c. $120,000 debit

d. The balance in the treasury stock account is reported as a deduction from the total of the paid-in capital and retained earnings.

Ex. 12–11

a.

Aug.	1	Treasury Stock....................................	432,000	
		Cash		432,000
Sept.	23	Cash..	285,000	
		Treasury Stock		270,000
		Paid-In Capital from Sale of		
		Treasury Stock		15,000
Dec.	29	Cash..	148,500	
		Paid-In Capital from Sale of		
		Treasury Stock.........................	13,500	
		Treasury Stock		162,000

b. $1,500 credit

c. Stockholders' Equity section

d. Aspen Inc. may have purchased the stock to support the market price of the stock, to provide shares for resale to employees, or for reissuance to employees as a bonus according to stock purchase agreements.

Ex. 12–12

a. 125,000 shares (25,000 × 5)

b. $33 per share ($165 ÷ 5)

Ex. 12–13

		Assets	Liabilities	Stockholders' Equity
(1)	Declaring a cash dividend	0	+	–
(2)	Paying the cash dividend declared in (1)	–	–	0
(3)	Authorizing and issuing stock certificates in a stock split	0	0	0
(4)	Declaring a stock dividend	0	0	0
(5)	Issuing stock certificates for the stock dividend declared in (4)	0	0	0

Ex. 12–14

Feb. 13	Cash Dividends..	120,000	
	Cash Dividends Payable...............................		120,000
Mar. 15	No entry required.		
Apr. 10	Cash Dividends Payable	120,000	
	Cash		120,000

Ex. 12–15

a. (1) Stock Dividends... 275,000*
    Stock Dividends Distributable 250,000
    Paid-In Capital in Excess of Par—
    Common Stock... 25,000
    *[($12,500,000 ÷ $100) × $110] × 2%

   (2) Stock Dividends Distributable.............................. 250,000
    Common Stock... 250,000

b. (1) $13,250,000
   (2) $30,578,000
   (3) $43,828,000

c. (1) $13,525,000
   (2) $30,303,000
   (3) $43,828,000

Ex. 12–16

Feb. 9 No entry required. The stockholders ledger would be revised to record the increased number of shares held by each stockholder.

Apr. 10	Cash Dividends..	57,000*	
	Cash Dividends Payable...............................		57,000

* [(12,000 shares × $1) + (900,000 shares × $0.05)]

May 1	Cash Dividends Payable	57,000	
	Cash		57,000

Oct. 12	Cash Dividends..	147,000*	
	Cash Dividends Payable...............................		147,000

* [(12,000 shares × $1) + (900,000 shares × $0.15)]

12	Stock Dividends..	432,000**	
	Stock Dividends Distributable		360,000
	Paid-In Capital in Excess of Par—Common Stock		72,000

** (900,000 shares × 1% × $48)

Nov. 14	Cash Dividends Payable	147,000	
	Cash		147,000

14	Stock Dividends Distributable............................	360,000	
	Common Stock..		360,000

Ex. 12–17

Stockholders' Equity

Paid-in capital:			
Preferred $2 stock, $100 par (80,000 shares authorized, 7,500 shares issued).................	$750,000		
Excess of issue price over par.......	90,000	$840,000	
Common stock, no par, $5 stated value (200,000 shares authorized, 112,500 shares issued).....	$562,500		
Excess of issue price over par.......	75,000	637,500	
From sale of treasury stock		63,750	
Total paid-in capital			$1,541,250

Ex. 12–18

Stockholders' Equity

Paid-in capital:

Common stock, $25 par (60,000 shares authorized, 30,000 shares issued)	$750,000	
Excess of issue price over par	120,000	$ 870,000
From sale of treasury stock		25,000
Total paid-in capital		$ 895,000
Retained earnings		1,350,000
Total		$ 2,245,000
Deduct treasury stock (2,000 shares at cost)		80,000
Total stockholders' equity			$2,165,000

Ex. 12–19

Stockholders' Equity

Paid-in capital:

Preferred $2 stock, $100 par (10,000 shares authorized, 4,800 shares issued)	$480,000	
Excess of issue price over par	78,000	$ 558,000
Common stock, $4 par (250,000 shares authorized 150,000 shares issued)	$600,000	
Excess of issue price over par	210,000	810,000
From sale of treasury stock		42,000
Total paid-in capital		$ 1,410,000
Retained earnings		3,903,000
Total		$ 5,313,000
Deduct treasury common stock (12,000 shares at cost)		120,000
Total stockholders' equity			$5,193,000

Ex. 12–20

BRAVO CORPORATION
Retained Earnings Statement
For the Year Ended July 31, 2006

Retained earnings, August 1, 2005		$2,213,400
Net income	$558,000	
Less dividends declared...	330,000	
Increase in retained earnings..		228,000
Retained earnings, July 31, 2006		$2,441,400

Ex. 12–21

1. Retained earnings is not part of paid-in capital.

2. The cost of treasury stock should be *deducted* from the *total* stockholders' equity.

3. Dividends payable should be included as part of current liabilities and not as part of stockholders' equity.

4. Common stock should be included as part of paid-in capital.

5. The amount of shares of common stock issued of 75,000 times the par value per share of $20 should be extended as $1,500,000, not $1,789,200. The difference, $289,200 probably represents paid-in capital in excess of par.

6. Organizing costs should be expensed when incurred and not included as a part of stockholders' equity.

One possible corrected stockholders' equity section of the balance sheet is as follows:

Stockholders' Equity

Paid-in capital:		
Preferred $1 stock, cumulative, $50 par		
(9,800 shares authorized and issued)...................	$ 490,000	
Excess of issue price over par...................................	84,000	$ 574,000
Common stock, $20 par (100,000 shares authorized,		
75,000 shares issued)..	$ 1,500,000	
Excess of issue price over par...................................	289,200	1,789,200
Total paid-in capital		$2,363,200
Retained earnings		806,000*
		$3,169,200
Deduct treasury stock (5,000 shares at cost)		105,000
Total stockholders' equity		$3,064,200

* $906,000 – $100,000. Since the organizing costs should have been expensed, the retained earnings should be $100,000 less.

Ex. 12–22

Investors are apparently attracted to eBay because they anticipate a rapid increase in the market price of the stock.

Ex. 12–23

a.   1.9% ($1.26 ÷ $67.44)

b.   Hershey's dividend yield is above average for similar companies. Thus, it is likely that most stockholders are looking for current dividends as well as an increase in market price.

PROBLEMS

Prob. 12–1A

1.

Year	Total Dividends	Preferred Dividends		Common Dividends	
		Total	Per Share	Total	Per Share
2002	$40,000	$30,000	$1.20	$10,000	$0.25
2003	18,000	18,000	0.72	0	0
2004	24,000	24,000	0.96	0	0
2005	27,000	27,000	1.08	0	0
2006	65,000	51,000*	2.04	14,000	0.35
2007	54,000	30,000	1.20	24,000	0.60
			$7.20		$1.20

* Arrears dividend, preferred

   (2003: $12,000; 2004: $6,000; 2005: $3,000) $21,000

   Current dividend, preferred 30,000

     Total $51,000

2. Average annual dividend for preferred: $1.20 per share ($7.20 ÷ 6)

   Average annual dividend for common: $0.20 per share ($1.20 ÷ 6)

3. a. 2.4% ($1.20 ÷ $50)

   b. 2.5% ($0.20 ÷ $8)

Prob. 12–2A

Nov.	5	Cash..	780,000	
		Mortgage Note Payable.................................		780,000
	20	Cash..	720,000	
		Preferred Stock		600,000
		Paid-In Capital in Excess of Par— Preferred Stock		120,000
	23	Building	900,000	
		Land..	120,000	
		Common Stock..		600,000
		Paid-In Capital in Excess of Par— Common Stock..		420,000

Prob. 12–2A   Concluded

This solution is applicable only if the P.A.S.S. Software that accompanies the text is used.

DIAMOND OPTICS
Balance Sheet
November 23, 20—

Assets

Cash	$ 2,152,223	
Accounts receivable	855,900	
Merchandise inventory	2,112,617	
Prepaid insurance	197,260	
Supplies	190,900	
Total current assets		$ 5,508,900
Land	$ 1,120,000	
Building	3,507,900	
Total plant assets		4,627,900
Total assets		$10,136,800

Liabilities

Accounts payable	$ 624,300	
Total current liabilities		$ 624,300
Mortgage note payable	$ 780,000	
Total long-term liabilities		780,000
Total liabilities		$ 1,404,300

Stockholders' Equity

Common stock	$ 2,400,000	
Paid-in capital in excess of par—common stock	660,000	
Preferred stock	1,800,000	
Paid-in capital in excess of par—preferred stock	300,000	
Retained earnings	3,572,500	
Total stockholders' equity		8,732,500
Total liabilities and stockholders' equity		$10,136,800

Prob. 12–3A

a.	Treasury Stock	1,080,000	
	Cash		1,080,000
b.	Cash	420,000	
	Treasury Stock		360,000
	Paid-In Capital from Sale of Treasury Stock		60,000
c.	Cash	756,000	
	Preferred Stock		700,000
	Paid-In Capital in Excess of Par—Preferred Stock		56,000
d.	Cash	920,000	
	Common Stock		400,000
	Paid-In Capital in Excess of Par—Common Stock		520,000
e.	Cash	595,000	
	Paid-In Capital from Sale of Treasury Stock	35,000	
	Treasury Stock		630,000
f.	Cash Dividends	135,600	
	Cash Dividends Payable		135,600
	[(25,000 × $2) + (535,000 × $0.16)]		
g.	Cash Dividends Payable	135,600	
	Cash		135,600

Prob. 12–3A   Concluded

This solution is applicable only if the P.A.S.S. Software that accompanies the text is used.

ELK RIVER CORPORATION
Balance Sheet
December 31, 2006

Assets

Cash...	$ 2,223,300	
Accounts receivable......................................	628,950	
Merchandise inventory..................................	4,627,650	
Prepaid insurance	439,650	
Supplies..	482,950	
Total current assets		$ 8,402,500

Equipment.......................................	$ 2,090,000		
Accumulated depreciation—equipment	(259,600)		
		$ 1,830,400	
Building	$ 7,405,000		
Accumulated depreciation—building	(972,000)		
Total plant assets		$ 6,433,000	8,263,400
Total assets..			$16,665,900

Liabilities

Accounts payable		$ 532,000

Stockholders' Equity

Preferred stock	$ 2,500,000	
Paid-in capital in excess of par—preferred stock	228,500	
Common stock...	5,400,000	
Paid-in capital in excess of par—common stock	1,756,000	
Paid-in capital from sale of treasury stock	25,000	
Treasury stock	(90,000)	
Retained earnings	6,314,400	
Total stockholders' equity		16,133,900
Total liabilities and stockholders' equity		$16,665,900

Prob. 12–4A

1. and 2.

Common Stock

	Jan. 1 Bal.	600,000
	Mar. 15	200,000
	Aug. 30	16,000
		816,000

Paid-In Capital in Excess of Stated Value

	Jan. 1 Bal.	150,000
	Mar. 15	280,000
	July 30	24,000
		454,000

Retained Earnings

Dec. 31	78,300	Jan. 1 Bal.	497,750
		Dec. 31	182,500
	601,950		*680,250*

Treasury Stock

Jan. 1 Bal.	120,000	Feb. 2	120,000
Oct. 10	105,000		
105,000	*225,000*		

Paid-In Capital from Sale of Treasury Stock

	Feb. 2	30,000

Stock Dividends Distributable

Aug. 30	16,000	July 30	16,000

Stock Dividends

July 30	40,000	Dec. 31	40,000

Cash Dividends

Dec. 30	38,300	Dec. 31	38,300

Prob. 12–4A   Continued

2.

Jan. 19	Cash Dividends Payable	31,500	
	Cash		31,500
Feb. 2	Cash	150,000	
	Treasury Stock		120,000
	Paid-In Capital from Sale of Treasury Stock.		30,000
Mar. 15	Cash	480,000	
	Common Stock		200,000
	Paid-In Capital in Excess of Stated Value.....		280,000
July 30	Stock Dividends	40,000*	
	Stock Dividends Distributable		16,000
	Paid-In Capital in Excess of Stated Value.....		24,000

*(60,000 + 20,000) × 2% × $25

Aug. 30	Stock Dividends Distributable	16,000	
	Common Stock		16,000
Oct. 10	Treasury Stock	105,000	
	Cash		105,000
Dec. 30	Cash Dividends	38,300**	
	Cash Dividends Payable		38,300

**(60,000 + 20,000 + 1,600 − 5,000) × $0.50

31	Income Summary	182,500	
	Retained Earnings		182,500
31	Retained Earnings	78,300	
	Stock Dividends		40,000
	Cash Dividends		38,300

Prob. 12–4A   Continued

3.

AEROTRONICS ENTERPRISES INC.
Retained Earnings Statement
For the Year Ended December 31, 2006

Retained earnings (beginning of period)............................		$497,750
Net income	$182,500	
Less: Cash dividends	(38,300)	
Stock dividends	(40,000)	
Increase in retained earnings..		104,200
Retained earnings (end of period)		$601,950

4.

Stockholders' Equity

Paid-in capital:		
Common stock, $10 stated value (100,000 shares authorized, 81,600 shares issued)...............................	$ 816,000	
Excess of issue price over stated value........................	454,000	
From sale of treasury stock...	30,000	
Total paid-in capital	$ 1,300,000	
Retained earnings	601,950	
Total..	$ 1,901,950	
Deduct treasury stock (5,000 shares at cost)	105,000	
Total stockholders' equity		$1,796,950

Prob. 12–4A   Concluded

This solution is applicable only if the P.A.S.S. Software that accompanies the text is used.

AEROTRONICS ENTERPRISES INC.
Balance Sheet
December 31, 2006

Assets

Cash	$ 615,500	
Accounts receivable	426,325	
Merchandise inventory	584,550	
Prepaid insurance	75,225	
Supplies	101,945	
Total current assets		$1,803,545
Land	$ 365,400	
Equipment	180,400	
Accumulated depreciation—equipment	(112,095)	
Total plant assets		433,705
Total assets		$2,237,250

Liabilities

Accounts payable	$ 357,500	
Cash dividends payable	82,800	
Total liabilities		$ 440,300

Stockholders' Equity

Common stock	$ 816,000	
Paid-in capital in excess of stated value	454,000	
Paid-in capital from sale of treasury stock	30,000	
Retained earnings	601,950	
Treasury stock	(105,000)	
Total stockholders' equity		1,796,950
Total liabilities and stockholders' equity		$2,237,250

Prob. 12–5A

Jan. 8 No entry required. The stockholders ledger would be revised to record the increased number of shares held by each stockholder.

Mar. 20

Cash Dividends..	104,000*	
Cash Dividends Payable..................................		104,000

*(20,000 × $1) + (600,000 × $0.14)

Apr. 20

Cash Dividends Payable	104,000	
Cash		104,000

May 8

Treasury Stock...	2,400,000	
Cash		2,400,000

Aug. 2

Cash...	1,680,000	
Treasury Stock		1,440,000
Paid-In Capital from Sale of Treasury Stock		240,000

Sept. 15

Cash Dividends...	60,600*	
Cash Dividends Payable..................................		60,600

*(20,000 × $1) + [(600,000 – 20,000) × $0.07]

15

Stock Dividends...	301,600**	
Stock Dividends Distributable		34,800
Paid-In Capital in Excess of Par—Common Stock		266,800

**(600,000 – 20,000) × 1% × $52

Oct. 15

Cash Dividends Payable	60,600	
Cash		60,600

15

Stock Dividends Distributable............................	34,800	
Common Stock..		34,800

Prob. 12–5A   Concluded

This solution is applicable only if the P.A.S.S. Software that accompanies the text is used.

SERRA DO MAR CORPORATION
Balance Sheet
December 31, 20—

Assets

Cash		$ 548,510
Accounts receivable		219,885
Merchandise inventory		505,642
Prepaid insurance		121,666
Office supplies		23,203
Equipment	$ 342,775	
Accumulated depreciation—equipment	(111,625)	231,150
Total assets		$1,650,056

Liabilities

Accounts payable		$ 188,755

Stockholders' Equity

Common stock	$ 34,800	
Paid-in capital in excess of par—common stock	266,800	
Paid-in capital from sale of treasury stock	240,000	
Retained earnings	1,879,701	
Treasury stock	(960,000)	
Total stockholders' equity		1,461,301
Total liabilities and stockholders' equity		$1,650,056

Prob. 12–1B

1.

Year	Total Dividends	Preferred Dividends		Common Dividends	
		Total	Per Share	Total	Per Share
2002	$18,000	$18,000	$ 0.90	$ 0	$ 0
2003	54,000	54,000	2.70	0	0
2004	70,000	48,000*	2.40	22,000	0.88
2005	75,000	40,000	2.00	35,000	1.40
2006	80,000	40,000	2.00	40,000	1.60
2007	90,000	40,000	2.00	50,000	2.00
			$12.00		$5.88

	Preferred Dividends
* Arrears dividend, preferred...	$ 8,000
Current dividend, preferred	40,000
Total	$48,000

2. Average annual dividend for preferred: $2 per share ($12 ÷ 6)

   Average annual dividend for common: $0.98 per share ($5.88 ÷ 6)

3. a. 2% ($2 ÷ $100)

   b. 2.5% ($0.98 ÷ $39.20)

Prob. 12–2B

April	3	Building	225,000	
		Land	45,000	
		Common Stock		240,000
		Paid-In Capital in Excess of Par—		
		Common Stock		30,000
	18	Cash	375,000	
		Preferred Stock		300,000
		Paid-In Capital in Excess of Par—		
		Preferred Stock		75,000
	28	Cash	155,000	
		Mortgage Note Payable		155,000

Prob. 12–2B   Concluded

This solution is applicable only if the P.A.S.S. Software that accompanies the text is used.

DAHOF CORP.
Balance Sheet
April 30, 20—

Assets

Cash	$ 1,030,000	
Accounts receivable	826,325	
Merchandise inventory	1,834,550	
Prepaid insurance	100,225	
Supplies	201,945	
Total current assets		$3,993,045
Land	$ 808,000	
Building	1,571,455	
Total plant assets		2,379,455
Total assets		$6,372,500

Liabilities

Accounts payable	$ 357,500	
Total current liabilities		$ 357,500
Mortgage note payable	$ 155,000	
Total long-term liabilities		155,000
Total liabilities		$ 512,500

Stockholders' Equity

Common stock	$ 2,740,000	
Paid-in capital in excess of par—common stock	350,000	
Preferred stock	900,000	
Paid-in capital in excess of par—preferred stock	195,000	
Retained earnings	1,675,000	
Total stockholders' equity		5,860,000
Total liabilities and stockholders' equity		$6,372,500

Prob. 12–3B

a.	Cash..	180,000	
	Common Stock		75,000
	Paid-In Capital in Excess of Par—Common		
	Stock...		105,000
b.	Cash..	64,800	
	Preferred Stock...		60,000
	Paid-In Capital in Excess of Par—Preferred		
	Stock...		4,800
c.	Treasury Stock...	66,000	
	Cash..		66,000
d.	Cash..	50,400	
	Treasury Stock..		39,600
	Paid-In Capital from Sale of Treasury Stock		10,800
e.	Cash..	14,250	
	Paid-In Capital from Sale of Treasury Stock	2,250	
	Treasury Stock..		16,500
f.	Cash Dividends	30,020	
	Cash Dividends Payable		30,020
	[(8,800 × $1.50) + (42,050 × $0.40)]		
g.	Cash Dividends Payable......................................	30,020	
	Cash..		30,020

Prob. 12–3B   Concluded

This solution is applicable only if the P.A.S.S. Software that accompanies the text is used.

KINGFISHER ENVIRONMENTAL
Balance Sheet
December 31, 2006

Assets

Cash	$ 626,730	
Accounts receivable	602,200	
Merchandise inventory	809,300	
Prepaid insurance	46,400	
Supplies	85,000	
Total current assets		$2,169,630
Equipment	$ 1,132,900	
Accumulated depreciation—equipment	(69,000)	
Total plant assets		1,063,900
Total assets		$3,233,530

Liabilities

Accounts payable		$ 835,100

Stockholders' Equity

Preferred stock	$ 660,000	
Paid-in capital in excess of par—preferred stock	104,800	
Common stock	425,000	
Paid-in capital in excess of par—common stock	190,000	
Paid-in capital from sale of treasury stock	8,550	
Retained earnings	1,019,980	
Treasury stock	(9,900)	
Total stockholders' equity		2,398,430
Total liabilities and stockholders' equity		$3,233,530

Prob. 12–4B   Continued

3.

SHOSHONE ENTERPRISES INC.
Retained Earnings Statement
For the Year Ended December 27, 2006

Retained earnings (beginning of period)........................		$725,000
Net income	$ 269,400	
Less: Cash dividends..	(64,575)	
Stock dividends	(129,600)	
Increase in retained earnings...		75,225
Retained earnings (end of period)		$800,225

4.

Stockholders' Equity

Paid-in capital:		
Common stock, $20 stated value (100,000 shares		
authorized, 93,600 shares issued)............................	$ 1,872,000	
Excess of issue price over stated value......................	417,600	
From sale of treasury stock...	25,000	
Total paid-in capital	$ 2,314,600	
Retained earnings	800,225	
Total..	$ 3,114,825	
Deduct treasury stock (7,500 shares at cost)	255,000	
Total stockholders' equity		$2,859,825

Prob. 12–4B   Concluded

This solution is applicable only if the P.A.S.S. Software that accompanies the text is used.

SHOSHONE ENTERPRISES INC.
Balance Sheet
December 27, 2006

Assets

Cash	$ 512,223	
Accounts receivable	385,900	
Merchandise inventory	822,300	
Prepaid insurance	72,260	
Supplies	90,900	
Total current assets		$1,883,583
Land	$ 636,400	
Equipment	668,717	
Accumulated depreciation—equipment	(98,500)	
Total plant assets		1,206,617
Total assets		$3,090,200

Liabilities

Accounts payable	$ 221,800	
Cash dividends payable	8,575	
Total liabilities		$ 230,375

Stockholders' Equity

Common stock	$ 1,872,000	
Paid-in capital in excess of stated value	417,600	
Paid-in capital from sale of treasury stock	25,000	
Retained earnings	800,225	
Treasury stock	(255,000)	
Total stockholders' equity		2,859,825
Total liabilities and stockholders' equity		$3,090,200

Prob. 12–5B

Jan. 20 No entry required. The stockholders ledger would be revised to record the increased number of shares held by each stockholder.

Apr. 1	Treasury Stock..	600,000	
	Cash		600,000
May 1	Cash Dividends...	108,000*	
	Cash Dividends Payable..................................		108,000

*(24,000 × $1.50) + [(500,000 – 20,000) × $0.15]

June 1	Cash Dividends Payable	108,000	
	Cash		108,000
Aug. 7	Cash..	456,000	
	Treasury Stock		360,000
	Paid-In Capital from Sale of Treasury Stock		96,000
Nov. 15	Cash Dividends..	75,360*	
	Cash Dividends Payable................................		75,360

*(24,000 × $1.50) + [(500,000 – 8,000) × $0.08]

15	Stock Dividends...	344,400**	
	Stock Dividends Distributable		98,400
	Paid-In Capital in Excess of Par—Common Stock		246,000

**(500,000 – 8,000) × 2% × $35

Dec. 15	Cash Dividends Payable	75,360	
	Cash		75,360
15	Stock Dividends Distributable............................	98,400	
	Common Stock..		98,400

Prob. 12–5B   Concluded

This solution is applicable only if the P.A.S.S. Software that accompanies the text is used.

MEAD BOATING SUPPLY CORPORATION
Balance Sheet
December 31, 20—

Assets

Cash	$ 309,099	
Accounts receivable	174,564	
Merchandise inventory	561,812	
Prepaid insurance	65,235	
Office supplies	73,601	
Total current assets		$1,184,311
Land	$ 447,221	
Equipment	492,850	
Accumulated depreciation—equipment	(152,623)	
Total property, plant and equipment		787,448
Total assets		$1,971,759

Liabilities

Accounts payable		$ 249,310

Stockholders' Equity

Common stock	$ 1,044,650	
Paid-in capital in excess of par—common stock	523,700	
Paid-in capital from sale of treasury stock	98,500	
Retained earnings	325,599	
Treasury stock	(270,000)	
Total stockholders' equity		1,722,449
Total liabilities and stockholders' equity		$1,971,759

SPECIAL ACTIVITIES

Activity 12–1

1. The name "7-Eleven" originated in 1946 when the stores were open from 7 a.m. until 11 p.m. Today, the majority of stores in the United States and Canada serve more than 7 million daily customers with 24-hour convenience, seven days a week.

2. An average 7-Eleven store carries between 2,300 to 2,800 items.

3. Based upon 2002 sales figures, the rankings are as follows:

    1. tobacco products
    2. beverages, such as soft drinks and coffee
    3. nonfood products and services, such as automobile oil, toothpaste, coolers, money orders, and lottery tickets
    4. beer and wine
    5.* baked and fresh foods, such as bread and rolls
    5.* candy and snacks
    7. dairy products

    *Note that there is a tie for the fifth-place ranking.

4. Some ways (strategies) that 7-Eleven is implementing to increase its same-store sales include the following:

    a. Offering differentiated merchandise that is not normally offered in convenience stores. Examples of such merchandise include fresh products—from baked goods to sandwiches—that are delivered daily and are tailored to the tastes of each store location.

    b. The implementation of a state-of-the-art, automated retail information system. This system analyzes sales of individual items, sales trends, and customer preferences. The system interfaces with an item-by-item inventory management system designed to keep fast-selling items in stock.

    c. Installing self-service kiosks that offer check cashing, money orders, and ATM services to customers.

    d. Periodically upgrading store facilities to improve lighting, signage, and cleanliness, so that customers are provided a safe, friendly environment in which to shop.

Activity 12–2

At the time of this decision, the WorldCom board had come under intense scrutiny. This was the largest loan by a company to its CEO in history. The SEC began an investigation into this loan, and Bernie Ebbers was eventually terminated as the CEO, with this loan being cited as part of the reason. The board indicated that the decision to lend Ebbers this money was to keep him from selling his stock and depressing the share price. Thus, its claim was that it was actually helping shareholders by keeping these shares from being sold. However, this argument wasn't well received, given that the share price dropped from around $15 per share at the time of the loan to about $2.50 per share when Ebbers was terminated. In addition, critics were scornful of the low "sweetheart" interest rate given to Ebbers for this loan. In addition, many critics viewed the loan as risky, given that it was not supported by any personal assets. WorldCom has since entered bankruptcy proceedings, with the Ebbers loan still uncollected as of this writing.

Some press comments:

1. *When he borrowed money personally, he used his WorldCom stock as collateral. As these loans came due, he was unwilling to sell at "depressed prices" of $10 to $15 (it's now around $2.50). So WorldCom lent him the money to consolidate his loans, to the tune of $366 million. How a board of directors, representing you and me at the table, allowed this to happen is beyond comprehension. They should resign with Bernie.* (Source: "Bernie Bites the Dust," By Andy Kessler, 05/01/2002, *The Wall Street Journal*, p. A18.)

2. *It was astonishing to read the other day that the board of directors of the United States' second-largest telecommunications company claims to have had its shareholders' interests in mind when it agreed to grant more than $430 million in low-interest loans to the company's CEO, mainly to meet margin calls on his stock.*

   Yet that's the level to which fiduciary responsibility seems to have sunk on the board of Clinton, Mississippi-based WorldCom, the deeply troubled telecom giant, as it sought to bail Bernard Ebbers out of the folly of speculating in shares of WorldCom itself. Sadly, WorldCom is hardly alone.

   "The very essence of why Mr. Ebbers was granted a loan was to protect shareholder value," said a WorldCom spokesman in mid-March, just as the U.S. Securities & Exchange Commission was unfurling a probe of the loan and 23 other matters related to WorldCom's finances.

Activity 12–2   Concluded

Yes, folks, you read that right. On March 14, 2002, a spokesman for a publicly traded, $20 billion company actually stood up and declared that of all the uses to which the company could have put almost half-a-billion dollars, the best one by far—at least from the point of view of the shareholders—was to spend it on some sort of stock-parking scheme in order to keep the CEO out of bankruptcy court. (Source: "Bernie's Bad Idea," By Christopher Byron, *Red Herring,* April 16, 2002.)

Activity 12–3

Lois and Keith are behaving in a professional manner as long as full and complete information is provided to potential investors in accordance with federal regulations for the sale of securities to the public. If such information is provided, the marketplace will determine the fair value of the company's stock.

Activity 12–4

1. This case involves a transaction in which a security has been issued that has characteristics of both stock and debt. The primary argument for classifying the issuance of the common stock as debt is that the investors have a legal right to an amount equal to the purchase price (face value) of the security. This is similar to a note payable or a bond payable. In addition, the $100 payment could be argued to be equivalent to an interest payment, whose payment has been deferred until a later date.

   Arguments against classifying the security as debt include the fact that the investors will not receive fixed "annual" interest payments. In fact, if Kilimanjaro Inc. does not generate any net sales, the investors do not have a right to receive any payments. One could argue that the payments of 2% of net sales are, in substance, a method of redeeming the stock. As indicated in the case, the stockholders must surrender their stock for $100 after the $20 million payment has been made. Overall, the arguments would seem to favor classifying the security as common stock.

Activity 12–4 Concluded

2. In practice, the $20 million stock issuance would probably be classified as common stock. However, full disclosure should be made of the 2% of net sales and $100 payment obligations in the notes to the financial statements. In addition, as Kilimanjaro Inc. generates net sales, a current liability should be recorded for the payment to stockholders. Such payments would be classified as dividend payments rather than as interest payments. Anita Sparks should also investigate whether such payments might violate any loan agreements with the banks. Banks often restrict dividend payments in loan agreements. If such an agreement has been violated, Kilimanjaro Inc. should notify the bank immediately and request a waiver of the violation.

Activity 12–5

1. Before a cash dividend is declared, there must be sufficient retained earnings and cash. On December 31, 2006, the retained earnings balance of $599,600 is available for use in declaring a dividend. This balance is sufficient for the payment of the normal quarterly cash dividend of $0.40 per share, which would amount to $8,000 ($0.40 × 20,000).

Matterhorn Inc.'s cash balance at December 31, 2006, is $32,000, of which $20,000 is committed as the compensating balance under the loan agreement. This leaves only $12,000 to pay the dividend of $8,000 and to finance normal operations in the future. Unless the cash balance can be expected to increase significantly in early 2007, it is questionable whether sufficient cash will be available to pay a cash dividend and to provide for future cash needs.

Other factors that should be considered include the company's working capital (current assets – current liabilities) position and the loan provision pertaining to the current ratio, resources needed for plant expansion or replacement of facilities, future business prospects of the company, and forecasts for the industry and the economy in general. The working capital is $403,600 ($503,600 – $100,000) on December 31, 2006. The current ratio is therefore 5:1 ($503,600 ÷ $100,000) on December 31, 2006. However, after deducting the $300,000 committed to store modernization and product-line expansion, the ratio drops to 2:1 ($203,600 ÷ $100,000). If the cash dividend were declared and paid and the other current assets and current liabilities remain unchanged, the current ratio would drop to 1.956:1 ($195,600 ÷ $100,000), and this would violate the loan agreement. Further, working capital commitments for 2007 and any additional funds that might be required, such as funds for the replacement of fixed assets, would suggest that the declaration of a cash dividend for the fourth quarter of 2006 might not be wise.

Activity 12–5   Concluded

2. Given the cash and working capital position of Matterhorn Inc. on December 31, 2006, a stock dividend might be an appropriate alternative to a cash dividend.

    a. From the point of view of a stockholder, the declaration of a stock dividend would continue the dividend declaration trend of Matterhorn Inc. In addition, although the amount of the stockholders' equity and proportional interest in the corporation would remain unchanged, the stockholders might benefit from an increase in the fair market value of their total holdings of Matterhorn Inc. stock after distribution of the dividend.

    b. From the point of view of the board of directors, a stock dividend would continue the dividend trend, while the cash and working capital position of the company would not be jeopardized. Many corporations use stock dividends as a way to "plow back" retained earnings for use in acquiring new facilities or for expanding their operations. Matterhorn Inc. has sufficient unissued common stock to declare a stock dividend without changing the amount authorized.

Activity 12–6

Note to Instructors: The purpose of this activity is to familiarize students with sources of information about corporations and how that information is useful in evaluating the corporation's activities.

CHAPTER 13
Accounting for Partnerships and Limited Liability Corporations

CLASS DISCUSSION QUESTIONS

1. Proprietorship: Ease of formation.
   Corporation: Limited liability to owners and ease of raising large amounts of equity capital.
   Partnership: Expanded owner expertise and capital and ease of formation.
   Limited liability corporation: Limited liability to owners.

2. The disadvantages of a partnership are its life is limited, each partner has unlimited liability, one partner can bind the partnership to contracts, and raising large amounts of capital is more difficult for a partnership than a corporation.

3. Yes. A partnership may incur losses in excess of the total investment of all partners. The division of losses among the partners would be made according to their agreement. In addition, because of the unlimited liability of each partner for partnership debts, a particular partner may actually lose a greater amount than his or her capital balance.

4. The partnership agreement (partnership) or operating agreement (LLC) establishes the income-sharing ratio among the partners (members), amounts to be invested, and buy-sell agreements between the partners (members).

5. Equally.

6. No. He would have to bear his share of losses. In the absence of any agreement as to division of net income or net loss, his share would be one-third. In addition, because of the unlimited liability of each partner, DiPano may lose more than one-third of the losses if one partner is unable to absorb his share of the losses.

7. The statement of stockholders' equity discloses the material changes in each stockholders' equity account, such as common stock, paid-in excess of par value, retained earnings, and treasury stock, for a specified period.

8. The statement of partners' equity (for a partnership) and statement of members' equity (for a LLC) both show the material changes in owner's equity for each ownership person or class for a specified period.

9. The delivery equipment should be recorded at $15,000, the valuation agreed upon by the partners.

10. The accounts receivable should be recorded by a debit of $200,000 to Accounts Receivable and a credit of $20,000 to Allowance for Doubtful Accounts.

11. Yes. Partnership net income is divided according to the income-sharing ratio, regardless of the amount of the withdrawals by the partners. Therefore, it is very likely that the partners' monthly withdrawals from a partnership will not exactly equal their shares of net income.

12. a. Debit the partner's drawing account and credit Cash.
    b. Debit the income summary account for the amount of the net income and credit the partners' capital accounts for their respective shares of the net income.
    c. No. Payments to partners and the division of net income are separate. The amount of one does not affect the amount of the other.

13. a. By purchase of an interest, the capital interest of the new partner is obtained from the old partner, and neither the total assets nor the total equity of the partnership are affected.
    b. By investment, both the total assets and the total equity of the partnership are increased.

14. It is important to state all partnership assets in terms of current prices at the time of the admission of a new partner because failure to do so might result in participation by the new partner in gains or losses attributable to the period prior to admission to the partnership. To illustrate, assume that A and B share net income and net loss equally and operate a partnership that owns land recorded at and costing $20,000. C is admitted to the partnership, and the three partners share in income equally. The day after C is admitted to the partnership, the land is sold for $35,000 and, since the land was not revalued, C receives one-third distri-

bution of the $15,000 gain. In this case, C participates in the gain attributable to the period prior to admission to the partnership.

15. A new partner who is expected to improve the fortunes (income) of the partnership might be given equity in excess of the amount invested to join the partnership.

16. **a.** Losses and gains on realization are divided among partners in the income-sharing ratio.

   b. Cash is distributed to the partners according to their ownership claims, as indicated by the credit balances in their capital accounts, after taking into consideration the potential deficiencies that may result from the inability to collect from a deficient partner.

17. The different advantages of each organizational form are related to the natural life cycle of a business. For example, during the initial stages of a business, ease of formation may be paramount, which favors a proprietorship. As a business grows and succeeds, the need for expertise and capital grows, giving rise to partnerships. If limited liability becomes paramount to outside investors, such as venture capitalists, then the business may take the form of a limited liability corporation. Lastly, a business may wish to obtain more extensive sources of capital, such as from the investing public. In this case, the corporate form is best suited for raising public capital with the help of an underwriter through an initial public offering.

EXERCISES

Ex. 13–1

TENDER HEART GREETING CARDS INC
Statement of Stockholders' Equity
For the Year Ended December 31, 2006

	Common Stock, $2 Par	Paid-In Capital in Excess of Par	Treasury Stock	Retained Earnings	Total
Balance, Jan. 1, 2006....	$500,000	$400,000	—	$1,075,000	$1,975,000
Issued 50,000 shares of common stock.....	100,000	45,000			145,000
Purchased 10,000 shares as treasury stock..........................			$(25,000)		(25,000)
Net income				240,000	240,000
Dividends				(50,000)	(50,000)
Balance, Dec. 31, 2006 .	$600,000	$445,000	$(25,000)	$1,265,000	$2,285,000

Ex. 13–2

Cash..	6,000	
Accounts Receivable...	91,000	
Merchandise Inventory...	76,500	
Equipment..	90,000	
Allowance for Doubtful Accounts.................................		8,000
Todd Jost, Capital		255,500

Ex. 13–3

	Moore	Knell
a.	$60,000	$60,000
b.	80,000	40,000
c.	57,600	62,400
d.	55,000	65,000
e.	61,000	59,000

Details

	Moore	Knell	Total
a. Net income (1:1)	$60,000	$60,000	$120,000
b. Net income (2:1)	$80,000	$40,000	$120,000
c. Interest allowance	$24,000	$12,000	$ 36,000
Remaining income (2:3)	33,600	50,400	84,000
Net income	$57,600	$62,400	$120,000
d. Salary allowance	$40,000	$50,000	$ 90,000
Remaining income (1:1)	15,000	15,000	30,000
Net income	$55,000	$65,000	$120,000
e. Interest allowance	$24,000	$12,000	$ 36,000
Salary allowance	40,000	50,000	90,000
Excess of allowances over income (1:1)	(3,000)	(3,000)	(6,000)
Net income	$61,000	$59,000	$120,000

Ex. 13–4

	Moore	Knell
a.	$ 90,000	$90,000
b.	120,000	60,000
c.	81,600	98,400
d.	85,000	95,000
e.	91,000	89,000

Details

	Moore	Knell	Total
a. Net income (1:1)	$ 90,000	$90,000	$180,000
b. Net income (2:1)	$120,000	$60,000	$180,000
c. Interest allowance	$ 24,000	$12,000	$ 36,000
Remaining income (2:3)...............................	57,600	86,400	144,000
Net income..	$ 81,600	$98,400	$180,000
d. Salary allowance	$ 40,000	$50,000	$ 90,000
Remaining income (1:1)...............................	45,000	45,000	90,000
Net income..	$ 85,000	$95,000	$180,000
e. Interest allowance	$ 24,000	$12,000	$ 36,000
Salary allowance	40,000	50,000	90,000
Remaining income (1:1).................................	27,000	27,000	54,000
Net income..	$ 91,000	$89,000	$180,000

Ex. 13–5

	Jane Williams	Y. Osaka	Total
Salary allowances..	$ 40,000	$ 60,000	$ 100,000
Remainder ($120,000)(net loss, $20,000 plus $100,000 salary allowances) divided equally	(60,000)	(60,000)	(120,000)
Net loss...	$ (20,000)	$ 0	$ (20,000)

Ex. 13-9

a.

(1) Income Summary... 160,000

      Walt Bigney, Capital...   80,000

      Dan Harris, Capital...   80,000

(2) Walt Bigney, Capital... 72,000

   Dan Harris, Capital 84,000

      Walt Bigney, Drawing...   72,000

      Dan Harris, Drawing..   84,000

b.

BIGNEY AND HARRIS
Statement of Partners' Equity
For the Year Ended December 31, 2006

	Walt Bigney	Dan Harris	Total
Capital, January 1, 2006...............................	$ 80,000	$ 95,000	$175,000
Additional investment during the year	10,000	—	10,000
	$ 90,000	$ 95,000	$185,000
Net income for the year................................	80,000	80,000	160,000
	$170,000	$175,000	$345,000
Withdrawals during the year.........................	72,000	84,000	156,000
Capital, December 31, 2006	$ 98,000	$ 91,000	$189,000

Ex 13–10

a.

Jan. 31	Partner Drawing	20,000,000
	Cash...		20,000,000

b.

Dec. 31	Income Summary...............................	200,000,000
	Partner Capital...............................		200,000,000

c.

Dec. 31	Partner Capital	240,000,000*
	Partner Drawing.............................		240,000,000

*12 months × 20,000,000

d.

Dec. 31	Cash..	40,000,000
	Partner Capital..............................		40,000,000

During the year, the partners withdrew 40 million pounds more than what was earned. This represents a distribution of capital beyond the current year's earnings. According to the operating agreement, this difference must be returned to the partnership.

Ex. 13–11

a. and b.

Kirk, Capital...	30,000
McCoy, Capital...		30,000

Ex. 13–12

a. $811,000 ($1,840,000,000 ÷ 2,270), rounded

b. $132,000 ($300,000,000 ÷ 2,270), rounded

c.   A new partner might contribute more than $132,000 because of goodwill attributable to the firm's reputation, future income potential, a strong client base, etc.

Ex. 13–13

a. (1) Susan Yu, Capital.. 25,000
       Ben Hardy, Capital 18,000
          Ken Mahl... 43,000

   (2) Cash 35,000
       Jeff Wood, Capital.. 35,000

b. Susan Yu 75,000
   Ben Hardy.. 72,000
   Ken Mahl.. 43,000
   Jeff Wood 35,000

Ex. 13–14

a. Cash.. 45,000
   Cecil Jacobs, Capital.. 5,000
   Maria Estaban, Capital 5,000
      Lee White, Capital... 55,000

b. Cecil Jacobs.. 56,000
   Maria Estaban 54,000
   Lee White.. 55,000

Ex. 13–15

a. Conway, Member Equity .... 5,600[1]
   Patel, Member Equity .... 8,400[2]
       Medical Equipment 14,000

   [1]$14,000 \times 2/5 = \$5,600$
   [2]$14,000 \times 3/5 = \$8,400$

b. 1. Cash 340,000
      Conway, Member Equity 20,080
      Patel, Member Equity 30,120
      Truet, Member Equity 289,800

   Supporting calculations for the bonus:

Equity of Conway	$294,400
Equity of Patel	331,600
Contribution by Truett	340,000
Total equity after admitting Truett............	$966,000
Truett's equity interest after admission...	30%
Truett's equity after admission.................	$289,800
Contribution by Truett..............................	$340,000
Truett's equity after admission.................	289,800
Bonus paid to Conway and Patel	$ 50,200

   Conway: $\$50,200 \times 2/5 = \$20,080$
   Patel: $\$50,200 \times 3/5 = \$30,120$

b. 2. Cash 190,000
      Conway, Member Equity 8,864
      Patel, Member Equity... 13,296
          Truet, Member Equity 212,160

   Supporting calculations for the bonus:

Equity of Conway	$294,400
Equity of Patel	331,600
Contribution by Truett..............................	190,000
Total equity after admitting Truett............	$816,000
Truett's equity interest after admission...	26%
Truett's equity after admission.................	$212,160
Contribution by Truett..............................	190,000
Bonus paid to Truett.................................	$ 22,160

   Conway: $\$22,160 \times 2/5 = \$8,864$
   Patel: $\$22,160 \times 3/5 = \$13,296$

Ex 13–16

ANGEL INVESTOR ASSOCIATES
Statement of Partnership Equity
For the Year Ended December 31, 2006

	Jan Strous, Capital	Cara Wright, Capital	Michael Black, Capital	Total Partner- ship Capital
Partnership Capital, January 1, 2006	$ 31,500	$ 58,500	$	$ 90,000
Revaluation of assets	(3,500)	(6,500)		(10,000)
Admission of Michael Black	2,800	5,200	22,000	30,000
Salary allowance	12,000			12,000
Remaining income	44,800	83,200	32,000	160,000
Less: Partner withdrawals	(28,400)	(41,600)	(16,000)	(86,000)
Partnership Capital, December 31, 2006..	$59,200	$98,800	$38,000	$196,000

Supporting Calculations

<u>Income-sharing ratio prior to admitting Black:</u>

Jan Strous: $\dfrac{\$31,500}{\$90,000} = 35\%$

Cara Wright: $\dfrac{\$58,500}{\$90,000} = 65\%$

<u>Revaluation of assets:</u>

Jan Strous: $10,000 × 35% = $3,500 reduction in capital account
Cara Wright: $10,000 × 65% = $6,500 reduction in capital account

Ex. 13–16   Concluded

Admission of Michael Black:

Equity of initial partners prior to admission	$ 80,000
Contribution by Black	30,000
Total	$110,000
Black's equity interest after admission	20%
Black's equity after admission	$ 22,000
Contribution by Black	$ 30,000
Black's equity after admission	22,000
Bonus paid to Strous and Wright..................................	$ 8,000

The bonus is distributed to Strous and Wright according to their income-sharing ratio prior to admitting Black:

Strous: $8,000 × 35% = $2,800
Wright: $8,000 × 65% = $5,200

Net income distribution:

The revised income-sharing ratio is equal to the proportion of the capital balances after admitting Black according to the partnership agreement:

Jan Strous: $\dfrac{\$30,800}{\$110,000} = 28\%$

Cara Wright: $\dfrac{\$57,200}{\$110,000} = 52\%$

Michael Black: $\dfrac{\$22,000}{\$110,000} = 20\%$

Alternatively, the original income-sharing ratios for Strous and Wright could be multiplied by 80% (100% less the 20% sold to Black) to obtain 28% and 52%, respectively. Leaving 20% for Black.

These ratios can be multiplied by the $160,000 remaining income ($172,000 – $12,000 salary allowance to Strous) to distribute the earnings to the respective partner capital accounts.

Withdrawals:

Half of the income distribution for Wright and Black and half of the income distribution plus salary allowance for Strous. Strous need not take the salary allowance as a withdrawal but may allow it to accumulate in the member equity account.

Ex. 13–17

a.	Merchandise Inventory	15,000	
	Allowance for Doubtful Accounts		3,100
	Glenn Otis, Capital		5,100
	Tammie Sawyer, Capital		3,400
	Joe Parrott, Capital		3,400
b.	Glenn Otis, Capital	205,100	
	Cash		55,100
	Notes Payable		150,000

Ex. 13–18

a. The income-sharing ratio is determined by dividing the net income for each member by the total net income. Thus, in 2005 the income-sharing ratio is as follows:

Golden Properties, LLC: $\dfrac{\$50,000}{\$125,000} = 40\%$

Aztec Holdings, Ltd.: $\dfrac{\$75,000}{\$125,000} = 60\%$

Or a 2:3 ratio

b. Following the same procedure as in (a):

Golden Properties, LLC: $\dfrac{\$106,880}{\$334,000} = 32\%$

Aztec Holdings, Ltd.: $\dfrac{\$160,320}{\$334,000} = 48\%$

Jason Fields: $\dfrac{\$66,800}{\$334,000} = 20\%$

Ex. 13–18   Concluded

c. The member withdrawal ratios do not match the income-sharing ratio, shown as follows:

Golden Properties, LLC: $\dfrac{\$32,000}{\$130,000} = 24.6\%$

Aztec Holdings, Ltd.: $\dfrac{\$48,000}{\$130,000} = 36.9\%$

Jason Fields: $\dfrac{\$50,000}{\$130,000} = 38.5\%$

Clearly, the distribution to Jason Fields is disproportionably higher while the distributions to Golden Properties and Aztec Holdings are lower than their respective income-sharing ratios. Distributions need not be in the same proportion as the income-sharing ratio. Members may make withdrawals from the business as long as their member equity remains positive and the operating agreement allows such withdrawals.

d. Jason Fields provided a $183,750 cash contribution to the business. The amount credited to his member equity account is this amount plus his bonus ($20,000), or $203,750.

e. The negative entries to Golden Properties and Aztec Holdings are the result of a bonus paid to Jason Fields.

f. Jason Fields acquired a 20% interest in the business, computed as follows:

Jason Fields' member equity after admission .	$ 203,750
Golden Properties, LLC, member equity	332,000
Aztec Holdings, Ltd. member equity	483,000
Total	$1,018,750
Fields' ownership interest after admission ($203,750 ÷ $1,018,750)..	20.00%

Ex. 13–19

a.

Cash balance..	$20,000
Sum of capital accounts.............................	25,000
Loss from sale of noncash assets	$ 5,000

b. and c.

	Hires	Bellman
Capital balances before realization..............	$ 5,000	$20,000
Division of loss on sale of noncash assets	2,500	2,500
Balances	$ 2,500	$17,500
Cash distributed to partners.........................	2,500	17,500
Final balances	$ 0	$ 0

Ex. 13–20

	Goldburg	Luce
Capital balances before realization.....................	$57,000	$40,000
Division of loss on sale of noncash assets ($97,000 – $67,000)	15,000	15,000
Capital balances after realization........................	$42,000	$25,000
Cash distributed to partners...............................	42,000	25,000
Final balances..	$ 0	$ 0

Ex. 13–21

a. Deficiency

b. $60,000 ($20,000 + $57,500 – $17,500)

c.

Cash...	17,500	
Nell, Capital		17,500

	Bakki	Towers	Nell
Capital balances after realization	$20,000	$57,500	$(17,500) Dr.
Receipt of partner deficiency.............			17,500
Capital balances after eliminating deficiency..	$20,000	$57,500	$ 0

Ex. 13–22

a. Cash should be distributed as indicated in the following tabulation:

	Meyer	Ball	David	Total
Capital invested	$ 175	$ 125	$ —	$ 300
Net income	+ 100	+ 100	+ 100	+ 300
Capital balances and cash distribution	$ 275	$ 225	$ 100	$ 600

b. David has a capital deficiency of $60, as indicated in the following tabulation:

	Meyer	Ball	David	Total
Capital invested	$ 175	$ 125	$ —	$ 300
Net loss	− 60	− 60	− 60	− 180
Capital balances	$ 115	$ 65	$ 60 Dr.	$ 120

Ex. 13–23

	Duncan	Tribe	Ho
Capital balances after realization	$(15,000)	$50,000	$40,000
Distribution of partner deficiency	15,000	(10,000)	(5,000)
Capital balances after deficiency distribution	$ 0	$40,000	$35,000

Ex. 13–24

GIBBS, HILL, AND MANSON
Statement of Partnership Liquidation
For the Period Ending July 1–29, 20—

	Cash	+	Noncash Assets	=	Liabilities	+	Gibbs (3/6)	+	Hill (2/6)	+	Manson (1/6)
									Capital		
Balances before realization	$ 11,000		$ 85,000		$ 30,000		$ 24,000		$ 28,000		$ 14,000
Sale of assets and division of loss	+ 61,000		– 85,000		—		– 12,000		– 8,000		– 4,000
Balances after realization	$ 72,000		$ 0		$ 30,000		$ 12,000		$ 20,000		$ 10,000
Payment of liabilities	– 30,000		—		– 30,000		—		—		—
Balances after payment of liabilities	$ 42,000		$ 0		$ 0		$ 12,000		$ 20,000		$ 10,000
Distribution of cash to partners	– 42,000		—		—		– 12,000		– 20,000		– 10,000
Final balances	$ 0		$ 0		$ 0		$ 0		$ 0		$ 0

Ex. 13–25

a.

CITY SIGNS, LLC
Statement of LLC Liquidation
For the Period March 1–31, 2006

	Cash	+	Noncash Assets	=	Liabilities	+	Member Equity Ellis (2/5)	+	Roane (2/5)	+	Clausen (1/5)
Balances before realization	$ 4,000		$125,000		$ 44,000		$ 28,000		$ 45,000		$ 12,000
Sale of assets and division of loss	+ 96,000		−125,000		—		− 11,600		− 11,600		− 5,800
Balances after realization	$100,000		$ 0		$ 44,000		$ 16,400		$ 33,400		$ 6,200
Payment of liabilities	− 44,000		—		− 44,000		—		—		—
Balances after payment of liabilities	$ 56,000		$ 0		$ 0		$ 16,400		$ 33,400		$ 6,200
Distribution of cash to members	− 56,000		—		—		− 16,400		− 33,400		− 6,200
Final balances	$ 0		$ 0		$ 0		$ 0		$ 0		$ 0

b.

Ellis, Member Equity	16,400	
Roane, Member Equity	33,400	
Clausen, Member Equity	6,200	
Cash		56,000

613

PROBLEMS

Prob. 13–1A

1.

Nov.	1	Cash..	15,000	
		Merchandise Inventory	55,000	
		E. Tsao, Capital		70,000
	1	Cash..	6,100	
		Accounts Receivable	31,500	
		Merchandise Inventory	42,900	
		Equipment..	25,000	
		Allowance for Doubtful Accounts..................		800
		Accounts Payable		9,700
		Notes Payable...		10,000
		Mark Ivens, Capital...		85,000

2.

TSAO AND IVENS
Balance Sheet
November 1, 2005

Assets

Current assets:			
Cash		$21,100	
Accounts receivable	$31,500		
Less allowance for doubtful accounts ...	800	30,700	
Merchandise inventory		97,900	
Total current assets............................			$149,700
Plant assets:			
Equipment..			25,000
Total assets...			$174,700

Liabilities

Current liabilities:		
Accounts payable.....................................	$ 9,700	
Notes payable...	10,000	
Total liabilities...		$ 19,700

Partners' Equity

E. Tsao, capital	$70,000	
Mark Ivens, capital...	85,000	
Total partners' equity		155,000
Total liabilities and partners' equity.............		$174,700

Prob. 13–1A   Concluded

3.

Oct. 31	Income Summary			75,500	
	E. Tsao, Capital				40,000*
	Mark Ivens, Capital				35,500*
31	E. Tsao, Capital			26,000	
	Mark Ivens, Capital			17,500	
	E. Tsao, Drawing				26,000
	Mark Ivens, Drawing				17,500

*Computations:

	Tsao	Ivens	Total
Interest allowance	$ 7,000	$ 8,500	$15,500
Salary allowance	24,000	18,000	42,000
Remaining income (1:1)	9,000	9,000	18,000
Net income	$40,000	$35,500	$75,500

Prob. 13–2A

Plan		(1) $150,000 Haddox	(1) $150,000 French	(2) $90,000 Haddox	(2) $90,000 French
a.	....	$ 75,000	$75,000	$45,000	$45,000
b.	....	60,000	90,000	36,000	54,000
c.	....	100,000	50,000	60,000	30,000
d.	....	84,000	66,000	48,000	42,000
e.	....	87,000	63,000	57,000	33,000
f.	....	93,000	57,000	57,000	33,000

Details

		$150,000 Haddox	$150,000 French	$90,000 Haddox	$90,000 French
a.	Net income (1:1).........................	$ 75,000	$ 75,000	$ 45,000	$ 45,000
b.	Net income (2:3).........................	$ 60,000	$ 90,000	$ 36,000	$ 54,000
c.	Net income (2:1).........................	$ 100,000	$ 50,000	$ 60,000	$ 30,000
d.	Interest allowance	$ 12,000	$ 18,000	$ 12,000	$ 18,000
	Remaining allowance (3:2)........	72,000	48,000	36,000	24,000
	Net income	$ 84,000	$ 66,000	$ 48,000	$ 42,000
e.	Interest allowance	$ 12,000	$ 18,000	$ 12,000	$ 18,000
	Salary allowance........................	60,000	30,000	60,000	30,000
	Excess of allowances over income (1:1)...........................			(15,000)	(15,000)
	Remaining income (1:1)	15,000	15,000		
	Net income	$ 87,000	$ 63,000	$ 57,000	$ 33,000
f.	Interest allowance	$ 12,000	$ 18,000	$ 12,000	$ 18,000
	Salary allowance........................	60,000	30,000	60,000	30,000
	Bonus allowance	12,000			
	Excess of allowances over income (1:1)...........................			(15,000)	(15,000)
	Remaining income (1:1)	9,000	9,000		
	Net income	$ 93,000	$ 57,000	$ 57,000	$ 33,000

Prob. 13–3A

1.

REEVES AND STRANGE
Income Statement
For the Year Ended December 31, 2006

Professional fees		$316,750
Operating expenses:		
Salary expense	$84,500	
Depreciation expense—building	10,500	
Property tax expense	10,000	
Heating and lighting expense	9,900	
Supplies expense	5,750	
Depreciation expense—office equipment	5,000	
Miscellaneous expense	6,100	
Total operating expenses		131,750
Net income		$185,000

	Dan Reeves	Ron Strange	Total
Division of net income:			
Salary allowance	$ 25,000	$ 35,000	$ 60,000
Interest allowance	9,000*	6,000**	15,000
Remaining income	55,000	55,000	110,000
Net income	$ 89,000	$ 96,000	$ 185,000

*$75,000 × 12%
**($55,000 – $5,000) × 12%

2.

REEVES AND STRANGE
Statement of Partners' Equity
For the Year Ended December 31, 2006

	Dan Reeves	Ron Strange	Total
Capital, January 1, 2006	$ 75,000	$ 50,000	$ 125,000
Additional investment during the year	—	5,000	5,000
	$ 75,000	$ 55,000	$ 130,000
Net income for the year	89,000	96,000	185,000
	$ 164,000	$ 151,000	$ 315,000
Withdrawals during the year	50,000	60,000	110,000
Capital, December 31, 2006	$ 114,000	$ 91,000	$ 205,000

Prob. 13–3A   Concluded

3.

REEVES AND STRANGE
Balance Sheet
December 31, 2006

Assets

Current assets:		
Cash	$ 24,500	
Accounts receivable	40,500	
Supplies	2,400	
Total current assets.............................		$ 67,400
Plant assets:		
Land...	$ 50,000	
Building.. $ 150,000		
Less accumulated depreciation........... 77,500	72,500	
Office equipment....................................... $ 40,000		
Less accumulated depreciation........... 22,400	17,600	
Total plant assets		140,100
Total assets..		$ 207,500

Liabilities

Current liabilities:		
Accounts payable.....................................	$ 1,000	
Salaries payable	1,500	
Total liabilities...		$ 2,500

Partners' Equity

Dan Reeves, capital..	$ 114,000	
Ron Strange, capital...	91,000	
Total partners' equity		205,000
Total liabilities and partners' equity...............		$ 207,500

Prob. 13–4A

1.

May	31	Asset Revaluations....................................	4,050	
		Accounts Receivable		3,250
		Allowance for Doubtful Accounts		800*

*[($29,250 – $3,250) × 5%] – $500

	31	Merchandise Inventory..............................	3,300	
		Asset Revaluations		3,300
	31	Accumulated Depreciation—Equipment..	72,500	
		Equipment..		54,000
		Asset Revaluations		18,500
	31	Asset Revaluations....................................	17,750	
		Adrian Capps, Capital		8,875
		Lisa Knight, Capital..............................		8,875

2.

June	1	Adrian Capps, Capital...............................	25,000	
		Todd Aguero, Capital		25,000
	1	Cash..	25,000	
		Todd Aguero, Capital		25,000

Prob. 13–4A   Concluded

3.

CAPPS, KNIGHT, AND AGUERO
Balance Sheet
June 1, 2006

Assets

Current assets:			
Cash		$ 34,500	
Accounts receivable	$ 26,000		
Less allowance for doubtful accounts	1,300	24,700	
Merchandise inventory		63,400	
Prepaid insurance		2,000	
Total current assets............................			$ 124,600
Plant assets:			
Equipment...			108,000
Total assets...			$ 232,600

Liabilities

Current liabilities:			
Accounts payable.....................................		$ 9,850	
Notes payable		20,000	
Total liabilities...			$ 29,850

Partners' Equity

Adrian Capps, capital.....................................		$ 103,875	
Lisa Knight, capital...		48,875	
Todd Aguero, capital......................................		50,000	
Total partners' equity			202,750
Total liabilities and partners' equity...............			$ 232,600

Prob. 13–5A

1.

WILSON, CROWDER, AND PATEL
Statement of Partnership Liquidation
For the Period May 10–30, 2006

| | Cash | + | Noncash Assets | = | Liabilities | + | Capital | | |
							Wilson (50%)	+ Crowder (25%)	+ Patel (25%)
Balances before realization	$ 6,500		$ 89,100		$ 45,600		$ 27,800	$ 8,300	$ 13,900
Sale of assets and division of loss	+ 37,500		– 89,100				– 25,800	– 12,900	– 12,900
Balances after realization	$ 44,000		$ 0		$ 45,600		$ 2,000	$ 4,600 (Dr.)	$ 1,000
Receipt of deficiency	+ 4,600		—		—		—	+ 4,600	—
Balance	$ 48,600		$ 0		$ 45,600		$ 2,000	$ 0	$ 1,000
Payment of liabilities	– 45,600		—		– 45,600		—	—	—
Balances after payment of liabilities	$ 3,000		$ 0		$ 0		$ 2,000	$ 0	$ 1,000
Cash distributed to partners	– 3,000		—		—		– 2,000	—	– 1,000
Final balances	$ 0		$ 0		$ 0		$ 0	$ 0	$ 0

2. The $4,600 deficiency of Crowder would be divided between the other partners, Wilson and Patel, in their income-sharing ratio (2:1 respectively). Therefore, Wilson would absorb 2/3 of the $4,600 deficiency, or $3,066.67, and Patel would absorb 1/3 of the $4,600 deficiency, or $1,533.33.

Prob. 13–6A

1.

IMHOFF, BAXTER, AND WISE
Statement of Partnership Liquidation
For Period May 3–29, 2006

| | Cash | + | Noncash Assets | = | Liabilities | + | Capital | | | | |
							Imhoff (1/5)	+	Baxter (2/5)	+	Wise (2/5)
Balances before realization	$ 10,000		$ 285,000		$ 55,000		$ 30,000		$ 90,000		$ 120,000
Sale of assets and division of gain	+ 345,000		– 285,000		—		+ 12,000		+ 24,000		+ 24,000
Balances after realization	$ 355,000		$ 0		$ 55,000		$ 42,000		$ 114,000		$ 144,000
Payment of liabilities	– 55,000		—		– 55,000		—		—		—
Balances after payment of liabilities	$ 300,000		$ 0		$ 0		$ 42,000		$ 114,000		$ 144,000
Distribution of cash to partners	– 300,000		—		—		– 42,000		– 114,000		– 144,000
Final balances	$ 0		$ 0		$ 0		$ 0		$ 0		$ 0

Prob. 13-6A   Continued

2.

IMHOFF, BAXTER, AND WISE
Statement of Partnership Liquidation
For Period May 3–29, 2006

	Cash	+	Noncash Assets	=	Liabilities	+	Imhoff (1/5)	+	Baxter (2/5)	+	Wise (2/5)
									Capital		
Balances before realization	$ 10,000		$ 285,000		$ 55,000		$ 30,000		$ 90,000		$ 120,000
Sale of assets and division of loss	+175,000		−285,000		—		−22,000		−44,000		−44,000
Balances after realization	$ 185,000		$ 0		$ 55,000		$ 8,000		$ 46,000		$ 76,000
Payment of liabilities	−55,000		—		−55,000		—		—		—
Balances after payment of liabilities	$ 130,000		$ 0		$ 0		$ 8,000		$ 46,000		$ 76,000
Distribution of cash to partners	−130,000		—		—		−8,000		−46,000		−76,000
Final balances	$ 0		$ 0		$ 0		$ 0		$ 0		$ 0

Prob. 13–6A   Concluded

3.

IMHOFF, BAXTER, AND WISE
Statement of Partnership Liquidation
For Period May 3–29, 2006

	Cash	+	Noncash Assets	=	Liabilities	+	Imhoff (1/5)	+	Baxter (2/5)	+	Wise (2/5)
									Capital		
Balances before realization	$ 10,000		$ 285,000		$ 55,000		$ 30,000		$ 90,000		$ 120,000
Sale of assets and division of loss	+ 105,000		– 285,000		—		– 36,000		– 72,000		– 72,000
Balances after realization	$ 115,000		$ 0		$ 55,000		$ 6,000 (Dr.)		$ 18,000		$ 48,000
Payment of liabilities	– 55,000		—		– 55,000		—		—		—
Balances after payment of liabilities	$ 60,000		$ 0		$ 0		$ 6,000 (Dr.)		$ 18,000		$ 48,000
Receipt of deficiency	+ 6,000		—		—		+ 6,000		—		—
Balances	$ 66,000		$ 0		$ 0		$ 0		$ 18,000		$ 48,000
Distribution of cash to partners	– 66,000		—		—		—		– 18,000		– 48,000
Final balances	$ 0		$ 0		$ 0		$ 0		$ 0		$ 0

624

Prob. 13–1B

1.

May	1	Cash	10,500	
		Merchandise Inventory	36,500	
		Crystal Hall, Capital		47,000
	1	Cash	12,000	
		Accounts Receivable	18,000	
		Equipment	40,000	
		Allowance for Doubtful Accounts		1,000
		Accounts Payable		14,000
		Notes Payable		15,000
		Doug Tucker, Capital		40,000

2.

HALL AND TUCKER
Balance Sheet
May 1, 2005

Assets

Current assets:		
Cash		$ 22,500
Accounts receivable	$ 18,000	
Less allowance for doubtful accounts	1,000	17,000
Merchandise inventory		36,500
Total current assets		$ 76,000
Plant assets:		
Equipment		40,000
Total assets		**$ 116,000**

Liabilities

Current liabilities:		
Accounts payable		$ 14,000
Notes payable		15,000
Total liabilities		$ 29,000

Partners' Equity

Crystal Hall, capital		$ 47,000
Doug Tucker, capital		40,000
Total partners' equity		87,000
Total liabilities and partners' equity		**$ 116,000**

Prob. 13–1B   Concluded

3.

Apr. 30	Income Summary	72,700	
	Crystal Hall, Capital		35,200*
	Doug Tucker, Capital		37,500*
30	Crystal Hall, Capital	20,000	
	Doug Tucker, Capital	26,000	
	Crystal Hall, Drawing		20,000
	Doug Tucker, Drawing		26,000

*Computations:

	Hall	Tucker	Total
Interest allowance	$ 4,700	$ 4,000	$ 8,700
Salary allowance	18,000	21,000	39,000
Remaining income (1:1)	12,500	12,500	25,000
Net income	$ 35,200	$ 37,500	$ 72,700

Prob. 13–2B

Plan		(1) $90,000 Garland	(1) $90,000 Driscoe	(2) $240,000 Garland	(2) $240,000 Driscoe
a.	....	$45,000	$45,000	$120,000	$120,000
b.	....	60,000	30,000	160,000	80,000
c.	....	30,000	60,000	80,000	160,000
d.	....	51,000	39,000	126,000	114,000
e.	....	36,000	54,000	111,000	129,000
f.	....	36,000	54,000	96,000	144,000

Details

		$90,000 Garland	$90,000 Driscoe	$240,000 Garland	$240,000 Driscoe
a.	Net income (1:1).........................	$ 45,000	$ 45,000	$ 120,000	$ 120,000
b.	Net income (2:1).........................	$ 60,000	$ 30,000	$ 160,000	$ 80,000
c.	Net income (1:2).........................	$ 30,000	$ 60,000	$ 80,000	$ 160,000
d.	Interest allowance	$ 24,000	$ 12,000	$ 24,000	$ 12,000
	Remaining allowance (1:1)........	27,000	27,000	102,000	102,000
	Net income	$ 51,000	$ 39,000	$ 126,000	$ 114,000
e.	Interest allowance	$ 24,000	$ 12,000	$ 24,000	$ 12,000
	Salary allowance........................	30,000	60,000	30,000	60,000
	Excess of allowances over income (1:1)............................	(18,000)	(18,000)		
	Remaining income (1:1)			57,000	57,000
	Net income	$ 36,000	$ 54,000	$ 111,000	$ 129,000
f.	Interest allowance	$ 24,000	$ 12,000	$ 24,000	$ 12,000
	Salary allowance........................	30,000	60,000	30,000	60,000
	Bonus allowance				30,000
	Excess of allowances over income (1:1)............................	(18,000)	(18,000)		
	Remaining income (1:1)			42,000	42,000
	Net income	$ 36,000	$ 54,000	$ 96,000	$ 144,000

Prob. 13–3B

1.

DIXON AND FAWLER
Income Statement
For the Year Ended December 31, 2006

Professional fees		$285,650
Operating expenses:		
Salary expense	$80,500	
Depreciation expense—building	10,500	
Property tax expense	8,000	
Heating and lighting expense	7,900	
Supplies expense	2,850	
Depreciation expense—office equipment	2,800	
Miscellaneous expense	6,100	
Total operating expenses		118,650
Net income		$167,000

	Peter Dixon	May Fawler	Total
Division of net income:			
Salary allowance	$ 30,000	$ 40,000	$ 70,000
Interest allowance	9,000*	6,000**	15,000
Remaining income	41,000	41,000	82,000
Net income	$ 80,000	$ 87,000	$ 167,000

*$75,000 × 12%
**($55,000 – $5,000) × 12%

2.

DIXON AND FAWLER
Statement of Partners' Equity
For the Year Ended December 31, 2006

	Peter Dixon	May Fawler	Total
Capital, January 1, 2006	$ 75,000	$ 50,000	$ 125,000
Additional investment during the year	—	5,000	5,000
	$ 75,000	$ 55,000	$ 130,000
Net income for the year	80,000	87,000	167,000
	$ 155,000	$ 142,000	$ 297,000
Withdrawals during the year	60,000	75,000	135,000
Capital, December 31, 2006	$ 95,000	$ 67,000	$ 162,000

Prob. 13–3B   Concluded

3.

DIXON AND FAWLER
Balance Sheet
December 31, 2006

Assets

Current assets:

Cash	$ 22,000	
Accounts receivable	38,900	
Supplies	1,900	
Total current assets		$ 62,800

Plant assets:

Land		$ 25,000	
Building	$ 130,000		
Less accumulated depreciation	69,200	60,800	
Office equipment	$ 39,000		
Less accumulated depreciation	21,500	17,500	
Total plant assets			103,300
Total assets			$ 166,100

Liabilities

Current liabilities:

Accounts payable	$ 2,100	
Salaries payable	2,000	
Total liabilities		$ 4,100

Partners' Equity

Peter Dixon, capital	$ 95,000	
May Fawler, capital	67,000	
Total partners' equity		162,000
Total liabilities and partners' equity		$ 166,100

Prob. 13–4B

1. **Apr.** **30** Asset Revaluations 2,380
       Accounts Receivable.................................. 1,900
       Allowance for Doubtful Accounts 480*
    *[($22,500 – $1,900) × 5%] – $550

       30 Merchandise Inventory 2,500
       Asset Revaluations.................................... 2,500

       30 Accumulated Depreciation—Equipment....... 65,000
       Equipment 45,000
       Asset Revaluations.................................... 20,000

       30 Asset Revaluations 20,120
       Tom Denney, Capital 10,060
       Cheryl Burks, Capital................................ 10,060

2. **May** **1** Cheryl Burks, Capital...................................... 20,000
       Sara Wold, Capital 20,000

       1 Cash 20,000
       Sara Wold, Capital 20,000

Prob. 13–4B   Concluded

3.

DENNEY, BURKS, AND WOLD
Balance Sheet
May 1, 2006

Assets

Current assets:		
Cash		$ 27,900
Accounts receivable	$ 20,600	
Less allowance for doubtful accounts	1,030	19,570
Merchandise inventory		53,100
Prepaid insurance		1,650
Total current assets.............................		$ 102,220
Plant assets:		
Equipment..		100,000
Total assets...		$ 202,220

Liabilities

Current liabilities:		
Accounts payable.....................................	$ 12,100	
Notes payable...	10,000	
Total liabilities..		$ 22,100

Partners' Equity

Tom Denney, capital......................................	$ 90,060	
Cheryl Burks, capital......................................	50,060	
Sara Wold, capital..	40,000	
Total partners' equity		180,120
Total liabilities and partners' equity...............		$ 202,220

Prob. 13–6B   Continued

2.

EWING, JOHNSON, AND LANDRY
Statement of Partnership Liquidation
For Period October 1–30, 2006

	Cash	+	Noncash Assets	=	Liabilities	+	Ewing (2/5)	+	Johnson (2/5)	+	Landry (1/5)
									Capital		
Balances before realization	$ 20,000		$ 250,000		$ 50,000		$ 100,000		$ 90,000		$ 30,000
Sale of assets and division of loss	+120,000		–250,000		—		– 52,000		– 52,000		– 26,000
Balances after realization	$ 140,000		$ 0		$ 50,000		$ 48,000		$ 38,000		$ 4,000
Payment of liabilities	– 50,000		—		– 50,000		—		—		—
Balances after payment of liabilities	$ 90,000		$ 0		$ 0		$ 48,000		$ 38,000		$ 4,000
Distribution of cash to partners	– 90,000		—		—		– 48,000		– 38,000		– 4,000
Final balances	$ 0		$ 0		$ 0		$ 0		$ 0		$ 0

Prob. 13–6B   Concluded

3.

EWING, JOHNSON, AND LANDRY
Statement of Partnership Liquidation
For Period October 1–30, 2006

	Cash	+	Noncash Assets	=	Liabilities	+	Ewing (2/5)	+	Johnson (2/5)	+	Landry (1/5)
									Capital		
Balances before realization	$ 20,000		$ 250,000		$ 50,000		$ 100,000		$ 90,000		$ 30,000
Sale of assets and division of loss	+ 50,000		− 250,000		—		− 80,000		− 80,000		− 40,000
Balances after realization	$ 70,000		$ 0		$ 50,000		$ 20,000		$ 10,000		$ 10,000 (Dr.)
Payment of liabilities	− 50,000		—		− 50,000		—		—		—
Balances after payment of liabilities	$ 20,000		$ 0		$ 0		$ 20,000		$ 10,000		$ 10,000 (Dr.)
Receipt of deficiency	+ 10,000		—		—		—		—		+ 10,000
Balances	$ 30,000		$ 0		$ 0		$ 20,000		$ 10,000		$ 0
Distribution of cash to partners	− 30,000		—		—		− 20,000		− 10,000		—
Final balances	$ 0		$ 0		$ 0		$ 0		$ 0		$ 0

SPECIAL ACTIVITIES

Activity 13–1

This scenario highlights one of the problems that arises in partnerships: attempting to align contribution with income division. Often disagreements are based upon honest differences of opinion. However, in this scenario, there is evidence that Harrison was acting unethically. Harrison apparently made no mention of his plans to "scale back" once the partnership was consummated. As a result, Miller agreed to an equal division of income based on the assumption that Harrison's past efforts would project into the future, while in fact, Harrison had no intention of this. As a result, Miller is now providing twice the effort, while receiving the same income as Harrison. This is clearly not sustainable in the long term. Harrison does not appear to be concerned about this inequity. Thus, the evidence points to some duplicity on Harrison's part. Essentially, he knows that he is riding on Miller's effort and had planned it that way.

Miller could respond to this situation by either withdrawing from the partnership or changing the partnership agreement. One possible change would be to provide a partner salary based on the amount of patient billings. This salary would be highly associated with the amount of revenue brought into the partnership, thus avoiding disputes associated with unequal contribution to the firm.

Activity 13–2

A good solution to this problem would be to divide income in three steps:
1. Provide interest on each partner's capital balance.
2. Provide a monthly salary for each partner.
3. Divide the remainder according to a partnership formula.

With this approach, the return on capital and effort will be separately calculated in the income division formula before applying the percentage formula. Thus, Adair will receive a large interest distribution based on the large capital balance, while Fontana should receive a large salary distribution based on the larger service contribution. The return on capital and salary allowances should be based on prevailing market rates. If both partners are pleased with their return on capital and effort, then the remaining income could be divided equally among them.

Activity 13–3

a.

PricewaterhouseCoopers	$2,893,678[1]	$240,808[2]
Deloitte & Touche	2,685,064	299,433
Ernst & Young	2,319,028	323,336
KPMG	2,155,676	303,794

[1] Revenue per partner for PricewaterhouseCoopers = $\dfrac{\$8,056,000,000}{2,784}$ = $2,893,678

[2] Revenue per staff for PricewaterhouseCoopers $\dfrac{\$8,056,000,000}{33,454}$ = $240,808

b. The amount earned per partner is highest with PricewaterhouseCoopers at $2,893,678 and lowest with KPMG at $2,155,676. However, the amount of revenue earned per professional staff member is only $240,808 for Pricewaterhouse-Coopers, while KPMG is higher, at $303,794. This unusual result suggests that PricewaterhouseCoopers has fewer partners but a greater number of staff to support their business than is the case for KPMG. The same pattern appears to hold for Deloitte & Touche and Ernst & Young as well. Interestingly, these results may be driven by the difference in the revenue mix between the two groups of firms. Both PricewaterhouseCoopers and Deloitte & Touche have significant revenues from management consulting operations, while Ernst & Young and KPMG have sold these operations and no longer perform consulting. It is possible that consulting requires fewer partners and more professional staff per revenue dollar earned than do tax and accounting services.

Note: The Sarbanes-Oxley Act has prohibited audit clients from using management consulting services from the same firm. As a result, public accounting firms are divesting their consulting operations.

Activity 13–4

a. A key distinction between a partnership and a corporation is that all of the partners (owners) are not only investors but also work in the partnership. The partners provide both capital and "sweat equity." This is a key distinction that provides insight about the performance of the firm. The expected income from the partnership is given as the country average, or $230,000.

 The following is what each partner actually earned from the partnership.

 Allocation of partnership income ($35,000,000 ÷ 200 partners) = $175,000 per partner

 Note that the partners' earnings are less than what might be expected from the expected, or average, income. Thus, the partnership has performed below the partners' expectations.

b. The income statement indicates some large litigation losses. These losses appear to be the major reason for the partnership's poor performance. Without the losses, the partnership net income allocation would have been $225,000 [($35,000,000 + $10,000,000) ÷ 200]. The $225,000 is much closer to the market-based compensation of $230,000 per year. In addition, the staff professional salaries of $80,000 per year ($120,000,000 ÷ 1,500) is slightly higher than average ($75,000). This would also have led to a smaller income to the partners than might have been expected.

Activity 13–5

1. Many of the Wall Street analysts during the late 1990s and early 2000s were not behaving like independent analysts. Rather, they were supporting the investment bankers in their firm. The investment bankers earned huge fees for selling new issues of common stock to the public. The research analysts curried favor with small emerging companies by providing glowing recommendations. The analysts were actively involved in, and received bonuses for, soliciting new investment banking clients. These recommendations, in turn, supported initial public offerings of common stock. After the common stock was issued, highly favorable analysis caused the stock prices to increase. In a sense, the analysts were acting like advertisers by promoting a company, rather than critically analyzing it. The Merrill e-mails have caused major criticism and launched reform in the investment banking business. Blodget was released from Merrill Lynch. At this writing, major firms and analysts are facing both civil suits and potential criminal actions.

2. Some have argued that nothing really needs to be done, because the marketplace will make the necessary adjustments. Namely, analysts from investment banking firms will no longer be trusted, giving rise to a new class of independent analysts that is separate from investment banking. These analysts would earn fees for their unbiased advice. This adjustment is already taking place to some degree. However, many are calling for additional reforms. Such reforms include separating investment banking from research by preventing analysts from engaging in, or being compensated by, the investment banking function. Under this scenario, the research analysts would not receive bonuses based on investment banking business, nor would they be involved in investment banking solicitation. The analyst would have no direct responsibility nor be under the authority of investment banking. Some are calling for additional regulation of the analyst community in order to monitor this separation.

Activity 13–6

a. Omidyar incorporated the business in order to likely accomplish two major objectives. First, incorporation limits his liability to his investment in the company. Second, incorporation eases raising additional capital through shares of stock. It is likely that eBay's stunning growth would require additional sources of capital, thus favoring the corporate form.

b.

Benchmark's assumed proceeds after IPO	
(3,000,000 shares × $18.00)	$54,000,000
Benchmark's initial investment	3,000,000
Assumed profit from sale after IPO	$51,000,000

This would represent a return of 1,700% in approximately one year.

c. The underwriters' discount is their compensation, or $4,410,000. Shown as follows:

Discount	$1.26
Number of shares issued	× 3,500,000*
Underwriters' compensation	$ 4,410,000

*$63,000,000 ÷ $18

Investment banking is known to be a very profitable industry when there are many IPO's and other capital market transactions.

Note: Goldman Sach's was the lead underwriter for this IPO.

d. Percent of voting shares received by public shareholders: $\dfrac{3,500,000}{39,739,076} = 8.8\%$

Shares issued to the public: 3,500,000 (of which 10,725 shares were from an existing shareholder exiting the investment through the IPO)

Shares outstanding after IPO: 39,739,076 (from prospectus)

Activity 13–6 Concluded

e. Percent of shareholders' equity provided by public shareholders:

$$\frac{\$58,410,463}{\$67,410,463} = 86.6\%$$

Shareholders' equity prior to the IPO	$ 9,000,000
Proceeds to the company from IPO	58,410,463
Total shareholders' equity after IPO	$67,410,463

Thus, the public shareholders have 8.8% of the common stock (d), yet have contributed 86.6% of the capital. This result is typical for a successful start-up company.

f. Omidyar's unrealized gain in 2003, when the stock price was $89 per share, would be calculated as follows:

Number of shares held by Omidyar	14,700,000
Market price in 2003..	× $89
Total value of shares held...	$1,308,300,000
Less initial investment	14,262
Unrealized gain	$1,308,285,738

Omidyar is a billionaire and has reaped the fruits of a very successful idea. The eBay story shows how the capitalist system rewards new initiatives, businesses, and ideas.

CHAPTER 14
INCOME TAXES, UNUSUAL INCOME ITEMS, AND INVESTMENTS IN STOCKS

CLASS DISCUSSION QUESTIONS

1. **a.** Current liability

    b. Long-term liability or deferred credit (following the Long-Term Liabilities section)

2. This is an example of a fixed asset impairment. Thus, a loss of $130 million should be disclosed on the income statement as a separate line item above the income from continuing operations, and the plant and equipment should be written down to their appraised value ($20 million).

3. The severance costs are a current period expense associated with downsizing operations. Thus, a restructuring charge should be recognized on the income statement (above income from continuing operations) and any liability recognized. As payments are made to employees, the liability is decreased.

4. Extraordinary items:

    Gain on condemnation of land, net of applicable income tax of $60,000 .... $90,000

5. The urban renewal agency's acquisition of the property may be viewed as a form of expropriation under paragraph 23 of Accounting Principles Board Opinion No. 30, *Reporting the Results of Operations—Reporting the Effects of Disposal of a Segment of a Business, and Extraordinary, Unusual and Infrequently Occurring Events and Transactions.* Paragraph 23 says a gain or loss from sale or abandonment of property, plant, or equipment used in the business should be included as an extraordinary item if it is the direct result of an expropriation. Accordingly, the gain should be reported as an extraordinary item in the income statement.

6. The "loss from discontinued operations" of $2.3 billion should be identified on the income statement as discontinued operations and should follow the presentation of the results of continuing operations (sales less the customary costs and expenses). The data on discontinued operations (identity of the segment, date of disposal, etc.) should be disclosed in a note.

7. Readers of the financial statements should be able to assume that the successive financial statements of a business are based consistently on the same generally accepted accounting principles. Therefore, significant changes in accounting methods must be disclosed so that the reader is alerted to the effect of those changes on the financial statements.

8. **a.** Yes, the $0.45-per-share gain should be reported as an extraordinary item.

    b. Operations appear to have declined. The earnings per share for the current year that is comparable to the preceding year's earnings per share of $1.10 is $0.93 ($1.38 – $0.45).

9. **a.** Examples of other comprehensive income items include foreign currency items, pension liability adjustments, and unrealized gains and losses on certain investments in debt and equity securities.

    b. No. Other comprehensive income does not affect the determination of net income or retained earnings.

10. A business may purchase stocks as a means of earning a return (income) on excess cash that it does not need for its normal operations. In other cases, a business may purchase the stock of another company as a means of developing or maintaining business relationships with the other company. A business may also purchase common stock as a means of gaining control of another company's operations.

11. On the balance sheet, temporary investments in marketable securities are reported at their fair market values, net of any applicable income taxes related to any unrealized gains or losses.

12. Unrealized gains or losses (net of applicable taxes) should be reported as either an addition to or deduction from net income in arriving at comprehensive income.

13. **a.** The equity method
    b. Investments

14. Investment in Gestalt Corporation

15. **a.** Minority interest
    b. Preceding stockholders' equity, usually in the Long-Term Liabilities section.

16. Investment in
    Affiliates 2,400,000
    Income of
    Affiliates   2,400,000

EXERCISES

Ex. 14–1

Apr.	15	Income Tax Expense..	70,000	
		Cash..		70,000
June	15	Income Tax Expense..	70,000	
		Cash..		70,000
Sept.	15	Income Tax Expense..	70,000	
		Cash..		70,000
Dec.	31	Income Tax Expense..	150,000*	
		Income Tax Payable		40,000
		Deferred Income Tax Payable.......................		110,000**

$$*[(\$900,000 \times 40\%) - (3 \times \$70,000)] = \$150,000$$
$$**[(\$800,000 \times 40\%) - (3 \times \$70,000)] = \$110,000$$

Jan.	15	Income Tax Payable...	110,000	
		Cash..		110,000

Ex. 14–2

2005

Dec.	31	Income Tax Expense..	920,000	
		Deferred Income Tax Payable.......................		120,000*
		Income Tax Payable		800,000**

$$*\$300,000 \times 40\% = \$120,000$$
$$**\$2,000,000 \times 40\% = \$800,000$$

2006

Dec.	31	Income Tax Expense..	880,000	
		Deferred Income Tax Payable	120,000	
		Income Tax Payable		1,000,000**

$$**\$2,500,000 \times 40\% = \$1,000,000$$

Ex. 14–3

a.

Depreciation expense per year: $\dfrac{\$100,000,000 - \$20,000,000}{10 \text{ years}} = \$8,000,000$ per year

December 31, 2006 net book value (carrying value) prior to impairment adjustment:

Fiber optic network cost	$100,000,000
Less accumulated depreciation	16,000,000
Fiber optic net book value	$ 84,000,000

b.

2006

Dec.	31	Loss from Fixed Asset Impairment 39,000,000*	
		Fixed Assets—Fiber Optic Network	39,000,000

*$84,000,000 – $45,000,000

c.

Balance sheet:

Fixed assets—Fiber optic network...........................	$61,000,000*
Less accumulated depreciation	16,000,000
Fixed assets—Fiber optic network net book value.	$45,000,000

*$100,000,000 – $39,000,000

Ex. 14–4

a.

2006

Dec. 31 Loss from Fixed Asset Impairment 99,000,000
           Fixed Assets—Buildings and Improvements   80,000,000
           Fixed Assets—Land......................................   8,000,000
           Fixed Assets—Equipment.............................   11,000,000

b. On December 31, 2006, management determined that one of the resort properties was permanently impaired due to the discovery of an adjacent toxic
chemical waste site. Bookings to this property have dropped significantly,
and it was determined that the property had to abandoned. As a result, a $99
million asset impairment loss was recognized in 2006, reflecting the fair value
of assets associated with this site, as detailed in the following table:

Buildings and improvements	$80,000,000
Land...	8,000,000
Equipment...	11,000,000
Total impairment..	$99,000,000

Ex. 14–6   **(Concluded)**

e.   Note disclosure:

On July 1, 2006, the board of directors of the company approved and announced a restructuring plan that resulted in a $3,039,200 charge in 2006 consisting of the following items:

Closing and relocation costs	$ 500,000
Employee severance costs	2,419,200
Contract termination costs	120,000
Total restructuring charge	$ 3,039,200

The restructuring was caused by unfavorable publicity regarding the caffeine content of our juice products. The adverse publicity reduced the demand for our products, requiring us to consolidate operations by closing one of our juice plants and eliminating 280 direct labor positions. On December 31, 2006, there remains a current restructuring obligation of $1,814,400, primarily related to employee severance agreements.

Note: While no information was provided in the exercise, it is likely that the factory building is also impaired requiring a write-down and appropriate disclosures.

Ex. 14–7

a.

2006

Dec. 31 Loss from Fixed Asset Impairment 15,000,000*
       Fixed Assets—Tractor-Trailers....................   15,000,000

    *($34,000,000 – $9,000,000) × 60%

Dec. 31 Restructuring Charge 650,000*
       Employee Termination Obligation................   650,000

    *65 employees × $10,000

b. December 31, 2006 balance sheet disclosures:

Fixed assets:
Tractor-trailers	$19,000,000
Less accumulated depreciation	(9,000,000)
Tractor-trailer net book value	$10,000,000

Current liabilities:
Employee termination obligation	$650,000

Note:

On December 31, 2006, the board of directors approved and communicated a restructuring plan in response to low-cost competition in the company's service market. The plan calls for the sale of 50 tractor-trailers and elimination of 50 drivers and 15 staff personnel. Due to the general overcapacity in the transportation market, tractor-trailer market values are estimated to be 40% of the existing book value, causing us to recognize an unrecoverable loss on fixed asset impairment of $15,000,000 in 2006 for the entire fleet. In addition, a severance plan was approved for the eliminated positions. The charge for employee severance was $650,000 for 2006, all of which is currently payable at the end of the fiscal year. It is estimated that all severance obligations will be satisfied by the end of the first quarter in 2007.

c.

2007

Mar. 14 Employee Termination Obligation 650,000
       Cash   650,000

Ex. 14–8

a.

Special Charges...	32,755,000	
Fixed Assets—Property, Plant, and Equipment ...		28,627,000
Employee Termination Obligation		4,128,000

b.

Accrued Liabilities..	4,629,000	
Cash		4,629,000

c. Balance sheet:

Current liabilities:

Accrued liabilities	$4,110,000*

*$6,903,000 + $4,128,000 – $4,629,000 – $2,292,000

Note: The noncash utilization of the employee severance was not described in the notes, but it could include pension, health, or other employee benefit increases. In addition, employee benefit obligations would be included with other accrued liabilities on the balance sheet.

Ex. 14–9

No. Extraordinary items are events and transactions that are unusual and occur infrequently. It is not unusual for a company to insure the life of its president or to receive the proceeds of the policy upon his or her death. Since it does not meet both criteria, this gain is not an extraordinary item.

Ex. 14–10

To be classified as an extraordinary item for income statement reporting purposes, the item (event) must be (1) unusual from the typical operating activities of the business and (2) occurring infrequently. Although it would seem that the income from the Stabilization Act would meet these criteria, the airline industry (including Delta) did not report the income as an extraordinary item. Indeed, the complete costs and income from the September 11, 2001 terrorist incident were not accounted for as extraordinary items as explained below.

The text from the Emerging Issues Task Force, "Accounting for the Impact of the Terrorist Attacks of September 11, 2001," explains the reason for the decision:

The EITF reached a consensus that losses or costs resulting from the September 11 events should be included in the determination of income from continuing operations; thus, they should not be classified as extraordinary items. In the opinion of the Task Force, it would not be possible to isolate the effects of the September 11 events in a single line item, because of the difficulty in distinguishing losses that are directly attributable to such events from those that are not. Losses or costs associated with the events of September 11 may, however, be reported as a separate component of income from continuing operations if they are deemed to be either unusual or infrequently occurring in nature.

In the final analysis, the Task Force reached the foregoing decision based on its conclusion that users of financial statements would not be well served by separate reporting as an extraordinary item of only a portion of the impact of the September 11 events that strictly qualify for extraordinary classification under APB No. 30, Reporting the Results of Operations. Pursuant to Opinion 30, only losses or costs that can be clearly measured and irrefutably attributed to a specific event may be shown as an extraordinary item.

The Task Force acknowledges that, while the September 11 events no doubt contributed to the pace and severity of the economic slowdown, identifying the impact of those events would be subjective and difficult—if at all possible. Moreover, the Task Force points out that the most significant financial statement impact for many affected companies might be lost or reduced revenues; in accordance with Opinion 30, the measurement of an extraordinary item does not reflect an estimate of forgone sales or income.

Ex. 14–11

a. NR	e. E
b. NR	f. NR
c. NR	g. E
d. NR	h. NR

Ex. 14–12

WAVE RUNNER, INC.
Income Statement
For the Year Ended June 30, 2006

Sales		$976,400
Cost of merchandise sold		431,900
Gross profit		$544,500
Operating expenses:		
Selling expenses	$125,100	
Administrative expenses	92,400	217,500
Other expenses:		
Fixed asset impairment		100,000
Restructuring charge		80,000
Income from continuing operations before income tax		$147,000
Income tax expense		58,800
Income from continuing operations		$ 88,200
Loss on discontinued operations, net of applicable income tax of $36,000		54,000
Income before extraordinary item and cumulative effect of a change in accounting principle		$ 34,200
Extraordinary item:		
Gain on condemnation of land, net of applicable income tax of $17,200		25,800
Less cumulative effect on prior years of changing to a different depreciation method, net of applicable income tax reduction of $24,000		(36,000)
Net income		$ 24,000
Earnings per common share:		
Income from continuing operations		$ 8.82
Loss on discontinued operations		5.40
Income before extraordinary item and cumulative effect of a change in accounting principle		$ 3.42
Extraordinary item		2.58
Less cumulative effect on prior years of changing to a different depreciation method		(3.60)
Net income		$ 2.40

Ex. 14–13

1. The order of presentation of the unusual items is incorrect. The order should be as follows:

   Income from continuing operations

   Loss on discontinued operations

   Income before extraordinary items and cumulative effect of a change in accounting method

   Extraordinary item

   Cumulative effect of change in accounting method

   Net income

2. The restructuring charge is not an extraordinary item but should be disclosed above income from continuing operations. The associated tax benefit should not be net against this amount but should be part of the tax on continuing operations.

3. The fixed asset impairment should be disclosed above income from continuing operations.

4. The earnings per share data are presented in the incorrect order—see (1) above.

5. The earnings per share computations are incorrect. The amount of preferred stock dividends ($20,000) should be subtracted from "income from continuing operations," "income before extraordinary item and cumulative effect of change in accounting principle," and "net income" in computing the earnings per share of common stock.

6. A corrected presentation appears on the next page.

Ex. 14–13   (Concluded)

AUDIO AFFECTION, INC.
Income Statement
For the Year Ended December 31, 2006

Net sales..		$ 9,450,000
Cost of merchandise sold..		7,100,000
Gross profit..		$ 2,350,000
Operating expenses:		
Selling expenses	$820,000	
Administrative expenses	320,000	1,140,000
Special charges:		
Restructuring charge	$ 85,000	
Fixed asset impairment..	30,000	115,000
Income from continuing operations before income tax		$ 1,095,000
Income tax expense		394,500*
Income from continuing operations		$ 700,500
Loss on discontinued operations (net of applicable		
income tax of $76,000)		(184,000)
Income before extraordinary items and cumulative effect		
of change in accounting method		$ 516,500
Extraordinary item:		
Gain on condemnation of land, net of applicable		
income tax of $80,000...		120,000
Cumulative effect on prior years' income (decrease) of		
changing to a different depreciation method (net of		
applicable income tax reduction of $86,000)		(204,000)
Net income		$ 432,500
Earnings per common share:		
Income from continuing operations		
[($700,500 – $20,000) ÷ 50,000 shares]		$ 13.61
Loss on discontinued operations		(3.68)
Income before extraordinary item and cumulative		
effect of change in accounting principle		$ 9.93
Extraordinary item..		2.40
Cumulative effect on prior years' income (decrease)		
of changing to a different depreciation method...		(4.08)
Net income		$ 8.25

*$420,000 – $25,500 tax benefit from restructuring charge

Ex. 14–14

Basic earnings per share when there is preferred stock is determined as,

$$\text{Earnings per Common Share} = \frac{\text{Net Income - Preferred Stock Dividends}}{\text{Number of Common Shares Outstanding}}$$

$$\text{Earnings per Common Share} = \frac{\$740{,}000 - (50{,}000 \text{ pref. shares} \times \$6 \text{ per share})}{125{,}000 \text{ common shares}}$$

Earnings per Common Share = $3.52 per share

Ex. 14–15

a. Other comprehensive income (in millions):

Foreign currency translation	$ 263
Net investment hedges,	
net of $238 tax benefit	(397)
Other, net of tax benefit	(106)
Total other comprehensive income (loss)................	$(240)

b. Percentage decline in net income due to other comprehensive losses:

$$\frac{\$240}{\$4{,}352} = 5.5\%$$

c. (1) Retained earnings: $11,980 = $10,451 + $4,352 – $2,823

    (2) Accumulated other comprehensive loss: ($2,360) = ($240) – ($2,120)

Ex. 14–16

a. $40,000 $180,000 – $140,000
b. $(3,000) $8,000 – $5,000
c. $37,000 $40,000 – $3,000
d. $23,000 $26,000 – $3,000
e. $38,000 $36,000 + $2,000
f. $25,000 $23,000 + $2,000
g. $216,000 $180,000 + $36,000
h. $(6,000)   –$8,000 + $2,000

Ex. 14–17

a.

COSBY CORPORATION
Statement of Comprehensive Income
For the Year Ended December 31, 2006

Net income	$145,000
Other comprehensive income:	
Unrealized gain on investment portfolio, net of tax	40,000
Total comprehensive income	$185,000

b.

COSBY CORPORATION
Stockholders' Equity
December 31, 2006

Common stock...	$ 35,000
Paid-in capital in excess of par value........................	350,000
Retained earnings	580,000*
Accumulated other comprehensive loss..................	(20,000)**
Total	$945,000

*$435,000 + $145,000
**($60,000) + $40,000

Ex. 14–18

a. 2006

Unrealized loss [10,000 shares × ($20 – $17)]..........	$30,000
Less tax benefit on unrealized loss (40% rate)........	12,000
Unrealized loss, net of income tax benefit...............	$18,000

2007

Unrealized gain [10,000 shares × ($27 – $17)]..........	$10,000
Less taxes on unrealized gain (40% rate)................	40,000
Unrealized gain, net of income tax	$60,000

Note: The tax benefit and expense give rise to temporary differences, since gains and losses are only included for tax purposes at the time of sale.

b.

Dec. 31, 2006

Other Accumulated Comprehensive Loss	$18,000

Dec. 31, 2007

Other Accumulated Comprehensive Income	$42,000*

*($18,000) + $60,000 = $40,000

c. The Other Accumulated Comprehensive Income or Deficit is disclosed in the stockholders' equity section of the balance sheet, separately from the retained earnings or paid-in capital accounts.

Ex. 14–19

a.	Marketable Securities..	74,000	
	Cash..		74,000
b.	Cash	2,500	
	Dividend Revenue		2,500

Ex. 14–20

a.

LYON RESEARCH CORPORATION
Balance Sheet
December 31, 2006

Assets

Current assets:

Temporary investments in marketable securities, at cost	$74,000	
Less unrealized loss (net of applicable income tax benefit of $4,400)	6,600*	$67,400

*Computation:

Market:

M-Labs, Inc.: 1,000 shares × $28	$ 28,000
Spectrum Corp.: 2,500 shares × $14	35,000
	$ 63,000
Cost ($29,000 + $45,000)	74,000
Unrealized loss	$(11,000)
Taxes on unrealized loss ($11,000 × 40%)	4,400
Unrealized loss, net of applicable tax benefit	$ (6,600)

b.

LYON RESEARCH CORPORATION
Statement of Comprehensive Income
For the Year Ended December 31, 2006

Net income	$ 80,000
Other comprehensive loss:	
Unrealized loss on temporary investments in marketable securities (net of applicable income tax benefit of $4,400)	(6,600)
Comprehensive income	$73,400

Ex. 14–21

a. Investment in Beach Co. Stock 122,400
   Cash.. 122,400

b. Cash... 4,500
   Dividend Revenue 4,500
   (No entry for stock dividends; carrying
   amount per share of stock is now
   $122,400 ÷ 3,060, or $40.)

c. Cash... 48,940
   Investment in Beach Co. Stock 40,000
   Gain on Sale of Investments 8,940

Ex. 14–22

a. Investment in Caleb Corp. Stock............................ 625,000
   Income of Caleb Corp. 625,000
   ($2,500,000 × 70,000/280,000)

b. Cash... 238,000
   Investment in Caleb Corp. Stock............................ 238,000
   (70,000 shares × $3.40)

Ex. 14–23

a.

Investment in Toys-Japan Feb. 3, 2001	$108
Plus equity in net earnings of Toys-Japan...............	29
Less dividends received or common stock sale	(14)*
Investment in Toys-Japan Feb. 2, 2002	$123

*Since the ending balance in the investment in Toys-Japan account is not equal to the beginning balance plus the equity earnings, there must be some explanation for the $14 million reduction. The two best explanations are a dividend by Toys-Japan to Toys "R" Us, which would reduce the investment account, or an outright sale of common stock, which would also reduce the investment. This exercise asks the student to identify these two possibilities. How could we determine which explanation is the correct one? Although not required in this exercise, the statement of cash flows will show if there are any investment activities from sale of common stock, or whether there were dividends received from the investee.

Ex. 14–23   (Concluded)

b. The Investment in Toys-Japan is not recognized at market value because Toys "R" Us has significant influence over the investee, by having an investment that exceeds 20% of the outstanding common stock of Toys-Japan. When the investor holds significant influence, the equity method is applied, rather than market value accounting. One reason for this is because such large percentage holdings in a company may not be easily sold at the market price shown in the secondary market.

Ex. 14–24

a. (1) $45,000

        Consolidated sales should be $966,000 ($845,000 + $166,000 – $45,000).

    (2) $45,000

        Consolidated cost of merchandise sold should be $413,000 ($390,000 + $68,000 – $45,000).

b. Consolidated net income can be determined as follows:

Sales [from a. (1)]	$966,000
Cost of merchandise sold [from a. (2)]	413,000
Selling expenses	159,000
Administrative expense	103,000
Net income	$291,000

Note: The interest revenue and interest expense should also be eliminated from the consolidated numbers.

Ex. 14–25

$$\text{Price-Earnings Ratio} = \frac{\text{Market Price per Share of Common Stock}}{\text{Earnings per Share of Common Stock (basic)}}$$

a. Price-earnings ratio, Jan. 28, 2001:
        55.83   ($16.75/$0.30)
    Price-earnings ratio, Feb. 3, 2002:
        76.33   ($37.40/$0.49)
    Price-earnings ratio, Feb. 2, 2003:
        49.85   ($30.41/0.6)

Ex. 14–25   **Concluded**

b. The price-earnings ratio increased in 2002 from 55.83 to 76.33, then declined to 49.85 by the end of fiscal 2003. These price-earnings ratios are over twice the average ratios of the overall market. This indicates that investors are optimistic about the prospects for this company. They expect strong earnings growth and have priced this expectation into the common stock. That is, investors are attracted to the common stock, and this has caused the price-earnings ratio to remain high. The doubling of earnings per share from 2001 to 2003 provides some evidence for this optimism. The stock price has begun to settle, allowing the earnings to "catch up" to the price, thus causing the price-earnings ratio to decline in 2003. Krispy Kreme's price-earnings ratio should also be compared with its industry competitors to assess how the market expects Krispy Kreme to perform relative to the market.

c. The diluted earnings per share includes the impact of potentially dilutive securities, such as convertible preferred stock, options, warrants, and contingently issuable shares.

Ex. 14–26

a.

$$\text{Price-Earnings Ratio} = \frac{\text{Market Price per Share of Common Stock}}{\text{Earnings per Share of Common Stock (basic)}}$$

Price-earnings ratio, 2002: $\dfrac{\$35}{\$1.69}$, 20.71

Price-earnings ratio, 2001: $\dfrac{\$39}{\$2.23}$, 17.49

Price-earnings ratio, 2000: $\dfrac{\$42}{\$2.55}$, 16.47

b. The price-earnings ratio grew by nearly 26% from 2000 to 2002. During this time, the overall stock market was declining, and the economy was headed for a recession. In the case of ExxonMobil, earnings per share fell by 34%, while the stock price dropped only 17%. Thus, the price-earnings ratio expanded. Market participants believe that the decline in earnings is not a trend; thus, the market price has not fallen proportionately. Apparently, market participants believe the stock price will increase in the future, thus increasing the price-earnings ratio over this time period. This expectation may be warranted due to the company's sensitivity to oil prices.

Prob. 14–3A

1.

SURF'S UP CORPORATION
Income Statement
For the Year Ended July 31, 2006

Sales		$2,600,000
Cost of merchandise sold		984,000
Gross profit		$1,616,000
Operating expenses:		
Selling expenses	$ 540,000	
Administrative expenses	140,000	
Total operating expenses		680,000
Income from operations before other items		$ 936,000
Other expenses, income, and special charges:		
Loss from restructuring charge	$(300,000)	
Fixed asset impairment	(60,000)	
Interest expense	(7,500)	
Interest revenue	1,500	366,000
Income from continuing operations before income tax		$ 570,000
Income tax expense		170,000
Income from continuing operations		$ 400,000
Loss from discontinued operations	$ 104,000	
Less applicable income tax	24,000	(80,000)
Income before extraordinary item		$ 320,000
Extraordinary item:		
Gain on condemnation of land	$ 30,000	
Less applicable income tax	10,000	20,000
Net income		$ 340,000
Earnings per common share:		
Income from continuing operations	$	1.20*
Loss on discontinued operations		(0.32)
Income before extraordinary item	$	0.88
Extraordinary item		0.08
Net income	$	0.96

*($400,000 − $100,000) ÷ 250,000 shares

Prob. 14–3A   (Continued)

2.

SURF'S UP CORPORATION
Retained Earnings Statement
For the Year Ended July 31, 2006

Retained earnings, August 1, 2005			$4,231,600
Net income		$340,000	
Less dividends declared:			
Cash dividends	$180,000		
Stock dividends	40,000	220,000	
Increase in retained earnings			120,000
Retained earnings, July 31, 2006			$4,351,600

3.

SURF'S UP CORPORATION
Balance Sheet
July 31, 2006

Assets

Current assets:			
Cash..		$ 115,500	
Temporary investments in marketable			
equity securities at cost....................	$ 95,000		
Plus unrealized gain..............................	15,000		
Temporary investments in marketable			
at market value		110,000	
Accounts receivable.............................	$276,050		
Less allowance for doubtful accounts	11,500	264,550	
Merchandise inventory, at lower of			
cost (FIFO) or market.........................		551,500	
Interest receivable		2,500	
Prepaid expenses.................................		15,900	
Total current assets..........................			$ 1,059,950
Property, plant, and equipment:			
Equipment..		$11,819,050	
Less accumulated depreciation		3,050,000	
Total property, plant, and equipment			8,769,050
Intangible assets:			
Patents			85,000
Total assets...			$ 9,914,000

Prob. 14–3A   (Concluded)

<u>Liabilities</u>

Current liabilities:

Accounts payable	$ 99,500	
Employee termination obligation	90,000	
Income tax payable	55,900	
Dividends payable	25,000	
Deferred income taxes payable	4,700	
Total current liabilities		$ 275,100
Deferred credits:		
Deferred income taxes payable		61,000
Total liabilities		$ 336,100

<u>Stockholders' Equity</u>

Paid-in capital:

Preferred 6 2/3% stock, $100 par (30,000 shares authorized; 15,000 shares issued)	$1,500,000		
Excess of issue price over par	240,000	$ 1,740,000	
Common stock, $10 par (500,000 shares authorized; 251,000 shares issued)	$2,510,000		
Excess of issue price over par	996,300	3,506,300	
From sale of treasury stock		5,000	
Total paid-in capital		$ 5,251,300	
Retained earnings		4,351,600	
		$ 9,602,900	
Deduct treasury common stock (1,000 shares at cost)		(40,000)	
Accumulated other comprehensive income		15,000	
Total stockholders' equity			9,577,900
Total liabilities and stockholders' equity			$9,914,000

Prob. 14–4A

2004

Feb. 10	Investment in Haslam Corporation Stock.........	192,168	
	Cash		192,168
June 15	Cash	2,800	
	Dividend Revenue		2,800
Dec. 15	Cash	3,000	
	Dividend Revenue		3,000

2007

Jan. 3	Investment in Jacob Inc. Stock..........................	1,250,000	
	Cash		1,250,000
Apr. 1	Cash	2,800	
	Dividend Revenue		2,800

Memo—Received a dividend of 80 shares
of Haslam Corporation stock. Number of
shares held, 4,080. Cost basis per share,
$192,168 ÷ 4,080 shares = $47.10.

July 20	Cash	40,950	
	Loss on Sales of Investments............................	6,150	
	Investment in Haslam Corporation Stock		47,100
Dec. 15	Cash	2,464	
	Dividend Revenue		2,464
	(4,080 – 1,000 = 3,080 shares; 3,080 × $0.80 = $2,464)		
31	Cash	40,000	
	Investment in Jacob Inc. Stock......................		40,000
31	Investment in Jacob Inc. Stock..........................	118,000	
	Income of Jacob Inc.		118,000
	($295,000 × 40% = $118,000)		

Prob. 14–3B

1.

SKATE N' SKI CORPORATION
Income Statement
For the Year Ended October 31, 2006

Sales		$2,020,000
Cost of merchandise sold...		732,000
Gross profit..		$1,288,000
Operating expenses:		
Selling expenses	$ 400,000	
Administrative expenses	100,000	
Total operating expenses..		500,000
Income from operations before other items		$ 788,000
Other expenses, income, and special charges:		
Loss from fixed asset impairment	$(200,000)	
Restructuring charge	(90,000)	
Interest expense	(8,000)	
Interest revenue...	5,000	293,000
Income from continuing operations before income tax.		$ 495,000
Income tax expense		206,000
Income from continuing operations		$ 289,000
Loss from discontinued operations................................	$ 76,800	
Less applicable income tax..	28,800	48,000
Income before extraordinary item...................................		$ 241,000
Extraordinary item:		
Gain on condemnation of land.................................	$ 60,000	
Less applicable income tax.......................................	24,000	36,000
Net income		$ 277,000
Earnings per common share:		
Income from continuing operations		$ 1.26*
Loss on discontinued operations		0.32
Income before extraordinary item............................		$ 0.94
Extraordinary item..		0.24
Net income		$ 1.18

*($289,000 – $100,000 preferred dividends) ÷ 150,000 common shares

2.

SKATE N' SKI CORPORATION
Retained Earnings Statement
For the Year Ended October 31, 2006

Retained earnings, November 1, 2005		$2,446,150
Net income	$277,000	
Less dividends declared:		
Cash dividends	$140,000	
Stock dividends	60,000	200,000
Increase in retained earnings		77,000
Retained earnings, October 31, 2006		$2,523,150

3.

SKATE N' SKI CORPORATION
Balance Sheet
October 31, 2006

Assets

Current assets:			
Cash...		$ 145,500	
Temporary investment in marketable			
equity securities—at cost	$145,000		
Less unrealized loss in temporary			
investments		24,000	121,000
Accounts receivable..............................	$309,050		
Less allowance for doubtful accounts	21,500	287,550	
Notes receivable		77,500	
Merchandise inventory, at lower of			
cost (FIFO) or market.........................		425,000	
Interest receivable		2,500	
Prepaid expenses		15,900	
Total current assets...........................			$1,074,950
Property, plant, and equipment:			
Equipment..		$9,541,050	
Less accumulated depreciation		3,050,000	
Total property, plant, and equipment			6,491,050
Intangible assets:			
Patents			55,000
Total assets...			$7,621,000

Prob. 14–3B   (Concluded)

Liabilities

Current liabilities:

Accounts payable	$ 89,500	
Employee benefit obligation	60,000	
Income tax payable	55,900	
Dividends payable	30,000	
Deferred income taxes payable	4,700	
Total current liabilities		$ 240,100
Deferred credits:		
Deferred income taxes payable		21,000
Total liabilities		$ 261,100

Stockholders' Equity

Paid-in capital:

Preferred 6 2/3% stock, $100 par (30,000 shares authorized; 15,000 shares issued)	$1,500,000		
Excess of issue price over par	240,000	$1,740,000	
Common stock, $15 par (400,000 shares authorized; 152,000 shares issued)	$2,280,000		
Excess of issue price over par	894,750	3,174,750	
From sale of treasury stock		16,000	
Total paid-in capital		$4,930,750	
Retained earnings		2,523,150	
		$7,453,900	
Deduct treasury common stock (2,000 shares at cost)		70,000	
Less accumulated other comprehensive loss		24,000	
Total stockholders' equity			7,359,900
Total liabilities and stockholders' equity			$7,621,000

Prob. 14–4B

2004

Jan. 3   Investment in Davidson Corporation Stock......   201,468
      Cash   201,468

July 2   Cash   3,900
      Dividend Revenue   3,900

Dec. 5   Cash   4,200
      Dividend Revenue   4,200

2007

Jan. 2   Investment in Comstock Inc. Stock...................   760,000
      Cash   760,000

July 6   Cash   3,900
      Dividend Revenue   3,900

      Memo—Received a dividend of 90 shares of
      Davidson Corporation stock. Number of shares
      held, 3,090. Cost basis per share,
      $201,468 ÷ 3,090 shares = $65.20.

Oct. 23   Cash   58,360
      Investment in Davidson Corporation Stock..   48,900
      Gain on Sale of Investments   9,460

Dec. 10   Cash   3,510
      Dividend Revenue   3,510
      (3,090 − 750 = 2,340 shares;
      2,340 × $1.50 = $3,510)

31   Cash   32,000
      Investment in Comstock Inc. Stock..............   32,000

31   Investment in Comstock Inc. Stock...................   105,000
      Income of Comstock Inc...............................   105,000
      ($350,000 × 30% = $105,000)

SPECIAL ACTIVITIES

Activity 14–1

Yes. In this case, the equity method is required because Goodyear owns enough of the voting stock of the investee to have a significant influence over its operating and financing policies.

Activity 14–2

1.

FLEET SHOES, INC.
Vertical Analysis of Income Statement
For the Years Ended December 31, 2005 and 2006

	2005		2006	
Sales	$430,000	100.0%	$510,000	100.0%
Cost of merchandise sold	193,500	45.0	224,400	44.0
Gross profit	$236,500	55.0	$285,600	56.0
Selling and administrative expenses	107,500	25.0	122,400	24.0
Loss on fixed asset impairment		0.0	102,000	20.0
Income from operations	$129,000	30.0	$ 61,200	12.0
Income tax expense	51,600	12.0	24,480	4.8
Net income	$ 77,400	18.0%	$ 36,720	7.2%

2. The operating income is 30% of sales in 2005, but only 12% of sales in 2006. Net income dropped from $77,400 to $36,720. This would seem to indicate a large reduction in performance in 2006. However, the loss on the fixed asset impairment, which is unusual, is 20% of sales. Without this loss, the income from operations would have been 32% of sales, or 2 points better than 2005. Combining this with growing sales from $430,000 to $510,000 would indicate that the company is doing well on a recurring basis.

There is some concern that management was unable to successfully complete the software project. Order management is an important capability for a retailer, so this event should not be completely ignored. The loss clearly indicates a failed effort at meeting an important operational objective. This need is still outstanding, will require future effort, and may limit future growth. However, the financial numbers would seem to indicate that the recurring, or core, earnings and growth are on track.

Activity 14–3

This was a controversial decision at the time. The FASB's position was not based on the infrequency or unusual character of the incident. The FASB is not saying that it views these as "normal" operating risks. Rather, the FASB was more practical in realizing that it would be very difficult to segregate 9/11 costs from normal business costs. The FASB was concerned that if the incident was allowed "extraordinary" treatment, then companies would put all costs, including the impact of reduced sales and other indirect impact, into this classification. It was concerned that nondirectly affected firms would disclose 9/11 extraordinary items for business downturn related events. Rather than facing this prospect, the FASB decided that it would be best to avoid the issue altogether by stating that this was not an extraordinary reporting event. In stating this, it was saying the economic impact of 9/11 was a general business condition that impacted many firms, and thus, not extraordinary. Furthermore, it avoided requiring auditors to distinguish between direct and indirect impacts.

Activity 14–4

a. The "other" comprehensive income or loss for the period is the difference in the accumulated other comprehensive income shown on the balance sheet [($249) − ($207)] between the two comparative periods, or a $42 other comprehensive loss.

b. The other comprehensive loss items are adjustments to stockholders' equity that do not flow through the income statement. The FASB created this category of disclosure to recognize economic events that impact stockholders' equity but are considered too controversial to be included in earnings. In a sense, this is a "middle ground" solution where the items are not ignored, nor are they considered part of net income.

Activity 14–5

As long as you pay your full amount of taxes owed on the due date of your return, plus any interest or penalty for underpaying estimated taxes, it is appropriate to intentionally underpay your estimated taxes. Most individuals attempt to pay only the minimum amount for estimated taxes for the very reason that Steph indicated. That is, paying the minimum allows you to use your money as long as possible. Since the Internal Revenue Service does not pay interest on overpayments, it does not make sense to pay more than the minimum of estimated taxes. If you pay less than the minimum required, however, you will be subject to paying IRS interest and penalties.

Activity 14–6

No. Although Reed will not be lying about the amount of total earnings per share of $1.05, it would be clearly misleading not to identify the impact of the extraordinary gain of $0.20 related to the selling of the land. In addition to being unethical and unprofessional, Reed may violate federal securities laws if he sells his stock after the announcement. In this case, it might be alleged that Reed traded on "insider" information for his own profit.

Activity 14–7

To be classified as an extraordinary item, an event must meet both of the following requirements:

a. Unusual nature—The event should be significantly different from the typical or the normal operating activities of the entity.

b. Infrequent occurrence—The event should not be expected to recur often.

Events that meet both of the preceding requirements are uncommon. Usually, extraordinary items result from natural disasters, such as floods, earthquakes, and fires. Thus, your first impression might be that the frost damage for Orlando Fruit would qualify as an extraordinary item. However, this is not the case. In an accounting interpretation of a similar case, it was ruled that frost damage experienced by a Florida citrus grower did not meet the criterion of "infrequent" in occurrence. Frost damage is normally experienced in Florida every three to four years. Thus, the history of past losses would suggest that such damage can be expected to occur again in the foreseeable future. The fact that Orlando Fruit had not had frost damage in the previous five years is not sufficient to meet the infrequency of occurrence criterion. It would, however, be acceptable to identify the losses from frost damage as a separate line item above the income from continuing operations.

Activity 14–8

Note to Instructors: The purpose of this activity is to familiarize students with extraordinary items and discontinued operations reported by real companies and to determine the impact of these items on earnings per share.

The following is an example from R.J. Reynolds' comparative income statements, beginning with income for continuing operations before taxes:

	2002/12/31	2001/12/31	2000/12/31
Income from continuing operations before income taxes..	$ 683,000,000	$ 892,000,000	$ 748,000,000
Provision for income taxes............................	265,000,000	448,000,000	396,000,000
Income from continuing operations	$ 418,000,000	$ 444,000,000	$ 352,000,000
Discontinued operations:			
Gain (loss) on sale of discontinued businesses, net of income taxes [(2002—$22; 2001—$(5)]............................	40,000,000	(9,000,000)	0
Income before extraordinary item and cumulative effect of accounting change ..	$ 458,000,000	$ 435,000,000	$ 352,000,000
Extraordinary item—gain on acquisition, net of $0 income taxes.............................	0	0	1,475,000,000
Cumulative effect of accounting change, net of $328 income taxes...........................	(502,000,000)	0	0
Net income (loss)...	$ (44,000,000)	$ 435,000,000	$1,827,000,000
Basic income (loss) per share:			
Income from continuing operations	$ 4.71	$ 4.57	$ 3.48
Gain (loss) on sale of discontinued businesses...	0.45	(0.09)	0
Extraordinary item—gain on acquisition.....................	0	0	14.56
Cumulative effect of accounting change	(5.66)	0	0
Net income (loss)...	$ (0.50)	$ 4.48	$18.04

The extraordinary item was related to the acquisition of Nabisco.

EXERCISES

Ex. 15–1

		Bridger Co.
a.	Earnings before bond interest and income tax...........	$ 1,600,000
	Bond interest..	640,000
	Balance	$ 960,000
	Income tax	384,000
	Net income..	$ 576,000
	Dividends on preferred stock	480,000
	Earnings available for common stock	$ 96,000
	Earnings per share on common stock.........................	$ 0.48
b.	Earnings before bond interest and income tax...........	$ 2,400,000
	Bond interest..	640,000
	Balance	$ 1,760,000
	Income tax	704,000
	Net income..	$ 1,056,000
	Dividends on preferred stock	480,000
	Earnings available for common stock	$ 576,000
	Earnings per share on common stock.........................	$ 2.88
c.	Earnings before bond interest and income tax...........	$ 4,000,000
	Bond interest..	640,000
	Balance	$ 3,360,000
	Income tax	1,344,000
	Net income..	$ 2,016,000
	Dividends on preferred stock	480,000
	Earnings available for common stock	$ 1,536,000
	Earnings per share on common stock.........................	$ 7.68

Ex. 15–2

Factors other than earnings per share that should be considered in evaluating financing plans include: bonds represent a fixed annual interest requirement, while dividends on stock do not; bonds require the repayment of principal, while stock does not; and common stock represents a voting interest in the ownership of the corporation, while bonds do not.

Ex. 15–3

Home Depot's major source of financing is common stock. It has long-term debt, excluding current installments, of $1,321,000,000, compared to stockholders' equity of $19,802,000,000.

Ex. 15–4

a. $100,000 ÷ 1.05 = $95,238
     $ 95,238 ÷ 1.05 = $90,703
     $ 90,703 ÷ 1.05 = $86,384

b. $100,000 × 0.86384 = $86,384

Ex. 15–5

a.   First Year: $50,000 × 0.94340 = $ 47,170.00
     Second Year: $50,000 × 0.89000 =   44,500.00
     Third Year: $50,000 × 0.83962 =   41,981.00
     Fourth Year: $50,000 × 0.79209 =   39,604.50
         Total present value $173,255.50

b. $50,000 × 3.46511 = $173,255.50

Ex. 15–6

$1,000,000 × 12.78336 = $12,783,360

Ex. 15–7

No. The present value of your winnings using an interest rate of 12% is $7,843,140 ($1,000,000 × 7.84314), which is more than one-half of the present value of your winnings using an interest rate of 6% ($12,783,360; see Ex. 15–6). This is because of the effect of compounding the interest. That is, compound interest functions are not linear functions, but use exponents.

Ex. 15–8

Present value of $1 for 10 (semiannual) periods at 6% (semiannual rate)	0.55840	
Face amount of bonds	× $12,000,000	$ 6,700,800
Present value of an annuity of $1 for 10 periods at 6%	7.36009	
Semiannual interest payment....................................	× $480,000	3,532,843
Total present value (proceeds).................................		$10,233,643

Ex. 15–9

Present value of $1 for 10 (semiannual) periods at 5% (semiannual rate)	0.61391	
Face amount of bonds	× $40,000,000	$24,556,400
Present value of an annuity of $1 for 10 periods at 5%	7.72174	
Semiannual interest payment....................................	× $2,200,000	16,987,828
Total present value (proceeds).................................		$41,544,228

Ex. 15–10

The bonds were selling at a premium. This is indicated by the selling price of 103.536, which is stated as a percentage of face amount and is more than par (100%). The market rate of interest for similar quality bonds was lower than 2.125%, and this is why the bonds were selling at a premium.

Ex. 15–11

May	1	Cash	18,000,000	
		Bonds Payable		18,000,000
Nov.	1	Interest Expense	630,000	
		Cash		630,000
Dec.	31	Interest Expense	210,000	
		Interest Payable...		210,000

Ex. 15–12

a. 1. Cash.. 7,095,482
Discount on Bonds Payable 904,518
   Bonds Payable 8,000,000

2. Interest Expense... 320,000
   Cash 320,000

3. Interest Expense... 320,000
   Cash 320,000

4. Interest Expense... 180,904
Discount on Bonds Payable.............................. 180,904
$904,518 ÷ 5 years = $180,904

b. Annual interest paid...................................... $ 640,000
Plus discount amortized 180,904
Interest expense for first year....................................... $ 820,904

Note: The following data in support of the proceeds of the bond issue stated in the exercise are presented for the instructor's information. Students are not required to make the computations.

Present value of $1 for 10 (semiannual)
periods at 5 1/2% (semiannual rate)................. 0.58543
Face amount.. × $8,000,000 $ 4,683,440

Present value of annuity of $1 for 10
periods at 5 1/2% 7.53763
Semiannual interest payment............................ × $320,000 2,412,042

Total present value of bonds payable.............. $ 7,095,482

Ex. 15–13

a. Cash 7,789,543
      Premium on Bonds Payable   289,543
      Bonds Payable   7,500,000

Note: The following data are in support of the determination of the proceeds of the bond issue stated in the exercise:

Present value of $1 for 10 (semiannual) periods at 5% (semiannual rate)	0.61391	
Face amount	× $7,500,000	$ 4,604,325
Present value of an annuity of $1 for 10 periods at 5%	7.72174	
Semiannual interest payment	× $412,500	3,185,218
Proceeds		$ 7,789,543

b. Interest Expense 383,546
    Premium on Bonds Payable 28,954*
      Cash   412,500

*$289,543 ÷ 10 semiannual payments

Ex. 15–14

2006
Apr. 1 Cash 12,000,000
          Bonds Payable   12,000,000

Oct. 1 Interest Expense 480,000
          Cash   480,000

2010
Oct. 1 Bonds Payable 12,000,000
      Loss on Redemption of Bonds 240,000
          Cash   12,240,000

Ex. 15–15

2006

Jan.	1	Cash	18,000,000	
		Bonds Payable		18,000,000
July	1	Interest Expense	810,000	
		Cash		810,000

2012

July	1	Bonds Payable.................................	18,000,000	
		Gain on Redemption of Bonds.......................		540,000
		Cash		17,460,000

Ex. 15–16

1. The significant loss on redemption of the series X bonds should be reported in the Other Income and Expense section of the income statement, rather than as an extraordinary loss.

2. The series Y bonds outstanding at the end of the current year should be reported as a noncurrent liability on the balance sheet because they are to be paid from funds set aside in a sinking fund.

Ex. 15–17

The discount of $811 ($1,000 – $189) is amortized as interest revenue over the life of the bonds, using the straight-line method (illustrated in this chapter) or the interest method (illustrated in the appendix to this chapter).

Ex. 15–18

a.	Investment in Pierce Co. Bonds	456,750	
	Interest Revenue	9,000	
	Cash		465,750
b.	Cash	18,000	
	Interest Revenue		18,000
c.	Interest Revenue	540	
	Investment in Pierce Co. Bonds		540
d.	Cash	448,500	
	Loss on Sale of Investments	8,250	
	Investment in Pierce Co. Bonds		453,750
	Interest Revenue		3,000

Ex. 15–19

a.	Investment in Theisen Co. Bonds	264,600	
	Interest Revenue	2,250	
	Cash		266,850
b.	Cash	6,750	
	Interest Revenue		6,750
c.	Investment in Theisen Co. Bonds	450	
	Interest Revenue		450
d.	Cash	274,500	
	Investment in Theisen Co. Bonds		267,250
	Gain on Sale of Investments		2,750
	Interest Revenue		4,500

Ex. 15–20

a. Current year:

Number of times interest charges earned: $4.7 = \dfrac{\$392,682,000 + \$106,023,000}{\$106,023,000}$

Preceding year:

Number of times interest charges earned: $12.6 = \dfrac{\$827,659,000 + \$69,827,000}{\$69,827,000}$

b. The number of times interest charges earned has declined from 12.6 to 4.7 in the current year. Although Southwest Airlines has adequate earnings to pay interest, the decline in this ratio would potentially cause concern among debtholders.

Appendix Ex. 15–21

a.

1. Cash.. 7,095,482
   Discount on Bonds Payable 904,518
      Bonds Payable 8,000,000

2. Interest Expense... 320,000
      Cash 320,000

3. Interest Expense... 320,000
      Cash 320,000

4. Interest Expense... 144,367
      Discount on Bonds Payable............................... 144,367

Computations:
$7,095,482 × 0.055 = $390,252
$390,252 – $320,000 = $70,252 first semiannual amortization
$7,095,482 + $70,252 = $7,165,734
$7,165,734 × 0.055 = $394,115
$394,115 – $320,000 = $74,115 second semiannual amortization
$70,252 + $74,115 = $144,367 amortization for first year

Note: The following data in support of the proceeds of the bond issue stated in the exercise are presented for the instructor's information. Students are not required to make the computations.

Present value of $1 for 10 (semiannual) periods at 5 1/2% (semiannual rate)........................	0.58543	
Face amount...	× $8,000,000	$ 4,683,440
Present value of annuity of $1 for 10 periods at 5 1/2%	7.53763	
Semiannual interest payment.................................	× $320,000	2,412,042
Total present value of bonds payable.....................		$ 7,095,482

b.

Annual interest paid..	$640,000
Plus discount amortized	144,367
Interest expense for first year...........................	$784,367

Appendix Ex. 15–22

a.	1. Interest Expense...	412,500	
	Cash		412,500
	2. Interest Expense...	412,500	
	Cash		412,500
	3. Premium on Bonds Payable	47,197	
	Interest Expense		47,197

Computations:
$7,789,543 × 5% = $389,477
$412,500 – $389,477 = $23,023 first semiannual amortization
$7,789,543 – $23,023 = $7,766,520
$7,766,520 × 5% = $388,326
$412,500 – $388,326 = $24,174 second semiannual amortization
$23,023 + $24,174 = $47,197 first year amortization

b.	Annual interest paid..	$825,000
	Less premium amortized...	47,197
	Interest expense for first year.......................................	$777,803

Appendix Ex. 15–23

a.	Present value of $1 for 10 (semiannual) periods at 5 1/2% (semiannual rate)	0.58543	
	Face amount..	× $32,500,000	$19,026,475
	Present value of annuity of $1 for 10 periods at 5 1/2%...	7.53763	
	Semiannual interest payment	× $1,950,000	14,698,378
	Proceeds of bond sale..		$33,724,853
b.	First semiannual interest payment..........................		$ 1,950,000
	5 1/2% of carrying amount of $33,724,853		1,854,867
	Premium amortized...		$ 95,133
c.	Second semiannual interest payment......................		$ 1,950,000
	5 1/2% of carrying amount of $33,629,720*..............		1,849,635
	Premium amortized...		$ 100,365

*$33,724,853 – $95,133 = $33,629,720

d.	Annual interest paid...	$ 3,900,000
	Less premium amortized...	195,498*
	Interest expense for first year....................................	$ 3,704,502

*$95,133 + $100,365 = $195,498

Appendix Ex. 15–24

a.
Present value of $1 for 10 (semiannual) periods at 6% (semiannual rate)	0.55840	
Face amount	× $17,500,000	$ 9,772,000
Present value of annuity of $1 for 10 periods at 6%....	7.36009	
Semiannual interest payment	× $875,000	6,440,079
Proceeds of bond sale		$16,212,079

b.
6% of carrying amount of $16,212,079	$ 972,725
First semiannual interest payment	875,000
Discount amortized	$ 97,725

c.
6% of carrying amount of $16,309,804*	$ 978,588
Second semiannual interest payment	875,000
Discount amortized	$ 103,588

*$16,212,079 + $97,725 = $16,309,804

d.
Annual interest paid	$ 1,750,000
Plus discount amortized	201,313*
Interest expense first year	$ 1,951,313

*$97,725 + $103,588 = $201,313

PROBLEMS

Prob. 15–1A

1.

	Plan 1	Plan 2	Plan 3
Earnings before interest and income tax	$15,000,000	$15,000,000	$15,000,000
Deduct interest on bonds	—	—	1,000,000
Income before income tax	$15,000,000	$15,000,000	$14,000,000
Deduct income tax..	6,000,000	6,000,000	5,600,000
Net income	$ 9,000,000	$ 9,000,000	$ 8,400,000
Dividends on preferred stock.........................	—	600,000	300,000
Available for dividends on common stock....	$ 9,000,000	$ 8,400,000	$ 8,100,000
Shares of common stock outstanding	÷ 4,000,000	÷ 2,000,000	÷ 1,000,000
Earnings per share on common stock	$ 2.25	$ 4.20	$ 8.10

2.

	Plan 1	Plan 2	Plan 3
Earnings before interest and income tax	$ 1,600,000	$ 1,600,000	$ 1,600,000
Deduct interest on bonds	—	—	1,000,000
Income before income tax	$ 1,600,000	$ 1,600,000	$ 600,000
Deduct income tax..	640,000	640,000	240,000
Net income	$ 960,000	$ 960,000	$ 360,000
Dividends on preferred stock.........................	—	600,000	300,000
Available for dividends on common stock....	$ 960,000	$ 360,000	$ 60,000
Shares of common stock outstanding	÷ 4,000,000	÷ 2,000,000	÷ 1,000,000
Earnings per share on common stock	$ 0.24	$ 0.18	$ 0.06

Prob. 15–1A   Concluded

3. The principal advantage of Plan 1 is that it involves only the issuance of common stock, which does not require a periodic interest payment or return of principal, and a payment of preferred dividends is not required. It is also more attractive to common shareholders than is Plan 2 or 3 if earnings before interest and income tax is $1,600,000. In this case, it has the largest EPS ($0.24). The principal disadvantage of Plan 1 is that it requires an additional investment by present common shareholders to retain their current interest in the company. Also, if earnings before interest and income tax is $15,000,000, this plan offers the lowest EPS ($2.25) on common stock.

    The principal advantage of Plan 3 is that little additional investment would need to be made by common shareholders for them to retain their current interest in the company. Also, it offers the largest EPS ($8.10) if earnings before interest and income tax is $15,000,000. Its principal disadvantage is that the bonds carry a fixed annual interest charge and require the payment of principal. It also requires a dividend payment to preferred stockholders before a common dividend can be paid. Finally, Plan 3 provides the lowest EPS ($0.06) if earnings before interest and income tax is $1,600,000.

    Plan 2 provides a middle ground in terms of the advantages and disadvantages described in the preceding paragraphs for Plans 1 and 3.

Prob. 15–2A

1. Cash 10,121,603*
       Premium on Bonds Payable   1,121,603
       Bonds Payable..   9,000,000

   *Present value of $1 for 20 (semiannual)
       periods at 5% (semiannual rate) 0.37689
   Face amount.. × $9,000,000 $ 3,392,010
   Present value of an annuity of $1 for 20
       periods at 5% 12.46221
   Semiannual interest payment .... × $540,000   6,729,593
   Proceeds of bond issue $10,121,603

2. a. Interest Expense..   483,920
       Premium on Bonds Payable ($1,121,603 ÷ 20)..   56,080
          Cash   540,000

   b. Interest Expense..   483,920
       Premium on Bonds Payable   56,080
          Cash   540,000

3. $483,920

4. Yes. Investors will be willing to pay more than the face amount of the bonds when the interest payments they will receive from the bonds exceed the amount of interest that they could receive from investing in other bonds.

Prob. 15–2A   Concluded

This solution is applicable only if the P.A.S.S. Software that accompanies the text is used.

REST-IN-PEACE CORPORATION
Balance Sheet
June 30, 2007

Assets

Cash	$10,434,403	
Accounts receivable	602,200	
Merchandise inventory	809,300	
Prepaid insurance	46,400	
Supplies	85,000	
Total current assets		$11,977,303
Equipment	$ 1,132,900	
Accumulated depreciation—equipment	(69,000)	
Total plant assets		1,063,900
Total assets		$13,041,203

Liabilities

Accounts payable		$ 835,100
Bonds payable	$ 9,000,000	
Premium on bonds payable	1,009,443	
Total long-term liabilities		10,009,443
Total liabilities		$10,844,543

Stockholders' Equity

Paid-in capital:		
Preferred stock	$ 600,000	
Excess of issue price over par—preferred stock	75,000	
Common stock	400,000	
Excess of issue price over par—common stock	200,000	
From sale of treasury stock	11,000	
Total paid-in capital	$ 1,286,000	
Retained earnings	931,660	
Total	$ 2,217,660	
Less treasury stock	21,000	
Total stockholders' equity		2,196,660
Total liabilities and equity		$13,041,203

Prob. 15–3A

1.

Cash	10,623,552*	
Discount on Bonds Payable	1,376,448	
Bonds Payable		12,000,000

*Present value of $1 for 20 (semiannual)		
periods at 6% (semiannual rate)	0.31180	
Face amount	× $12,000,000	$ 3,741,600
Present value of an annuity of $1 for 20		
periods at 6%	11.46992	
Semiannual interest payment	× $600,000	6,881,952
		$10,623,552

2.

a.

Interest Expense	668,822	
Discount on Bonds Payable		
($1,376,448 ÷ 20)		68,822
Cash		600,000

b.

Interest Expense	668,822	
Discount on Bonds Payable		68,822
Cash		600,000

3. $668,822

4. Yes. Investors will not be willing to pay the face amount of the bonds when the interest payments they will receive from the bonds are less than the amount of interest that they could receive from investing in other bonds.

Prob. 15–4A

1.

2005					
July	1	Cash...	7,382,236	
		Discount on Bonds Payable	617,764	
		Bonds Payable		8,000,000
Dec.	31	Interest Expense................................	320,000	
		Cash		320,000
	31	Interest Expense................................	61,776	
		Discount on Bonds Payable...................		61,776
	31	Income Summary................................	381,776	
		Interest Expense		381,776
2006					
June	30	Interest Expense................................	320,000	
		Cash		320,000
Dec.	31	Interest Expense................................	320,000	
		Cash		320,000
	31	Interest Expense................................	123,552	
		Discount on Bonds Payable...................		123,552
	31	Income Summary................................	763,552	
		Interest Expense		763,552
2007					
June	30	Bonds Payable....................................	8,000,000	
		Loss on Redemption of Bonds...................	290,660	
		Discount on Bonds Payable...................		370,660
		Cash		7,920,000

2. a. 2005: $381,776

b. 2006: $763,552

3.

Initial carrying amount of bonds	$7,382,236
Discount amortized on December 31, 2005.................	61,776
Discount amortized on December 31, 2006.................	123,552
Carrying amount of bonds, December 31, 2006..........	$7,567,564

Prob. 15–4A   Concluded

This solution is applicable only if the P.A.S.S. Software that accompanies the text is used.

PRAIRIE RENAISSANCE INC.
Balance Sheet
June 30, 2007

Assets

Cash	$10,206,812	
Accounts receivable	1,352,200	
Merchandise inventory	809,300	
Prepaid insurance	46,400	
Supplies	85,000	
Total current assets		$12,499,712
Equipment	$ 1,882,900	
Accumulated depreciation—equipment	(69,000)	
Total plant assets		1,813,900
Total assets		$14,313,612

Liabilities

Accounts payable		$ 835,100

Stockholders' Equity

Paid-in capital:		
Preferred stock	$ 4,600,000	
Excess of issue price over par—preferred stock	1,075,000	
Common stock	4,400,000	
Excess of issue price over par—common stock	1,200,000	
From sale of treasury stock	11,000	
Total paid-in capital	$11,286,000	
Retained earnings	2,213,512	
Total	$13,499,512	
Less treasury stock	21,000	
Total stockholders' equity		13,478,512
Total liabilities and equity		$14,313,612

Prob. 15–5A

2005

Sept. 1	Investment in Sheehan Company Bonds	494,750	
	Interest Revenue ($480,000 × 8% × 2/12)...........	6,400	
	Cash		501,150
Dec. 31	Cash	19,200	
	Interest Revenue		19,200
31	Interest Revenue	500	
	Investment in Sheehan Company Bonds		500

2011

June 30	Cash	19,200	
	Interest Revenue		19,200
Aug. 31	Interest Revenue	500	
	Investment in Sheehan Company Bonds		500
31	Cash	247,600*	
	Gain on Sale of Investments		1,525
	Investment in Sheehan Company Bonds		242,875
	Interest Revenue		3,200

*($240,000 × 1.02) + ($240,000 × 8% × 2/12) − $400

Dec. 31	Cash	9,600	
	Interest Revenue		9,600
31	Interest Revenue	750	
	Investment in Sheehan Company Bonds		750

Appendix Prob. 15–6A

1. a. Interest Expense.. 506,080
        Premium on Bonds Payable
        [$540,000 – (5% × $10,121,603)] 33,920
            Cash 540,000

    b. Interest Expense.. 504,384
        Premium on Bonds Payable
        [$540,000 – (5% × $10,087,683)] 35,616
            Cash 540,000

2. $506,080

Appendix Prob. 15–7A

1. a. Interest Expense.. 637,413
        Discount on Bonds Payable
        [($10,623,552 × 6%) – $600,000] 37,413
            Cash 600,000

    b. Interest Expense.. 639,658
        Discount on Bonds Payable
        [($10,660,965 × 6%) – $600,000] 39,658
            Cash 600,000

2. $637,420

Prob. 15–1B

1.

	Plan 1	Plan 2	Plan 3
Earnings before interest and income tax	$ 4,500,000	$ 4,500,000	$ 4,500,000
Deduct interest on bonds	—	—	1,350,000
Income before income tax	$ 4,500,000	$ 4,500,000	$ 3,150,000
Deduct income tax	1,800,000	1,800,000	1,260,000
Net income	$ 2,700,000	$ 2,700,000	$ 1,890,000
Dividends on preferred stock	—	1,080,000	720,000
Available for dividends on common stock	$ 2,700,000	$ 1,620,000	$ 1,170,000
Shares of common stock outstanding	÷ 1,800,000	÷ 900,000	÷ 450,000
Earnings per share on common stock	$ 1.50	$ 1.80	$ 2.60

2.

	Plan 1	Plan 2	Plan 3
Earnings before interest and income tax	$ 2,700,000	$ 2,700,000	$ 2,700,000
Deduct interest on bonds	—	—	1,350,000
Income before income tax	$ 2,700,000	$ 2,700,000	$ 1,350,000
Deduct income tax	1,080,000	1,080,000	540,000
Net income	$ 1,620,000	$ 1,620,000	$ 810,000
Dividends on preferred stock	—	1,080,000	720,000
Available for dividends on common stock	$ 1,620,000	$ 540,000	$ 90,000
Shares of common stock outstanding	÷ 1,800,000	÷ 900,000	÷ 450,000
Earnings per share on common stock	$ 0.90	$ 0.60	$ 0.20

This solution is applicable only if the P.A.S.S. Software that accompanies the text is used.

FRONTIER INC.
Balance Sheet
June 30, 2006

Assets

Cash...		$23,784,131
Accounts receivable............................		228,950
Merchandise inventory..........................		2,681,650
Prepaid insurance		139,650
Supplies...		182,950
Total current assets		$27,017,331
Equipment..	$ 1,390,000	
Accumulated depreciation—equipment	(109,600) $	1,280,400
Building	$ 5,405,000	
Accumulated depreciation—building	(672,000)	4,733,000
Total plant assets		6,013,400
Total assets......................................		$33,030,731

Liabilities

Accounts payable		$ 32,000
Bonds payable	$20,000,000	
Premium on bonds payable.....................	1,121,607	
Total long-term liabilities		21,121,607
Total liabilities..................................		$21,153,607

Stockholders' Equity

Paid-in capital:		
Preferred stock	$ 2,100,000	
Excess of issue price over par—preferred stock	172,500	
Common stock...............................	4,500,000	
Excess of issue price over par—common stock	1,100,000	
From sale of treasury stock.................	2,000	
Total paid-in capital............................	$ 7,874,500	
Retained earnings	4,222,624	
Total...	$ 12,097,124	
Less treasury stock.............................	220,000	
Total stockholders' equity		11,877,124
Total liabilities and equity.....................		$33,030,731

Prob. 15–3B

1.
Cash	16,878,410*	
Discount on Bonds Payable.................................	1,121,590	
Bonds Payable..		18,000,000

*Present value of $1 for 20 (semiannual) periods at 5% (semiannual rate)	0.37689	
Face amount...	× $18,000,000	$ 6,784,020
Present value of an annuity of $1 for 20 periods at 5%	12.46221	
Semiannual interest payment	× $810,000	10,094,390
Proceeds of bond issue		$16,878,410

2.
a.
Interest Expense..	866,080	
Discount on Bonds Payable ($1,121,590 ÷ 20)...		56,080
Cash		810,000

b.
Interest Expense..	866,080	
Discount on Bonds Payable..........................		56,080
Cash		810,000

3. $866,080

4. Yes. Investors will not be willing to pay the face amount of the bonds when the interest payments they will receive from the bonds are less than the amount of interest that they could receive from investing in other bonds.

Prob. 15–4B

1.

				Debit	Credit
2005					
July	1	Cash...		16,104,095	
		Premium on Bonds Payable..................			1,104,095
		Bonds Payable			15,000,000
Dec.	31	Interest Expense.................................		1,050,000	
		Cash			1,050,000
	31	Premium on Bonds Payable		110,409	
		Interest Expense			110,409
	31	Income Summary.................................		939,591	
		Interest Expense			939,591
2006					
June	30	Interest Expense.................................		1,050,000	
		Cash			1,050,000
Dec.	31	Interest Expense.................................		1,050,000	
		Cash			1,050,000
	31	Premium on Bonds Payable		220,818	
		Interest Expense			220,818
	31	Income Summary.................................		1,879,182	
		Interest Expense			1,879,182
2007					
July	1	Bonds Payable...................................		15,000,000	
		Premium on Bonds Payable		662,459	
		Gain on Redemption on Bonds.............			512,459
		Cash			15,150,000

2. a. 2005: $939,591

   b. 2006: $1,879,182

3.
Initial carrying amount of bonds	$16,104,095
Premium amortized on December 31, 2005................	(110,409)
Premium amortized on December 31, 2006................	(220,818)
Carrying amount of bonds, December 31, 2006..........	**$15,772,868**

Prob. 15–4B   Concluded

This solution is applicable only if the P.A.S.S. Software that accompanies the text is used.

ABSAROKA CO.
Balance Sheet
July 1, 2007

Assets

Cash..	$ 2,931,604	
Accounts receivable....................................	728,950	
Merchandise inventory...............................	4,681,650	
Prepaid insurance	139,650	
Supplies..	182,950	
Total current assets		$ 8,664,804
Equipment.................................. $ 2,390,000		
Accumulated depreciation—equipment.. (109,600)	$ 2,280,400	
Building .... $ 7,405,000		
Accumulated depreciation—building ...... (772,018)	6,632,982	
Total plant assets		8,913,382
Total assets...		$17,578,186

Liabilities

Accounts payable	$ 32,000	

Stockholders' Equity

Paid-in capital:		
Preferred stock...	$ 4,100,000	
Excess of issue price over par—preferred stock	672,500	
Common stock..	6,500,000	
Excess of issue price over par—common stock.....	1,600,000	
From sale of treasury stock.............................	2,000	
Total paid-in capital......................................	$12,874,500	
Retained earnings	4,891,686	
Total...	$17,766,186	
Less treasury stock.......................................	220,000	
Total stockholders' equity		17,546,186
Total liabilities and equity..		$17,578,186

Prob. 15–5B

2005

Sept. 1   Investment in Churchill Company Bonds   385,720
       Interest Revenue ($400,000 × 9% × 2/12)...........   6,000
           Cash   391,720

Dec. 31   Cash   18,000
           Interest Revenue   18,000

    31   Investment in Churchill Company Bonds   240
           Interest Revenue   240

2010

June 30   Cash   18,000
           Interest Revenue   18,000

Oct. 31   Investment in Churchill Company Bonds   300
           Interest Revenue   300

    31   Cash 198,600*
       Loss on Sale of Investments.............................   2,120
           Investment in Churchill Company Bonds   194,720
           Interest Revenue   6,000
       *($200,000 × 0.965) + ($200,000 × 9% × 4/12) − $400

Dec. 31   Cash   9,000
           Interest Revenue   9,000

    31   Investment in Churchill Company Bonds   360
           Interest Revenue   360

Appendix Prob. 15–6B

1. a. Interest Expense... 1,062,312
   Premium on Bonds Payable
   [$1,100,000 – (5% × $21,246,231)] 37,688
      Cash 1,100,000

   b. Interest Expense... 1,060,427
   Premium on Bonds Payable
   [$1,100,000 – (5% × $21,208,543)] 39,573
      Cash 1,100,000

2. $1,062,312

Appendix Prob. 15–7B

1. a. Interest Expense... 843,921
   Discount on Bonds Payable
   [($16,878,410 × 5%) – $810,000] 33,921
      Cash 810,000

   b. Interest Expense... 845,617
   Discount on Bonds Payable
   [($16,912,331 × 5%) – $810,000] 35,617
      Cash 810,000

2. $843,921

COMPREHENSIVE PROBLEM 4

1. a. Cash.. 520,000

      Common Stock.. 250,000

      Paid-in Capital in Excess of Par—

      Common Stock... 270,000

  b. Cash.. 1,000,000

      Preferred Stock 800,000

      Paid-in Capital in Excess of Par—

      Preferred Stock 200,000

  c. Cash.. 12,747,739

      Bonds Payable 12,000,000

      Premium on Bonds Payable....................... 747,739

Computations:

Present value of face amount: $12,000,000 × 0.37689

   [present value of $1 for 20 (semiannual) periods

   at 5% (semiannual rate)]..................................... $ 4,522,680

Present value of semiannual interest payments of

   $660,000 at 5% compounded semiannually:

   $660,000 × 12.46221 (present value of annuity

   of $1 for 20 periods at 5%) 8,225,059

Total present value of bonds................................... $12,747,739

  d. Cash Dividends.. 55,000

      Cash Dividends Payable............................. 55,000

  e. Cash Dividends Payable 55,000

      Cash 55,000

  f. Bonds Payable... 400,000

     Premium on Bonds Payable 4,920

      Cash 404,000

      Gain on Redemption of Bonds.................... 920

  g. Treasury Stock.. 250,000

      Cash 250,000

h. Stock Dividends... 96,900*
   Cash Dividends.. 30,000
      Stock Dividends Distributable   47,500
      Paid-In Capital in Excess of Par—
      Common Stock...   49,400
      Cash Dividends Payable...................................   30,000

   *100,000 – 5,000 = 95,000
   95,000 × 2% = 1,900
   1,900 × $51 = $96,900

i. Stock Dividends Distributable............................... 47,500
   Cash Dividends Payable 30,000
      Common Stock..   47,500
      Cash   30,000

j. Investment in Athens Sports Inc. Bonds................ 116,400
   Interest Revenue... 4,500
      Cash   120,900

k. Cash... 174,000
      Treasury Stock   150,000
      Paid-In Capital from Sale of Treasury Stock.....   24,000

l. Interest Expense.. 622,613
   Premium on Bonds Payable 37,387
      Cash   660,000

   Computations:
   Semiannual interest payment................................. $660,000
   Amortization premium [($747,739 ÷ 120 months) ×
     6 months, rounded]   37,387
   Interest expense $622,613

m. Interest Receivable... 6,000
      Interest Revenue   6,000

   Computation: $120,000 × 15% × 4/12 = $6,000

   Investment in Athens Sports Inc. Bonds................ 120
      Interest Revenue   120

SPECIAL ACTIVITIES

Activity 15–1

1. a. Gatorade® was developed in the 1960s by scientists at the University of Florida for use by the University's football team, the Florida Gators; hence, the name Gatorade. Gatorade was designed to replace fluid and electrolytes that the players lost through sweat during practices and games. In the 1967 Orange Bowl, the football team used Gatorade to overpower its dehydrated opponent, Georgia Tech, 27 to 12.

    b. Gatorade has approximately 85% of the sports-drink market.

2. a. Some overlap in descriptions exists; however, sports, lifestyle, and active thirst drinks are normally defined as follows:

    Sports drinks are designed to replace fluid and electrolytes consumed during athletic activities.

    Lifestyle drinks are designed to be appropriate for any occasion.

    Active thirst drinks are drinks that people consume when they are "hot and thirsty."

    b. Although drinks can cross over into more than one category, examples include the following:

    Sports drinks: Gatorade, Powerade®, Red Bull®

    Lifestyle drinks: Coke®, Pepsi®, iced tea, bottled water, coffee, beer, wine, various liquors

    Active thirst drinks: Tap water, bottled water, Coke, Pepsi, iced tea, beer, Gatorade, Powerade

3. PepsiCo decided to emphasize the origins of Gatorade as a sports drink in its advertising campaign. Rather than lose its identity, PepsiCo decided to "stay true" to its user base and strength as a sports drink. Thus, Gatorade's new advertising campaign emphasizes the origins of the development of Gatorade to enhance player performance.

    Note: A survey conducted by PepsiCo on Gatorade's origin revealed that 26% thought it was developed by Dr. Gator, while over 2% thought it contained a "secret ingredient" of alligator juice.

    Source: Betsy McKay, "Gatorade Seeks to Dominate Sports Drink Realm With Ads," *The Wall Street Journal*, June 11, 2002; http://gatorade.com.

Activity 15–2

GE Capital's action was legal, but caused a great public relations stir at the time. Some quotes:

"A lot of people feel like they have been sorely used," said one bond fund manager. "There was nothing illegal about it, but it was nasty."

The fund manager said that GE Capital's decision to upsize its bond issue to $11 billion from $6 billion midway through the offering ordinarily wouldn't have upset bondholders.

"But then to find out two days later that they had filed a $50 billion shelf?" he said. "People buy GE because it's like buying Treasurys, not because they want to get jerked around."

GE Capital's action was probably ethical, even though it caused some stir. In its own defense it stated:

In a statement released late Thursday, GE Capital said "with the $11 billion bond issuance of March 13, GE Capital exhausted its existing debt shelf registration; consequently, on March 20, GE Capital filed a $50 billion shelf registration."

The release said the shelf filing was not an offering and that it would be used in part to roll over $31 billion in maturing long term debt.

In retrospect, GE Capital could have been a little more forthcoming about its financing plans prior to selling the $11 billion on bonds, but there was nothing unethical or illegal about its disclosures.

Source: "GE Capital Timing On $50B Shelf Filing Added To Backlash," Dow Jones Capital Markets Report, March 22, 2002, Copyright (c) 2002, Dow Jones & Company, Inc.

Activity 15–3

Without the consent of the bondholders, Terry Holter's use of the sinking fund cash to temporarily alleviate the shortage of funds would violate the bond indenture contract and the trust of the bondholders. It would therefore be unprofessional. In addition, the use of Terry's brother-in-law as trustee of the sinking fund is a potential conflict of interest that could be considered unprofessional.

CHAPTER 16
STATEMENT OF CASH FLOWS

CLASS DISCUSSION QUESTIONS

1. It is costly to accumulate the data needed.

2. It focuses on the differences between net income and cash flows from operating activities, and the data needed are generally more readily available and less costly to obtain than is the case for the direct method.

3. In a separate schedule of noncash investing and financing activities accompanying the statement of cash flows.

4. **a.** No effect
   b. No

5. The $25,000 increase must be added to income from operations because the amount of cash paid to merchandise creditors was $25,000 less than the amount of purchases included in the cost of goods sold.

6. The $10,000 decrease in salaries payable should be deducted from income to determine the amount of cash flows from operating activities. The effect of the decrease in the amount of salaries owed was to pay $10,000 more cash during the year than had been recorded as an expense.

7. **a.** $5,000 gain
   b. Cash inflow of $80,000

   c. The gain of $5,000 would be deducted from net income in determining net cash flow from operating activities; $80,000 would be reported as cash flow from investing activities.

8. Cash flow from financing activities— issuance of bonds, $5,250,000

9. **a.** Cash flow from investing activities— disposal of fixed assets, $5,000

   The $5,000 gain on asset disposal should be deducted from net income in determining cash flow from operating activities under the indirect method.

   b. No effect

10. The same. The amount reported as the net cash flow from operating activities is not affected by the use of the direct or indirect method.

11. Cash received from customers, cash payments for merchandise, cash payments for operating expenses, cash payments for interest, cash payments for income taxes.

12. Reported in a separate schedule, as follows:
    Schedule of noncash financing activities:
    Issuance of stock for
    acquisitions.......................... $128 million

EXERCISES

Ex. 16–1

There were net additions, such as depreciation and amortization of intangible assets of $10.2 billion, to the net loss reported on the income statement to convert the net loss from the accrual basis to the cash basis. For example, depreciation is an expense in determining net income, but it does not result in a cash outflow. Thus, depreciation is added back to the net loss in order to determine cash flow from operations.

The cash from operating activities detail is provided as follows for class discussion:

AOL Time Warner
Cash Flows from Operating Activities
(selected from Statement of Cash Flows)
(in millions)

OPERATING ACTIVITIES	
Net income (loss)	$(4,921)
Adjustments for noncash and nonoperating items:	
Depreciation and amortization	9,203
Amortization of film costs	2,380
Loss on writedown of investments	2,537
Net gains on sale of investments	(34)
Equity in losses of other investee companies net of cash distributions	975
Changes in operating assets and liabilities, net of acquisitions:	
Receivables	(484)
Inventories	(2,801)
Accounts payable and other liabilities	(1,952)
Other balance sheet changes	391
Cash provided by operating activities	$ 5,294

Ex. 16–2

a. Cash receipt, $225,000
b. Cash receipt, $41,000
c. Cash payment, $120,000
d. Cash payment, $250,000
e. Cash receipt, $101,000
f. Cash payment, $37,500
g. Cash payment, $501,000
h. Cash payment, $30,000

Ex. 16–3

a. investing
b. investing
c. financing
d. investing
e. operating
f. financing
g. financing
h. financing
i. investing
j. financing
k. financing

Ex. 16–4

a. added

b. added

c. deducted

d. deducted

e. deducted

f. added

g. added

h. added

i. added

j. deducted

k. deducted

Ex. 16–5

a. Cash flows from operating activities:

Net income		$255,800
Add: Depreciation...	$53,500	
Decrease in accounts receivable	1,600	
Decrease in prepaid expenses	200	
Increase in salaries payable	400	55,700
		$311,500
Deduct:		
Increase in inventories.........................	$13,300	
Decrease in accounts payable	6,100	19,400
Cash from operations....................................		$292,100

b. Yes. The amount of cash flows from operating activities reported on the statement of cash flows is not affected by the method of reporting such flows.

Ex. 16–6

Cash flows from operating activities:

Net income			$ 75,000
Add:	Depreciation	$22,500	
	Decrease in accounts receivable	3,700	
	Increase in wages payable	3,000	29,200
			$104,200
Deduct:	Increase in inventories	$ 5,500	
	Increase in prepaid expenses	400	
	Decrease in accounts payable	1,900	7,800
Cash from operations			$96,400

Ex. 16–7

Dividends declared	$80,000
Add decrease in dividends payable	5,000
Dividends paid to stockholders during the year	$85,000

The company probably had four quarterly payments—the first one being $25,000 declared in the preceding year and three payments of $20,000 each—of dividends declared and paid during the current year. Thus, $85,000 [$25,000 + (3 × $20,000)] is the amount of cash payments to stockholders. The $20,000 of dividends payable at the end of the year will be paid in the next year.

Ex. 16–8

Cash flows from investing activities:

Cash received from sale of equipment	$25,000

[The gain on the sale, $5,000 ($25,000 proceeds from sale less $20,000 book value), would be deducted from net income in determining the cash flows from operating activities if the indirect method of reporting cash flows from operations is used.]

Ex. 16–9

Cash flows from investing activities:

Cash received from sale of equipment	$75,000

[The loss on the sale, $5,000 ($75,000 proceeds from sale less $80,000 book value), would be added to net income in determining the cash flows from operating activities if the indirect method of reporting cash flows from operations is used.]

Ex. 16–10

Cash flows from investing activities:

Cash received from sale of land....................................	$310,000
Less: Cash paid for purchase of land..........................	300,000

(The gain on the sale of land, $60,000, would be deducted from net income in determining the cash flows from operating activities if the indirect method of reporting cash flows from operations is used.)

Ex. 16–11

Cash flows from financing activities:

Cash received from sale of common stock................	$480,000
Less: Cash paid for dividends......................................	240,000

Note: The stock dividend is not disclosed on the statement of cash flows.

Ex. 16–12

Cash flows from investing activities:

Cash paid for purchase of land....................................	$290,000

A separate schedule of noncash investing and financing activities would report the purchase of $200,000 land with a long-term mortgage note, as follows:

Purchase of land by issuing long-term mortgage note.....	$200,000

Ex. 16–13

Cash flows from financing activities:

Cash paid to redeem bonds payable	$ 48,000
Cash received from issuing bonds payable...............	185,000

Note: The discount amortization of $1,200 and the loss on retirement of the bonds of $2,000 ($48,000 less the bond carrying value of $46,000 on January 1) would be shown as adjusting items (increases) in the cash flows from operating activities section under the indirect method.

Ex. 16–14

Net cash flow from operating activities..............			$105,700
Add:	Increase in accounts receivable...............	$ 6,500	
	Increase in prepaid expenses...................	2,000	
	Decrease in income taxes payable...........	2,100	
	Gain on sale of investments	3,600	14,200
			$119,900
Deduct:	Depreciation...	$11,000	
	Decrease in inventories	6,400	
	Increase in accounts payable..............	4,700	22,100
Net income, per income statement.....................			$ 97,800

Note to Instructors: The net income must be determined by working backward through the cash flows from operating activities section of the statement of cash flows. Hence, those items which were added (deducted) to determine net cash flow from operating activities must be deducted (added) to determine net income.

Ex. 16–15

Cash flows from operating activities*:

Net income, per income statement			$ 75,096
Add:	Depreciation	$81,594	
	Loss on sale of fixed assets	3,950	
	Decrease in accounts receivable	6,025	
	Decrease in merchandise inventories	33,793	
	Increase in accounts payable and other accrued expenses.................................	4,156	
	Increase in income tax payable	12,145	141,663
			$216,759
Deduct:	Increase in prepaid expenses...............	$ 4,511	
	Other noncash income..........................	7,242	11,753
Cash from operations			$205,006

*Dollars in thousands

Ex. 16–16

a.	Sales	$510,000
	Plus decrease in accounts receivable balance	27,000
	Cash received from customers	$537,000
b.	Income tax expense	$ 29,000
	Plus decrease in income tax payable	3,900
	Cash payments for income tax	$ 32,900

Ex. 16–17

Cost of merchandise sold	$7,604*
Add: Decrease in accounts payable	274
Deduct: Decrease in merchandise inventories	(266)
Cash paid for merchandise	$7,612

*In millions

Ex. 16–18

a.	Cost of merchandise sold	$450,000
	Add decrease in accounts payable	4,700
		$454,700
	Deduct decrease in inventories	11,700
	Cash payments for merchandise	$443,000
b.	Operating expenses other than depreciation	$ 80,000
	Add decrease in accrued expenses	600
		$ 80,600
	Deduct decrease in prepaid expenses	1,000
	Cash payments for operating expenses	$ 79,600

Ex. 16–19

Cash flows from operating activities:

Cash received from customers......................			$657,000[1]
Deduct: Cash payments for merchandise...	$380,400[2]		
Cash payments for operating expenses	150,600[3]		
Cash payments for income tax	29,000[4]	560,000	
Net cash flow from operating activities			$ 97,000

Computations:

1.

Sales...		$645,000
Add decrease in accounts receivable		12,000
Cash received from customers...		$657,000

2.

Cost of merchandise sold		$367,800
Add: Increase in inventories..	$ 4,200	
Decrease in accounts payable	8,400	12,600
Cash payments for merchandise......................................		$380,400

3.

Operating expenses other than depreciation		$155,400
Deduct: Decrease in prepaid expenses.........................	$ 2,500	
Increase in accrued expenses	2,300	4,800
Cash payments for operating expenses		$150,600

4.

Income tax expense		$ 25,400
Add decrease in income tax payable...............................		3,600
Cash payments for income tax		$ 29,000

Ex. 16–20

Cash flows from operating activities:

Cash received from customers......................			$262,700[1]
Deduct: Cash payments for merchandise...	$ 97,500[2]		
Cash payments for operating expenses	125,800[3]		
Cash payments for income tax	12,300	235,600	
Net cash flow from operating activities			$ 27,100

Computations:

1. | Sales.. | $265,000 |
|---|---|
| Deduct increase in accounts receivable .... | 2,300 |
| Cash received from customers.. | $262,700 |

2. | Cost of merchandise sold .... | $ 95,800 |
|---|---|
| Add increase in inventories .... | 5,300 |
| | $101,100 |
| Deduct increase in accounts payable .... | 3,600 |
| Cash payments for merchandise.. | $ 97,500 |

3. | Operating expenses other than depreciation .... | $125,700 |
|---|---|
| Add decrease in accrued expenses .... | 500 |
| | $126,200 |
| Deduct decrease in prepaid expenses................................. | 400 |
| Cash payments for operating expenses .... | $125,800 |

Ex. 16–21

CONTEMPORARY MILLWORKS INC.
Statement of Cash Flows
For the Year Ended December 31, 2006

Cash flows from operating activities:

Net income, per income statement.......................		$30
Add: Depreciation...	$3	
Decrease in accounts receivable	2	
Loss on sale of land	2	7
		$37
Deduct: Increase in inventories...........................	$5	
Decrease in accounts payable	3	8
Net cash flow from operating activities		$29

Cash flows from investing activities:

Cash received from sale of land	$13	
Less cash paid for purchase of equipment	17	
Net cash flow used for investing activities...........		(4)

Cash flows from financing activities:

Cash received from sale of common stock	$12	
Less cash paid for dividends................................	3*	
Net cash flow from financing activities.................		9
Increase in cash..		$34
Cash at the beginning of the year		16
Cash at the end of the year..................................		$50

*$4 + $0 – $1 = $3

Ex. 16–22

1. The increase in accounts receivable should be deducted from net income in the cash flows from operating activities section.

2. The gain from sale of investments should be deducted from net income in the cash flows from operating activities section.

3. The increase in accounts payable should be added to net income in the cash flows from operating activities section.

4. Cash paid for dividends should be deducted from cash received from the sale of common stock in the cash flows from financing activities section.

5. The correct amount of cash at the beginning of the year, $70,700, should be added to the increase in cash.

6. The final amount should be the amount of cash at the end of the year, $96,100.

Ex. 16–22   Concluded

A correct statement of cash flows would be as follows:

HEALTHY CHOICE NUTRITION PRODUCTS, INC.
Statement of Cash Flows
For the Year Ended December 31, 2006

Cash flows from operating activities:			
Net income, per income statement...................		$100,500	
Add: Depreciation	$ 49,000		
Increase in accounts payable	4,400	53,400	
		$153,900	
Deduct: Increase in accounts receivable	$ 10,500		
Increase in inventories.........................	18,300		
Gain on sale of investments...............	5,000		
Decrease in accrued expenses	1,600	35,400	
Net cash flow from operating activities			$118,500
Cash flows from investing activities:			
Cash received from sale of investments..........		$ 85,000	
Less: Cash paid for purchase of land..............	$ 90,000		
Cash paid for purchase of equipment...	150,100	240,100	
Net cash flow used for investing			
activities			(155,100)
Cash flows from financing activities:			
Cash received from sale of common			
stock		$107,000	
Less: Cash paid for dividends		45,000	
Net cash flow provided by financing			
activities			62,000
Increase in cash..			$ 25,400
Cash at the beginning of the year			70,700
Cash at the end of the year....................................			$ 96,100

Ex. 16–23

Cash flows from operating activities	$120,000
Less: Cash paid for common dividends	20,000
Cash paid for preferred dividends	8,000
Cash paid for maintaining property, plant, and equipment	27,000
Free cash flow	$ 65,000

Supporting calculations:

Common dividends: 100,000 shares × $0.20 per share = $20,000
Preferred dividends: 1,000 × $100 × 8% = $8,000
Property, plant, and equipment to maintain productive capacity: $45,000 × 60% = $27,000

Ex. 16–24

a. and b.

	(all numbers in millions)			
		2003		2002
Sales		$58,247		$53,553
Cash flows from operating activities		$ 4,802		$ 5,963
Less: Capital expenditure to maintain existing capacity:				
Capital expenditures	$2,749		$3,393	
Percent to maintain productive capacity	× 20%	(550)	× 20%	(679)
Cash dividends		(492)		(396)
Free cash flow		$ 3,760		$ 4,888
Free cash flow as a percent of cash flows from operating activities......................		78.3%		81.9%
Free cash flow as a percent of sales		6.4%		9.1%

c. Home Depot has had strong free cash flows for both years. For example, the free cash flow has been more than sufficient to fund store expansion (80% of capital expenditures). However, the free cash flow for the year ended February 2, 2003, has dropped by 23% [($4,888 − $3,760)/$4,888] from the previous year. In addition, the free cash flow as a percent of sales has also dropped from 9.1% of sales to 6.4% of sales. The free cash flow as a percent of cash flow from operating activities has remained near 80%. Thus, while the free-cash-flow-generating ability of Home Depot is excellent, it has experienced some deterioration in between the two years. The statement of cash flows reveals that much of the decline in cash flows from operating activities was caused by a significant increase in inventories during the year.

PROBLEMS

Prob. 16–1A

WINNER'S EDGE SPORTING GOODS, INC.
Statement of Cash Flows
For the Year Ended December 31, 2006

Cash flows from operating activities:

Net income, per income statement.............		$180,600	
Add: Depreciation...	$ 26,000		
Increase in accounts payable............	18,200	44,200	
		$224,800	
Deduct: Increase in accounts receivable.	$ 17,500		
Increase in inventories	27,100		
Gain on sale of investments........	12,000		
Decrease in accrued			
expenses..............................	4,900	61,500	
Net cash flow from operating activities			$163,300

Cash flows from investing activities:

Cash received from sale of investments....		$132,000	
Less: Cash paid for purchase of land........	$160,000		
Cash paid for purchase of			
equipment......................................	120,000	280,000	
Net cash flow used for investing			
activities			(148,000)

Cash flows from financing activities:

Cash received from sale of			
common stock		$105,000	
Less cash paid for dividends.....................		52,000*	
Net cash flow provided by financing			
activities			53,000
Increase in cash...			$ 68,300
Cash at the beginning of the year			395,800
Cash at the end of the year.............................			$464,100

*$56,000 + $10,000 – $14,000 = $52,000

WINNER'S EDGE SPORTING GOODS, INC.
Work Sheet for Statement of Cash Flows
For the Year Ended December 31, 2006

	Balance Dec. 31, 2005		Transactions Debit		Transactions Credit	Balance Dec. 31, 2006
Cash....................................	395,800	(m)	68,300			464,100
Accounts receivable......................	145,700	(l)	17,500			163,200
Inventories	367,900	(k)	27,100			395,000
Investments.................................	120,000			(j)	120,000	0
Land...	0	(i)	160,000			160,000
Equipment...................................	575,500	(h)	120,000			695,500
Accumulated depreciation— equipment.................................	(168,000)			(g)	26,000	(194,000)
Accounts payable	(210,500)			(f)	18,200	(228,700)
Accrued expenses	(21,400)	(e)	4,900			(16,500)
Dividends payable	(10,000)			(d)	4,000	(14,000)
Common stock..............................	(60,000)			(c)	15,000	(75,000)
Paid-in capital in excess of par— common stock	(175,000)			(c)	90,000	(265,000)
Retained earnings.........................	(960,000)	(b)	56,000	(a)	180,600	(1,084,600)
Totals.......................................	0		453,800		453,800	0
Operating activities:						
Net income		(a)	180,600			
Decrease in accrued expenses				(e)	4,900	
Increase in accounts payable ..		(f)	18,200			
Depreciation		(g)	26,000			
Gain on sale of investments				(j)	12,000	
Increase in inventories				(k)	27,100	
Increase in accounts receivable				(l)	17,500	
Investing activities:						
Purchase of equipment				(h)	120,000	
Purchase of land.....................				(i)	160,000	
Sale of investments		(j)	132,000			
Financing activities:						
Declaration of cash dividends				(b)	56,000	
Sale of common stock.............		(c)	105,000			
Increase in dividends payable		(d)	4,000			
Net increase in cash				(m)	68,300	
Totals.......................................			465,800		465,800	

Prob. 16–2A

MEDALIST ATHLETIC APPAREL CO.
Statement of Cash Flows
For the Year Ended December 31, 2006

Cash flows from operating activities:			
Net income, per income statement................		$ 61,500	
Add: Depreciation..	$17,900		
Increase in accounts payable..............	1,700		
Decrease in accounts receivable	4,200	23,800	
		$ 85,300	
Deduct: Increase in merchandise			
inventory......................................	$ 5,400		
Increase in prepaid expenses	1,500	6,900	
Net cash flow from operating activities			$ 78,400
Cash flows from investing activities:			
Cash paid for equipment...............................		$ 47,500	
Net cash flow used for investing			
activities			(47,500)
Cash flows from financing activities:			
Cash received from sale of common stock ..		$104,000	
Less: Cash paid for dividends.......................	$48,000		
Cash paid to retire mortgage			
note payable	95,000	143,000	
Net cash flow used in financing			
activities			(39,000)
Decrease in cash			$ (8,100)
Cash at the beginning of the year			45,300
Cash at the end of the year..................................			$ 37,200

Prob. 16–2A Concluded

MEDALIST ATHLETIC APPAREL CO.
Work Sheet for Statement of Cash Flows
For the Year Ended December 31, 2006

	Balance Dec. 31, 2005	Transactions Debit		Transactions Credit		Balance Dec. 31, 2006
Cash...	45,300			(l)	8,100	37,200
Accounts receivable.........................	65,400			(k)	4,200	61,200
Merchandise inventory.....................	85,600	(j)	5,400			91,000
Prepaid expenses............................	4,000	(i)	1,500			5,500
Equipment.......................................	155,500	(h)	47,500	(g)	12,500	190,500
Accumulated depreciation—						
equipment..................................	(35,800)	(g)	12,500	(f)	17,900	(41,200)
Accounts payable............................	(65,400)			(e)	1,700	(67,100)
Mortgage note payable.....................	(95,000)	(d)	95,000			0
Common stock.................................	(10,000)			(c)	4,000	(14,000)
Paid-in capital in excess of par—						
common stock.............................	(100,000)			(c)	100,000	(200,000)
Retained earnings............................	(49,600)	(b)	48,000	(a)	61,500	(63,100)
Totals...	0		209,900		209,900	0
Operating activities:						
Net income		(a)	61,500			
Increase in accounts payable ..		(e)	1,700			
Depreciation.............................		(f)	17,900			
Increase in prepaid expenses ..				(i)	1,500	
Increase in merchandise						
inventory.............................				(j)	5,400	
Decrease in accounts						
receivables		(k)	4,200			
Investing activities:						
Purchase of equipment				(h)	47,500	
Financing activities:						
Payment of cash dividends......				(b)	48,000	
Sale of common stock..............		(c)	104,000			
Payment of mortgage note						
payable..............................				(d)	95,000	
Net decrease in cash......................		(l)	8,100			
Totals...			197,400		197,400	

Prob. 16–3A

SUNRISE JUICE COMPANY
Statement of Cash Flows
For the Year Ended, December 31, 2006

Cash flows from operating activities:			
Net loss, per income statement			$ (43,800)
Add: Depreciation..	$ 27,100		
Decrease in prepaid expenses	2,000		
Loss on sale of land	9,000	38,100	
		$ (5,700)	
Deduct: Increase in accounts receivable	$ 18,400		
Increase in inventory	25,400		
Decrease in accounts payable....	3,500	47,300	
Net cash flow from operating activities			$ (53,000)
Cash flows from investing activities:			
Cash received from land sold		$ 81,000	
Less: Cash paid for acquisition			
of building......................................	$250,000		
Cash paid for purchase			
of equipment...................................	32,900	282,900	
Net cash flow used for investing			
activities			(201,900)
Cash flows from financing activities:			
Cash received from issuance of			
bonds payable...	$ 80,000		
Cash received from issuance of			
common stock	160,000	$ 240,000	
Less: Cash paid for dividends.....................		12,000	
Net cash flow provided by financing			
activities			228,000
Decrease in cash			$ (26,900)
Cash at the beginning of the year			432,100
Cash at the end of the year...............................			$405,200

Prob. 16–3A   Concluded

SUNRISE JUICE COMPANY
Work Sheet for Statement of Cash Flows
For the Year Ended December 31, 2006

	Balance Dec. 31, 2005	Transactions Debit	Transactions Credit	Balance Dec. 31, 2006
Cash..	432,100		(o) 26,900	405,200
Accounts receivable	305,700	(n) 18,400		324,100
Inventories	576,900	(m) 25,400		602,300
Prepaid expenses	12,000		(l) 2,000	10,000
Land..	190,000		(k) 90,000	100,000
Buildings	400,000	(j) 250,000		650,000
Accumulated depreciation— buildings..................................	(155,000)		(i) 17,500	(172,500)
Equipment..................................	210,700	(h) 32,900	(g) 18,000	225,600
Accumulated depreciation— equipment................................	(56,500)	(g) 18,000	(f) 9,600	(48,100)
Accounts payable	(402,600)	(e) 3,500		(399,100)
Bonds payable	0		(d) 80,000	(80,000)
Common stock.............................	(50,000)		(c) 10,000	(60,000)
Paid-in capital in excess of par— common stock	(200,000)		(c) 150,000	(350,000)
Retained earnings.........................	(1,263,300)	(a) 43,800		(1,207,500)
		(b) 12,000		
Totals..	0	404,000	404,000	0
Operating activities:				
Net loss......................................			(a) 43,800	
Decrease in accounts payable.			(e) 3,500	
Depreciation—equipment.........		(f) 9,600		
Depreciation—buildings...........		(i) 17,500		
Loss on sale of land		(k) 9,000		
Decrease in prepaid expenses.		(l) 2,000		
Increase in inventories			(m) 25,400	
Increase in accounts receivable			(n) 18,400	
Investing activities:				
Purchase of equipment			(h) 32,900	
Acquisition of building			(j) 250,000	
Sale of land................................		(k) 81,000		
Financing activities:				
Payment of cash dividends......			(b) 12,000	
Issuance of bonds payable		(d) 80,000		
Issuance of common stock......		(c) 160,000		
Net decrease in cash		(o) 26,900		
Totals..		386,000	386,000	

Prob. 16–4A

VILLAGE MARKETS, INC.
Statement of Cash Flows
For the Year Ended December 31, 2007

Cash flows from operating activities:

Cash received from customers...................			$4,336,300[1]
Deduct: Cash payments for merchandise............................	$2,552,900[2]		
Cash payments for operating expenses	1,263,200[3]		
Cash payments for income tax ...	175,000	3,991,100	
Net cash flow from operating activities			$345,200

Cash flows from investing activities:

Cash received from sale of investments....		$ 150,000	
Less: Cash paid for purchase of land........	$ 230,000		
Cash paid for purchase of equipment......................................	140,000	370,000	
Net cash flow used for investing activities			(220,000)

Cash flows from financing activities:

Cash received from sale of common stock		$ 78,000	
Less: Cash paid for dividends....................		238,000*	
Net cash flow used for financing activities			(160,000)
Decrease in cash			$ (34,800)
Cash at the beginning of the year			456,700
Cash at the end of the year.............................			$421,900

Reconciliation of Net Income with Cash Flows from Operating Activities:

Net income, per income statement.............		$330,300	
Add: Depreciation.......................................	$ 47,600		
Increase in accounts payable...........	14,900		
Loss on sale of investments	25,000	87,500	
		$417,800	
Deduct: Increase in accounts receivable	$ 31,500		
Increase in inventories	35,800		
Decrease in accrued expenses...	5,300	72,600	
Net cash flow from operating activities		$345,200	

*Dividends paid: $241,000 + $58,000 − $61,000 = $238,000

Prob. 16–4A   Continued

Computations:

1.	Sales	$4,367,800
	Deduct increase in accounts receivable	31,500
	Cash received from customers	$4,336,300
2.	Cost of merchandise sold	$2,532,000
	Add increase in inventories	35,800
		$2,567,800
	Deduct increase in accounts payable	14,900
	Cash payments for merchandise	$2,552,900
3.	Operating expenses other than depreciation	$1,257,900
	Add decrease in accrued expenses	5,300
	Cash payments for operating expenses	$1,263,200

Prob. 16–4A   Continued

VILLAGE MARKETS, INC.
Work Sheet for Statement of Cash Flows
For the Year Ended December 31, 2007

	Balance Dec. 31, 2006	Transactions Debit		Transactions Credit		Balance Dec. 31, 2007
Balance Sheet						
Cash..	456,700			(q)	34,800	421,900
Accounts receivable......................	365,700	(p)	31,500			397,200
Inventories	623,100	(o)	35,800			658,900
Investments.................................	175,000			(e)	175,000	0
Land..	0	(n)	230,000			230,000
Equipment..................................	450,000	(m)	140,000			590,000
Accumulated depreciation	(234,500)			(c)	47,600	(282,100)
Accounts payable	(456,300)			(l)	14,900	(471,200)
Accrued expenses	(45,300)	(k)	5,300			(40,000)
Dividends payable	(58,000)			(j)	3,000	(61,000)
Common stock..............................	(20,000)			(i)	3,000	(23,000)
Paid-in capital in excess of par— common stock	(120,000)			(i)	75,000	(195,000)
Retained earnings.........................	(1,136,400)	(h)	241,000	(g)	330,300	(1,225,700)
Totals..	0		683,600		683,600	0

Prob. 16–4A   Concluded

	Balance Dec. 31, 2006	Transactions Debit	Transactions Credit	Balance Dec. 31, 2007
Income Statement				
Sales...			(a) 4,367,800	
Cost of merchandise sold..............		(b) 2,532,000		
Depreciation expense.....................		(c) 47,600		
Other operating expenses..............		(d) 1,257,900		
Loss on sale of investments..........		(e) 25,000		
Income tax.....................................		(f) 175,000		
Net income		(g) 330,300		
Cash Flows				
Operating activities:				
Cash received from customers		(a) 4,367,800	(p) 31,500	
Cash payments:				
Merchandise............................		(l) 14,900	(b) 2,532,000	
			(o) 35,800	
Operating expenses.................			(d) 1,257,900	
			(k) 5,300	
Income taxes			(f) 175,000	
Investing activities:				
Purchase of equipment			(m) 140,000	
Sale of investments		(e) 150,000		
Purchase of land......................			(n) 230,000	
Financing activities:				
Declaration of cash dividends			(h) 241,000	
Increase in dividends payable		(j) 3,000		
Issuance of common stock......		(i) 78,000		
Net decrease in cash......................		(q) 34,800		
Totals...		9,016,300	9,016,300	

Prob. 16–5A   Continued

WINNER'S EDGE SPORTING GOODS, INC.
Work Sheet for Statement of Cash Flows
For the Year Ended December 31, 2006

	Balance Dec. 31, 2005		Debit		Credit	Balance Dec. 31, 2006
Balance Sheet						
Cash...	395,800	(q)	68,300			464,100
Accounts receivable........................	145,700	(p)	17,500			163,200
Inventories	367,900	(o)	27,100			395,000
Investments......................................	120,000			(e)	120,000	0
Land..	0	(n)	160,000			160,000
Equipment...	575,500	(m)	120,000			695,500
Accumulated depreciation..............	(168,000)			(c)	26,000	(194,000)
Accounts payable	(210,500)			(l)	18,200	(228,700)
Accrued expenses	(21,400)	(k)	4,900			(16,500)
Dividends payable	(10,000)			(j)	4,000	(14,000)
Common stock..................................	(60,000)			(i)	15,000	(75,000)
Paid-in capital in excess of par—						
common stock	(175,000)			(i)	90,000	(265,000)
Retained earnings............................	(960,000)	(h)	56,000	(g)	180,600	(1,084,600)
Totals..	0		453,800		453,800	0

Prob. 16–5A   Concluded

	Balance Dec. 31, 2005	Transactions Debit	Transactions Credit	Balance Dec. 31, 2006
Income Statement				
Sales			(a) 1,580,500	
Cost of merchandise sold		(b) 957,300		
Depreciation expense		(c) 26,000		
Other operating expenses		(d) 329,400		
Gain on sale of investments			(e) 12,000	
Income tax		(f) 99,200		
Net income		(g) 180,600		
Cash Flows				
Operating activities:				
Cash received from customers		(a) 1,580,500	(p) 17,500	
Cash payments:				
Merchandise		(l) 18,200	(b) 957,300	
			(o) 27,100	
Operating expenses			(d) 329,400	
			(k) 4,900	
Income taxes			(f) 99,200	
Investing activities:				
Purchase of equipment			(m) 120,000	
Sale of investments		(e) 132,000		
Purchase of land			(n) 160,000	
Financing activities:				
Declaration of cash dividends			(h) 56,000	
Increase in dividends payable		(j) 4,000		
Issuance of common stock		(i) 105,000		
Net increase in cash			(q) 68,300	
Totals		3,432,200	3,432,200	

Prob. 16–1B

TRUE-TREAD FLOORING CO.
Statement of Cash Flows
For the Year Ended June 30, 2006

Cash flows from operating activities:			
Net income, per income statement................		$ 46,100	
Add: Depreciation	$ 7,700		
Increase in accounts payable...............	4,100		
Increase in accrued expenses..............	900		
Loss on sale of investments................	4,000	16,700	
		$ 62,800	
Deduct: Increase in accounts receivable	$ 3,800		
Increase in inventories....................	13,100	16,900	
Net cash flow from operating activities			$ 45,900
Cash flows from investing activities:			
Cash received from sale of investments.......		$ 41,000	
Less: Cash paid for purchase of land...........	$105,500		
Cash paid for purchase of equipment...	25,200	130,700	
Net cash flow used for investing activities			(89,700)
Cash flows from financing activities:			
Cash received from sale of common stock ..		$105,000	
Less cash paid for dividends		46,000*	
Net cash flow provided by financing activities			59,000
Increase in cash...			$ 15,200
Cash at the beginning of the year			53,700
Cash at the end of the year.................................			$ 68,900

*$48,000 + $10,000 – $12,000 = $46,000

TRUE-TREAD FLOORING CO.
Work Sheet for Statement of Cash Flows
For the Year Ended June 30, 2006

	Balance June 30, 2005	Transactions Debit	Transactions Credit	Balance June 30, 2006
Cash....................................	53,700	(m) 15,200		68,900
Accounts receivable......................	85,400	(l) 3,800		89,200
Inventories	132,700	(k) 13,100		145,800
Investments...................................	45,000		(j) 45,000	0
Land..	0	(i) 105,500		105,500
Equipment.....................................	185,600	(h) 25,200		210,800
Accumulated depreciation—				
equipment................................	(45,100)		(g) 7,700	(52,800)
Accounts payable	(100,200)		(f) 4,100	(104,300)
Accrued expenses	(14,300)		(e) 900	(15,200)
Dividends payable	(10,000)		(d) 2,000	(12,000)
Common stock...............................	(50,000)		(c) 5,000	(55,000)
Paid-in capital in excess of par—				
common stock	(100,000)		(c) 100,000	(200,000)
Retained earnings..........................	(182,800)	(b) 48,000	(a) 46,100	(180,900)
Totals...	0	210,800	210,800	0
Operating activities:				
Net income		(a) 46,100		
Increase in accrued expenses		(e) 900		
Increase in accounts payable ..		(f) 4,100		
Depreciation		(g) 7,700		
Loss on sale of investments		(j) 4,000		
Increase in inventories			(k) 13,100	
Increase in accounts receivable			(l) 3,800	
Investing activities:				
Purchase of equipment			(h) 25,200	
Purchase of land			(i) 105,500	
Sale of investments		(j) 41,000		
Financing activities:				
Declaration of cash dividends ..			(b) 48,000	
Sale of common stock..............		(c) 105,000		
Increase in dividends payable ..		(d) 2,000		
Net increase in cash......................			(m) 15,200	
Totals...		210,800	210,800	

Prob. 16–2B

SKY-MATE LUGGAGE COMPANY
Statement of Cash Flows
For the Year Ended December 31, 2006

Cash flows from operating activities:			
Net income, per income statement................		$ 140,500	
Add: Depreciation	$29,500		
Amortization of patents	4,000		
Decrease in inventories..........................	48,500	82,000	
		$ 222,500	
Deduct: Increase in accounts receivable	$27,800		
Increase in prepaid expenses	1,500		
Decrease in accounts payable	11,400		
Decrease in salaries payable...........	3,000	43,700	
Net cash flow from operating activities			$178,800
Cash flows from investing activities:			
Cash paid for construction of building		$ 175,000	
Net cash flow used for investing activities...			(175,000)
Cash flows from financing activities:			
Cash received from issuance of			
mortgage note		$ 70,000	
Less: Cash paid for dividends......................		55,000*	
Net cash flow provided by			
financing activities......................................			15,000
Increase in cash..			$ 18,800
Cash at the beginning of the year			165,400
Cash at the end of the year................................			$184,200
Schedule of noncash financing and investing activities:			
Issuance of common stock to retire bonds ..			$ 102,000

*$60,000 + $10,000 – $15,000 = $55,000

SKY-MATE LUGGAGE COMPANY
Work Sheet for Statement of Cash Flows
For the Year Ended December 31, 2006

	Balance Dec. 31, 2005	Transactions Debit	Transactions Credit	Balance Dec. 31, 2006
Cash..	165,400	(p) 18,800		184,200
Accounts receivable (net)	224,300	(o) 27,800		252,100
Inventories	348,700		(n) 48,500	300,200
Prepaid expenses	8,000	(m) 1,500		9,500
Land...	120,000			120,000
Buildings	425,000	(l) 175,000		600,000
Accumulated depreciation— buildings...................................	(194,000)		(k) 21,000	(215,000)
Machinery and equipment..............	310,000			310,000
Accumulated depreciation— machinery and equipment........	(75,000)		(j) 8,500	(83,500)
Patents	54,000		(i) 4,000	50,000
Accounts payable	(295,700)	(h) 11,400		(284,300)
Dividends payable	(10,000)		(g) 5,000	(15,000)
Salaries payable............................	(22,500)	(f) 3,000		(19,500)
Mortgage note payable...................	0		(e) 70,000	(70,000)
Bonds payable	(102,000)	(d) 102,000		—
Common stock...............................	(20,000)		(c) 2,000	(22,000)
Paid-in capital in excess of par— common stock	(50,000)		(c) 100,000	(150,000)
Retained earnings..........................	(886,200)	(b) 60,000	(a) 140,500	(966,700)
Totals...	0	399,500	399,500	0

	Balance Dec. 31, 2005	Transactions		Balance Dec. 31, 2006
		Debit	Credit	
Operating activities:				
Net income		(a) 140,500		
Decrease in salaries payable ...			(f) 3,000	
Decrease in accounts payable			(h) 11,400	
Amortization of patents		(i) 4,000		
Depreciation—machinery and equipment............................		(j) 8,500		
Depreciation—buildings...........		(k) 21,000		
Increase in prepaid expenses			(m) 1,500	
Decrease in inventories............		(n) 48,500		
Increase in accounts receivable			(o) 27,800	
Investing activities:				
Construction of building			(l) 175,000	
Financing activities:				
Declaration of cash dividends			(b) 60,000	
Issuance of mortgage note payable................................		(e) 70,000		
Increase in dividends payable		(g) 5,000		
Schedule of noncash investing and financing activities:				
Issuance of common stock to retire bonds		(c) 102,000	(d) 102,000	
Net increase in cash			(p) 18,800	
Totals...		399,500	399,500	

Prob. 16–3B

BUILDER'S SUPPLY CO.
Statement of Cash Flows
For the Year Ended December 31, 2006

Cash flows from operating activities:			
Net income, per income statement.............		$ 72,800	
Add: Depreciation	$ 31,400		
Increase in income tax payable	700		
Decrease in prepaid expenses	1,100	33,200	
		$106,000	
Deduct: Increase in accounts receivable ..	$ 7,200		
Increase in inventories..................	17,900		
Decrease in accounts payable	3,500		
Gain on sale of land	6,000	34,600	
Net cash flow from operating activities			$ 71,400
Cash flows from investing activities:			
Cash received from land sold		$ 31,000	
Less: Cash paid for acquisition			
of building.....................................	$175,000		
Cash paid for purchase			
of equipment.................................	39,200	214,200	
Net cash flow used for investing			
activities			(183,200)
Cash flows from financing activities:			
Cash received from issuance of			
bonds payable...	$ 40,000		
Cash received from issuance of			
common stock	82,000	$122,000	
Less: Cash paid for dividends....................		15,000	
Net cash flow provided by financing			
activities			107,000
Decrease in cash			$ (4,800)
Cash at the beginning of the year			45,200
Cash at the end of the year..............................			$ 40,400

BUILDER'S SUPPLY CO.
Work Sheet for Statement of Cash Flows
For the Year Ended December 31, 2006

	Balance Dec. 31, 2005	Transactions Debit		Transactions Credit		Balance Dec. 31, 2006
Cash...	45,200			(p)	4,800	40,400
Accounts receivable	87,900	(o)	7,200			95,100
Inventories	122,800	(n)	17,900			140,700
Prepaid expenses	5,000			(m)	1,100	3,900
Land..	100,000			(l)	25,000	75,000
Buildings	140,000	(k)	175,000			315,000
Accumulated depreciation— buildings...................................	(58,300)			(j)	11,900	(70,200)
Equipment......................................	210,400	(i)	39,200	(h)	24,000	225,600
Accumulated depreciation— equipment................................	(85,900)	(h)	24,000	(g)	19,500	(81,400)
Accounts payable	(100,500)	(f)	3,500			(97,000)
Income tax payable........................	(6,400)			(e)	700	(7,100)
Bonds payable	0			(d)	40,000	(40,000)
Common stock...............................	(30,000)			(c)	2,000	(32,000)
Paid-in capital in excess of par— common stock	(120,000)			(c)	80,000	(200,000)
Retained earnings..........................	(310,200)	(b)	15,000	(a)	72,800	(368,000)
Totals...	0		281,800		281,800	0
Operating activities:						
Net income		(a)	72,800			
Increase in income tax payable		(e)	700			
Decrease in accounts payable				(f)	3,500	
Depreciation—equipment.........		(g)	19,500			
Depreciation—buildings...........		(j)	11,900			
Gain on sale of land.................				(l)	6,000	
Decrease in prepaid expenses		(m)	1,100			
Increase in inventories				(n)	17,900	
Increase in accounts receivable				(o)	7,200	
Investing activities:						
Purchase of equipment				(i)	39,200	
Acquisition of building				(k)	175,000	
Sale of land..............................		(l)	31,000			
Financing activities:						
Payment of cash dividends......				(b)	15,000	
Issuance of bonds payable		(d)	40,000			
Issuance of common stock......		(c)	82,000			
Net decrease in cash		(p)	4,800			
Totals...			263,800		263,800	

Prob. 16–4B

HEAVEN'S BOUNTY NURSERY INC.
Statement of Cash Flows
For the Year Ended December 31, 2007

Cash flows from operating activities:			
Cash received from customers...................		$951,500[1]	
Deduct: Cash payments for			
merchandise	$510,700[2]		
Cash payments for operating			
expenses	260,500[3]		
Cash payments for income tax.....	69,400	840,600	
Net cash flow from operating activities			$110,900
Cash flows from investing activities:			
Cash received from sale of investments....		$132,000	
Less: Cash paid for land	$140,000		
Cash paid for equipment	80,000	220,000	
Net cash flow used for investing			
activities			(88,000)
Cash flows from financing activities:			
Cash received from sale of			
common stock		$ 82,000	
Less: Cash paid for dividends.....................		125,000*	
Net cash flow used for			
financing activities................................			(43,000)
Decrease in cash			$ (20,100)
Cash at the beginning of the year....................			154,300
Cash at the end of the year...............................			$134,200

Schedule Reconciling Net Income with Cash Flows from Operating Activities:

Net income, per income statement.............		$137,200	
Add: Depreciation	$18,900		
Increase in accounts payable	16,700	35,600	
		$172,800	
Deduct: Increase in accounts receivable ..	$13,500		
Increase in inventories..................	24,200		
Decrease in accrued expenses	2,200		
Gain on sale of investments.........	22,000	61,900	
Net cash flow from operating activities		$110,900	

*Dividends paid: $126,700 + $30,400 – $32,100 = $125,000

Prob. 16–4B   Continued

Computations:

1. Sales.. $965,000
   Deduct increase in accounts receivable 13,500
   Cash received from customers...................................... $951,500

2. Cost of merchandise sold $503,200
   Add increase in inventories 24,200
                                              $527,400
   Deduct increase in accounts payable 16,700
   Cash payments for merchandise................................... $510,700

3. Operating expenses other than depreciation $258,300
   Add decrease in accrued expenses 2,200
   Cash payments for operating expenses $260,500

Prob. 16–4B   Continued

HEAVEN'S BOUNTY NURSERY INC.
Work Sheet for Statement of Cash Flows
For the Year Ended December 31, 2007

	Balance Dec. 31, 2006	Transactions Debit		Transactions Credit		Balance Dec. 31, 2007
Balance Sheet						
Cash....................................	154,300			(q)	20,100	134,200
Accounts receivable.......................	189,700	(p)	13,500			203,200
Inventories	243,700	(o)	24,200			267,900
Investments..................................	110,000			(e)	110,000	0
Land..	0	(n)	140,000			140,000
Equipment......................................	210,000	(m)	80,000			290,000
Accumulated depreciation	(93,400)			(c)	18,900	(112,300)
Accounts payable	(175,400)			(l)	16,700	(192,100)
Accrued expenses	(14,600)	(k)	2,200			(12,400)
Dividends payable	(30,400)			(j)	1,700	(32,100)
Common stock..............................	(8,000)			(i)	2,000	(10,000)
Paid-in capital in excess of par—						
common stock	(100,000)			(i)	80,000	(180,000)
Retained earnings..........................	(485,900)	(h)	126,700	(g)	137,200	(496,400)
Totals...	0		386,600		386,600	0

	Balance Dec. 31, 2006	Transactions Debit	Transactions Credit	Balance Dec. 31, 2007
Income Statement				
Sales			(a) 965,000	
Cost of merchandise sold		(b) 503,200		
Depreciation expense		(c) 18,900		
Other operating expenses		(d) 258,300		
Gain on sale of investments			(e) 22,000	
Income tax		(f) 69,400		
Net income		(g) 137,200		
Cash Flows				
Operating activities:				
Cash received from customers		(a) 965,000	(p) 13,500	
Cash payments:				
Merchandise		(l) 16,700	(b) 503,200	
			(o) 24,200	
Operating expenses			(d) 258,300	
			(k) 2,200	
Income taxes			(f) 69,400	
Investing activities:				
Purchase of equipment			(m) 80,000	
Sale of investments		(e) 132,000		
Purchase of land			(n) 140,000	
Financing activities:				
Declaration of cash dividends			(h) 126,700	
Increase in dividends payable		(j) 1,700		
Issuance of common stock		(i) 82,000		
Net decrease in cash		(q) 20,100		
Totals		2,204,500	2,204,500	

Prob. 16–5B

TRUE-TREAD FLOORING CO.
Statement of Cash Flows
For the Year Ended June 30, 2006

Cash flows from operating activities:			
Cash received from customers..................		$ 941,400[1]	
Deduct: Cash payments for merchandise	$674,900[2]		
Cash payments for operating expenses.....................................	192,500[3]		
Cash payments for income tax.....	28,100	895,500	
Net cash flow from operating activities			$ 45,900
Cash flows from investing activities:			
Cash received from sale of investments....		$ 41,000	
Less: Cash paid for purchase of land........	$105,500		
Cash paid for purchase of equipment.....................................	25,200	130,700	
Net cash flow used for investing activities			(89,700)
Cash flows from financing activities:			
Cash received from sale of common stock		$ 105,000	
Less cash paid for dividends.......................		46,000*	
Net cash flow provided by financing activities			59,000
Increase in cash...			$ 15,200
Cash at the beginning of the year			53,700
Cash at the end of the year.............................			$ 68,900

Schedule Reconciling Net Income with Cash Flows from Operating Activities:

Net income, per income statement.............		$46,100	
Add: Depreciation.......................................	$ 7,700		
Increase in accounts payable...........	4,100		
Increase in accrued expenses..........	900		
Loss on sale of investments	4,000	16,700	
		$62,800	
Deduct: Increase in accounts receivable ..	$ 3,800		
Increase in inventories..................	13,100	16,900	
Net cash flow from operating activities		$45,900	

*Dividends paid: $48,000 + $10,000 – $12,000 = $46,000

Prob. 16–5B   Continued

Computations:

1. Sales... $945,200
   Deduct increase in accounts receivable........................ 3,800
   Cash received from customers..................................... $941,400

2. Cost of merchandise sold $665,900
   Add increase in inventories 13,100
                                        $679,000
   Deduct increase in accounts payable 4,100
   Cash payments for merchandise.................................. $674,900

3. Operating expenses other than depreciation $193,400
   Deduct increase in accrued expenses 900
   Cash payments for operating expenses $192,500

Prob. 16–5B   Continued

TRUE-TREAD FLOORING CO.
Work Sheet for Statement of Cash Flows
For the Year Ended June 30, 2006

	Balance June 30, 2005	Transactions Debit		Transactions Credit		Balance June 30, 2006
Balance Sheet						
Cash..	53,700	(q)	15,200			68,900
Accounts receivable........................	85,400	(p)	3,800			89,200
Inventories	132,700	(o)	13,100			145,800
Investments.....................................	45,000			(e)	45,000	0
Land..	0	(n)	105,500			105,500
Equipment..	185,600	(m)	25,200			210,800
Accumulated depreciation	(45,100)			(c)	7,700	(52,800)
Accounts payable	(100,200)			(l)	4,100	(104,300)
Accrued expenses	(14,300)			(k)	900	(15,200)
Dividends payable	(10,000)			(j)	2,000	(12,000)
Common stock................................	(50,000)			(i)	5,000	(55,000)
Paid-in capital in excess of par—						
common stock	(100,000)			(i)	100,000	(200,000)
Retained earnings...........................	(182,800)	(h)	48,000	(g)	46,100	(180,900)
Totals...	0		210,800		210,800	0

	Balance June 30, 2005	Transactions		Balance June 30, 2006
		Debit	Credit	
Income Statement				
Sales			(a) 945,200	
Cost of merchandise sold		(b) 665,900		
Depreciation expense		(c) 7,700		
Other operating expenses		(d) 193,400		
Loss on sale of investments		(e) 4,000		
Income tax		(f) 28,100		
Net income		(g) 46,100		
Cash Flows				
Operating activities:				
Cash received from customers		(a) 945,200	(p) 3,800	
Cash payments:				
Merchandise		(l) 4,100	(b) 665,900	
			(o) 13,100	
			(d) 193,400	
Operating expenses		(k) 900		
Income taxes			(f) 28,100	
Investing activities:				
Purchase of equipment			(m) 25,200	
Sale of investments		(e) 41,000		
Purchase of land			(n) 105,500	
Financing activities:				
Declaration of cash dividends			(h) 48,000	
Increase in dividends payable		(j) 2,000		
Issuance of common stock		(i) 105,000		
Net increase in cash			(q) 15,200	
Totals		2,043,400	2,043,400	

SPECIAL ACTIVITIES

Activity 16–1

Although this situation might seem harmless at first, it is, in fact, a gross violation of generally accepted accounting principles. The operating cash flow per share figure should not be shown on the face of the income statement. The income statement is constructed under accrual accounting concepts, while operating cash flow "undoes" the accounting accruals. Thus, unlike Karen's assertion that this information would be useful, more likely the information could be confusing to users. Some users might not be able to distinguish between earnings and operating cash flow per share—or how to interpret the difference. By agreeing with Karen, Jeff has breached his professional ethics because the disclosure would violate generally accepted accounting principles. On a more subtle note, Karen is being somewhat disingenuous. Apparently, Karen is not pleased with this year's operating performance and would like to cover the earnings "bad news" with some cash flow "good news" disclosures. An interesting question is: Would Karen be as interested in the dual per share disclosures in the opposite scenario—with earnings per share improving and cash flow per share deteriorating? Probably not.

Activity 16–2

Start-up companies are unique in that they frequently will have negative retained earnings and operating cash flows. The negative retained earnings are often due to losses from high start-up expenses. The negative operating cash flows are typical because growth requires cash. Growth must be financed with cash before the cash returns. For example, a company must expend cash to make the service in Period 1 before selling it and receiving cash in Period 2. The start-up company constantly faces spending cash today for the next period's growth. For OmniTech Inc., the money spent on salaries to develop the business is a cash outflow that must occur before the service provides revenues. In addition, the company must use cash to market its service to potential customers. In this situation, the only way the company stays in business is from the capital provided by the owners. This owner-supplied capital is the lifeblood of a start-up company. Banks will not likely lend money on this type of venture (except with assets as security). OmniTech Inc. could be a good investment. It all depends on whether the new service has promise. The financial figures will not reveal this easily. Only actual sales will reveal if the service is a hit. Until this time the company is at risk. If the service is not popular, the company will have no cash to fall back on—it will likely go bankrupt. If, however, the service is successful, then OmniTech Inc. should become self-sustaining and provide a good return for the shareholders.

Activity 16–3

The senior vice president is very focused on profitability but has been bleeding cash. The increase in accounts receivable and inventory is striking. Apparently, the new credit card campaign has found many new customers, since the accounts receivable is growing. Unfortunately, it appears as though the new campaign has done a poor job of screening creditworthiness in these new customers. In other words, there are many new credit card purchasers—unfortunately, they do not appear to be paying off their balances. The new merchandise purchases appear to be backfiring. The company has received some "good deals," except that they are only "good deals" if it can resell the merchandise. If the merchandise has no customer appeal, then that would explain the inventory increase. In other words, the division is purchasing merchandise that sits on the shelf, regardless of pricing. The reduction in payables is the result of the division becoming overdue on payments. The memo reports that most of the past due payables have been paid. This situation is critical in the retailing business. A retailer cannot afford a poor payment history, or it will be denied future merchandise shipments. This is a signal of severe cash problems. Overall, the picture is of a retailer having severe operating cash flow difficulties.

Note to Instructors: This scenario is essentially similar to KMART's path to eventual bankruptcy. It reported earnings, while having significant negative cash flows from operations due to expanding credit too liberally (increases in accounts receivable) and purchasing too much unsaleable inventory (increases in inventory). Eventually, KMART's inventory write-down resulted in significant losses about the time it entered bankruptcy.

Activity 16–4

a. 1. Normal practice for determining the amount of cash flows from operating activities during the year is to begin with the reported net income. This net income must ordinarily be adjusted upward and/or downward to determine the amount of cash flows. Although many operating expenses decrease cash, depreciation does not do so. The amount of net income understates the amount of cash flows provided by operations to the extent that depreciation expense is deducted from revenue. Accordingly, the depreciation expense for the year must be added back to the reported net income in arriving at cash flows from operating activities.

2. Generally accepted accounting principles require that significant transactions affecting future cash flows should be reported in a separate schedule to the statement, even though they do not affect cash. Accordingly, even though the issuance of the common stock for land does not affect cash, the transaction affects future cash flows and must be reported.

3. The $42,500 cash received from the sale of the investments is reported in the cash flows from investing activities section. Since the sale included a gain of $7,500, to avoid double reporting of this amount, the gain is deducted from net income to remove it from the determination of cash flows from operating activities.

4. The balance sheets for the last two years will indicate the increase in cash but will not indicate the firm's activities in meeting its financial obligations, paying dividends, and maintaining and expanding operating capacity. Such information, as provided by the statement of cash flows, assists creditors in assessing the firm's solvency and profitability—two very important factors bearing on the evaluation of a potential loan.

b. The statement of cash flows indicates a strong liquidity position for Kitchens By Design, Inc. The increase in cash of $76,400 for the past year is more than adequate to cover the $50,000 of new building and store equipment costs that will not be provided by the loan. Thus, the statement of cash flows most likely will enhance the company's chances of receiving a loan. However, other information, such as a projection of future earnings, a description of collateral pledged to support the loan, and an independent credit report, would normally be considered before a final loan decision is made.

CHAPTER 17
FINANCIAL STATEMENT ANALYSIS

CLASS DISCUSSION QUESTIONS

1. Horizontal analysis is the percentage analysis of increases and decreases in corresponding statements. The percent change in the cash balances at the end of the preceding year from the end of the current year is an example. Vertical analysis is the percentage analysis showing the relationship of the component parts to the total in a single statement. The percent of cash as a portion of total assets at the end of the current year is an example.

2. Comparative statements provide information as to changes between dates or periods. Trends indicated by comparisons may be far more significant than the data for a single date or period.

3. Before this question can be answered, the increase in net income should be compared with changes in sales, expenses, and assets devoted to the business for the current year. The return on assets for both periods should also be compared. If these comparisons indicate favorable trends, the operating performance has improved; if not, the apparent favorable increase in net income may be offset by unfavorable trends in other areas.

4. You should first determine if the expense amount in the base year (denominator) is significant. A 100% or more increase of a very small expense item may be of little concern. However, if the expense amount in the base year is significant, then over a 100% increase may require further investigation.

5. Generally, the two ratios would be very close, because most service businesses sell services and hold very little inventory.

6. The amount of working capital and the change in working capital are just two indicators of the strength of the current position. A comparison of the current ratio and the quick ratio, along with the amount of working capital, gives a better analysis of the current position. Such a comparison shows:

	Current Year	Preceding Year
Working capital	$42,500	$37,500
Current ratio	2.0	2.5
Quick ratio..............	0.8	1.2

It is apparent that, although working capital has increased, the current ratio has fallen from 2.5 to 2.0, and the quick ratio has fallen from 1.2 to 0.8.

7. The bulk of Wal-Mart sales are to final customers that pay with credit cards or cash. In either case, there is no accounts receivable. Procter and Gamble, in contrast, sells almost exclusively to other businesses, such as Wal-Mart. Such sales are "on account," and thus, create accounts receivable that must be collected. A recent financial statement showed Wal-Mart's accounts receivable turning 109 times, while Procter and Gamble's turned only 13 times.

8. No, an accounts receivable turnover of 6 with sales on a n/30 basis is not satisfactory. It indicates that accounts receivable are collected, on the average, in one-sixth of a year, or approximately 60 days from the date of sale. Assuming that some customers pay within the 30-day term, it indicates that other accounts are running beyond 60 days. It is also possible that there is a substantial amount of past-due accounts of doubtful collectibility on the books.

9. a. A high inventory turnover minimizes the amount invested in inventories, thus freeing funds for more advantageous use. Storage costs, administrative expenses, and losses caused by obsolescence and adverse changes in prices are also kept to a minimum.

   b. Yes. The inventory turnover could be high because the quantity of inventory on hand is very low. This condition might result in the lack of sufficient goods on hand to meet sales orders.

c. Yes. The inventory turnover relates to the "turnover" of inventory during the year, while the number of days' sales in inventory relates to the amount of inventory on hand at the end of the year. Therefore, a business could have a high inventory turnover *for the year*, yet have a high number of days' sales in inventory at the *end of the year.*

10. The ratio of fixed assets to long-term liabilities increased from 2 for the preceding year to 2.5 for the current year, indicating that the company is in a stronger position now than in the preceding year to borrow additional funds on a long-term basis.

11. a. Due to leverage, the rate on stockholders' equity will often be greater than the rate on total assets. This occurs because the amount earned on assets acquired through the use of funds provided by creditors exceeds the interest charges paid to creditors.

    b. Higher. The concept of leverage applies to preferred stock as well as debt. The rate earned on common stockholders' equity ordinarily exceeds the rate earned on total stockholders' equity because the amount earned on assets acquired through the use of funds provided by preferred stockholders normally exceeds the dividends paid to preferred stockholders.

12. The earnings per share in the preceding year were $20 per share ($40/2), adjusted for the stock split in the latest year.

13. A share of common stock is currently selling at 10 times current annual earnings.

14. The dividend yield on common stock is a measure of the rate of return to common stockholders in terms of cash dividend distributions. Companies in growth industries typically reinvest a significant portion of the amount earned in common stockholders' equity to expand operations rather than to return earnings to stockholders in the form of cash dividends.

15. During periods when sales are increasing, it is likely that a company will increase its inventories and expand its plant. Such situations frequently result in an increase in current liabilities out of proportion to the increase in current assets and thus lower the current ratio.

EXERCISES

Ex. 17–1

a.

HOME-MATE APPLIANCE CO.
Comparative Income Statement
For the Years Ended December 31, 2006 and 2005

	2006		2005	
	Amount	Percent	Amount	Percent
Sales	$500,000	100.0%	$450,000	100.0%
Cost of goods sold	275,000	55.0	234,000	52.0
Gross profit...............................	$225,000	45.0%	$216,000	48.0%
Selling expenses	$ 90,000	18.0%	$ 94,500	21.0%
Administrative expenses	60,000	12.0	63,000	14.0
Total operating expenses	$150,000	30.0%	$157,500	35.0%
Income from operations............	$ 75,000	15.0%	$ 58,500	13.0%
Income tax expense	25,000	5.0	22,500	5.0
Net income	$ 50,000	10.0%	$ 36,000	8.0%

b. The vertical analysis indicates that the cost of goods sold as a percent of
    sales increased by 3 percentage points (55% – 52%) between 2005 and 2006.
    However, the selling expenses and administrative expenses improved by 5
    percentage points. Thus, the net income as a percent of sales improved by 2
    percentage points.

Ex. 17–10

a. (1) Accounts receivable turnover: $\dfrac{\text{Net sales on account}}{\text{Average accounts receivable}}$

Sears: $\dfrac{\$35,698}{(\$28,155 + \$30,759)/2} = 1.2$

Federated: $\dfrac{\$15,434}{(\$2,379 + \$2,945)/2} = 5.8$

(2) Number of days' sales in receivables: $\dfrac{\text{Accounts receivable, end of year}}{\text{Average daily sales on account}}$

Sears: $\dfrac{\$30,759}{\$97.8^1} = 314.5$ days

Federated: $\dfrac{\$2,945}{\$42.3^2} = 69.6$ days

$^1\$97.8 = \$35,698 \div 365$ days
$^2\$42.3 = \$15,434 \div 365$ days

b. Sears' accounts receivable turnover is much less than Federated's (1.2 for Sears vs. 5.8 for Federated). Likewise, the number of days' sales in receivables is much greater for Sears than for Federated (314.4 days for Sears vs. 69.6 days for Federated). These differences must be interpreted with care. Sears has significant MasterCard receivables with customers who have not made purchases from Sears, which represent receivables that do no correspond to Sears' sales. Thus, it is not surprising that Sears has a much lower turnover than does Federated, since the accounts receivable include receivables that are outside of the Sears retail network. In addition, we do not know how much of the Sears or Federated sales are on credit; thus, it is not possible to accurately compare the number of days' sales in receivables with credit terms.

Note to Instructors: The annual 10-K for Federated indicated that the sales through its proprietary credit card was $4,128. Thus, the accounts receivable turnover based on this number would be 1.6 ($4,128 ÷ $2,662), while the number of days' sales in receivables would be 260.6 days ($2,945 ÷ $11.3). Thus, the calculations in part a. above actually overstate Federated's accounts receivable turnover and understates Federated's credit card days' sales in receivables. This exercise helps the student see the importance of interpreting these ratios carefully. In the case of Sears, much of the receivables are not related to Sears' sales, which distorts the ratio. In the case of Federated, only $4,128 million in sales were on account, thus actually overstating its accounts receivable turnover and understating its days' sales in receivable, relative to the sales on account.

Ex. 17–11

a. (1) Inventory turnover: $\dfrac{\text{Cost of goods sold}}{\text{Average inventory}}$

2006: $\dfrac{\$328,000}{(\$42,000 + \$40,000)/2} = 8.0$

2005: $\dfrac{\$430,000}{(\$44,000 + \$42,000)/2} = 10.0$

(2) Number of days' sales in inventory: $\dfrac{\text{Inventory, end of year}}{\text{Average daily cost of goods sold}}$

2006: $\dfrac{\$40,000}{\$899^{1}} = 44.49$ days

2005: $\dfrac{\$42,000}{\$1,178^{2}} = 35.65$ days

[1] $\$899 = \$328,000 \div 365$ days

[2] $\$1,178 = \$430,000 \div 365$ days

b. The inventory position of the business has deteriorated. The inventory turnover has decreased, while the number of days' sales in inventory has increased. The sales volume has declined faster than the inventory has declined, thus resulting in the deteriorating inventory position.

Ex. 17–16

a. Ratio of net sales to total assets: $\dfrac{\text{Net sales}}{\text{Total assets}}$

Yellow Corp.: $\dfrac{\$3,276,651}{\$1,285,777} = 2.55$

Union Pacific: $\dfrac{\$11,973,000}{\$31,551,000} = 0.38$

C.H. Robinson Worldwide: $\dfrac{\$3,090,072}{\$683,490} = 4.52$

b. The ratio of net sales to assets measures the number of sales dollars earned for each dollar of assets. The greater the number of sales dollars earned for every dollar of assets, the more efficient a firm is in using assets. Thus, the ratio is a measure of the efficiency in using assets. The three companies are different in their efficiency in using assets, because they are different in the nature of their operations. Union Pacific earns only 38 cents for every dollar of assets. This is because Union Pacific is very asset intensive. That is, Union Pacific must invest in locomotives, railcars, terminals, tracks, right-of-way, and information systems in order to earn revenues. These investments are significant. Yellow Corp. is able to earn $2.55 for every dollar of assets, and thus, is able to earn more revenue for every dollar of assets than the railroad. This is because the motor carrier invests in trucks, trailers, and terminals, which require less investment per dollar of revenue than does the railroad. Moreover, the motor carrier does not invest in the highway system, because the government owns the highway system. Thus, the motor carrier has no investment in the transportation network itself unlike the railroad. The transportation arranger hires transportation services from motor carriers and railroads, but does not own these assets itself. The transportation arranger has assets in accounts receivable and information systems but does not require transportation assets; thus, it is able to earn the highest revenue per dollar of assets.

Ex. 17–16   Concluded

Note to Instructors: Students may wonder how asset intensive companies overcome their asset efficiency disadvantages to competitors with better asset efficiencies, as in the case between railroads and motor carriers. Asset efficiency is part of the financial equation; the other part is the profit margin made on each dollar of sales. Thus, companies with high asset efficiency often operate on thinner margins than do companies with lower asset efficiency. For example, the motor carrier must pay highway taxes, which lowers its operating margins when compared to railroads that own their right-of-way, and thus do not have the tax expense of the highway. In this exercise the railroad has the highest profit margins, the motor carrier is in the middle, while the transportation arranger operates on very thin margins.

Ex. 17–17

a.   Rate earned on total assets: $\dfrac{\text{Net income plus interest}}{\text{Average total assets}}$

2007: $\dfrac{\$150,000 + \$15,000}{\$1,375,000 *} = 12.0\%$ 2006: $\dfrac{\$180,000 + \$15,000}{\$1,200,000 **} = 16.25\%$

*($1,300,000 + $1,450,000) ÷ 2   **($1,100,000 + $1,300,000) ÷ 2

Rate earned on stockholders' equity: $\dfrac{\text{Net income}}{\text{Average stockholders' equity}}$

2007: $\dfrac{\$150,000}{\$1,080,000 *} = 13.89\%$ 2006: $\dfrac{\$180,000}{\$935,000 **} = 19.25\%$

*($1,015,000 + $1,145,000) ÷ 2   **($855,000 + $1,015,000) ÷ 2

Rate earned on
common stockholders' equity: $\dfrac{\text{Net income less preferred dividends}}{\text{Average common stockholders' equity}}$

2007: $\dfrac{\$150,000 - \$20,000}{\$880,000 *} = 14.77\%$ 2006: $\dfrac{\$180,000 - \$20,000}{\$735,000 **} = 21.77\%$

*($815,000 + $945,000) ÷ 2   **($655,000 + $815,000) ÷ 2

b.   The profitability ratios indicate that Yellowstone's profitability has deteriorated. Most of this change is from net income falling from $180,000 in 2006 to $150,000 in 2007. The cost of debt is 8%. Since the rate of return on assets exceeds this amount in either year, there is positive leverage from use of debt. However, this leverage is greater in 2006 because the rate of return on assets exceeds the cost of debt by a greater amount in 2006.

Ex. 17–18

a. Rate earned on total assets: $\dfrac{\text{Net income} + \text{interest expense}}{\text{Average total assets}}$

2002: $\dfrac{\$80,158 + \$6,886}{(\$883,166 + \$1,010,826)/2} = 9.2\%$ 2001: $\dfrac{\$29,105 + \$6,869}{(\$883,166 + \$848,115)/2} = 4.2\%$

b. Rate earned on stockholders' equity: $\dfrac{\text{Net income}}{\text{Average stockholders' equity}}$

2002: $\dfrac{\$80,158}{(\$883,166 + \$1,010,826)/2} = 12.1\%$ 2001: $\dfrac{\$29,105}{(\$883,166 + \$848,115)/2} = 4.9\%$

c. Both the rate earned on total assets and the rate earned on stockholders' equity have improved over the two-year period. The rate earned on total assets improved from 4.2% to 9.2%, which is over twice the return of the prior year. The rate earned on stockholders' equity improved from 4.9% to 12.1%. The rate earned on stockholders' equity exceeds the rate earned on total assets due to the positive use of leverage.

d. Fiscal year 2002 was a difficult time for the apparel industry. The rate earned on total assets for Ann Taylor, however, exceeded the industry average (9.2% vs. 6%). The rate earned on stockholders' equity was also greater than the industry average (12.1% vs. 7.8%). These relationships suggest that Ann Taylor has more leverage than the industry, on average.

Ex. 17–19

a. Ratio of fixed assets to long-term liabilities: $\dfrac{\text{Fixed assets}}{\text{Long-term liabilities}}$

$$\frac{\$950{,}000}{\$680{,}000} = 1.40$$

b. Ratio of liabilities to stockholders' equity: $\dfrac{\text{Total liabilities}}{\text{Total stockholders' equity}}$

$$\frac{\$725{,}000}{\$1{,}466{,}000} = 0.49$$

c. Ratio of net sales to assets: $\dfrac{\text{Net sales}}{\text{Average total assets (excluding investments)}}$

$$\frac{\$3{,}000{,}000}{\$1{,}900{,}000\,^*} = 1.58$$

*[($2,009,000 + $2,191,000) ÷ 2] – $200,000. The end-of-period total assets are equal to the sum of total liabilities ($725,000) and stockholders' equity ($1,466,000).

d. Rate earned on total assets: $\dfrac{\text{Net income plus interest}}{\text{Average total assets}}$

$$\frac{\$180{,}000 + \$51{,}000}{\$2{,}100{,}000\,^*} = 11.00\%$$

*($2,009,000 + $2,191,000) ÷ 2

e. Rate earned on stockholders' equity: $\dfrac{\text{Net income}}{\text{Average stockholders' equity}}$

$$\frac{\$180{,}000}{\$1{,}408{,}000\,^*} = 12.78\%$$

*[($200,000 + $650,000 + $500,000) + $1,466,000] ÷ 2

f. Rate earned on common stockholders' equity: $\dfrac{\text{Net income less preferred dividends}}{\text{Average common stockholders' equity}}$

$$\frac{\$180{,}000 - \$16{,}000}{\$1{,}208{,}000\,^*} = 13.58\%$$

* [($650,000 + $500,000) + ($650,000 + $616,000)] ÷ 2

Ex. 17–20

a. Number of times bond interest charges were earned: $\dfrac{\text{Income before tax } + \text{ Interest expense}}{\text{Interest expense}}$

$\dfrac{\$450{,}000 + \$180{,}000}{\$180{,}000} = 3.5 \text{ times}$

b. Number of times preferred dividends were earned: $\dfrac{\text{Net income}}{\text{Preferred dividends}}$

$\dfrac{\$325{,}000}{\$25{,}000} = 13 \text{ times}$

c. Earnings per share on common stock: $\dfrac{\text{Net income } - \text{ Preferred dividends}}{\text{Common shares outstanding}}$

$\dfrac{\$325{,}000 - \$25{,}000}{125{,}000 \text{ shares}} = \$2.40$

d. Price-earnings ratio: $\dfrac{\text{Market price per share}}{\text{Earnings per share}}$

$\dfrac{\$50}{\$2.40} = 20.83$

e. Dividends per share of common stock: $\dfrac{\text{Common dividends}}{\text{Common shares outstanding}}$

$\dfrac{\$100{,}000}{125{,}000 \text{ shares}} = \$0.80$

f. Dividend yield: $\dfrac{\text{Common dividend per share}}{\text{Share price}}$

$\dfrac{\$0.80}{\$50.00} = 1.6\%$

Ex. 17–21

a. Earnings per share: $\dfrac{\text{Net income} - \text{Preferred dividends}}{\text{Common shares outstanding}}$

$$\dfrac{\$444{,}000 - \$54{,}000}{200{,}000 \text{ shares}} = \$1.95$$

b. Price-earnings ratio: $\dfrac{\text{Market price per share}}{\text{Earnings per share}}$

$$\dfrac{\$39.00}{\$1.95} = 20$$

c. Dividends per share: $\dfrac{\text{Common dividends}}{\text{Common shares outstanding}}$

$$\dfrac{\$156{,}000}{200{,}000 \text{ shares}} = \$0.78$$

d. Dividend yield: $\dfrac{\text{Common dividend per share}}{\text{Share price}}$

$$\dfrac{\$0.78}{\$39.00} = 2.0\%$$

Ex. 17–22

a. Earnings per share on income before extraordinary items:

Net income..	$ 890,000
Less gain on condemnation	(256,000)
Plus loss from flood damage.......................................	166,000
Income before extraordinary items	$ 800,000

Earnings before extraordinary items per share on common stock:

$\dfrac{\text{Income before extraordinary items} - \text{Preferred dividends}}{\text{Common shares outstanding}}$

$$\dfrac{\$800{,}000 - \$320{,}000}{500{,}000 \text{ shares}} = \$0.96 \text{ per share}$$

b. Earnings per share on common stock: $\dfrac{\text{Net income} - \text{Preferred dividends}}{\text{Common shares outstanding}}$

$$\dfrac{\$890{,}000 - \$320{,}000}{500{,}000 \text{ shares}} = \$1.14 \text{ per share}$$

Ex. 17–23

a. Price-earnings ratio: $\dfrac{\text{Market price per share}}{\text{Earnings per share}}$

Bank of America: $\dfrac{\$68.20}{\$5.91} = 11.54$

eBay: $\dfrac{\$73.56}{\$0.85} = 86.54$

Coca-Cola: $\dfrac{\$40.06}{\$1.68} = 23.85$

Dividend yield: $\dfrac{\text{Dividend per share}}{\text{Market price per share}}$

Bank of America: $\dfrac{\$2.56}{\$68.20} = 3.75\%$

eBay: $\dfrac{\$0}{\$73.56} = 0$

Coca-Cola: $\dfrac{\$0.80}{\$40.06} = 2.0\%$

b. Bank of America has the largest dividend yield, but the smallest price-earnings ratio. Stock market participants value Bank of America common stock on the basis of its dividend. The dividend is an attractive yield at this date. Because of this attractive yield, stock market participants do not expect the share price to grow significantly, hence the low price-earnings valuation. This is a typical pattern for companies that pay high dividends. eBay shows the opposite extreme. eBay pays no dividend, and thus has no dividend yield. However, eBay has the largest price-earnings ratio of the three companies. Stock market participants are expecting a return on their investment from appreciation in the stock price. Some would say that the stock is priced very aggressively at 86.54 times earnings. Coca-Cola is priced in between the other two companies. Coca-Cola has a moderate dividend producing a yield of 2%. The price-earnings ratio is near 24, which is close to the market average at this writing. Thus, Coca-Cola is expected to produce shareholder returns through a combination of some share price appreciation and a small dividend.

PROBLEMS

Prob. 17–1A

1.

TURNBERRY COMPANY
Comparative Income Statement
For the Years Ended December 31, 2006 and 2005

	2006	2005	Increase (Decrease) Amount	Increase (Decrease) Percent
Sales	$482,000	$429,000	$ 53,000	12.35%
Sales returns and allowances	6,000	4,000	2,000	50.00%
Net sales...	$476,000	$425,000	$ 51,000	12.00%
Cost of goods sold	216,000	180,000	36,000	20.00%
Gross profit.....................................	$260,000	$245,000	$ 15,000	6.12%
Selling expenses	$109,250	$ 95,000	$ 14,250	15.00%
Administrative expenses	52,500	30,000	22,500	75.00%
Total operating expenses	$161,750	$125,000	$ 36,750	29.40%
Income from operations...............	$ 98,250	$120,000	$ (21,750)	(18.13)%
Other income	2,000	2,000	0	0.00%
Income before income tax	$100,250	$122,000	$ (21,750)	(17.83)%
Income tax expense	30,000	40,000	(10,000)	(25.00)%
Net income	$ 70,250	$ 82,000	$ (11,750)	(14.33)%

2. Net income has declined from 2005 to 2006. Net sales have increased by 12%; however, cost of goods sold has increased by 20%, causing the gross profit to grow at a rate less than sales relative to the base year. In addition, total operating expenses have increased over twice as fast as sales (29.4% increase vs. 12% net sales increase). Increases in costs and expenses that are higher than the increase in sales have caused the net income to decline by approximately 14%.

Prob. 17–2A

1.

AUDIO TONE COMPANY
Comparative Income Statement
For the Years Ended December 31, 2006 and 2005

	2006 Amount	2006 Percent	2005 Amount	2005 Percent
Sales	$ 664,000	100.61%	$ 526,000	101.15%
Sales returns and allowances ..	4,000	0.61	6,000	1.15
Net sales.....................................	$ 660,000	100.00%	$ 520,000	100.00%
Cost of goods sold	257,400	39.00	213,200	41.00
Gross profit................................	$ 402,600	61.00%	$ 306,800	59.00%
Selling expenses	$ 138,600	21.00%	$ 124,800	24.00%
Administrative expenses	72,600	11.00	67,600	13.00
Total operating expenses	$ 211,200	32.00%	$ 192,400	37.00%
Income from operations............	$ 191,400	29.00%	$ 114,400	22.00%
Other income	2,500	0.38	2,000	0.38
Income before income tax	$ 193,900	29.38%	$ 116,400	22.38%
Income tax expense	54,000	8.18	30,000	5.77
Net income	$ 139,900	21.20%	$ 86,400	16.61%*

*Rounded to next lowest hundredth of a percent

2. The vertical analysis indicates that the costs (cost of goods sold, selling expenses, and administrative expenses) as a percent of sales improved from 2005 to 2006. As a result, net income as a percent of sales increased from 16.61% to 21.20%. The sales promotion campaign appears successful. The selling expenses as a percent of sales declined, suggesting that the increased cost was more than made up by increased sales.

Prob. 17–3A

1. a. Working capital = Current assets – Current liabilities

   $1,255,000 – $590,000 = $665,000

   b. Current ratio = $\dfrac{\text{Current assets}}{\text{Current liabilities}}$

   $\dfrac{\$1,255,000}{\$590,000} = 2.13$

   c. Quick ratio = $\dfrac{\text{Quick assets}}{\text{Current liabilities}}$

   $\dfrac{\$240,000 + \$110,000 + \$380,000}{\$590,000} = 1.24$

2.

| | | | | Supporting Calculations | | |
Transaction	Working Capital	Current Ratio	Quick Ratio	Current Assets	Quick Assets	Current Liabilities
a.	$665,000	2.13	1.24	$1,255,000	$730,000	$590,000
b.	665,000	2.25	1.26	1,195,000	670,000	530,000
c.	665,000	1.99	1.09	1,335,000	730,000	670,000
d.	665,000	2.21	1.25	1,215,000	690,000	550,000
e.	640,000	2.04	1.19	1,255,000	730,000	615,000
f.	665,000	2.13	1.24	1,255,000	730,000	590,000
g.	785,000	2.33	1.44	1,375,000	850,000	590,000
h.	665,000	2.13	1.24	1,255,000	730,000	590,000
i.	915,000	2.55	1.66	1,505,000	980,000	590,000
j.	665,000	2.13	1.22	1,255,000	720,000	590,000

Prob. 17–4A

1. Working capital: $871,000 − $290,000 = $581,000

Ratio	Numerator	Denominator	Calculated Value
2. Current ratio	$871,000	$290,000	3.0
3. Quick ratio	$762,000	$290,000	2.6
4. Accounts receivable turnover	$1,050,000	($165,000 + $199,000)/2	5.8
5. Number of days' sales in receivables	$199,000	($1,050,000/365)	69.2
6. Inventory turnover	$400,000	($84,000 + $52,000)/2	5.9
7. Number of days' sales in inventory..........	$84,000	($400,000/365)	76.7
8. Fixed assets to long-term liabilities................	$1,040,000	$900,000	1.2
9. Liabilities to stock-holders' equity...............	$1,190,000	$1,021,000	1.2
10. Number of times interest charges earned..........................	$109,000 + $96,000	$96,000	2.1
11. Number of times preferred dividends earned..........................	$68,000	$15,000	4.5
12. Ratio of net sales to assets............................	$1,050,000	($1,911,000 + $1,375,000)/2	0.6
13. Rate earned on total assets............................	$68,000 + $96,000	($2,211,000 + $1,575,000)/2	8.7%
14. Rate earned on stock-holders' equity...............	$68,000	($1,021,000 + $925,000)/2	7.0%
15. Rate earned on common stock-holders' equity...............	($68,000 − $15,000)	($771,000 + $725,000)/2	7.1%
16. Earnings per share on common stock	($68,000 − $15,000)	35,000	$1.51
17. Price-earnings ratio	$20.00	$1.51	13.2
18. Dividends per share of common stock	$7,000	35,000	$0.20
19. Dividend yield................	$0.20	$20.00	1.0%

Prob. 17–5A

1.   a.

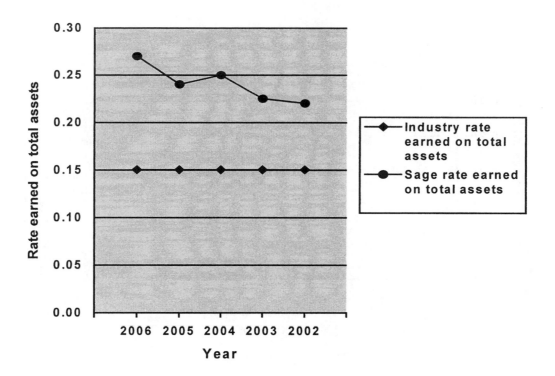

Rate earned on total assets: $\dfrac{\text{Net income} + \text{interest expense}}{\text{Average total assets}}$

2006: $\dfrac{\$1,400,000}{\$5,250,000} = 0.27$ 2003: $\dfrac{\$520,000}{\$2,300,000} = 0.23$

2005: $\dfrac{\$970,000}{\$4,000,000} = 0.24$ 2002: $\dfrac{\$400,000}{\$1,800,000} = 0.22$

2004: $\dfrac{\$750,000}{\$3,050,000} = 0.25$

Prob. 17–5A   Continued

1.   b.

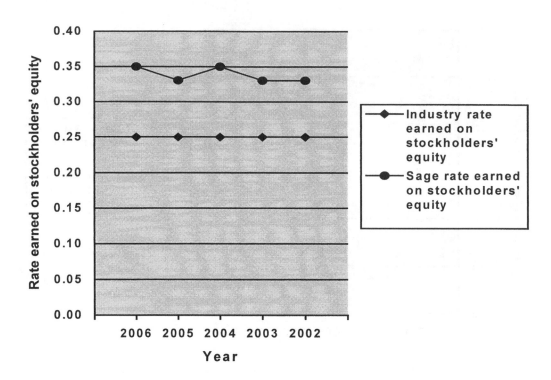

Rate earned on stockholders' equity: $\dfrac{\text{Net income}}{\text{Average stockholders' equity}}$

2006: $\dfrac{\$1,200,000}{\$3,400,000} = 0.35$ 2003: $\dfrac{\$400,000}{\$1,200,000} = 0.33$

2005: $\dfrac{\$800,000}{\$2,400,000} = 0.33$ 2002: $\dfrac{\$300,000}{\$900,000} = 0.33$

2004: $\dfrac{\$600,000}{\$1,700,000} = 0.35$

Prob. 17–5A   Continued

1.   c.

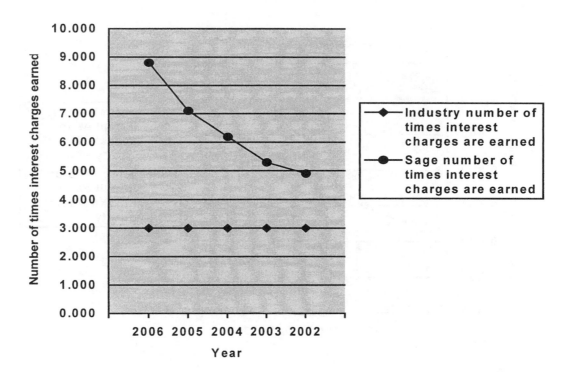

$$\text{Number of times interest charges were earned} = \frac{\text{Net income} + \text{Income tax expense} + \text{Interest expense}}{\text{Interest expense}}$$

2006: $\dfrac{\$1,760,000}{\$200,000} = 8.80$ 2003: $\dfrac{\$640,000}{\$120,000} = 5.33$

2005: $\dfrac{\$1,210,000}{\$170,000} = 7.12$ 2002: $\dfrac{\$490,000}{\$100,000} = 4.90$

2004: $\dfrac{\$930,000}{\$150,000} = 6.20$

Prob. 17–5A   Continued

1. d.

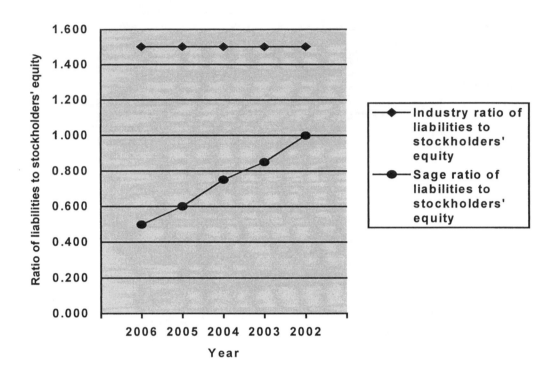

Ratio of liabilities to stockholders' equity: $\dfrac{\text{Total liabilities}}{\text{Total stockholders' equity}}$

2006: $\dfrac{\$2,000,000}{\$4,000,000} = 0.50$ 2003: $\dfrac{\$1,200,000}{\$1,400,000} = 0.86$

2005: $\dfrac{\$1,700,000}{\$2,800,000} = 0.61$ 2002: $\dfrac{\$1,000,000}{\$1,000,000} = 1.00$

2004: $\dfrac{\$1,500,000}{\$2,000,000} = 0.75$

Note: The total liabilities are the difference between the total assets and total stockholders' equity ending balances.

Prob. 17–5A   Concluded

2. Both the rate earned on total assets and rate earned on stockholders' equity are above the industry average for all five years. The rate earned on total assets is actually improving gradually. The rate earned on stockholders' equity exceeds the rate earned on total assets, providing evidence of the positive use of leverage. The company is clearly growing earnings as fast as the asset and equity base. In addition, the ratio of liabilities to stockholders' equity indicates that the proportion of debt to stockholders' equity has been declining over the period. The firm is adding to debt at a slower rate than the assets are growing from earnings. The number of times interest charges were earned ratio is improving during this time period. Again, the firm is increasing earnings faster than the increase in interest charges. Overall, these ratios indicate excellent financial performance coupled with appropriate use of debt (leverage).

Prob. 17–1B

1.

PET CARE, INC.
Comparative Income Statement
For the Years Ended December 31, 2006 and 2005

	2006	2005	Increase (Decrease) Amount	Percent
Sales	$76,200	$61,000	$15,200	24.92%
Sales returns and allowances	1,200	1,000	200	20.00%
Net sales..	$75,000	$60,000	$15,000	25.00%
Cost of goods sold	42,000	35,000	7,000	20.00%
Gross profit.......................................	$33,000	$25,000	$ 8,000	32.00%
Selling expenses	$13,800	$12,000	$ 1,800	15.00%
Administrative expenses	9,000	8,000	1,000	12.50%
Total operating expenses	$22,800	$20,000	$ 2,800	14.00%
Income from operations...................	$10,200	$ 5,000	$ 5,200	104.00%
Other income	500	500	0	0.00%
Income before income tax	$10,700	$ 5,500	$ 5,200	94.55%
Income tax expense	2,400	1,200	1,200	100.00%
Net income	$ 8,300	$ 4,300	$ 4,000	93.02%

2. The profitability has significantly improved. Net sales have increased by 25% over the 2005 base year. In addition, however, cost of goods sold, selling expenses, and administrative expenses grew at a slower rate. Increasing sales combined with costs that increase at a slower rate results in strong earnings growth. In this case, net income grew in excess of 93% over the base year.

Prob. 17–2B

1.

INDUSTRIAL SANITATION SYSTEMS, INC.
Comparative Income Statement
For the Years Ended December 31, 2006 and 2005

	2006		2005	
	Amount	Percent	Amount	Percent
Sales	$ 144,000	102.86%	$ 128,000	102.40%
Sales returns and allowances	4,000	2.86	3,000	2.40
Net sales	$ 140,000	100.00%	$ 125,000	100.00%
Cost of goods sold	80,000	57.14	72,000	57.60
Gross profit	$ 60,000	42.86%	$ 53,000	42.40%
Selling expenses	$ 56,000	40.00%	$ 30,000	24.00%
Administrative expenses	14,000	10.00	12,000	9.60
Total operating expenses	$ 70,000	50.00%	$ 42,000	33.60%
Income from operations	$ (10,000)	(7.14)%	$ 11,000	8.80%
Other income	2,000	1.43	1,800	1.44
Income before income tax	$ (8,000)	(5.71)%	$ 12,800	10.24%
Income tax expense (benefit)	(2,000)	(1.43)	3,000	2.40
Net income (loss)	$ (6,000)	(4.28)%*	$ 9,800	7.84%

*Rounded down

2. The net income as a percent of sales has declined. All the costs and expenses, other than selling expenses, have maintained their approximate cost as a percent of sales relationship between 2005 and 2006. Selling expenses as a percent of sales, however, have grown from 24% to 40% of sales. Apparently, the new advertising campaign has not been successful. The increased expense has not produced sufficient sales to maintain relative profitability. Thus, selling expenses as a percent of sales have increased.

Prob. 17–3B

1. a. Working capital = Current assets – Current liabilities

$$\$594,000 - \$269,000 = \$325,000$$

b. Current ratio = $\dfrac{\text{Current assets}}{\text{Current liabilities}}$

$$\frac{\$594,000}{\$269,000} = 2.21$$

c. Quick ratio = $\dfrac{\text{Quick assets}}{\text{Current liabilities}}$

$$\frac{\$120,000 + \$56,000 + \$185,000}{\$269,000} = 1.34$$

2.

				Supporting Calculations		
Transaction	Working Capital	Current Ratio	Quick Ratio	Current Assets	Quick Assets	Current Liabilities
a.	$325,000	2.21	1.34	$594,000	$361,000	$269,000
b.	325,000	2.56	1.44	534,000	301,000	209,000
c.	325,000	2.05	1.17	634,000	361,000	309,000
d.	325,000	2.31	1.37	574,000	341,000	249,000
e.	300,000	2.02	1.23	594,000	361,000	294,000
f.	325,000	2.21	1.34	594,000	361,000	269,000
g.	445,000	2.65	1.79	714,000	481,000	269,000
h.	325,000	2.21	1.34	594,000	361,000	269,000
i.	425,000	2.58	1.71	694,000	461,000	269,000
j.	325,000	2.21	1.31	594,000	352,000	269,000

Prob. 17–4B

1. Working capital: $945,000 – $285,000 = $660,000

Ratio	Numerator	Denominator	Calculated Value
2. Current ratio	$945,000	$285,000	3.3
3. Quick ratio	$600,000	$285,000	2.1
4. Accounts receivable turnover	$2,800,000	($158,000 + $172,000)/2	17.0
5. Number of days' sales in receivables	$172,000	($2,800,000/365)	22.4
6. Inventory turnover	$1,250,000	($265,000 + $325,000)/2	4.2
7. Number of days' sales in inventory....................	$325,000	($1,250,000/365)	94.9
8. Fixed assets to long-term liabilities................	$2,100,000	$900,000	2.3
9. Liabilities to stock-holders' equity...............	$1,185,000	$2,110,000	0.6
10. Number of times interest charges earned	$501,000 + $79,000	$79,000	7.3
11. Number of times preferred dividends earned...........................	$361,000	$32,000	11.3
12. Ratio of net sales to assets............................	$2,800,000	($3,045,000 + $2,170,000)/2	1.1
13. Rate earned on total assets...........................	$361,000 + $79,000	($3,295,000 + $2,370,000)/2	15.5%
14. Rate earned on stock-holders' equity...............	$361,000	($2,110,000 + $1,745,000)/2	18.7%
15. Rate earned on common stock-holders' equity...............	($361,000 – $32,000)	($1,710,000 + $1,445,000)/2	20.9%
16. Earnings per share on common stock	($361,000 – $32,000)	80,000	$4.11
17. Price-earnings ratio	$64.00	$4.11	15.6
18. Dividends per share of common stock	$64,000	80,000	$0.80
19. Dividend yield................	$0.80	$64.00	1.25%

Prob. 17–5B

1.   a.

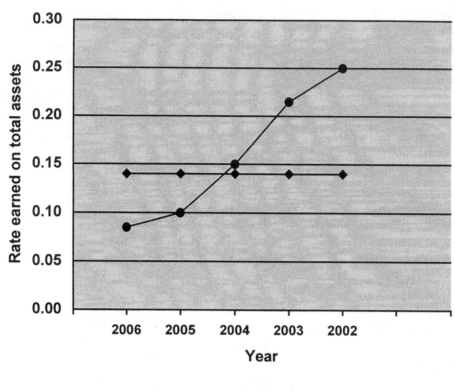

$$\text{Rate earned on total assets} = \frac{\text{Net income} + \text{Interest expense}}{\text{Average total assets}}$$

2006: $\dfrac{\$132,000}{\$1,550,000} = 0.09$ 2003: $\dfrac{\$230,000}{\$1,100,000} = 0.21$

2005: $\dfrac{\$145,000}{\$1,425,000} = 0.10$ 2002: $\dfrac{\$225,000}{\$900,000} = 0.25$

2004: $\dfrac{\$185,000}{\$1,275,000} = 0.15$

Prob. 17–5B   Continued

1.   b.

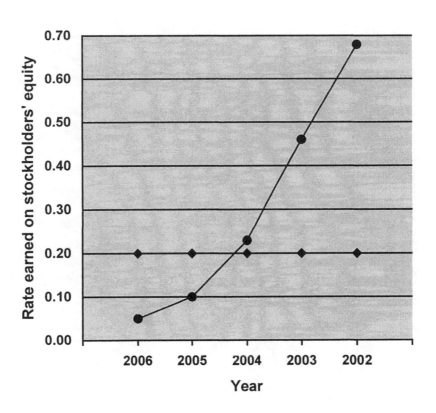

Rate earned on stockholders' equity = $\dfrac{\text{Net income}}{\text{Stockholders' equity}}$

2006: $\dfrac{\$30,000}{\$565,000} = 0.05$ 2003: $\dfrac{\$150,000}{\$325,000} = 0.46$

2005: $\dfrac{\$50,000}{\$525,000} = 0.10$ 2002: $\dfrac{\$150,000}{\$225,000} = 0.67$

2004: $\dfrac{\$100,000}{\$450,000} = 0.22$

Prob. 17–5B Continued

1. c.

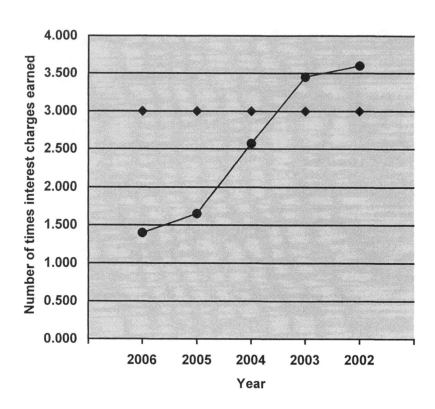

———◆——— Industry number of times interest charges are earned
———●——— Crane number of times interest charges are earned

Number of times
interest charges = $\dfrac{\text{Net Income} + \text{Income tax expense} + \text{Interest expense}}{\text{Interest expense}}$
were earned

2006: $\dfrac{\$141,000}{\$102,000} = 1.38$ 2003: $\dfrac{\$275,000}{\$80,000} = 3.44$

2005: $\dfrac{\$160,000}{\$95,000} = 1.68$ 2002: $\dfrac{\$270,000}{\$75,000} = 3.60$

2004: $\dfrac{\$215,000}{\$85,000} = 2.53$

Prob. 17–5B   Continued

1.   d.

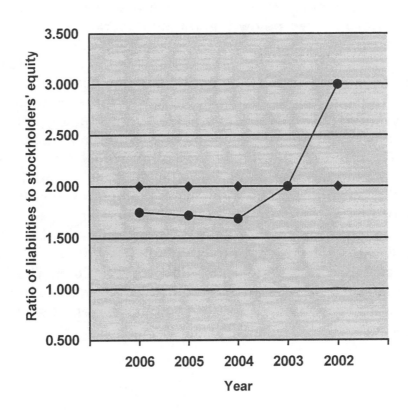

──◆── Industry ratio of liabilities to stockholders' equity
──●── Crane ratio of liabilities to stockholders' equity

$$\text{Ratio of liabilities to stockholders' equity} = \frac{\text{Total liabilities}}{\text{Total stockholders' equity}}$$

2006: $\dfrac{\$1,020,000}{\$580,000} = 1.76$ 2003: $\dfrac{\$800,000}{\$400,000} = 2.00$

2005: $\dfrac{\$950,000}{\$550,000} = 1.73$ 2002: $\dfrac{\$750,000}{\$250,000} = 3.00$

2004: $\dfrac{\$850,000}{\$500,000} = 1.70$

Note: Total liabilities are determined by subtracting stockholders' equity (ending balance) from the total assets (ending balance).

Prob. 17–5B   Concluded

2. Both the rate earned on total assets and the rate earned on stockholders' equity have been moving in a negative direction in the last five years. Both measures have moved below the industry average over the last two years. The cause of this decline is driven by a rapid decline in earnings. The use of debt can be seen from the ratio of liabilities to stockholders' equity. The ratio has declined over the time period and has declined below the industry average. Thus, the level of debt relative to the stockholders' equity has gradually improved over the five years. Unfortunately, the earnings have declined at a faster rate, causing the rate earned on stockholders' equity to decline. The rate earned on total assets ran below the interest cost on debt in 2006, causing the rate earned on stockholders' equity to drop below the rate earned on total assets. This is an example of negative leverage. The number of times interest charges were earned has been falling below the industry average for several years. This is the result of low profitability combined with high interest costs (10%). The number of times interest is earned has fallen to a dangerously low level in 2006. The low profitability and time interest charges are earned in 2006, as well as the five-year trend, should be a major concern to the company's management, stockholders, and creditors.

HOME DEPOT, INC., PROBLEM

1. a. **Working capital (in millions):**
        2003: $3,882 ($11,917 – $8,035)
        2002: $3,860 ($10,361 – $6,501)

    b. **Current ratio:**
        2003: 1.48 ($11,917 ÷ $8,035)
        2002: 1.59 ($10,361 ÷ $6,501)

    c. **Quick ratio:**
        2003: 0.41 ($3,325 ÷ $8,035)
        2002: 0.53 ($3,466 ÷ $6,501)

    d. **Accounts receivable turnover:**
        2003: 58.48 {$58,247 ÷ [($920 + $1,072)/2]}
        2002: 61.03 {$53,553 ÷ [($835 + $920)/2]}

    e. **Number of days' sales in receivables:**
        2003: 6.72 [$1,072 ÷ (58,247/365)]
        2002: 6.27 [$920 ÷ (53,553/365)]

    f. **Inventory turnover:**
        2003: 5.33 {$40,139 ÷ [($8,338 + $6,725)/2]}
        2002: 5.63 {$37,406 ÷ [($6,725 + $6,556)/2]}

    g. **Number of days' sales in inventory:**
        2003: 75.82 days [$8,338 ÷ ($40,139/365)]
        2002: 65.62 days [$6,725 ÷ ($37,406/365)]

    h. **Ratio of liabilities to stockholders' equity:**
        2003: 0.52 ($10,209 ÷ $19,802)
        2002: 0.46 ($8,312 ÷ $18,082)

    i. **Ratio of net sales to average total assets:**
        2003: 2.07 {$58,247 ÷ [($30,011 + $26,394)/2]}
        2002: 2.24 {$53,553 ÷ [($26,394 + $21,385)/2]}

    j. **Rate earned on average total assets:**
        2003: 13.12% {($3,664 + 37) ÷ [($30,011 + $26,394)/2)]}
        2002: 12.86% {($3,044 + 28) ÷ [($26,394 + $21,385)/2)]}

    k. **Rate earned on average common stockholders' equity:**
        2003: 19.34% {$3,664 ÷ [($19,802 + $18,082)/2]}
        2002: 18.4% {$3,044 ÷ [($18,082 + $15,004)/2]}

Home Depot, Inc., Problem   Concluded

l. Price-earnings ratio:
    2003: 13.66 ($21.31 ÷ $1.56)
    2002: 38.53 ($49.70 ÷ $1.29)

m. Percentage relationship of net income to net sales:
    2003: 6.29% ($3,664 ÷ $58,247)
    2002: 5.68% ($3,044 ÷ $53,553)

2. Before reaching definitive conclusions, each measure should be compared with past years, industry averages, and similar firms in the industry.

    a. The working capital increased slightly.

    b. and c. The working capital and the quick ratio declined modestly during 2003.

    d. and e. The accounts receivable turnover and number of days' sales in receivables indicate a slight decrease in the efficiency of collecting accounts receivable. The accounts receivable turnover decreased from 61.03 to 58.48. The number of days' sales in receivables increased from 6.27 to 6.72. Both measures indicate, however, that Home Depot has significant cash sales, since the turnover is so high and the average collection period is so short. If the credit sales were known, these ratios could be calculated with net credit sales on account in the numerator. The resulting calculations could be compared to Home Depot's credit policy.

    f. and g. The results of these two analyses showed a decrease in the inventory turnover and an increase in the number of days' sales in inventory. Both trends are unfavorable. Inventory management is critical to a retailer, so this ratio trend would warrant further analysis.

    h. The margin of protection to the creditors improved slightly in 2003. Overall, there is excellent protection to creditors.

    i. These analyses indicate a decrease in the effectiveness in the use of the assets to generate revenues.

    j. The rate earned on average total assets improved slightly during 2003. Overall, rates earned on assets that exceed 10% is usually considered good performance.

    k. The rate earned on average common stockholders' equity in 2003 also increased. This is also evidence of the positive use of leverage, since the rate earned on stockholders' equity exceeds the rate earned on assets. The rates earned on average common stockholders' equity shown for these two years would be considered excellent performance.

l. The price-earnings ratio dropped significantly from 2002 to 2003. This drop accompanied an overall drop in price-earnings ratios for the whole market during this time. In addition, market participants are revaluing Home Depot's growth prospects downward in light of the competition from Lowe's. Thus, even though earnings increased, the stock price declined.

m. The percent of net income to net sales increased, from 5.68% to 6.29%, a favorable trend.

Activity 17–6

1.

a.   Rate earned on total assets: $\dfrac{\text{Net income}}{\text{Average total assets}}$

Marriott: $\dfrac{\$236}{\$8,673} = 2.72\%$

Hilton: $\dfrac{\$176}{\$8,963} = 1.96\%$

b.   Rate earned on total stockholders' equity: $\dfrac{\text{Net income}}{\text{Average total stockholders' equity}}$

Marriott: $\dfrac{\$236}{\$3,373} = 7.00\%$

Hilton: $\dfrac{\$176}{\$1,713} = 10.27\,\%$

c.   Number of times interest charges are earned: $\dfrac{\text{Income before income tax expense} + \text{Interest expense}}{\text{Interest expense}}$

Marriott: $\dfrac{\$370 + \$109}{\$109} = 4.39$

Hilton: $\dfrac{\$306 + \$237}{\$237} = 2.29$

d.   Ratio of liabilities to stockholders' equity: $\dfrac{\text{Total liabilities}}{\text{Total stockholders' equity}}$

Marriott: $\dfrac{\$5,629}{\$3,478} = 1.62$

Hilton: $\dfrac{\$7,498}{\$1,642} = 4.57$

Activity 17–6   Concluded

Summary Table:

	Marriott	Hilton
Rate earned on total assets	2.72%	1.96%
Rate earned on stockholders' equity	7.00%	10.27%
Number of times interest charges are earned	4.39	2.29
Ratio of liabilities to stockholders' equity	1.62	4.57

2. Marriott earns a higher rate earned on total assets (2.72% vs. 1.96%), but a lower rate on stockholders' equity (7.00% vs. 10.27%), compared to Hilton. The reason can be seen with the leverage formula. Marriott has less leverage than does Hilton. This is confirmed by the ratio of liabilities to stockholders' equity, which shows the relative debt held by Marriott is 1.62 times the stockholders' equity, compared to 4.57 times for Hilton. Can Hilton manage this much debt? The number of times interest charges are earned shows that Marriott covers its interest charges 4.39 times. The comparable ratio for Hilton is 2.29. Hilton's operating income (before interest and taxes) is over twice its interest charges, which is marginal, but sufficient. Hilton's debt capacity is near a maximum. In sum, Hilton earns a higher return for stockholders, but with greater risk.

Ex. C–6

a. Income Summary 300,000
       Merchandise Inventory...   300,000

    Merchandise Inventory 275,000
       Income Summary...   275,000

b. Sales 1,450,000
    Purchases Returns and Allowances   9,000
    Purchases Discounts 14,000
       Income Summary...   1,473,000

    Income Summary 1,206,000
       Sales Returns and Allowances   32,000
       Sales Discounts...   18,000
       Purchases 820,000
       Transportation In   21,300
       Selling Expenses... 240,200
       Administrative Expenses   72,000
       Interest Expense..   2,500

    Income Summary 242,000
       Connie Sorum, Capital   242,000

    Connie Sorum, Capital 40,000
       Connie Sorum, Drawing..   40,000

Prob. C–1

			Debit	Credit
Nov.	2	Purchases	18,000	
		Accounts Payable—Loftin Co.		18,000
	8	Cash	8,100	
		Sales		8,100
	9	Purchases	12,000	
		Transportation In	180	
		Accounts Payable—Chestnut Co.		12,180
	10	Accounts Payable—Loftin Co.	3,000	
		Purchases Returns and Allowances		3,000
	11	Accounts Receivable—Fawcett Co.	2,000	
		Sales		2,000
	12	Accounts Payable—Loftin Co.	15,000	
		Cash		14,700
		Purchases Discounts		300
	15	Accounts Receivable—American Express	9,850	
		Sales		9,850
	19	Accounts Payable—Chestnut Co.	12,180	
		Cash		11,940
		Purchases Discounts		240
	21	Cash	1,980	
		Sales Discounts	20	
		Accounts Receivable—Fawcett Co.		2,000
	25	Accounts Receivable—Clemons Co.	3,000	
		Sales		3,000
	28	Cash	9,470	
		Nonbank Credit Card Expense	380	
		Accounts Receivable—American Express ...		9,850
	30	Sales Returns and Allowances	1,700	
		Accounts Receivable—Clemons Co.		1,700

Prob. C–4   Continued

3.

SUNSHINE SPORTS CO.
Statement of Owner's Equity
For the Year Ended December 31, 2006

Sherri Vogel, capital, January 1, 2006		$ 159,600
Net income for the year...	$222,950	
Less withdrawals...	40,000	
Increase in owner's equity..		182,950
Sherri Vogel, capital, December 31, 2006............................		$ 342,550

Prob. C–4   Continued

4.

SUNSHINE SPORTS CO.
Balance Sheet
December 31, 2006

Assets

Current assets:

Cash	$ 28,000	
Accounts receivable	142,500	
Merchandise inventory	215,000	
Prepaid insurance	4,900	
Store supplies	1,300	
Office supplies	750	
Total current assets		$392,450

Fixed assets:

Store equipment	$132,000		
Less accumulated depreciation	47,800	$ 84,200	
Office equipment	$ 50,000		
Less accumulated depreciation	21,000	29,000	
Total fixed assets			113,200
Total assets			$505,650

Liabilities

Current liabilities:

Accounts payable	$ 56,700	
Note payable (current portion)	10,000	
Salaries payable	6,000	
Unearned rent	400	
Total current liabilities		$ 73,100

Long-term liabilities:

Note payable (final payment, 2013)		90,000
Total liabilities		$163,100

Owner's Equity

Sherri Vogel, capital		342,550
Total liabilities and owner's equity		$505,650

Prob. D–1

1.

				Debit	Credit
Feb.	10	Accounts Receivable—Manco Company		10,800	
		Sales			10,800
		Cost of Merchandise Sold		6,000	
		Merchandise Inventory			6,000
Mar.	12	Cash		10,200	
		Exchange Loss		600	
		Accounts Receivable—Manco Company			10,800
	20	Merchandise Inventory		13,000	
		Accounts Payable—Fossum Inc.			13,000
Apr.	11	Accounts Payable—Fossum Inc.		13,000	
		Cash			12,600
		Exchange Gain			400
June	27	Accounts Receivable—Hu Company		6,400	
		Sales			6,400
		Cost of Merchandise Sold		3,800	
		Merchandise Inventory			3,800
July	27	Cash		6,800	
		Accounts Receivable—Hu Company			6,400
		Exchange Gain			400
Oct.	8	Merchandise Inventory		32,000	
		Accounts Payable—Chevalier Company			32,000
Nov.	7	Accounts Payable—Chevalier Company		32,000	
		Exchange Loss		500	
		Cash			32,500

Prob. D–1   **Concluded**

Dec.	15	Accounts Receivable—Cassandra Company	78,000	
		Sales		78,000
		Cost of Merchandise Sold	50,000	
		Merchandise Inventory		50,000
	16	Merchandise Inventory	8,500	
		Accounts Payable—Juan Company		8,500
	31	Accounts Receivable—Cassandra Company	1,200	
		Exchange Gain..		1,200
		$120,000 Canadian × $0.01 increase in exchange rate.		
	31	Exchange Loss..	500	
		Accounts Payable—Juan Company..............		500
		500,000 pesos × $0.001 increase in exchange rate.		
2. Jan.	15	Accounts Payable—Juan Company	9,000	
		Cash..		8,000
		Exchange Gain..		1,000
	17	Cash	80,400	
		Accounts Receivable—Cassandra Company		79,200
		Exchange Gain..		1,200